Author

Darlene Misconish Tyler, M.A.Ed.

Consultant

Angela Gallo, M.A.Ed.
Richardson Independent School District Program

Credits

Corinne Burton, M.A.Ed., *President and Publisher*
Emily R. Smith, M.A.Ed., *SVP of Content Development*
Véronique Bos, *VP of Creative*
Lynette Ordoñez, *Content Manager*
Melissa Laughlin, *Editor*
Avery Rabedeaux, *Assistant Editor*
Jill Malcolm, *Graphic Designer*

Image Credits: all images from Shutterstock and/or iStock

Standards

A division of Teacher Created Materials
5482 Argosy Avenue
Huntington Beach, CA 92649
www.tcmpub.com/shell-education
ISBN 979-8-7659-5278-8

Printed by: 51497
Printed in: China

Table of Contents

Math Education Today

As many adults can attest, whether they are teaching in a classroom or supporting children learning math at home, mathematics does not seem to be the same as how they learned it growing up. Instruction today focuses on critical thinking, problem solving, and using a variety of strategies to find answers. Current mathematics instruction might look different, but math still focuses on helping students become skillful problem solvers. Students are encouraged to think like mathematicians. Mathematics instruction seeks to build students' mathematical reasoning skills and to ensure students can apply concepts to real-world problems.

Prior to the 1990s, individual states created their own standards for student learning. This created a disparity in achievement among graduating high school seniors. To help make student education more consistent across the country, the National Governor's Association and the Council of Chief State School Offices set out to develop national standards with the intent of improving student learning and achievement (Marchitello and Wilhelm 2014). Over time, these standards were honed, improved, and updated using cognitive science and research regarding children's learning.

That research became a cornerstone in the philosophy of current math education—making sure students have a conceptual understanding of something before moving to the more abstract ways to solve problems. In the past, students might have learned only one way to solve a math problem. Research from Vanderbilt University shows it is more beneficial to introduce students to more than one problem-solving strategy (Durkin, Rittle-Johnson, and Star 2017). Knowing multiple strategies allows students to better understand a concept and helps them find efficient approaches that make the best sense to them.

Though mathematics education may look different today, the solutions to mathematical problems remain the same. Students today are taking time to think deeply, reason abstractly, and understand numbers in ways that will prepare them to be successful in college and their careers.

Refining Math Skills

Children learn math best when they can see, organize, and interpret through tools or models. Learning begins with concrete representations of mathematical concepts (Cathcart et al. 2014). Manipulatives, such as counters, base-ten blocks, and coins, are effective tools for students to use to build concrete representations. Students can then progress to drawing pictorial models of concrete objects, such as tallies, circles, and dots. These steps prepare students to learn the abstract qualities of mathematical concepts, making connections between the objects, pictures, and equations or formulas.

Problem-solving is the context in which students can extend current understanding to new situations and make connections between mathematical ideas and the real world. Rote practice in mathematics limits students' creativity and hinders their ability to problem solve and apply math in real-life situations. Problems are easier to solve when students can draw upon their practical, real-world knowledge (McNeil and Jarvin 2007).

Math Education Today *(cont.)*

Building Math Fluency

There is an emphasis on national mathematics standards for students to be able to solve math problems accurately and efficiently. While this mathematical fluency is certainly expected, it is important to realize that conceptual understanding is the basis for developing fluency. When a student understands combinations of tens, developed through many experiences using a ten frame, they can extend that understanding to learn more difficult addition facts. For example, a student can think about 9 + 6 as taking 1 from the 6 and adding it to the 9, so the fact now becomes 10 + 5, which equals 15. To assess students' fluency, evaluate their flexibility, accuracy, efficiency, and appropriate strategy use when solving math problems.

Learning math is not a "one and done" achievement. A spiral curriculum model was introduced by psychologist Jerome Bruner in 1960, and continuing research agrees that it greatly benefits students (Ireland and Mouthaan 2020). A spiral approach means concepts are spread out over time and reviewed frequently. When students have repeated exposure to a skill, they are more likely to understand and remember it.

Research to Practice

180 Days of Math incorporates a balanced approach to develop both conceptual understanding and mathematical fluency.

- Practice pages encourage students to find and use manipulatives, such as those provided in the digital resources, when solving problems.
- Instructional pages and practice pages provide students numerous opportunities to learn concepts through visual models and showcase their understanding by drawing their own pictorial representations.
- A variety of rich math tasks, or word problems, allow students to apply mathematical concepts and operations to real-world situations.
- Instructional pages and sidebars on practice pages model a variety of strategies to help students build proficiency.
- Five-day spiral reviews at the end of each unit touch on concepts taught throughout the entire book up to that point, not just the current unit.

How to Use This Resource

Instructional Pages

The math concepts in this resource are organized into five units. Each unit is divided into sections that focus on specific standards-based topics. To introduce mathematical concepts, there are instructional pages at the beginnings of the sections. These pages support students so they can complete the practice pages with confidence and accuracy.

An overview of big ideas, important concepts, and key vocabulary essential to the upcoming pages is explained in grade-appropriate language.

Example problems model problem-solving steps and strategies that students can follow.

Students answer guiding questions, attempt the modeled strategies, and solve problems with support.

UNIT 1

Learn about Ratio and Percent Problems

Percents are part-to-whole comparisons in which the whole amount is 100.
Ratios are comparisons and can be part-to-part or part-to-whole comparisons. You can use proportional relationships to solve percent problems. Set them up like this.

$\frac{\text{Part}}{\text{Whole}} = \frac{\text{Percent}}{100}$

Example: What is 25% of 90?
Since 90 is the total amount, and 25 is the percent, we can set it up as shown: $\frac{x}{90} = \frac{25}{100}$
To solve this, you can cross multiply, or multiply diagonally.
$90 \cdot 25 = 100 \cdot x$
$2{,}250 = 100x$
To solve this, we divide 2,250 by 100.
$x = 22.5$

Total with Tip

The Howard family went out to dinner, and the bill was $65. They want to leave a 20% tip. How much should they leave for the tip? What is the total amount the Howards have to pay, including the tip?

1. Set up a proportional relationship. $\frac{x}{65} = \frac{20}{100}$
2. Multiply diagonally. $65 \cdot 20 = 100 \cdot x$
3. Solve the equation.
   $100x = 1{,}300$
   $x = 13$
4. The Howard family should leave $_______ for a tip.
5. To find the total amount the Howard family has to pay, add $65 + the tip. What is the total amount they must pay?
   $_______

Discounted Price

Teddy has a coupon for 10% off a new baseball hat. The original price of the hat is $25. What is the discounted price?

1. Set up a proportional relationship. $\frac{x}{25} = \frac{10}{100}$
2. Cross multiply (multiply diagonally). $100 \cdot x = 25 \cdot 10$
3. Solve the equation.
   $100x = 250$
   $x = 2.5$ or $2.50
4. Subtract the original price by the discounted amount to find the new price.
   $25 – $2.50 = _______

44 142249—180 Days of Math © Shell Education

How to Use This Resource *(cont.)*

Practice Pages

Practice pages are provided for every day of the school year to reinforce grade-level concepts and skills. The practice pages can be easily prepared and implemented as part of a morning routine, at the beginning of each math lesson, or as homework. Each day's math skills are aligned to state mathematics standards. (A chart with these standards can be found on pages 226–227.)

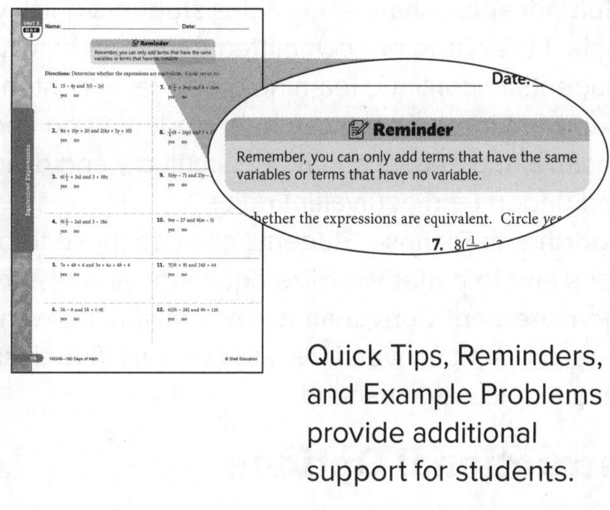

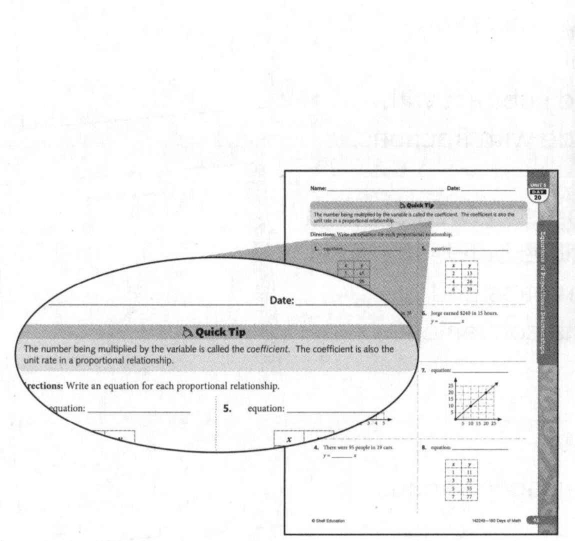

Quick Tips, Reminders, and Example Problems provide additional support for students.

Review Pages

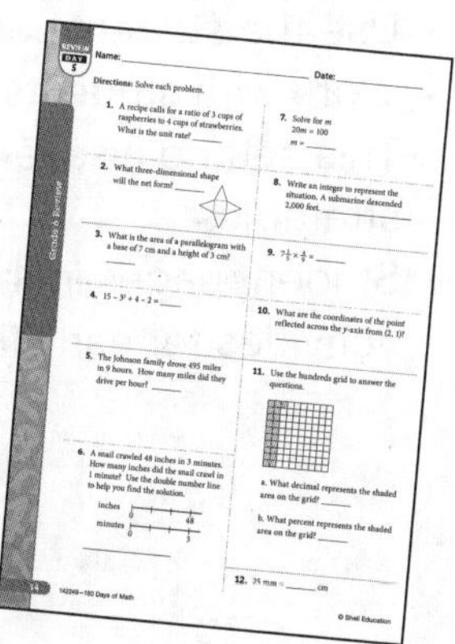

Review is embedded throughout this resource to support students' retention of mathematical concepts.

The first section of practice pages in this resource reviews the math concepts from the previous grade. This activates students' prior knowledge after summer break and offers teachers and families a quick view of students' grade-level readiness.

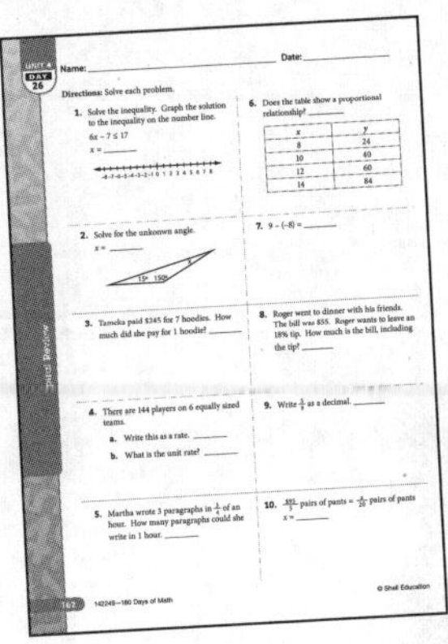

Spiral review pages at the end of each unit include additional practice in the concepts learned. This helps ensure that students' skills and content knowledge remain fresh, and it helps them build fluency as the year goes on.

A cumulative review serves as the last section of practice pages in this resource, allowing students to showcase their understanding of all grade-level math concepts practiced throughout the year.

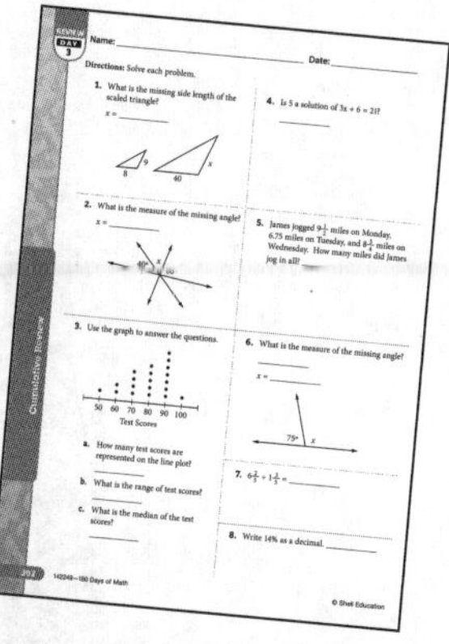

How to Use This Resource *(cont.)*

Digital Math Learning Resources

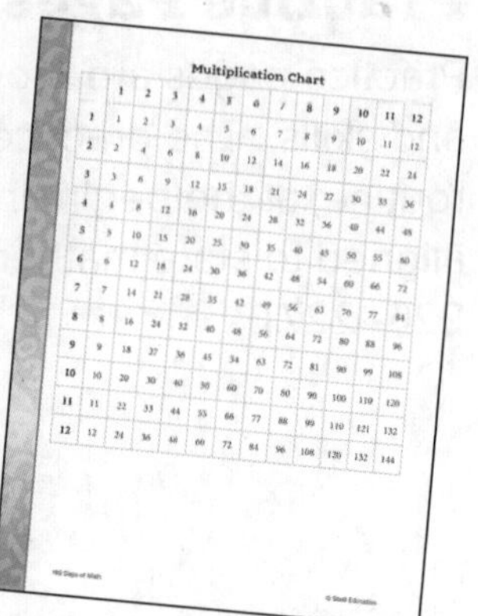

Multiplication Chart

	1	2	3	4	5	6	7	8	9	10	11	12
1	1	2	3	4	5	6	7	8	9	10	11	12
2	2	4	6	8	10	12	14	16	18	20	22	24
3	3	6	9	12	15	18	21	24	27	30	33	36
4	4	8	12	16	20	24	28	32	36	40	44	48
5	5	10	15	20	25	30	35	40	45	50	55	60
6	6	12	18	24	30	36	42	48	54	60	66	72
7	7	14	21	28	35	42	49	56	63	70	77	84
8	8	16	24	32	40	48	56	64	72	80	88	96
9	9	18	27	36	45	54	63	72	81	90	99	108
10	10	20	30	40	50	60	70	80	90	100	110	120
11	11	22	33	44	55	66	77	88	99	110	121	132
12	12	24	36	48	60	72	84	96	108	120	132	144

A variety of math resources are provided digitally (see page 248 for instructions on how to download these pages). These quick references and tools support students in understanding and solving many different problem types. You may choose to print the resources ahead of time or as needed. Some of the resources available include the following:

- **Multiplication Chart**—This helps students quickly reference math facts if they have not committed them to memory. This allows students to continue learning grade-level content.
- **Number Lines**—These can help students add and subtract with positive and negative numbers, multiply and divide with fractions, and understand equivalent ratios.
- **Coordinate Planes**—Students can use these to practice with ordered pairs and to better visualize equations and distances between points.
- **Measurement Conversions**—When working with ratios and measurement conversions, students will find this a convenient resource to have on hand.

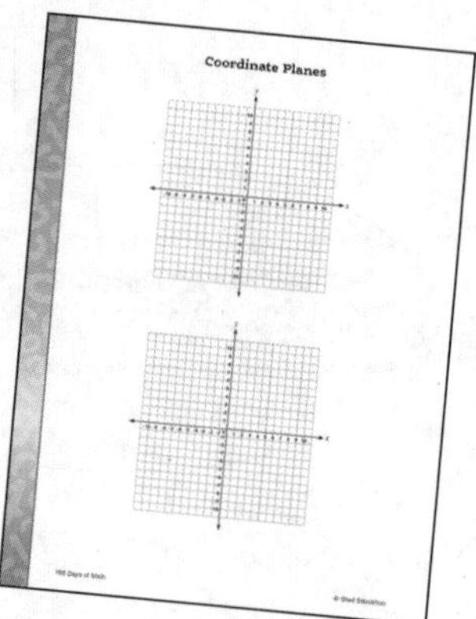

Instructional Options

180 Days of Math is a flexible resource that can be used in various instructional settings for different purposes.

- Use the student pages as daily warm-up activities or as review.
- Work with students in small groups, allowing them to focus on specific concepts and skills. This setting also lends itself to partner and group discussions about problem-solving strategies.
- Student pages in this resource can be completed independently during center times and as activities for early finishers.

How to Use This Resource *(cont.)*

Diagnostic Assessment

The practice pages in this book can be used as diagnostic assessments. These activity pages require students to think critically, use problem-solving strategies, and utilize mathematical skills and content knowledge. (An answer key is provided starting on page 229.)

The diagnostic analysis tools included in the digital resources allow for quick evaluation and ongoing monitoring of student work. See at a glance which math topics students may need to focus on further to develop proficiency.

Analysis sheets are provided as *Microsoft Word®* files in the digital resources. There is a *Class Analysis Sheet* and an *Individual Analysis Sheet*. Use the file that matches your assessment needs. After each review section, record how many answers each student got correct on the analysis sheet. Then, analyze the data on the analysis sheet to determine instructional needs for your child or class.

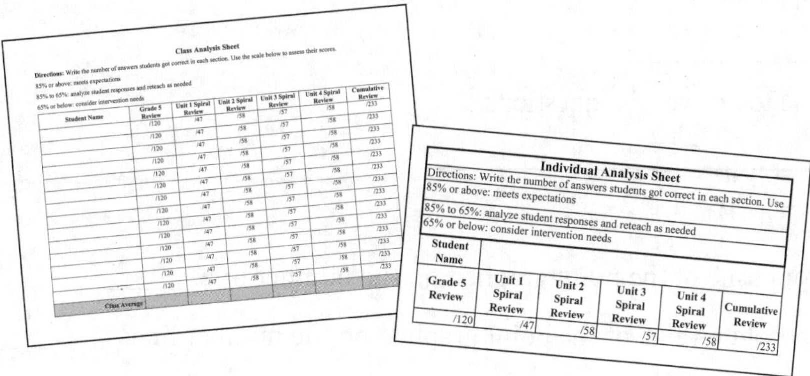

Class Analysis Sheet

Directions: Write the number of answers students got correct in each section. Use the scale below to assess their scores.

85% or above: meets expectations

85% to 65%: analyze student responses and reteach as needed

65% or below: consider intervention needs

Student Name	Grade 5 Review	Unit 1 Spiral Review	Unit 2 Spiral Review	Unit 3 Spiral Review	Unit 4 Spiral Review	Cumulative Review
	/120	/47	/58	/57	/58	/233
	/120	/47	/58	/57	/58	/233
	/120	/47	/58	/57	/58	/233
	/120	/47	/58	/57	/58	/233
	/120	/47	/58	/57	/58	/233
	/120	/47	/58	/57	/58	/233
	/120	/47	/58	/57	/58	/233
	/120	/47	/58	/57	/58	/233
	/120	/47	/58	/57	/58	/233
	/120	/47	/58	/57	/58	/233
	/120	/47	/58	/57	/58	/233
	/120	/47	/58	/57	/58	/233
	/120	/47	/58	/57	/58	/233
	/120	/47	/58	/57	/58	/233
Class Average						

Individual Analysis Sheet

Directions: Write the number of answers students got correct in each section. Use

85% or above: meets expectations

85% to 65%: analyze student responses and reteach as needed

65% or below: consider intervention needs

Student Name	

Grade 5 Review	Unit 1 Spiral Review	Unit 2 Spiral Review	Unit 3 Spiral Review	Unit 4 Spiral Review	Cumulative Review
/120	/47	/58	/57	/58	/233

Using the Results to Differentiate Instruction

Once results are gathered and analyzed, use the data to inform differentiation. The data can help determine which concepts are the most difficult for students and which students need additional instructional support and continued practice. The results of the diagnostic analysis may show that the class is struggling with a particular topic.

The results of the diagnostic analysis may also show that an individual or small group of students is struggling with a particular concept or group of concepts. Consider pulling aside these students while others are working independently to instruct further on the concept(s). You can also use the results to help identify individuals or groups of proficient students who are ready for enrichment or above-grade-level instruction. These students may benefit from independent learning contracts or more challenging activities.

REVIEW DAY 1

Name: ______________________ Date: ____________

Grade 6 Review

Directions: Solve each problem.

1. Write the ratio of bananas to strawberries in three ways.

a. ____________

b. ____________

c. ____________

2. Thomas cleaned $\frac{2}{5}$ of the garage. Mauricio cleaned 0.5 of the garage. Henry cleaned the rest of the garage. What percent of the garage did Henry clean? ____________

3. Write an equivalent expression.

$5x + 2y + 2x + 3y =$ ____________

4. Gina wants to find the volume of a box. The box is a rectangular prism and measures 5 inches by $2\frac{1}{2}$ inches by 3 inches. What is the volume (V) of the box?

$V =$ ________ cubic inches

5. $19 - (-8) =$ ____________

6. Use the number line to answer the questions.

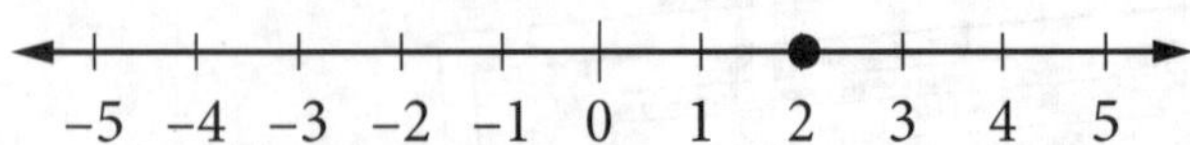

a. What is the opposite of the point graphed on the number line? ________

b. What is the absolute value of the point graphed on the number line? ________

7. What is the median of this set of data?

40, 50, 60, 70, 80 ________

8. $5^2 \div 5 \cdot 2 =$ ________

9. Solve for d.

$31d = 93$

$d =$ ________

10. In which quadrant on a coordinate plane is the point (–3, 4) located?

____

11. Sara bought a box of 24 ceramic mugs for $54. What is the price of one mug?

____

12. Which is the better deal? Circle it.

a. 12 bottles of water for $11.88

b. 28 bottles of water for $28.28

Name: ______________________ Date: ______________

Directions: Solve each problem.

1. What is the volume (V) of the prism?

$V =$ _______

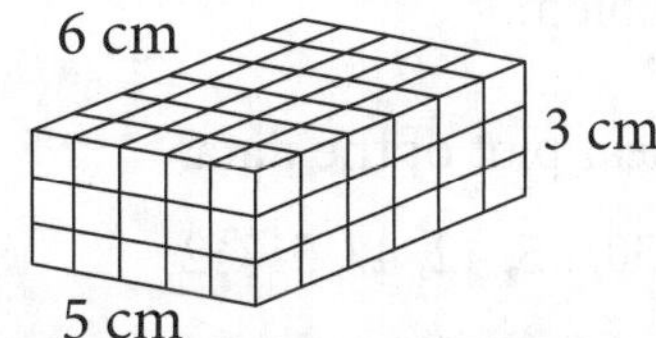

2. $41\overline{)10{,}086}$

3. $\begin{array}{r} 125 \\ \times\ 13.3 \\ \hline \end{array}$

4. What is the area of a rectangle that measures 4 m by 7 m? _______

5. Solve for x.

$5x = 230$

$x =$ _______

6. Graph the inequality on the number line.

$x > 4$

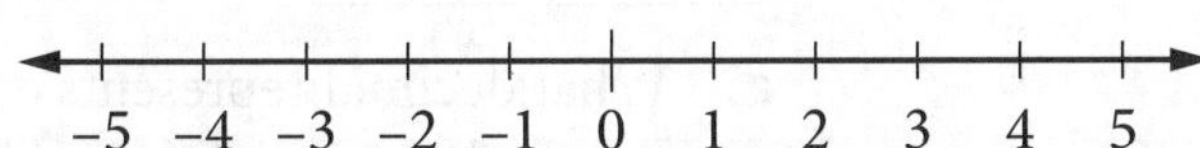

7. Can side lengths of 3, 5, and 9 form a triangle? How do you know?

____

8. What is the least common multiple (LCM) of 5 and 30? _______

9. Write an expression for *a number decreased by 3*. _______

10. $-9 \div 3 =$ _______

11. Use the table to answer the questions.

x	y
0	4
1	5
2	6
3	7

a. Is the relationship between x and y additive or multiplicative? _______

b. Write an equation to represent the table. $y =$ _______

12. Write 24 as a product of prime factors. ___________

Name: ______________________ Date: ____________

Directions: Solve each problem.

1. Make a stem and leaf plot of the data.

22, 22, 23, 24, 28, 30, 35, 42, 47, 51, 62

Stem	Leaf

2. Draw a net for the triangular prism.

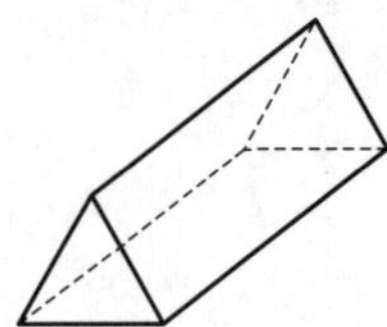

3. The Rocker family drove 1,760 miles in 32 hours. How many miles did they drive in 1 hour? ______

4. Find the unit rate, and use it to complete the table.

number of oranges	cost
1	
15	$12.75
25	

5. Li finished 10% of the running race. He ran 3 miles. How long is the race? Use the tape diagram to help you.

____

6.

$$\begin{array}{r} 140.3 \\ \times \quad 11.3 \\ \hline \end{array}$$

7. Use the hundreds grid to answer the questions.

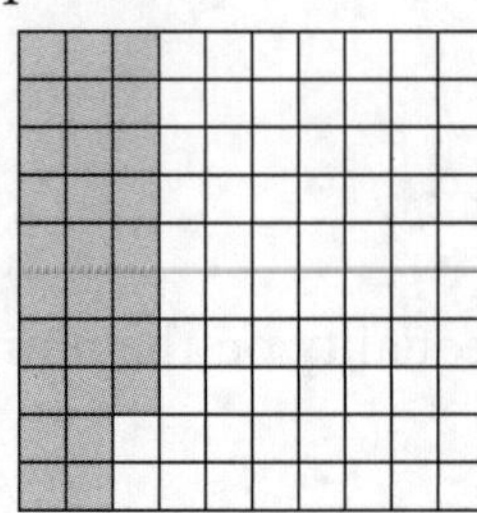

a. What decimal represents the shaded area on the grid?

______

b. What percent represents the shaded area on the grid?

______

8. A triangle has a base of 10 cm and a height of 4 cm. What is the area?

____

9. 4 kilometers = ______ meters

10. Write an integer to represent the situation.

An elevator went up 6 floors.

______

Name: ______________________________ Date: ________________

Directions: Solve each problem.

Use the dot plot to answer questions 1 through 3.

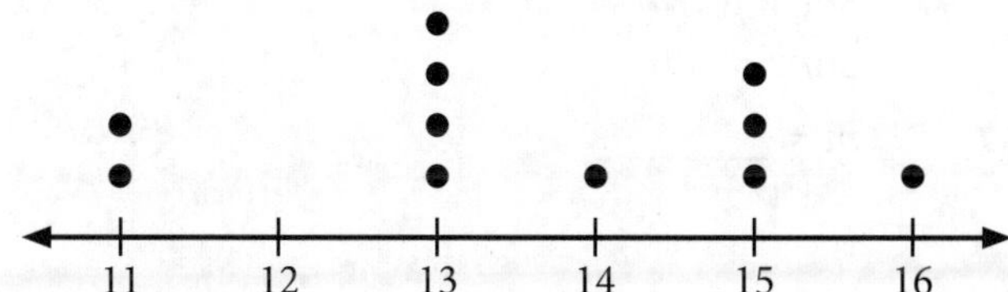

1. What is the median of the data on the dot plot? _______

2. What is the mode of the data on the dot plot? _______

3. What is the range of the data on the dot plot? _______

4. List the factors of 36 and 42. Circle the greatest common factor.

36: ______________________________

42: ______________________________

5. Look at the table. Is the relationship between *x* and *y* proportional? _______

x	*y*
1	4
2	8
3	12
4	16

6. Rectangle *ABCD* is graphed on a coordinate plane. Three of the points are *A*(–4, 2), *B*(4, 2), and *C*(4, –2). What are the coordinates of point *D*? __________

7. $-90 \div 9 =$ __________

8. Ike bought 4 shirts for $28. What was the price of 1 shirt? _______

9. Write an equivalent expression using the Distributive Property.

14 + 20 = _______ (_______ + _______)

10. $7\frac{1}{2} \times \frac{5}{10} =$ _______

11. 4 hours = _______ minutes

12. What is 25% as a decimal? _______

Name: ______________________________ Date: ______________

Directions: Solve each problem.

1. A recipe calls for a ratio of 3 cups of raspberries to 4 cups of strawberries. What is the unit rate? ________

2. What three-dimensional shape will the net form?

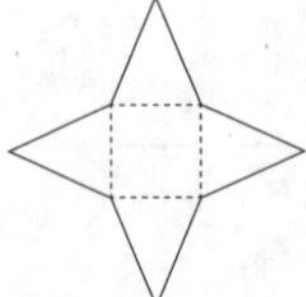

____

3. What is the area of a parallelogram with a base of 7 cm and a height of 3 cm?

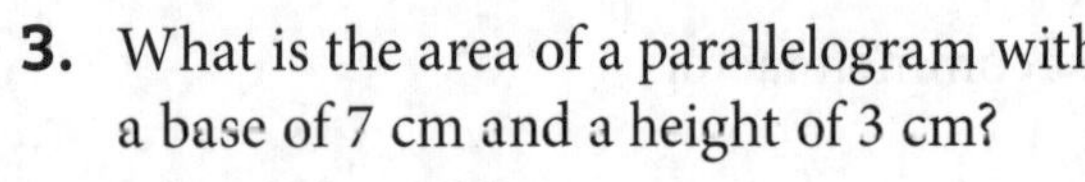

____

4. $15 - 3^2 + 4 - 2 =$ ________

5. The Johnson family drove 495 miles in 9 hours. How many miles did they drive per hour?

____

6. A snail crawled 48 inches in 3 minutes. How many inches did the snail crawl in 1 minute? Use the double number line to help you find the solution.

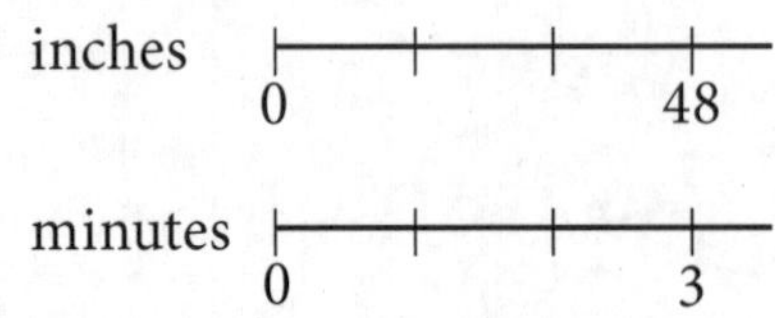

____

7. Solve for m.

$20m = 100$

$m =$ ________

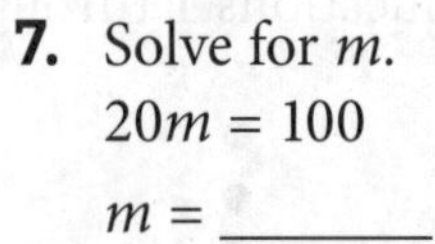

8. Write an integer to represent the situation. A submarine descended 2,000 feet.

____

9. $7\frac{1}{5} \times \frac{4}{9} =$ ________

10. What are the coordinates of the point reflected across the y-axis from (2, 1)?

____

11. Use the hundreds grid to answer the questions.

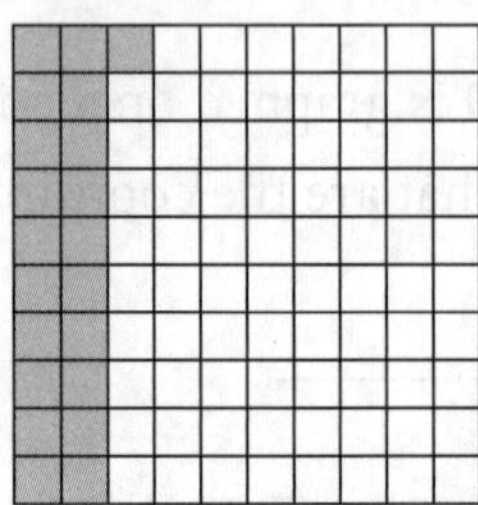

a. What decimal represents the shaded area on the grid? ________

b. What percent represents the shaded area on the grid? ________

12. 25 mm = ________ cm

Name: ______________________________ Date: ______________

Directions: Solve each problem.

1. What is the interquartile range (IQR) from the box plot?

____

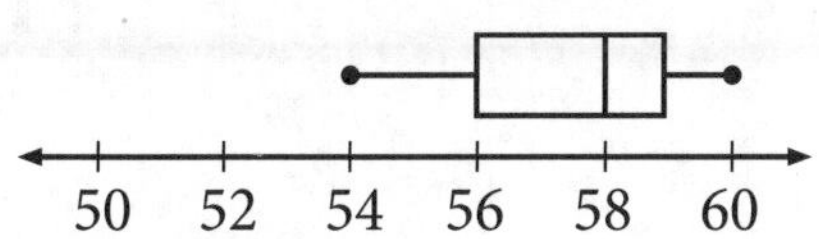

2. $30 \times \frac{4}{5} =$ ______

3. $3^3 - 2^2 =$ ______

4. Write 50 as a product of prime factors.

____

5. $18\overline{)3,870}$

6. Beth is mixing paint to make green. She uses the ratio 3 blue to 5 yellow.

a. What percent of the paint Beth is using is blue?

______

b. What fraction of the paint is yellow?

______

7. 7 yards = ______ feet

8. Write a ratio for shaded parts to unshaded parts in three ways.

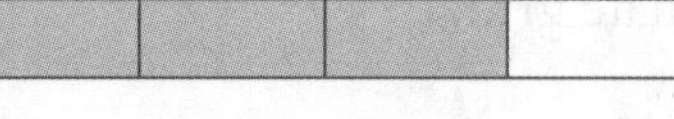

a. ______

b. ______

c. ______

9. What is 40% as a fraction? ______

10. What is the area of a triangle with a base of 8 inches and a height of 10 inches?

______ square inches

11. Rick is making miniature figures. Each figure requires $\frac{1}{4}$ of a tube of paint. Rick has $\frac{5}{8}$ of a tube of paint. Use the diagrams to help you answer the questions.

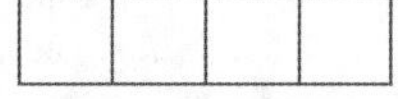 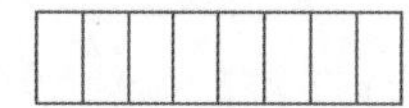

a. How many figures can Rick make? ______

b. Will Rick have any paint left over? ______

c. Write a division equation to represent the situation. __________

12. The 12 players on Lim's baseball team all hit the same number of home runs. As a team, they hit a total of 144 home runs. How many home runs did each player hit?

a. Write a division equation with a variable to represent the problem.

____

b. Write a multiplication equation with a variable to represent the problem.

____

c. What is the solution? __________

REVIEW DAY 7

Name: ______________________________ Date: ________________

Directions: Solve each problem.

1. Write an equation to represent the table. Then, graph the relationship on the coordinate grid.

$y =$ ________

x	y
0	0
1	3
2	6
3	9

2. Becca made a fruit smoothie using a ratio of 2 bananas to 6 strawberries.

a. What percent of the smoothie is banana? ________

b. What fraction of the smoothie is strawberries? ________

c. What decimal represents the amount of bananas in the smoothie? ________

3. Maril mowed $9\frac{4}{5}$ lawns. Sean mowed $\frac{2}{3}$ as many lawns. Who mowed more lawns? How do you know?

____

4. Complete the table.

Fraction	Decimal	Percent
		11%
	0.1	
$\frac{1}{5}$		

5. $\frac{2}{5} \div 3\frac{1}{4} =$ ________

6.
$$\begin{array}{r} 4.622 \\ 3.768 \\ +\ 0.247 \\ \hline \end{array}$$

7. Plot and label each number and its opposite on the number line. –2, 1, 4

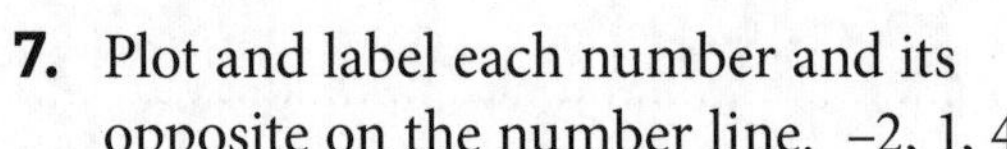

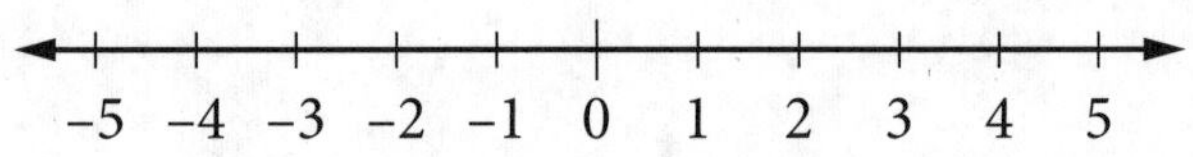

8. $5^3 =$ ________

9. Which quadrant on a coordinate grid is (4, –1) located in?

____

10. Graph and label the points on the coordinate grid. Then, find and write the distance between the points.

$A(2, 1)$ and $B(6, 1)$ distance: ________

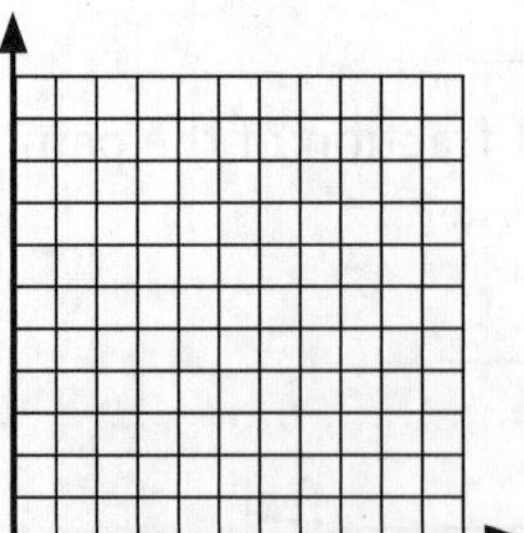

Name: ______________________________ Date: ________________

Directions: Solve each problem.

1. Mariah and Lynette were picking cherries for a pie. Mariah picked $\frac{1}{4}$ of the cherries. Lynette picked 0.75 of the cherries.

a. What is the decimal for the amount of cherries Mariah picked? ______

b. What is the percent for the cherries Lynette picked? ______

2. Which quadrant on a coordinate grid is (–4, –5) located in? ______________

3. What is the measure of the missing angle? ______

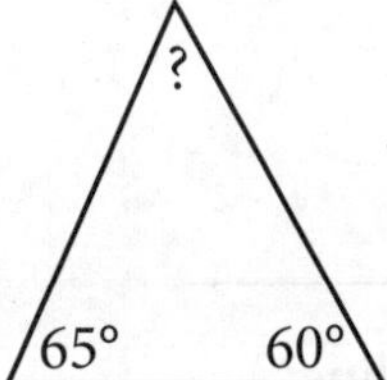

4. What are the coordinates of the new point if the graphed point is reflected over the *y*-axis?

____

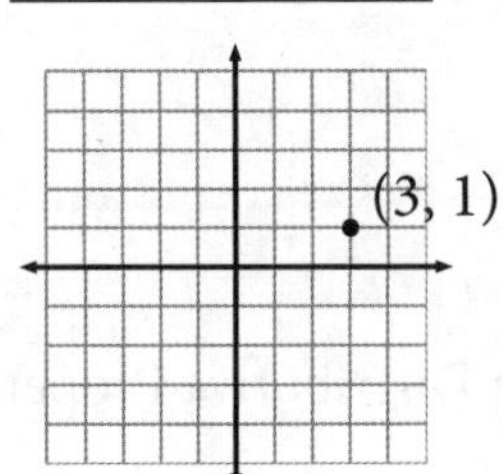

5. Use the shape to complete the tasks.

a. Draw a net for the square pyramid.

b. Find and record the surface area of the square pyramid.

______ square centimeters

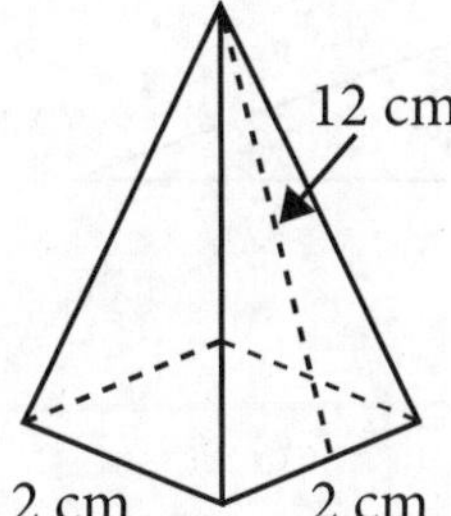

6. Use the graph to answer the questions.

a. How many people were surveyed according to the histogram? ______

b. Which age group was the mode? ______

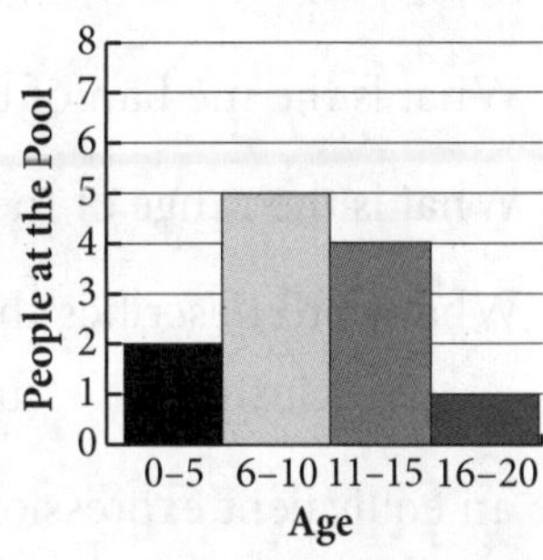

7. 15 – (–9) = ______

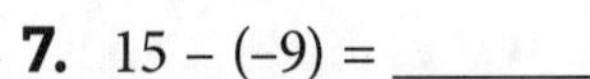

8. $8^2 + 1^5 =$ ______

Name: ________________________________ Date: ______________

Directions: Solve each problem.

1. Luka is making orange juice. He uses 4 cups of concentrate and the rest water in a batch of 10 cups of orange juice.

a. What percent of the orange juice is concentrate? _______

b. What is the ratio of concentrate to water? _______

2. What are the coordinates of the point reflected over the x-axis from (3, 2)? _______

3. Use the number line to answer the questions.

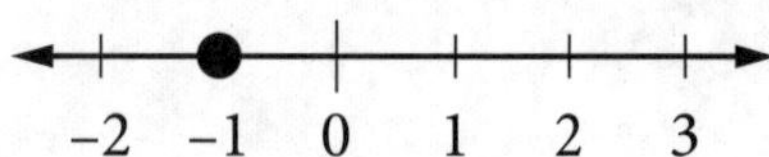

a. What is the opposite of the number graphed on the number line? _______

b. What is the absolute value of the number graphed on the number line? _______

4. Draw a net for the triangular prism.

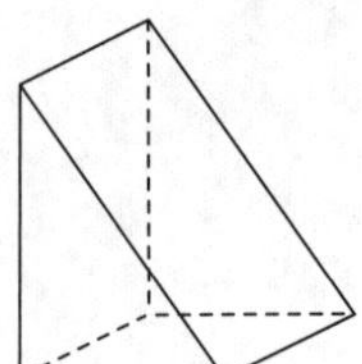

5. Write an equivalent expression for the area of the diagram using the Distributive Property.

$8(x + 10) =$ _______ + _______

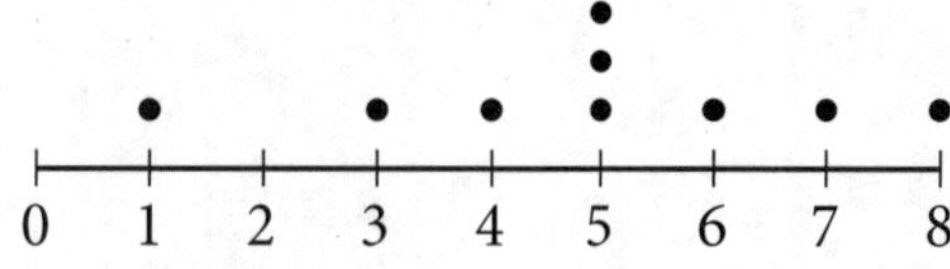

6. What is the measure of the missing angle? _______

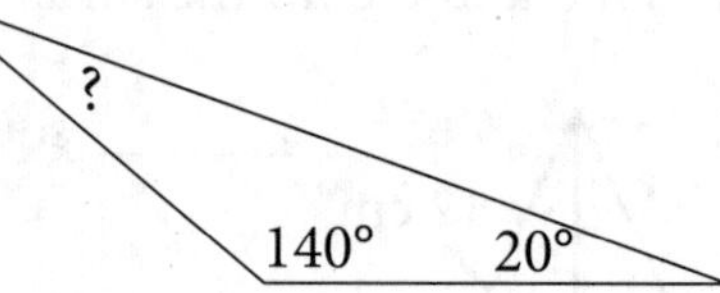

7. Use the dot plot to answer the questions.

0 1 2 3 4 5 6 7 8

a. What is the median of the data on the dot plot? _______

b. What is the range of the data on the dot plot? _______

c. What word describes the line plot? Circle your answer.

clustered uniform skewed

8. Write an equivalent expression using the Distributive Property.

$16 + 24x =$ _______ (_______ + _______)

Name: ______________________ Date: ______________

Directions: Solve each problem.

1. Use the hundreds grid to answer the questions.

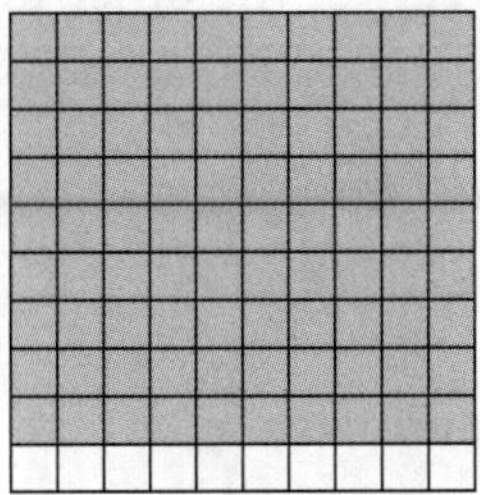

a. What decimal represents the shaded area on the grid? ________

b. What percent represents the shaded area on the grid? ________

2. Harry used 10 gallons of water to fill up his fish tank. Hallie used $\frac{9}{8}$ as much water. Who used more water to fill their fish tank? How do you know?

____

____

3. Write an equivalent expression using the Distributive Property.

10 + 35

______ (______ + ______)

4. The recipe calls for 3 cups of chocolate chips for every 5 cups of flour. How many cups of chocolate chips are needed for every 1 cup of flour?

____

5. Complete the table.

Number	Absolute Value	Opposite
6		
		–10
–3		

6. Write an expression for *a number increased by 9.*

____

7. What are the coordinates of the fourth point needed to form a rectangle on the graph? ______________

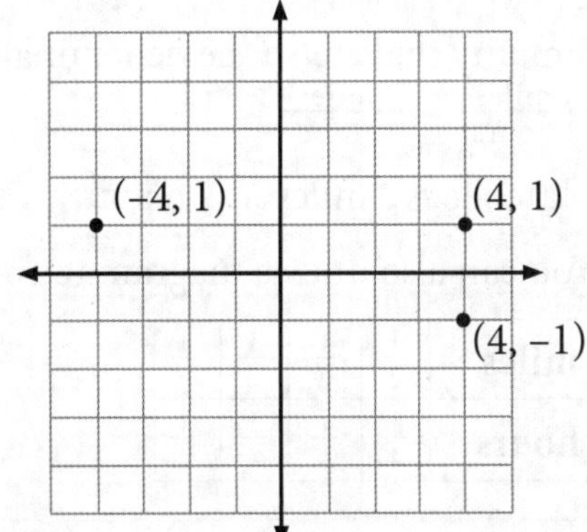

8. Write an expression, using the Distributive Property, to represent the area of the rectangle.

____

4x	20

Learn about Unit Rates

A **rate** is a comparison of two quantities of different units.

A **unit rate** is a comparison of a quantity to 1. Unit rates have a denominator of 1. Unit rates are found by dividing a ratio of different units to find the amount of a unit per 1 of the other unit.

Example 1

What is the rate and the unit rate for the given phrase?

40 sandwiches for 5 campers

1. Write the comparison as a fraction. Label the numerator and denominator.
   Rate: $\frac{\text{40 sandwiches}}{\text{5 campers}}$
2. To find the unit rate, divide the numerator of the rate by the denominator.
   40 ÷ 5 = ________
3. You can write it two ways. $\frac{\text{8 sandwiches}}{\text{1 camper}}$ or 8 $\frac{\text{sandwiches}}{\text{camper}}$

Example 2

Marco jogs $\frac{1}{2}$ of a mile in $\frac{1}{4}$ of an hour. How far does he jog in one hour?

1. Divide the distance Marco jogs by the time it takes him.
   $\frac{1}{2} \div \frac{1}{4}$ is the same as $\frac{1}{2} \times \frac{4}{1}$
   $\frac{1}{2} \times \frac{4}{1} = \frac{\text{4 miles}}{\text{2 hours}}$
2. Simplify the rate so the denominator is 1 hour.
   $\frac{\text{4 miles}}{\text{2 hours}} = \frac{\text{2 miles}}{\text{1 hour}}$
3. Marco jogs 2 miles in 1 hour.
4. You can also draw a diagram to find the answer or check your work.

miles	$\frac{1}{2}$	$\frac{1}{2}$	$\frac{1}{2}$	$\frac{1}{2}$
hours	$\frac{1}{4}$	$\frac{1}{4}$	$\frac{1}{4}$	$\frac{1}{4}$

Example 3

Frank ran 4 miles in $\frac{2}{3}$ of an hour. Find his unit rate.

1. To find Frank's unit rate, we can divide the number of miles he ran by the amount of time it took him to run the distance.
2. To divide by a fraction, we can multiply by the reciprocal.
   $4 \div \frac{2}{3} = \frac{4}{1} \times \frac{3}{2} = \frac{12}{2} = 6$
3. Frank ran ________ miles per hour.

Name: ______________________________ Date: ______________

Quick Tip

Be sure to label both the numerator and the denominator in a rate. When writing the unit rate, label the answer in the number of units in the numerator per one unit of the denominator.

Directions: Write the rate and the unit rate for each phrase.

1. 150 students for 15 tables

Rate: ______________

Unit Rate: ______________

2. 56 party hats in 8 packages

Rate: ______________

Unit Rate: ______________

3. 36 peaches in 3 boxes

Rate: ______________

Unit Rate: ______________

4. 120 campers in 10 tents

Rate: ______________

Unit Rate: ______________

5. 81 golf balls in 9 boxes

Rate: ______________

Unit Rate: ______________

6. $400 for 20 hours of work

Rate: ______________

Unit Rate: ______________

7. 90 students in 3 classrooms

Rate: ______________

Unit Rate: ______________

8. 12 birds in 4 nests

Rate: ______________

Unit Rate: ______________

9. 48 pounds of potatoes in 6 bags

Rate: ______________

Unit Rate: ______________

10. 60 books on 5 shelves

Rate: ______________

Unit Rate: ______________

11. 35 juice boxes in 7 packages

Rate: ______________

Unit Rate: ______________

12. 125 candles in 5 boxes

Rate: ______________

Unit Rate: ______________

Name: ______________________________ Date: ______________

Directions: Find each unit rate.

1. $\frac{\$1,050}{\text{50 hours}} = \frac{}{\text{1 hour}}$

2. $\frac{\text{45 dogs}}{\text{15 houses}} = \frac{}{\text{1 house}}$

3. $\frac{\$333}{\text{6 video games}} - \frac{}{\text{1 video game}}$

4. $\frac{\$48}{\text{6-month membership}} = \frac{}{\text{1-month membership}}$

5. $\frac{\text{40 driveways snowplowed}}{\text{4 hours}} = \frac{}{\text{1 hour}}$

6. $\frac{\text{80 gallons}}{\text{10 minutes}} = \frac{}{\text{1 minute}}$

7. $\frac{\text{3 miles}}{\frac{1}{4}\text{ hour}} = \frac{}{\text{1 hour}}$

8. $\frac{\text{112 pages}}{2\frac{1}{2}\text{ hours}} = \frac{}{\text{1 hour}}$

9. $\frac{\$216}{\text{18 hours}} = \frac{}{\text{1 hour}}$

10. $\frac{\text{8 pizzas}}{\text{16 teammates}} = \frac{}{\text{1 teammate}}$

11. $\frac{\text{400 miles}}{\text{16 gallons}} = \frac{}{\text{1 gallon}}$

12. $\frac{\$192}{\text{6 sweaters}} = \frac{}{\text{1 sweater}}$

13. $\frac{\text{450 words}}{\text{9 minutes}} = \frac{}{\text{1 minute}}$

14. $\frac{\text{54 wins}}{\text{6 seasons}} = \frac{}{\text{1 season}}$

Name: ____________________ Date: ____________

Directions: Solve each problem.

1. Tamyra bought 8 pairs of shoes for \$256. How much was 1 pair of shoes?

______

2. Li ate 2 hot dogs in $\frac{1}{3}$ of a minute. How many hot dogs could Li eat in 1 minute?

______

3. Bart bought 8 candy bars for \$4. How how much did each candy bar cost?

______

4. Camille read 84 pages of her book in 4 hours. At that speed, how many pages did Camille read in 1 hour?

______

5. Yan used 12 cups of sugar to make 6 pies. How many cups of sugar did Yan use for 1 pie?

______

6. Devin earned \$186 for $15\frac{1}{2}$ hours of work. How much did Devin earn in 1 hour?

______

7. Patty finished 16 math problems in $\frac{2}{3}$ of an hour. At this rate, how many problems will Patty complete in 1 hour?

______

8. Lonnie bought 4 pounds of oranges for \$6. How much was each pound of oranges?

______

9. Diana drove $942\frac{1}{2}$ miles in $14\frac{1}{2}$ hours. How many miles did Diana drive in 1 hour?

______

10. Grant can run $\frac{1}{2}$ miles in $5\frac{1}{2}$ minutes. How many miles can Grant run in 1 minute?

______

11. Walt mowed 5 lawns in his neighborhood in $2\frac{1}{3}$ hours. Each lawn was the same size. How many lawns could Walt mow in 1 hour?

______

12. At the movies, Ron bought 4 buckets of popcorn for \$43.96. How much was 1 bucket of popcorn?

______

Name: ____________________ Date: ____________

Directions: Solve each problem.

1. Geno swam 3 miles at the same speed in $\frac{1}{4}$ of an hour. How many miles could Geno swim in 1 hour?

____

2. Keith rode his bicycle 15 miles at the same speed in $1\frac{1}{4}$ hours. How many miles could Keith ride in 1 hour?

____

3. Wendy made 5 ceramic bowls in $\frac{1}{4}$ of an hour. How many bowls could she make in 1 hour?

____

4. Lance skateboarded $\frac{1}{2}$ of a mile in $\frac{1}{3}$ of an hour. How many miles could he skateboard in 1 hour?

____

5. Carol folded 16 origami animals in $\frac{2}{5}$ of an hour. How many animals could she fold in 1 hour?

____

6. Darci cut out 10 character drawings in $\frac{1}{5}$ of an hour. How many character drawings could she cut out in 1 hour?

____

7. Marci needed $\frac{1}{4}$ of a cup of chocolate chips for $\frac{1}{3}$ of a cookie recipe. How many cups of chocolate chips does Marci need for 1 full cookie recipe?

____

8. Rob's plant grew $\frac{1}{8}$ of an inch in $\frac{1}{2}$ of a week. How many inches will Rob's plant grow in 1 week?

____

9. Connie kept score at $\frac{1}{6}$ of her softball games for $\frac{1}{2}$ of the season. If there were 36 games this season, for how many games did Connie keep score?

____

10. Ling's garden takes $\frac{1}{8}$ of a bag of flower seeds for $\frac{1}{16}$ of the garden. How many bags of seeds will Ling need to fill the entire garden?

____

11. Angus ran 9 miles in $\frac{4}{5}$ of an hour. How many miles will Angus run in 1 hour?

____

12. Gus mows 7 lawns in $2\frac{1}{4}$ hours. How many lawns does Gus mow in 1 hour?

____

Unit Rates

Name: ______________________ Date: ______________

Reminder

You can divide the numerator by the denominator to find the unit rate.

Directions: Solve each problem.

1. Marcella takes her sister for a walk in the stroller every day. She walks $\frac{1}{3}$ of a mile in $\frac{1}{6}$ of an hour. How many miles can she walk in 1 hour?

   ____

2. Kenny walks his dog after school every day. He walks $\frac{3}{5}$ of a mile in $\frac{1}{10}$ of an hour. How many miles can he walk in 1 hour?

   ____

3. Michael runs $\frac{4}{5}$ of a mile in $\frac{1}{10}$ of an hour. How many miles can Michael run in 1 hour?

   ____

4. Gracie bakes $\frac{1}{2}$ a dozen cupcakes with $1\frac{1}{2}$ cups of flour. How many cupcakes can Gracie bake with 1 cup of flour?

   ____

5. Manny makes pillows. He sews $2\frac{1}{2}$ pillows in $\frac{2}{4}$ of an hour. How many pillows can Manny make in 1 hour?

   ____

6. Jennifer frosts $3\frac{1}{5}$ cakes in $\frac{1}{5}$ of an hour. How many cakes can Jennifer frost in 1 hour?

   ____

7. A plant grew $\frac{2}{3}$ of an inch in $\frac{1}{6}$ of a week. How many inches will the plant grow in 1 week?

   ____

8. Pears cost $14 for $3\frac{1}{2}$ pounds. How much is the cost of 1 pound of pears?

   ____

9. Pizzas cost $109.50 for 6 pizzas. How much does 1 pizza cost?

   ____

10. Stan paints $4\frac{1}{4}$ walls in $2\frac{1}{2}$ hours. How many walls does Stan paint per hour?

    ____

11. Justine needs $4\frac{1}{2}$ cups of strawberries for 3 cakes. How many cups of strawberries does she need for 1 cake?

    ____

12. There are 130 students in $4\frac{1}{3}$ classes. If the number of students is the same in each class, how many students are in 1 class?

    ____

Learn about Proportional Relationships

A **proportional relationship** is a relationship between two variables where the ratios are equivalent.

Example 1

A recipe calls for 2 cups of sugar to 4 cups of flour. How much flour do we need if we use 4 cups of sugar?

1. Write the ratios as fractions.

$$\frac{\text{2 cups of sugar}}{\text{4 cups of flour}} = \frac{\text{4 cups of sugar}}{?}$$

2. You can multiply or divide the numerator and denominator of one ratio by the same amount to get an equivalent ratio. So, if you multiply the 2 cups of sugar by 2, we get 4 cups of sugar. So, multiply the 4 cups of flour by the same amount.

$$\frac{\text{2 cups of sugar}}{\text{4 cups of flour}} \overset{\times 2}{\underset{\times 2}{=}} \frac{\text{4 cups of sugar}}{\text{8 cups of flour}}$$

For 4 cups of sugar, you need ________ cups of flour.

Example 2

Determine if the relationship between *x* and *y* is proportional.

x	*y*
2	8
4	16
6	24

1. Divide each *y* value by the corresponding *x* value. If the quotient is the same for each pair of numbers, the relationship is proportional. If the quotients are not all equal, the relationship is not proportional.

   $8 \div 2 =$ ________

   $16 \div 4 =$ ________

   $24 \div 6 =$ ________

2. Are all of the quotients the same? ________

   So, is the relationship proportional? ________

Proportional Relationships on Graphs

The graph of a proportional relationship will always be a straight line that starts at or passes through the origin, (0, 0).

Examples

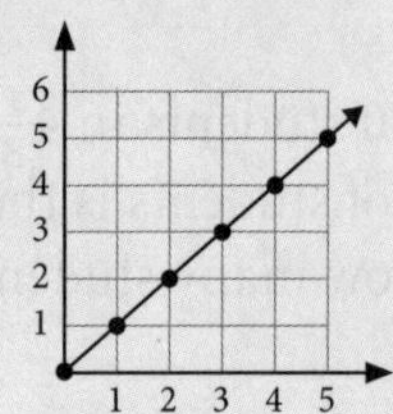

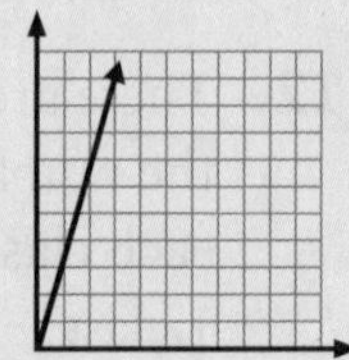

Non-examples

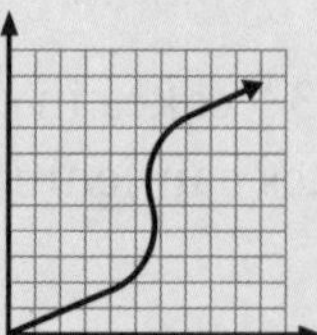

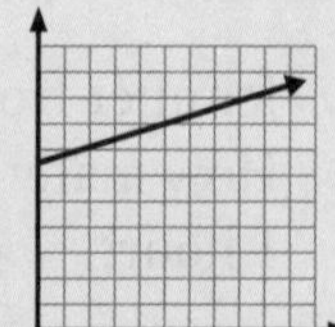

Name: ______________________________ Date: ______________

Reminder

When finding a missing number in a proportional relationship, you can multiply the numerator and denominator in one ratio by the same factor. You can also divide by the same amount.

Directions: Write the missing numbers to make proportional relationships.

1. $\frac{\text{5 dogs}}{\text{3 cats}} = \frac{\text{20 dogs}}{\text{\_\_\_\_\_ cats}}$

2. $\frac{\text{\$65}}{\text{5 hours}} = \frac{\text{\$\_\_\_\_\_}}{\text{30 hours}}$

3. $\frac{\text{18 pens}}{\text{16 pencils}} = \frac{\text{9 pens}}{\text{\_\_\_\_\_ pencils}}$

4. $\frac{\text{8 worksheets}}{\text{80 problems}} = \frac{\text{24 worksheets}}{\text{\_\_\_\_\_ problems}}$

5. $\frac{\text{28 points}}{\text{2 football games}} = \frac{\text{\_\_\_\_\_ points}}{\text{8 football games}}$

6. $\frac{\text{16 songs}}{\text{2 hours}} = \frac{\text{48 songs}}{\text{\_\_\_\_\_ hours}}$

7. $\frac{\text{24 candy bars}}{\text{3 boxes}} = \frac{\text{\_\_\_\_\_ candy bars}}{\text{12 boxes}}$

8. $\frac{\text{36 donuts}}{\text{4 boxes}} = \frac{\text{18 donuts}}{\text{\_\_\_\_\_ boxes}}$

9. $\frac{\text{2 cups chocolate chips}}{\text{3 cups sugar}} = \frac{\text{20 cups chocolate chips}}{\text{\_\_\_\_\_ cups sugar}}$

10. $\frac{\text{32 muffins}}{\text{4 batches}} = \frac{\text{\_\_\_\_\_ muffins}}{\text{16 batches}}$

11. $\frac{\text{14 players}}{\text{1 team}} = \frac{\text{\_\_\_\_\_ players}}{\text{6 teams}}$

12. $\frac{\text{104 cards}}{\text{2 decks}} = \frac{\text{728 cards}}{\text{\_\_\_\_\_ decks}}$

UNIT 1 DAY 7

Proportional Relationships

Name: ____________________ Date: ____________

Directions: Divide each pair of numbers in the table to determine whether the relationship is proportional. Circle your answer.

1. Is the relationship proportional?

yes no

x	y
5	15
6	18
7	24

2. Is the relationship proportional?

yes no

x	y
1	3
2	6
3	9
4	12

3. Is the relationship proportional?

yes no

x	y
8	4
10	5
12	6
14	7

4. Is the relationship proportional?

yes no

x	y
2	5
4	7
6	9
8	11

5. Is the relationship proportional?

yes no

x	y
5	5
10	10
15	15
20	20

6. Is the relationship proportional?

yes no

x	y
3	6
6	9
9	12
12	15

7. Is the relationship proportional?

yes no

x	y
2	11
4	13
6	15
8	17

8. Is the relationship proportional?

yes no

x	y
1	12
2	24
3	36
4	48

Name: ______________________________ Date: ________________

Directions: Determine whether the relationship represented on each graph is proportional. Circle your answer.

1. Is the relationship proportional?

yes no

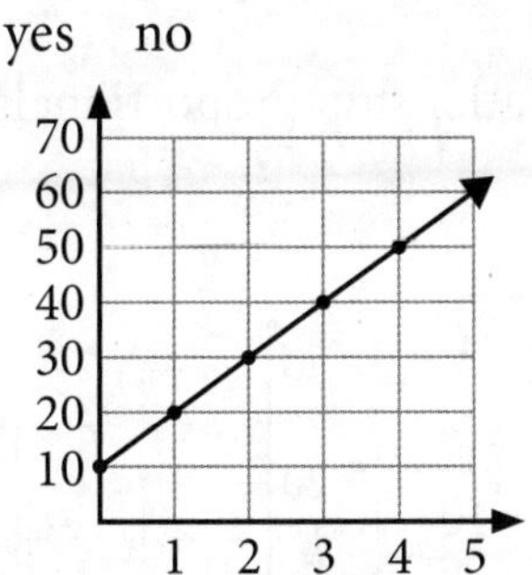

2. Is the relationship proportional?

yes no

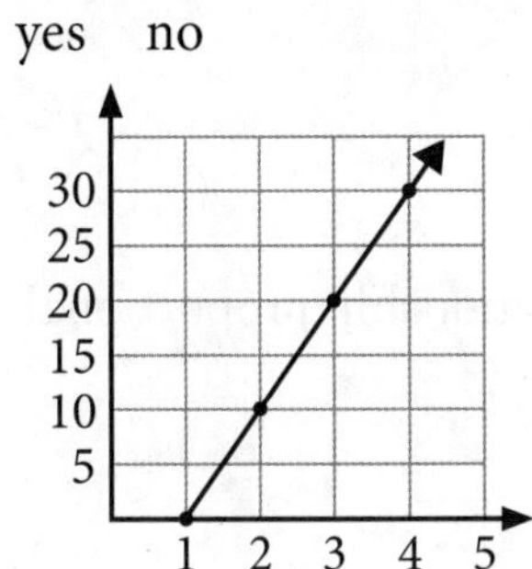

3. Is the relationship proportional?

yes no

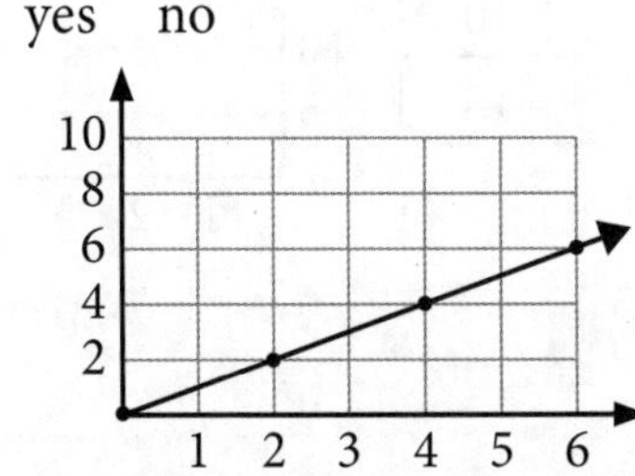

4. Is the relationship proportional?

yes no

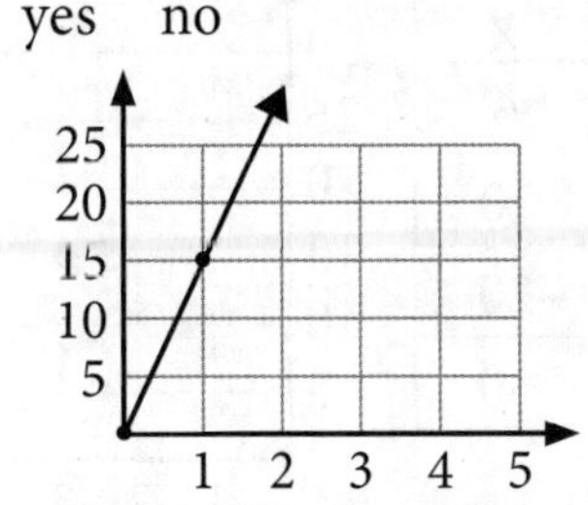

5. Is the relationship proportional?

yes no

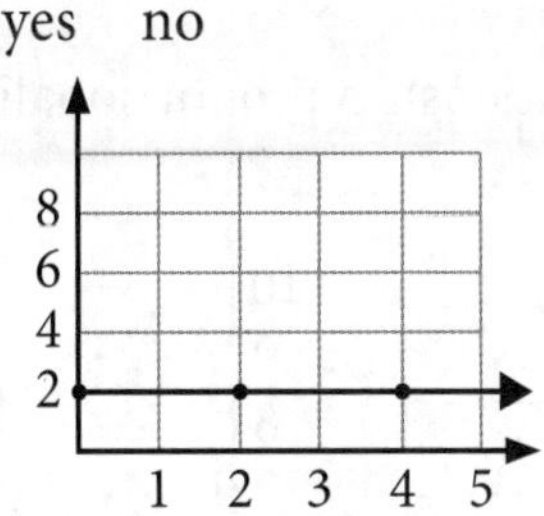

6. Is the relationship proportional?

yes no

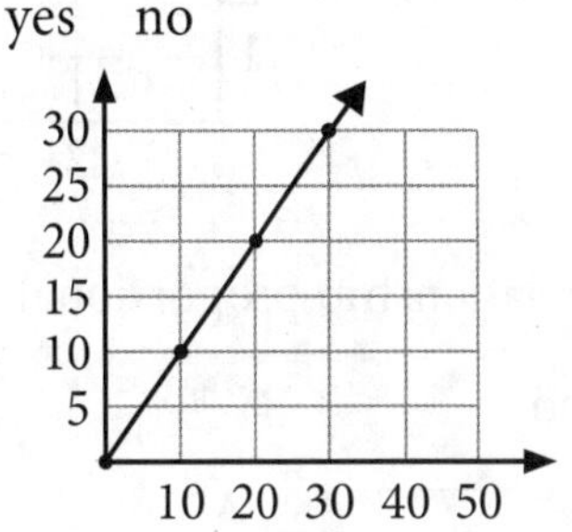

7. Is the relationship proportional?

yes no

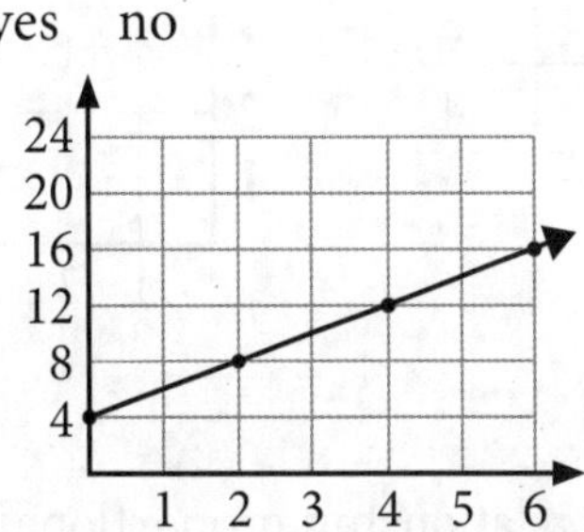

8. Is the relationship proportional?

yes no

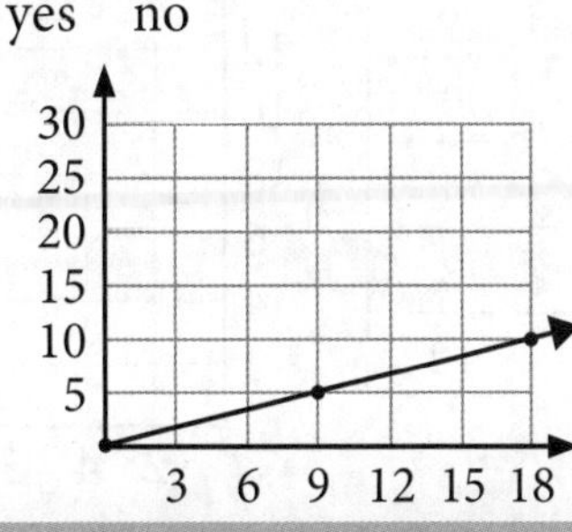

Math Talk

How did you determine whether a graph showed a proportional relationship?

Name: ______________________________ Date: ______________

Reminder

For a graph to be proportional, it must be a straight line and start at or pass through the origin.

Directions: Graph the values in each table. Then, circle whether the relationship is proportional.

1. Is the relationship proportional?

yes no

x	*y*
0	0
1	3
2	6
3	9

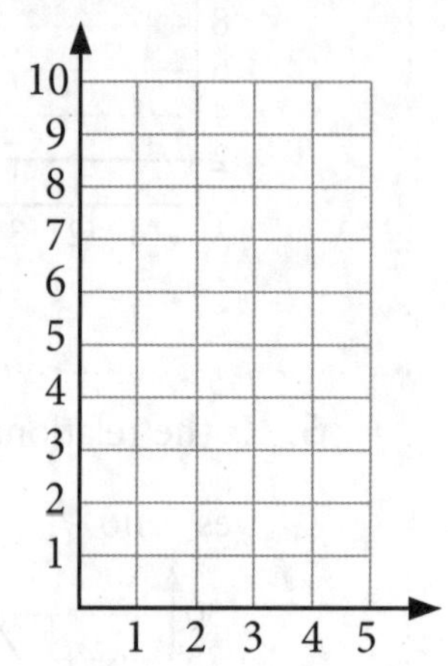

2. Is the relationship proportional?

yes no

x	*y*
0	1
1	2
2	3
3	4

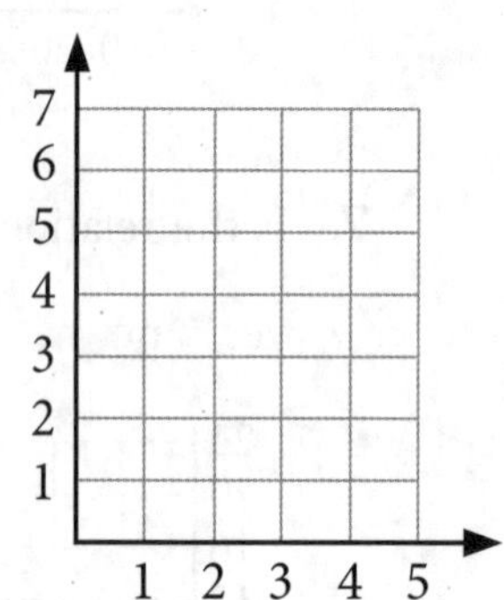

3. Is the relationship proportional?

yes no

x	*y*
0	0
2	4
4	8
6	12

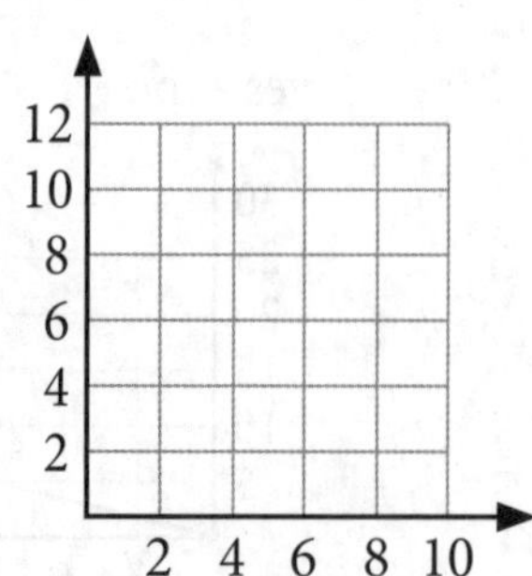

4. Is the relationship proportional?

yes no

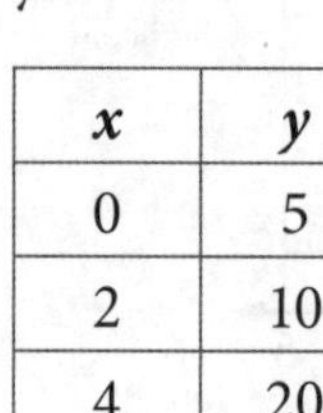

x	*y*
0	5
2	10
4	20
6	30

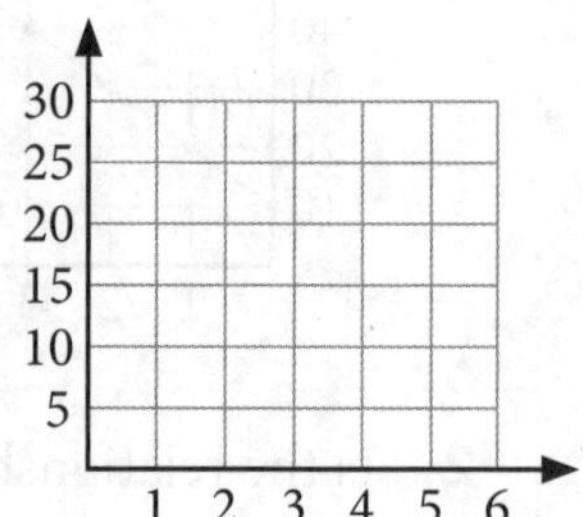

5. Is the relationship proportional?

yes no

x	*y*
0	0
1	5
2	10
3	15

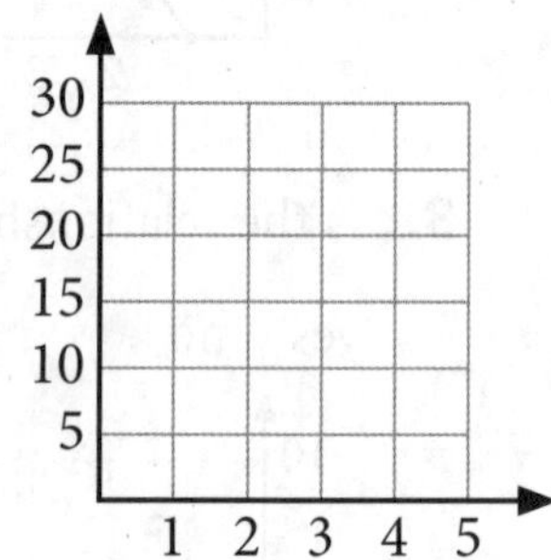

6. Is the relationship proportional?

yes no

x	*y*
0	6
1	10
2	20
3	30

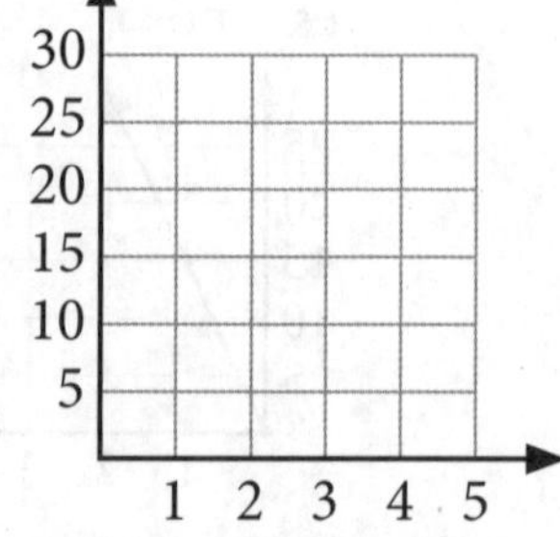

Name: ______________________ Date: ______________

Directions: Solve each problem.

1. Max is making muffins. One recipe calls for 2 cups of sugar and 3 cups of flour. How much flour would Max need to make 4 recipes?

   ____

2. The camp counselors need 40 sandwiches to feed 30 campers. How many sandwiches would they need for 90 campers?

   ____

3. Molly is painting her bedroom. She used 2 gallons of paint for 3 walls. How many gallons would she need for 6 walls?

   ____

4. Robert is filling a pool for his little brother. The pool takes 150 gallons of water. How many gallons would he need to fill the pool 4 times?

   ____

5. Irma earned $576 for 32 hours of work. How much would she earn if she worked 8 hours?

   ____

6. Tyrese made 4 ceramic mugs in 3 hours. How many mugs could Tyrese make in 12 hours?

   ____

7. Cami drew 8 chalk drawings on her driveway in 3 hours. How many chalk drawings could she do in 9 hours?

   ____

8. Peter mowed 4 lawns in 3 hours. How many lawns could he mow in 18 hours?

   ____

9. Linda baked 12 pies in 8 hours. How many pies could Linda bake in 2 hours?

   ____

10. Garrett buys 6 equally priced books for $24. How much would it cost him to buy 3 books?

    ____

11. Ming bought 10 shirts for $120. How many shirts could she buy for $60?

    ____

12. A car travels 210 miles in 3 hours. At this rate, how long would it take the car to travel 420 miles?

    ____

Learn about Constant of Proportionality

constant of proportionality—the number that one variable is multiplied by to get the other variable in a proportional relationship

- The constant of proportionality is typically represented by the variable k and is calculated by dividing $y \div x$.
- All proportional relationships begin at or pass through the origin, (0, 0).
- For any proportional relationship, the point where $x = 1$, also written as $(1, r)$, contains the constant of proportionality. The number 1 represents 1 unit and the r represents the rate, so the point $(1, r)$ represents the unit rate where r is the constant of proportionality.
- Constant of proptionality, unit rate, and slope are equivalent.

From a Table

1. Divide any y value by the corresponding x value. All of the quotients should be the same for the relationship to be proportional. The answer will be the same for every pair.

Pounds of Peanuts (x)	Cost (y)	Cost ÷ Pounds of Peanuts
2	$2.50	2.50 ÷ 2 = ________
4	$5.00	5.00 ÷ 4 = ________
6	$7.50	7.50 ÷ 6 = ________
8	$10.00	10.00 ÷ 8 = ________

2. What is the constant of proportionality? k = ________

From a Graph

Find the coordinates for the constant of proportionality. Explain what the point means in terms of the unit rate.

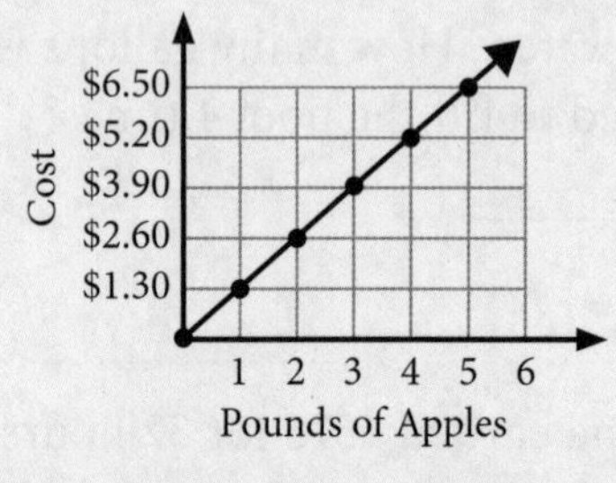

1. To find the constant of proportionality, look to see if $(1, r)$ is on the graph. If it is, then r is the constant of proportionality. What are the coordinates of the constant of proportionality? (1, 1.30)
2. If $(1, r)$ is not on the graph, or you want to check your answer, choose any point and divide $y \div x$. Choose and write a point on the graph. (________, ________)

   y = ________ x = ________ $y \div x$ = ________
3. What is the constant of proportionality? k = ________
4. What does the point mean? For every 1 pound of apples, the cost is $1.30.

From an Equation

Find the constant of proportionality from the equation. $y = 5x$

1. In an equation, the constant of proportionality is the coefficient of x. A coefficient is a number being multiplied by a variable. Circle the coefficient in the equation. $y = 5x$

   k = ________

Name: ______________________ Date: ______________

Quick Tip

Remember, k represents the constant of proportionality and $k = y \div x$.

Directions: Find the constant of proportionality for each table.

1. k = ________

x	y
0	0
2	3
4	6
6	9

2. k = ________

x	y
0	0
1	2.5
2	5
3	7.5

3. k = ________

x	y
0	0
1	9.3
2	18.6
3	27.9

4. k = ________

x	y
0	0
3	60
6	120
9	180

5. k = ________

x	y
0	0
5	22.5
10	45
15	67.5

6. k = ________

x	y
0	0
4	24
8	48
12	72

Name: ______________________ Date: ______________

Directions: Find the constant of proportionality for each graph.

1. $k =$ ________

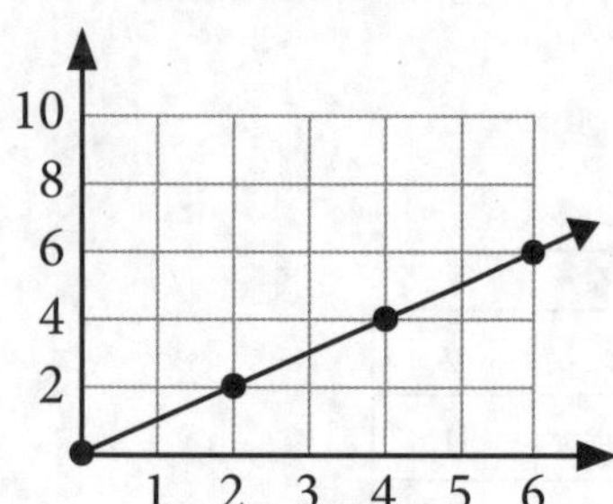

4. $k =$ ________

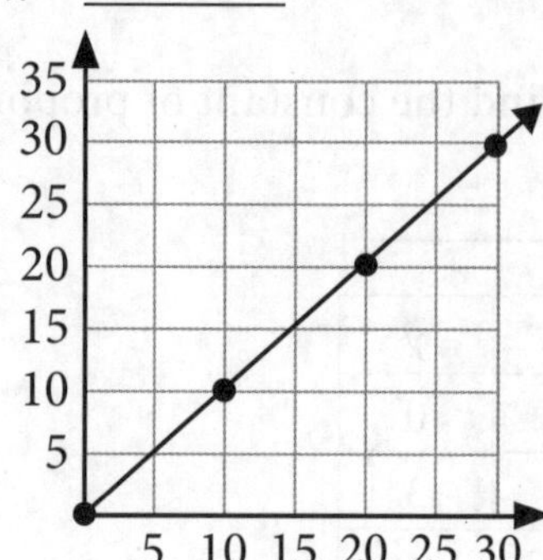

2. $k =$ ________

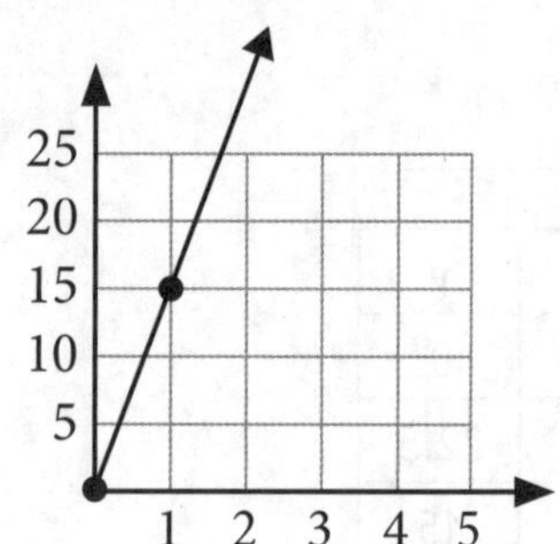

5. $k =$ ________

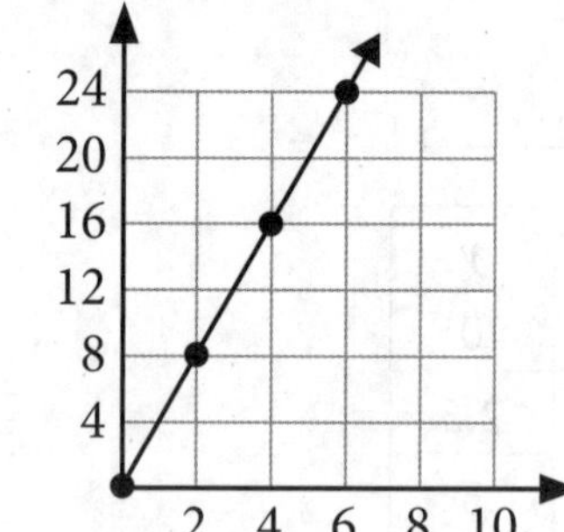

3. $k =$ ________

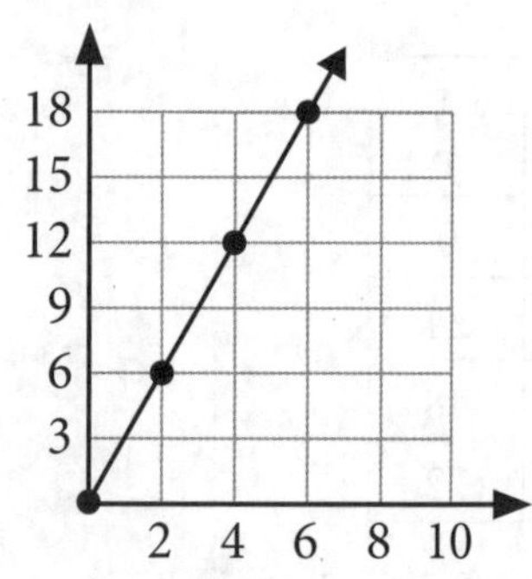

6. $k =$ ________

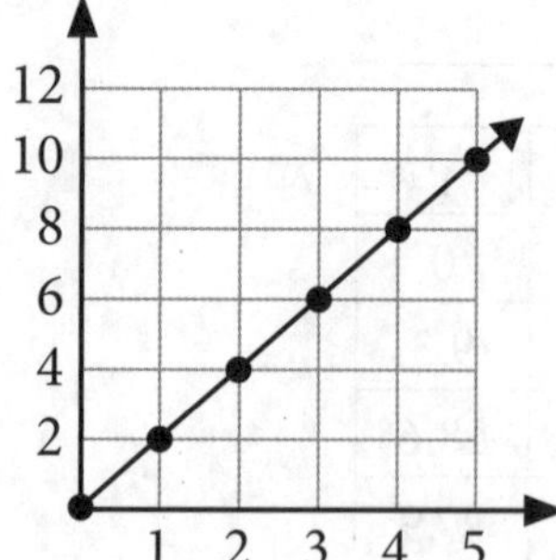

Name: ______________________________ Date: ________________

Reminder

Remember, if the point (1, *r*) is not shown on the graph, divide $y \div x$ for any point on the line to find the constant of proportionality. The variable *r* also represents the unit rate for the relationship.

Directions: Find the constant of proportionality for each graph. Then, complete the sentences to explain what the point means in terms of the unit rate.

1. **a.** $k =$ ________

b. Every 1 ________ costs ________.

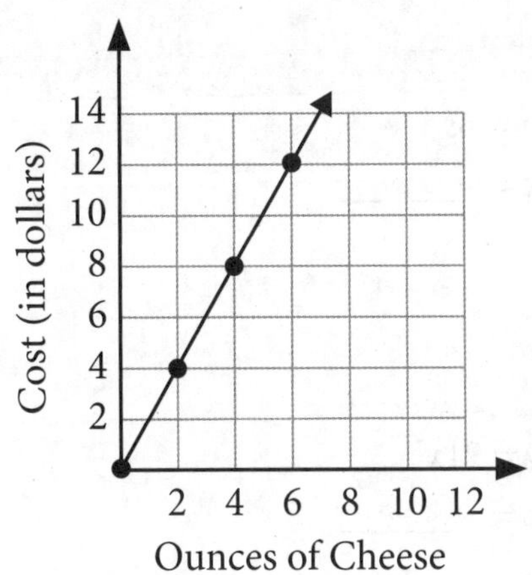

2. **a.** $k =$ ________

b. Every 1 ________ costs ________.

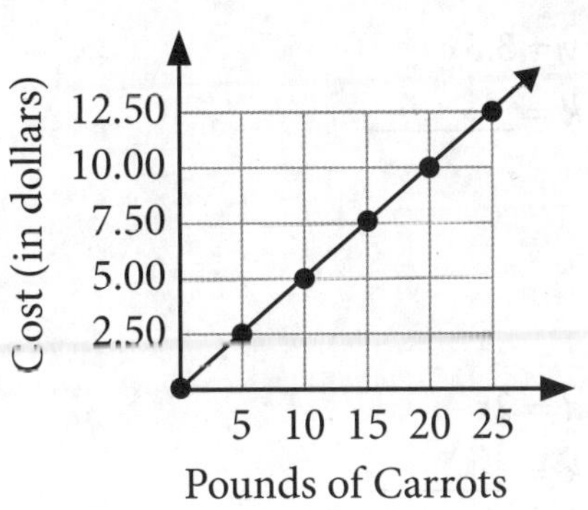

3. **a.** $k =$ ________

b. Every 1 ________ costs ________.

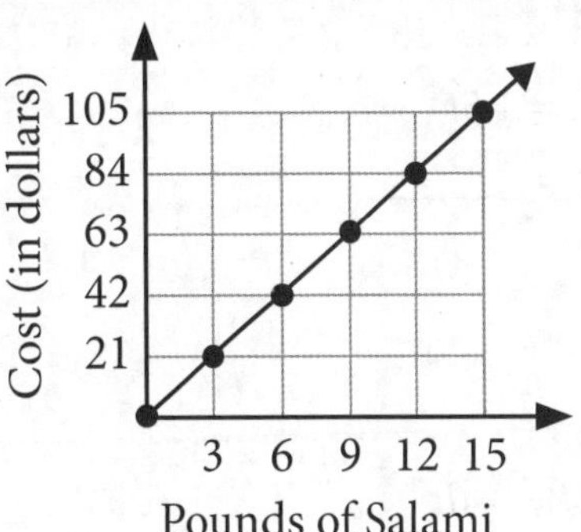

4. **a.** $k =$ ________

b. Every 1 ________ costs ________.

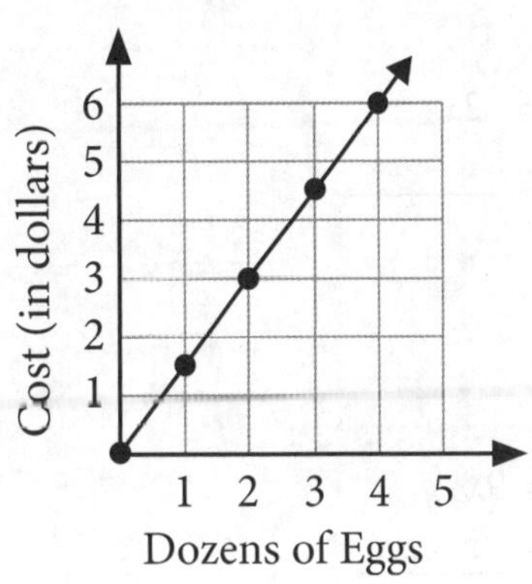

Name: ______________________ Date: ______________

Directions: Write the constant of proportionality for each problem.

1. $y = 3x$
$k =$ ______

2. $d = 6t$
$k =$ ______

3. $C = 1.5t$
$k =$ ______

4. $M = -4h$
$k =$ ______

5. $A = 4s$
$k =$ ______

6. $y = -2x$
$k =$ ______

7. $y = 9x$
$k =$ ______

8. $h = 5b$
$k =$ ______

9. $y = 1x$
$k =$ ______

10. $p = 4s$
$k =$ ______

11. $y = 21x$
$k =$ ______

12. $f = 15x$
$k =$ ______

13. $y = 3.5x$
$k =$ ______

14. $d = 2r$
$k =$ ______

Name: ______________________________ Date: ____________________

Directions: Write the constant of proportionality for each problem.

1. k = ________

Hours	Income
3	$36
6	$72
9	$108
12	$144

2. k = ________

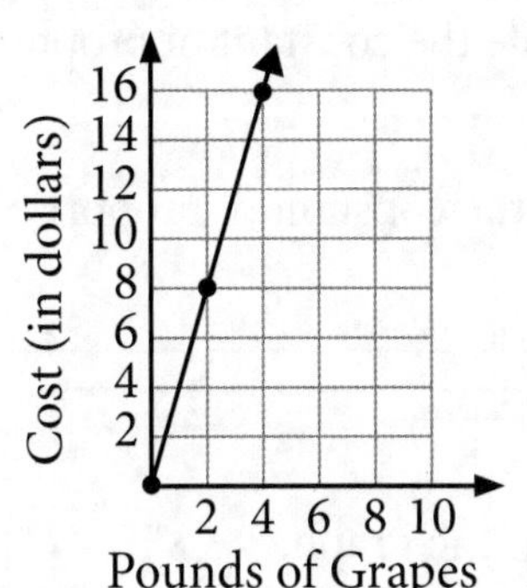

3. $y = -5x$

k = ________

4. k = ________

Hours	Laps Ran
2	18
4	36
6	54
8	72

5. k = ________

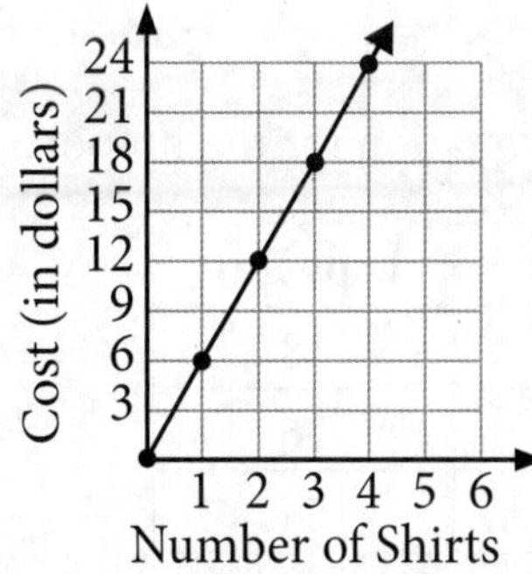

6. $y = 11x$

k = ________

7. k = ________

Hours	Cookies Baked
2	48
4	96
6	144
8	192

8. k = ________

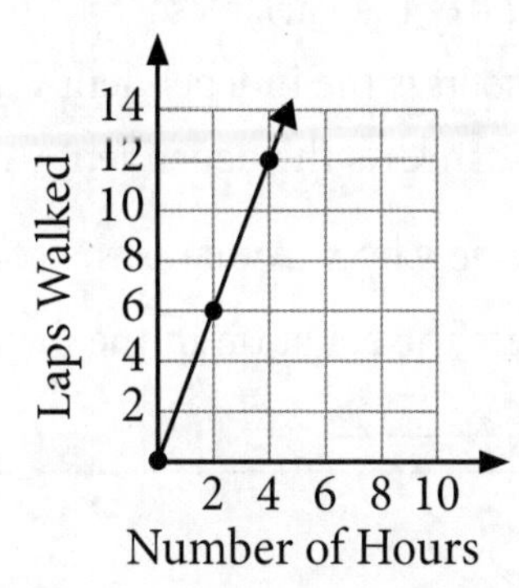

Constant of Proportionality

Learn about Equations of Proportional Relationships

The graphs of all proportional relationships must pass through the origin. The equations for proportional relationships are in the form $y = kx$, where k is the constant of proportionality.

Example 1

Write an equation for the proportional relationship.

Hours	Laps Ran
3	18
6	36
9	54

1. First, identify the variables. *Hours* is the independent variable, or x, and *Laps Ran* is the dependent variable, or y.
2. Divide a y value by the corresponding x value to calculate the constant of proportionality.
   $18 \div 3 =$ ________
3. Write the equation in the form $y = kx$, replacing k with the constant of proportionality.
   $y =$ ________x

Example 2

Write an equation for the proportional relationship shown on the graph.

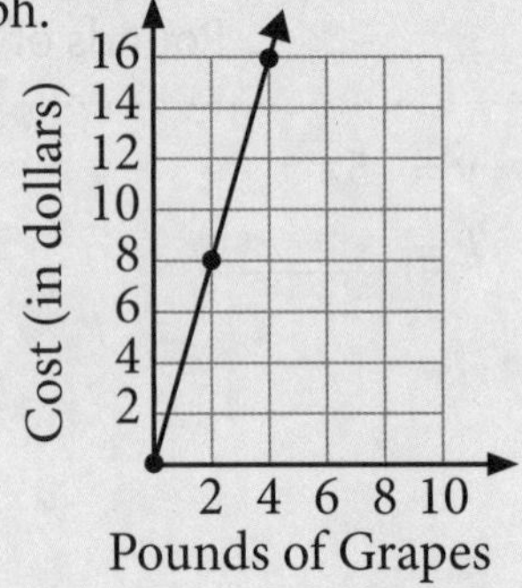

1. First, identify the variables. *Pounds of grapes* is the independent variable, or x, and *cost* is the dependent variable, or y.
2. Choose a point from the graph, and divide $y \div x$.
   What is the constant of proportionality? ________
3. Write the equation in the form $y = kx$, replacing k with the constant of proportionality.
   $y =$ ________x

Example 3

Write an equation for the proportional relationship.

The Jones family drove 1,820 miles in 28 hours.

1. Identify the variables.
   28 hours is the independent variable. (x)
   1,820 miles is the dependent variable. (y)
2. Divide y by x. What is the constant of proportionality? ________
3. Write the equation in the form $y = kx$, replacing k with the constant of proportionality.
   $y =$ ________x

Name: ______________________________ Date: ____________

Directions: Write the missing number in each equation for the proportional relationship.

1. $y =$ ________ x

Hula Hoops	Cost
1	$2
2	$4
3	$6
4	$8

4. $y =$ ________ x

Pounds of Peaches	Cost
5	$19.00
10	$38.00
15	$57.00
20	$76.00

2. $y =$ ________ x

Hours	Money Earned
2	$14
4	$28
6	$42
8	$56

5. $y =$ ________ x

Pounds of Almonds	Cost
3	$7.50
6	$15.00
9	$22.50
12	$30.00

3. $y =$ ________ x

Hours	Laps Swam
3	30
6	60
9	90
12	120

6. $y =$ ________ x

Hours	Miles Walked
3	12
5	20
7	28
9	36

Name: ______________________ Date: ______________

Directions: Write the missing number in each equation for the proportional relationship.

1. $y =$ ________ x

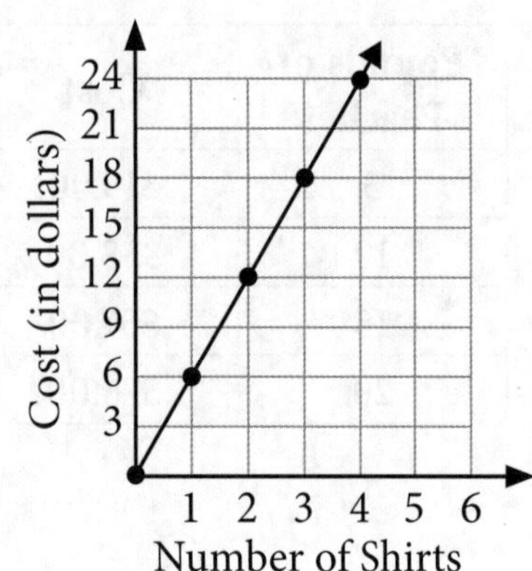

2. $y =$ ________ x

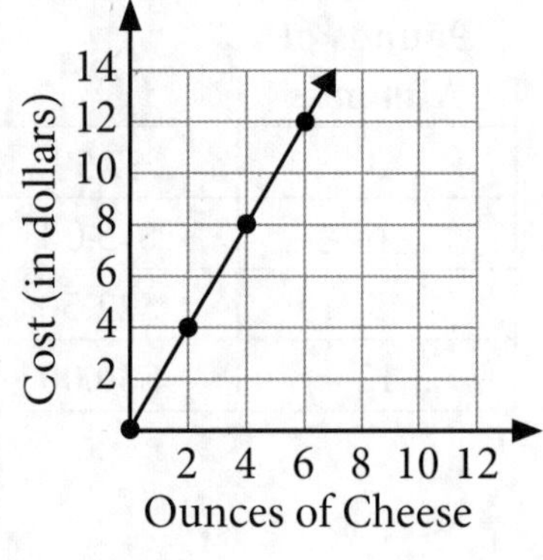

3. $y =$ ________ x

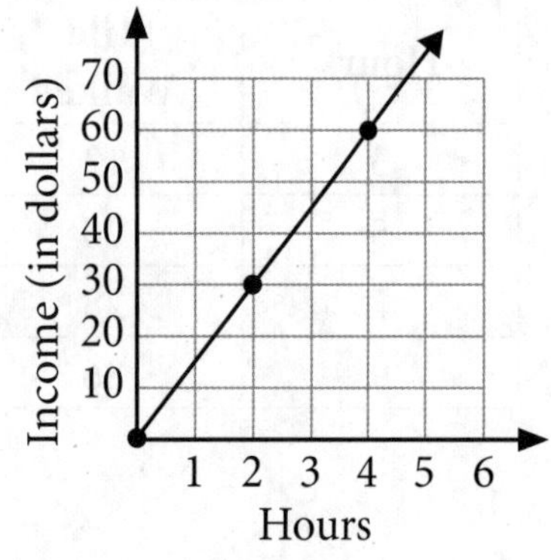

4. $y =$ ________ x

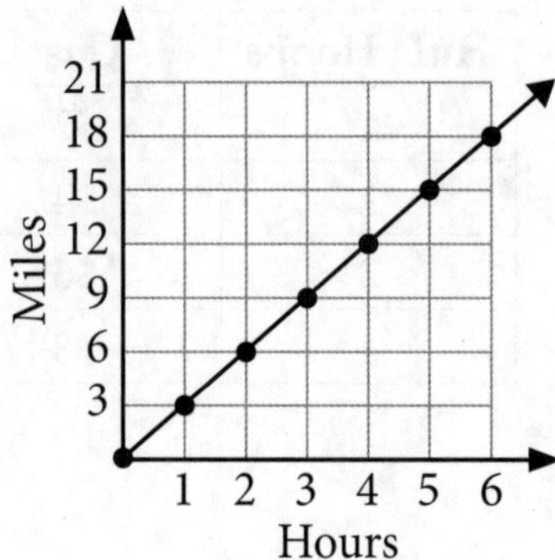

5. $y =$ ________ x

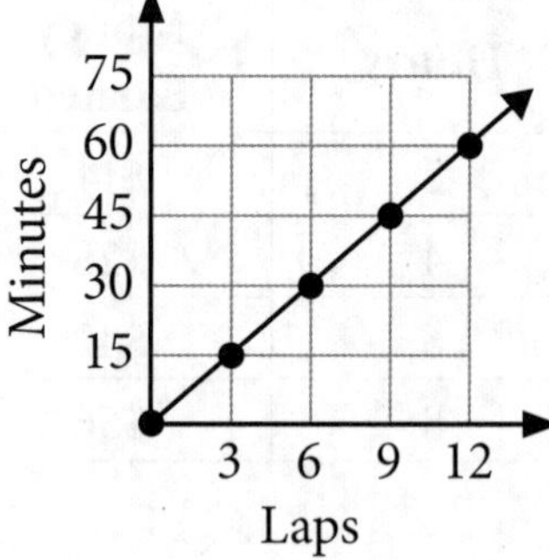

6. $y =$ ________ x

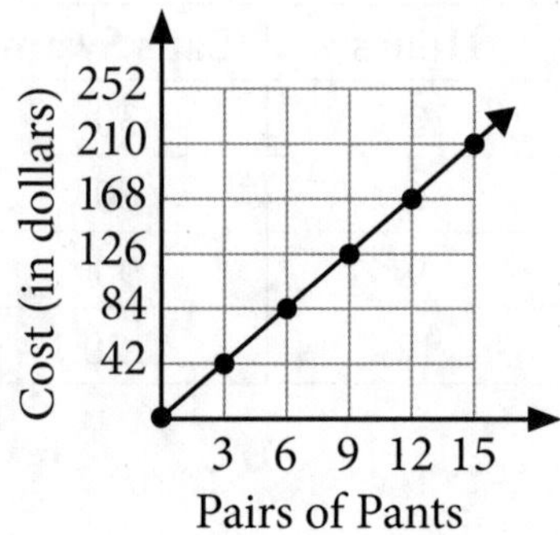

Name: ______________________ Date: ____________

Directions: Write the missing number in each equation for the proportional relationship.

1. Kevin and his friends paid $30 for 10 hot dogs at the baseball game.

$y =$ ________ x

2. Jamie ran 28 miles in 4 days.

$y =$ ________ x

3. The Lee family drove 1,500 miles in 6 days.

$y =$ ________ x

4. Mylee paid $55.50 for 3 shirts.

$y =$ ________ x

5. Mason earned $88 watching his neighbor's dog for 8 hours.

$y =$ ________ x

6. Ryan paid $22.50 for 9 packs of gum.

$y =$ ________ x

7. Aaron bought 36 golf balls for $117.

$y =$ ________ x

8. There were 300 balloons blown up by 30 people.

$y =$ ________ x

9. In Michelle's class, 64 cupcakes were baked by 4 students.

$y =$ ________ x

10. Roger read 108 books in 12 weeks.

$y =$ ________ x

11. There were 280 pieces of candy in 7 packages.

$y =$ ________ x

12. Lena has 120 stickers in 4 packs.

$y =$ ________ x

13. Paul walked 24 dogs in 8 hours.

$y =$ ________ x

14. Jermaine rode 14 miles in 2 hours.

$y =$ ________ x

Name: ______________________ Date: ______________

Quick Tip

To complete the table, multiply the unit rate by each value in the x (left) column. This will give you the y-value (right column).

Directions: Complete each table. Then, write an equation for the proportional relationship.

1. Garrett makes $25 an hour waiting tables.

equation: ______________________

Hours	Income
0	
1	
2	
3	

2. Lysa earns $7.50 an hour babysitting.

equation: ______________________

Hours	Income
0	
1	
2	
3	

3. The 150 campers drink 1,800 ounces of juice.

equation: ______________________

Campers	Ounces of Juice
0	
1	
10	
20	
50	

4. Denise spent $210 on 6 new pairs of pants.

equation: ______________________

Pairs of Pants	Cost
0	
2	
4	
6	

5. Marcel mowed 9 lawns and earned $270.

equation: ______________________

Number of Lawns	Income
0	
3	
6	
9	

6. Michael shoveled 7 driveways and earned $105.

equation: ______________________

Number of Driveways	Income
0	
2	
4	
6	

Name: ______________________ Date: ______________

Quick Tip

The number being multiplied by the variable is called the **coefficient**. The coefficient is also the unit rate in a proportional relationship.

Directions: Write an equation for each proportional relationship.

1. equation: ______________

x	y
5	45
10	90
15	135

2. The Ryan family drove 2,275 miles in 35 days.

$y =$ ________ x

3. equation: ______________

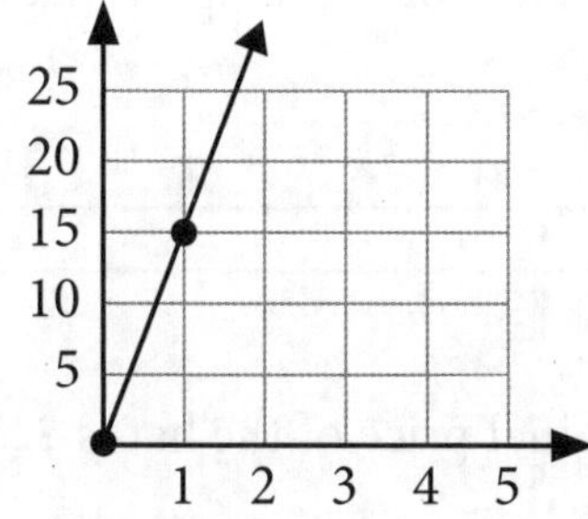

4. There were 95 people in 19 cars.

$y =$ ________ x

5. equation: ______________

x	y
2	13
4	26
6	39

6. Jorge earned $240 in 15 hours.

$y =$ ________ x

7. equation: ______________

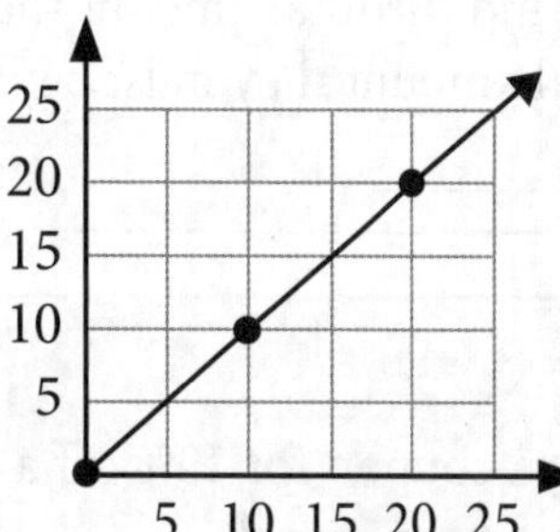

8. equation: ______________

x	y
1	11
3	33
5	55
7	77

Equations of Proportional Relationships

Learn about Ratio and Percent Problems

Percents are part-to-whole comparisons in which the whole amount is 100.
Ratios are comparisons and can be part-to-part or part-to-whole comparisons. You can use proportional relationships to solve percent problems. Set them up like this.

$\frac{\text{Part}}{\text{Whole}} = \frac{\text{Percent}}{100}$

Example: What is 25% of 90?

Since 90 is the total amount, and 25 is the percent, we can set it up as shown: $\frac{x}{90} = \frac{25}{100}$

To solve this, you can cross multiply, or multiply diagonally.

$90 \cdot 25 = 100 \cdot x$

$2{,}250 = 100x$

To solve this, we divide 2,250 by 100.

$x = 22.5$

Total with Tip

The Howard family went out to dinner, and the bill was $65. They want to leave a 20% tip. How much should they leave for the tip? What is the total amount the Howards have to pay, including the tip?

1. Set up a proportional relationship. $\frac{x}{65} = \frac{20}{100}$
2. Multiply diagonally. $65 \cdot 20 = 100 \cdot x$
3. Solve the equation.

   $100x = 1{,}300$

   $x = 13$
4. The Howard family should leave $________ for a tip.
5. To find the total amount the Howard family has to pay, add $65 + the tip. What is the total amount they must pay?

   $ ________

Discounted Price

Teddy has a coupon for 10% off a new baseball hat. The original price of the hat is $25. What is the discounted price?

1. Set up a proportional relationship. $\frac{x}{25} = \frac{10}{100}$
2. Cross multiply (multiply diagonally). $100 \cdot x = 25 \cdot 10$
3. Solve the equation.

   $100x = 250$

   $x = 2.5$ or $2.50
4. Subtract the original price by the discounted amount to find the new price.

   $25 – $2.50 = ________

Percent Increase

Gary sold \$40 in raffle tickets for the fundraiser last year. This year, Gary sold \$65 in raffle tickets. What is the percent of increase in Gary's raffle ticket sales?

1. Subtract the two numbers. $65 - 40 = 25$
2. Divide the difference by the original amount. $25 \div 40 = 0.625$
3. Multiply your answer by 100. $0.625 \times 100 =$ ________

Converting Units

When converting from a smaller unit to a larger unit, divide. When converting from a larger unit to the next smaller unit, multiply.

How many inches are in 4 feet?

1. Set up a proportional relationship using the unit rate.
   We know that 12 inches = 1 foot, so:
   $\frac{4 \text{ feet}}{1 \text{ foot}} = \frac{x}{12 \text{ inches}}$ This reads: 4 feet is to 1 foot as x inches is to 12 inches.
2. Since we are going from larger units of feet to smaller units of inches, we multiply. Because $1 \times 12 = 12$ in the denominator, we can multiply the numerator by 12 as well.
   $$\frac{4 \text{ feet}}{1 \text{ foot}} \overset{\times 12}{=} \frac{x \text{ inches}}{12 \text{ inches}} \quad (\times 12)$$
   $4 \times 12 =$ ________
3. 4 feet = ________ inches.

Converting Units with Multiple Steps

How many seconds are in 1 day?

1. Multiply by the conversion rates.
   $$\frac{60 \text{ seconds}}{1 \text{ minute}} \times \frac{60 \text{ minutes}}{1 \text{ hour}} = \frac{3{,}600 \text{ seconds}}{1 \text{ hour}}$$
   $$\frac{3{,}600 \text{ seconds}}{1 \text{ hour}} \times \frac{24 \text{ hours}}{1 \text{ day}} = \frac{\_\_\_\_ \text{ seconds}}{1 \text{ day}}$$

Name: ______________________ Date: ______________

Quick Tip

Remember to multiply or divide both the numerator and denominator by the same factor. If you multiply or divide by different factors, then the relationship is not proportional.

Directions: Write the missing number in each proportional relationship.

1. $\frac{3}{8} = \frac{x}{40}$

$x =$ ________

2. $\frac{9}{55} = \frac{x}{220}$

$x =$ ________

3. $\frac{x}{6} = \frac{7.5}{9}$

$x =$ ________

4. $\frac{x}{15} = \frac{28}{60}$

$x =$ ________

5. $\frac{2}{3} = \frac{14}{x}$

$x =$ ________

6. $\frac{8}{11} = \frac{56}{x}$

$x =$ ________

7. $\frac{x}{25} = \frac{40}{125}$

$x =$ ________

8. $\frac{15}{35} = \frac{3}{x}$

$x =$ ________

9. $\frac{250}{600} = \frac{x}{12}$

$x =$ ________

10. $\frac{x}{3} = \frac{16}{24}$

$x =$ ________

11. $\frac{5}{x} = \frac{100}{160}$

$x =$ ________

12. $\frac{7}{9} = \frac{x}{72}$

$x =$ ________

Name: ____________________ Date: ____________

Directions: Write a proportional relationship to model each problem. Then, solve for the unknown in each problem. Be sure to label the units in the numerator and denominator. The first problem has been done for you.

1. If 30 students ate 75 sandwiches, how many sandwiches would 120 students eat?

a. $\frac{30 \text{ students}}{75 \text{ sandwiches}} = \frac{120 \text{ students}}{x \text{ sandwiches}}$

b. $x =$ ______

2. If 9 dogs ate 31.5 pounds of dog food, how many pounds of dog food would 40 dogs eat?

a. ______ = ______

b. $x =$ ______

3. Marcia made $207 after 18 hours of work. How much money would Marcia make if she worked 54 hours?

a. ______ = ______

b. $x =$ ______

4. If Ryan picked 8 pounds of strawberries in 3 hours, how many pounds of strawberries could Ryan pick in 12 hours?

a. ______ = ______

b. $x =$ ______

5. The Smith family drove 1,625 miles in 25 hours. How many hours would it take them to drive 2,925 miles?

a. ______ = ______

b. $x =$ ______

6. A cake recipe needs 15 cups of flour for 6 cakes. How many cups of flour are needed for 1 cake?

a. ______ = ______

b. $x =$ ______

7. Isaac grilled 16 hamburgers in 45 minutes. How many hamburgers could he grill in 180 minutes?

a. ______ = ______

b. $x =$ ______

8. Frannie bought 4 packages of hot dog buns for $5.56. How many packages can she buy with $16.68?

a. ______ = ______

b. $x =$ ______

Name: ____________________ Date: ____________

Directions: Set up each proportional relationship. Then, solve for the unknown.

1. Theresa wants to give the babysitter a 15% tip. The babysitter earned $90. How much should Theresa pay the babysitter, including the tip?

a. ________ = ________

b. x = ______

2. Garrett is buying a new pair of jeans that are regularly $40. He has a 25% off coupon. What is the discounted price of the jeans?

a. ________ = ________

b. x = ______

3. Ryan has a stamp collection of 250 stamps, and 22% of them have animals on them. How many of Ryan's stamps have animals on them?

a. ________ = ________

b. x = ______

4. Mary weighed 130 pounds. She lost 10% of her weight. What is her new weight?

a. ________ = ________

b. x = ______

5. Henry loaned his brother $400 plus 5% interest. What is the total amount, including interest, that Henry's brother will have to pay back?

a. ________ = ________

b. x = ______

6. Monique wants to buy a new bicycle, and she has a coupon for 30% off. The original price of the bicycle is $350. What is the new price, with the discount?

a. ________ = ________

b. x = ______

7. Carl and his friends go out for pizza. The bill is $72. Carl wants to leave an 18% tip. How much will Carl and his friends pay, including the tip?

a. ________ = ________

b. x = ______

8. Riley's college tuition is $20,000. Riley gets a discount of 15% off his tuition because his dad also went to college there. How much money will Riley save on his tuition?

a. ________ = ________

b. x = ______

Name: ______________________ Date: ______________

Directions: Find the percent of increase or decrease for each problem. Round answers to the nearest tenth of a percent if necessary.

1. The class size increased from 125 to 140 students. What is the percent of increase in class size?

____

2. The ice cream store workers went from 18 workers to 12 workers. What is the percent of decrease in the number of workers?

____

3. Macie's savings account balance went from $360 to $500. What is the percent of increase in Macie's savings account?

____

4. Mark was earning $12 an hour. His boss gave him a raise up to $15 an hour. What is the percent of increase in Mark's earnings?

____

5. Ling had 36 peaches in a bushel at the first harvest. When it came time for the second harvest, Ling had 20 peaches. What is the percent of decrease in the number of peaches?

____

6. In September, the price of a new video game was $60. One month later, the price was $45. What is the percent of decrease in price?

____

7. Last week, Annabelle sent 250 text messages. This week, she sent 145 text messages. What is the percent of decrease in Annabelle's text messages?

____

8. Quinn had a 16-foot board. He cut 6 feet off. What is the percent of decrease in the length of the board?

____

9. A pizza at Pizza Pi is $9. After a sale, the pizzas were marked down to $7. What is the percent of decrease in pizza price?

____

10. The population in Small Town went from 120,000 to 135,000. What is the percent of increase in population?

____

Name: ______________________ Date: ______________

Directions: Solve each problem. Show your work. The first one has been modeled for you.

1. How many minutes are in 1 week?

$$\frac{24 \text{ hours}}{1 \text{ day}} \times \frac{60 \text{ minutes}}{1 \text{ hour}} = \frac{1{,}440 \text{ minutes}}{1 \text{ day}}$$

$$\frac{1{,}440 \text{ minutes}}{1 \text{ day}} \times \frac{7 \text{ days}}{1 \text{ week}} = \frac{10{,}080 \text{ minutes}}{1 \text{ week}}$$

10,080 minutes

2. How many seconds are in 3 hours?

________ seconds

3. How many hours are in 2 weeks?

________ hours

4. How many hours are in 9 days?

________ hours

5. How many minutes are in 6 days?

________ minutes

6. How many inches are in 1 mile?

________ inches

7. How many feet are in 8 miles?

________ feet

8. How many feet are in 12 yards?

________ feet

9. How many seconds are in 3 weeks?

________ seconds

10. How many inches are in 4 miles?

________ inches

11. How many hours are in one 30-day month?

________ hours

12. How many hours are in 1 year?

________ hours

Name: ____________________ Date: ____________

Directions: Solve each problem.

1. Harvey's tuition is $36,000 this year. Next year, his tuition will be $38,000. What is the percent of increase in Harvey's tuition?

____

2. Cathy paid $80 for 4 pairs of equally priced shoes. What was the cost of 1 pair?

____

3. There are 48 people in 4 equally sized groups.

a. What is the rate? ________

b. What is the unit rate? ________

4. Warren completed 30 problems in $\frac{5}{6}$ of an hour. How many problems could he complete in 1 hour?

____

5. What is the constant of proportionality shown in the graph?

$k =$ ________

6. Ben paid $140 for 7 packages of baseballs. What was the price of 1 package?

____

7. Lenny's bill is $53, but he wants to leave an 18% tip. How much should Lenny leave for the tip?

____

8. How many minutes are in 4 days?

____

9. $\frac{15 \text{ cats}}{40 \text{ houses}} = \frac{x \text{ cats}}{8 \text{ houses}}$

$x =$ ________

10. Marcus uses 15 gallons of water to fill 3 fish tanks. How many gallons does it take to fill 9 fish tanks?

____

11. What is the constant of proportionality shown in the table?

$k =$ ________

x	y
2	7
4	14
6	21
8	28

12. What is the constant of proportionality in the following equation?

$y = 4.1x$

$k =$ ________

Name: ______________________ Date: ____________

Directions: Solve each problem.

1. Does the graph show a proportional relationship?

Circle yes no

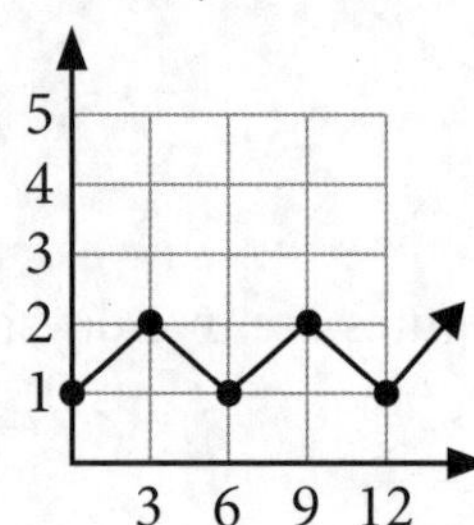

5. What is the constant of proportionality in the following equation?

$y = 9x$

$k =$ ________

2. Keith read 12 books in 6 weeks. How many books did he read in 1 week?

____

6. What is the constant of proportionality shown on the graph?

$k =$ ________

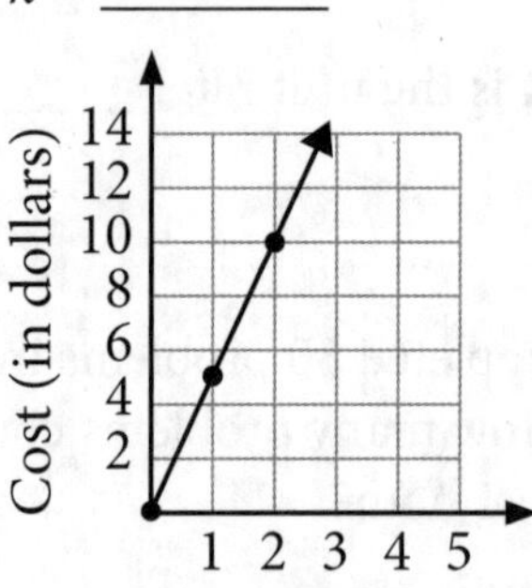

3. Does the table show a proportional relationship?

Circle yes no

x	y
1	9
2	18
3	27
4	36

7. Anna is buying new clothes for school that total $75, but she has to pay tax of 8%. What is the total that Anna has to pay, including tax?

____

4. Tyrone bought 5 hot dogs for $6.75. How many hot dogs could Tyrone buy with $16.20?

____

8. Holly is paying $12,000 for college this year. Next year, the tuition is increasing 5%. How many dollars will the tuition be increasing by next year?

____

Spiral Review

Name: ____________________ Date: ____________

Directions: Solve each problem.

1. What is the constant of proportionality shown on the graph?

____

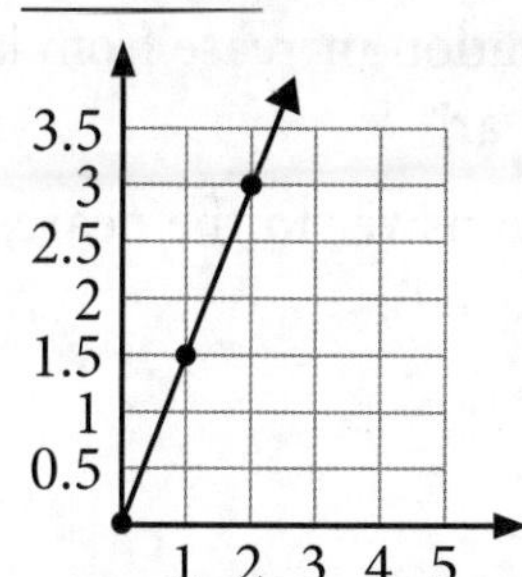

2. Raelyn runs 6 miles in $\frac{3}{4}$ of an hour. How many miles can she run in 1 hour?

____

3. What is the constant of proportionality from the table?

$k =$ ________

x	y
15	105
30	210
45	315
60	420

4. Sarah bought 4 bags of potatoes for $31.96. What is the cost of 1 bag of potatoes?

____

5. Does the graph show a proportional relationship?

Circle yes no

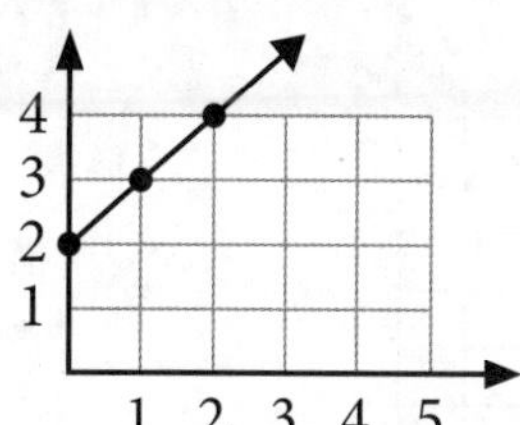

6. Theresa goes to lunch with her friends. The bill is $56, but they want to leave a tip of 20%.

a. What is the amount of the tip?

____

b. What is the total bill, including the tip? ________

7. $\frac{30 \text{ apples}}{2 \text{ pies}} = \frac{x \text{ apples}}{16 \text{ pies}}$

$x =$ ________

8. Jeffery made $81 for mowing 9 lawns. Find the constant of proportionality, and use it to complete the table.

x	y
1	
3	
6	
12	

Spiral Review

Name: ____________________ Date: ____________

Directions: Solve each problem.

1. Write an equation to represent the proportional relationship.

$y =$ ________ x

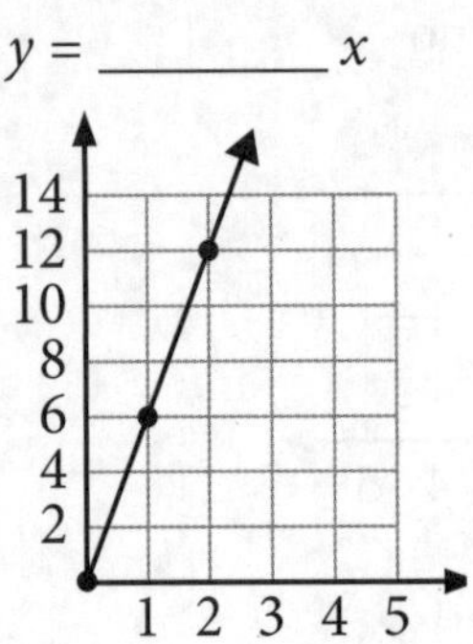

5. Today, Petra's town has a population of 140,000 people. Last year, the population was 130,000. What percent did the population increase from last year to this year?

(Round your answer to the nearest percent if needed).

____

2. Jenny earned $437.50 after working 35 hours. How much money does Jenny earn per hour?

____

6. What is the constant of proportionality shown on the graph? ________

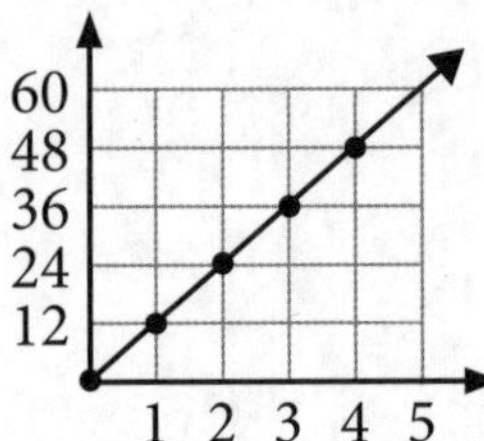

3. Does the graph show a proportional relationship?

Circle yes no

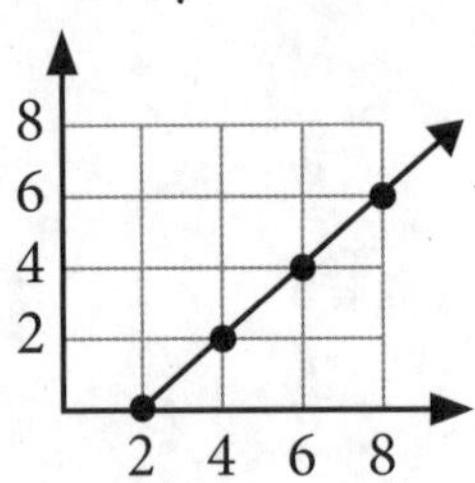

7. The Jacobs family drove 1,300 miles in 20 hours. Write an equation to represent the proportional relationship.

$y =$ ________ x

4. Does the table show a proportional relationship?

Circle yes no

x	y
3	24
6	54
9	90
12	132

8. How many seconds are in 5 days?

____

Name: ______________________ Date: ____________

Directions: Solve each problem.

1. Yvette runs 6 miles in $\frac{4}{5}$ of an hour. How many miles can she run in 1 hour?

____

2. Write an equation to represent the proportional relationship shown on the graph.

$y =$ _______ x

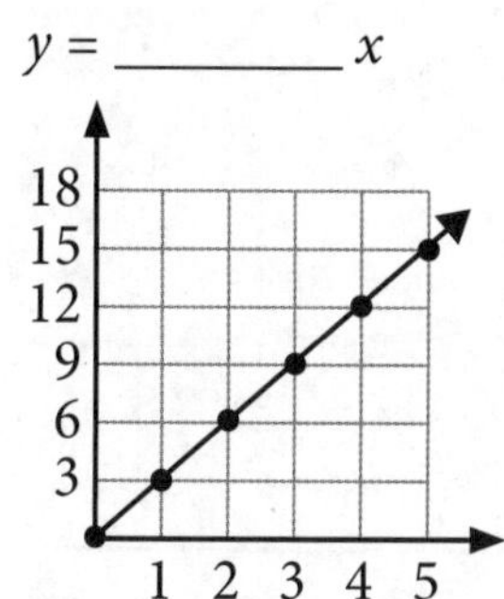

3. Rico is looking for a new car. The price of the car is $25,000, but Rico gets a discount of 10%. What is the new price of the car, with the discount?

____

4. How many yards are in 5 miles?

____

5. Marissa makes $15 an hour. Complete the table, and graph the points.

x	y
1	
2	
3	
4	

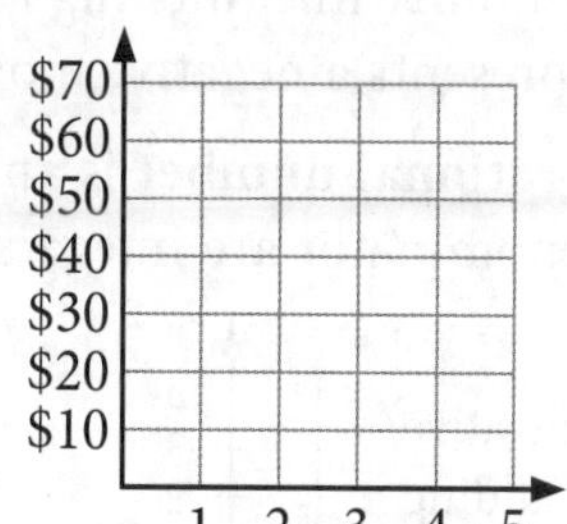

6. $\frac{16 \text{ beads}}{4 \text{ bracelets}} = \frac{x \text{ beads}}{32 \text{ bracelets}}$

$x =$ _______

7. Cheyenne is buying wood to build a birdhouse. The wood is $45, but she has to pay tax of 8%.

a. How much is the tax on the wood?

____

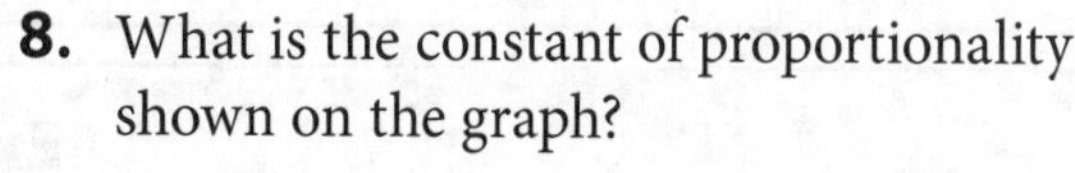

b. What is the total cost, including tax? _______

8. What is the constant of proportionality shown on the graph?

$k =$ _______

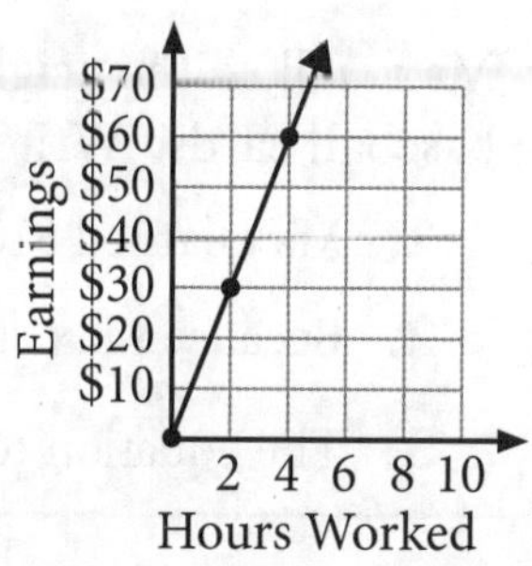

Spiral Review

Learn about Adding and Subtracting Rational Numbers

An **integer** is any positive whole number, negative whole number, and the number 0.

A **number line** is a drawn representation used to add and subtract rational numbers. When using a number line, moving right or up represents a positive move, or addition. Moving left or down represents a negative move, or subtraction.

A **rational number** is any number that can be written as a fraction where the numerator and denominator are integers and the denominator is not equal to 0.

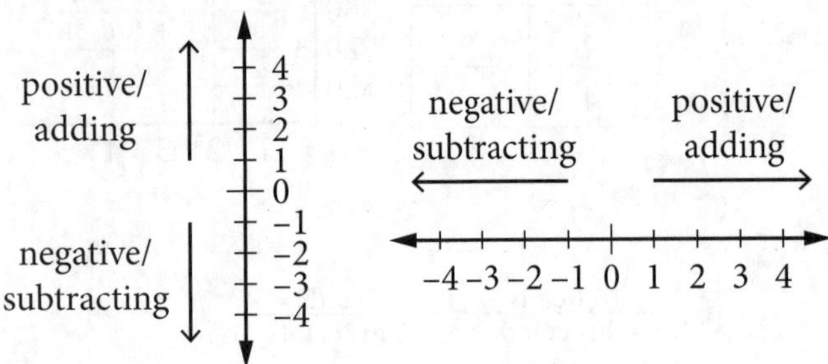

A number and its opposite are **additive inverses** and have a sum of 0.
The additive inverse of 4 is −4.

Subtraction is adding the additive inverse.

For example: 8 − 9 = 8 + (−9)
Subtracting 9 and adding −9 are equivalent.

Absolute value is the distance a number is from 0 on a number line.
Absolute value is always positive.

Example 1

Write the equation represented by the number line. Then, solve the equation.

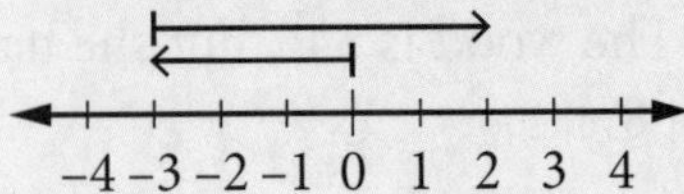

1. The arrow starts at 0 and moves to the left 3 spaces, so the number is −3.
2. Next, move from −3 to the right. The number of spaces moved to the right is the number being added, which is 5.
3. Write the equation, and solve it. The number that the arrow ends on is the answer.

   −3 + 5 = ________

Example 2

Max walked the neighbor's dog and earned $10. He then went to the store and spent $10 on baseball cards. Write and solve an equation that represents the situation.

1. Max earned $10, so that means it is +10.
2. Because Max spent $10, it is represented by −10.
3. The equation to represent the situation is: $10 − $10 = $0.

Example 3

Rewrite the subtraction problem as adding the additive inverse. Then, solve the problem.
$-7 - 4 = ?$

1. Rewrite the problem: $-7 + (-4)$
   -7 -4
2. Solve the problem. ________

Example 4

Find the difference between the points on the line.

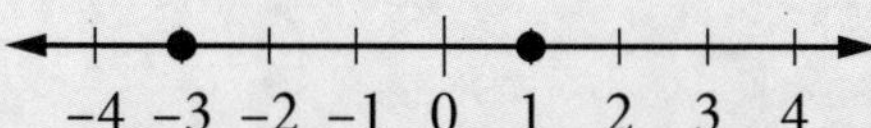

1. Identify the two numbers on the number line. ________ and ________
2. Subtract the numbers to find the distance. You can subtract them in either order because the absolute value of both answers is the same.
   $-3 - 1 = -4$
   Absolute value: ________
   $1 - (-3) = 4$
   Absolute value: ________
3. You can check your answer by counting from one point to the other.

Example 5

Is $a - b$ positive or negative?

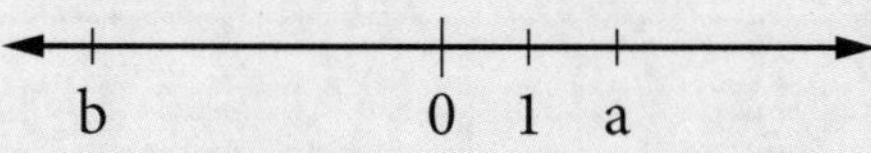

1. We can see that a is larger than 1 because it is to the right of 1 on the number line.
2. We can see that b is a negative number, and it is farther away from 0 than a.
3. Since a is positive and b is negative, we can write the expression $a - (-b)$.
4. The problem can be rewritten using additive inverse as $a + b$, so the answer will be positive.

Name: ______________________ Date: ______________

Quick Tip

Use the arrow closest to the number line to determine the first number in the equation.

Directions: Write and solve the equation for the problem represented on each number line.

1. ______ + ______ = ______

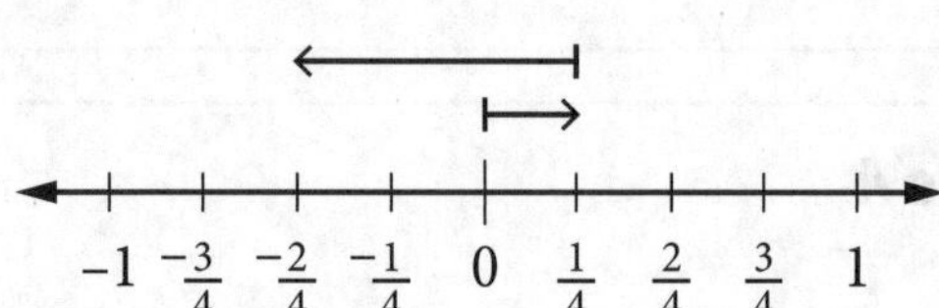

4. ______ + ______ = ______

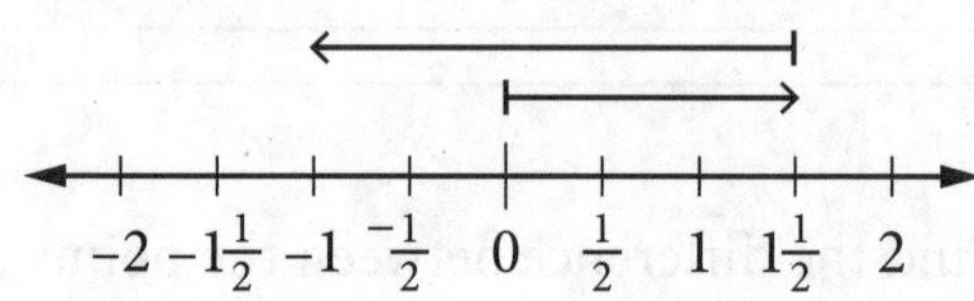

2. ______ + ______ = ______

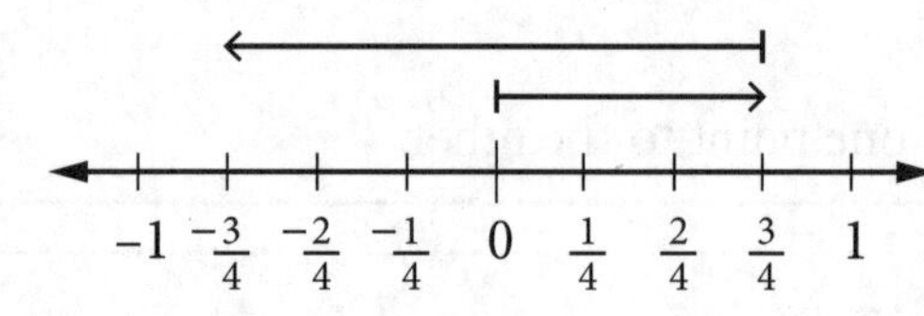

5. ______ + ______ = ______

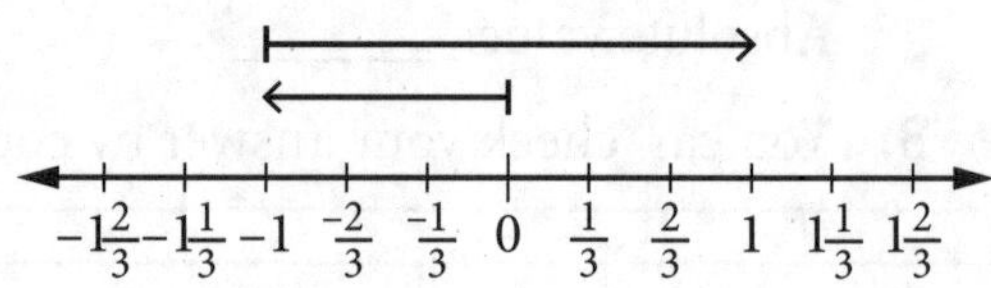

3. ______ + ______ = ______

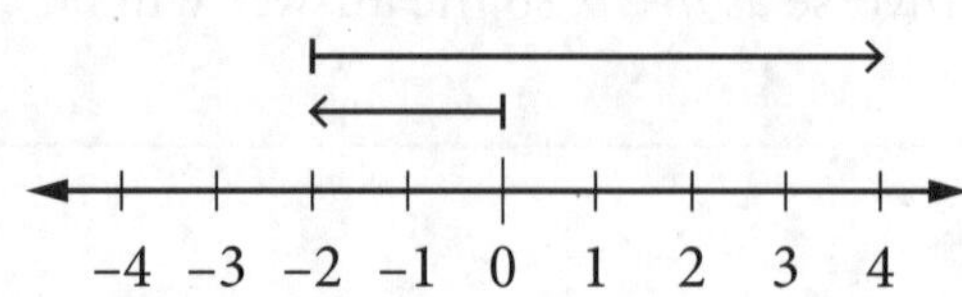

6. ______ + ______ = ______

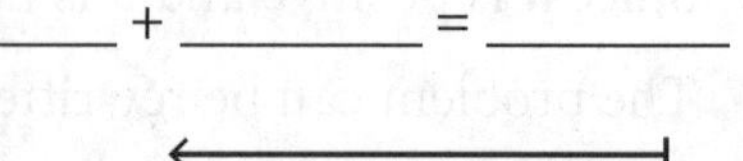

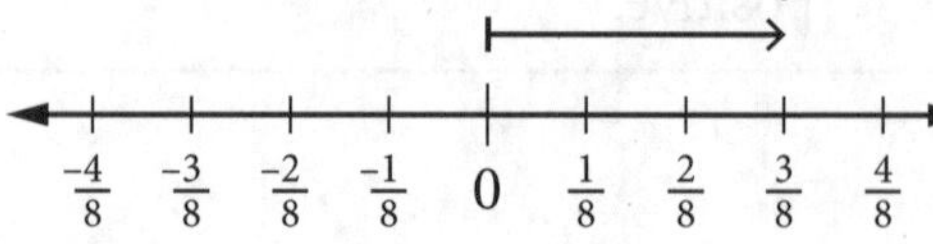

Name: ______________________________ Date: __________________

Directions: Write and solve the equation for each problem represented on the vertical number line.

1. ________ + ________ = ________

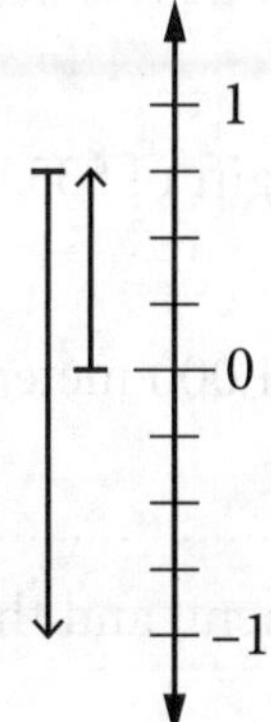

2. ________ + ________ = ________

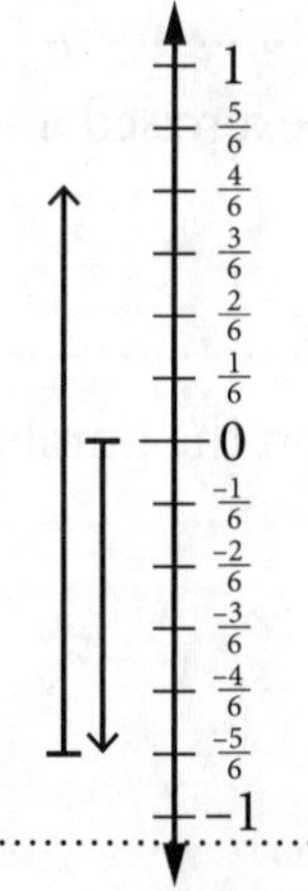

3. ________ + ________ = ________

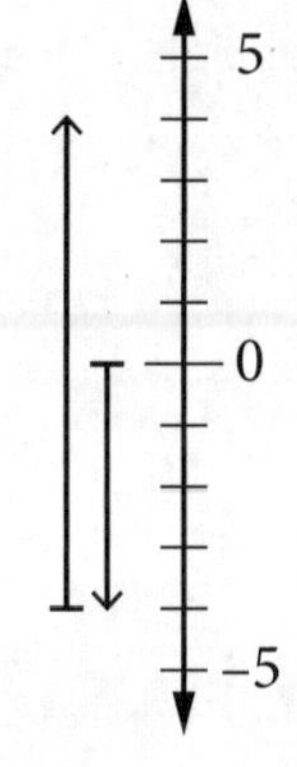

4. ________ + ________ = ________

1
$\frac{1}{4}$
0
$\frac{-1}{4}$
–1

5. ________ + ________ = ________

5
4
3
2
1
0
–1
–2
–3
–4
–5

6. ________ + ________ = ________

3
2
1
0
–1
–2
–3

Name: ____________________ Date: ____________

Quick Tip

Remember, the additive inverse of a number is the opposite of the number. So, subtracting a positive number is the same as adding a negative number.

Directions: Write an equation to represent each problem. The first one has been modeled for you.

1. Valerie spent $35 at the mall, but then she received a birthday gift of $35. _–35_ + _35_ = _0_

2. The submarine descended 1,000 meters, and then it ascended 1,000 meters.
   ________ + ________ = ________

3. Jerome went up 8 floors in the elevator to his dentist appointment, and then he went down 8 floors to leave the building.
   ________ + ________ = ________

4. The airplane rose 30,000 feet after takeoff. The airplane descended 30,000 feet before landing.
   ________ + ________ = ________

5. Tony gained 6 pounds while he was on vacation, but then he exercised and lost 6 pounds when he returned home.
   ________ + ________ = ________

6. Wade found 50 cents at the park, but then he spent 50 cents on the gumball machine.
   ________ + ________ = ________

Directions: Answer the questions.

7. What is the additive inverse of 9? ________

8. What is the additive inverse of –3? ________

9. What is the additive inverse of 25? ________

10. What is the additive inverse of –100? ________

Name: ______________________________ Date: ____________________

Directions: Rewrite each expression as adding the additive inverse. Then, solve.

1. 9 – 7 ________ + ________ = ________

2. –12 – 6 ________ + ________ = ________

3. –7 – (–3) ________ + ________ = ________

4. 14 – 15 ________ + ________ = ________

5. –11 – 12 ________ + ________ = ________

6. 24 – 30 ________ + ________ = ________

7. 18 – (–6) ________ + ________ = ________

8. 14 – (–6) ________ + ________ = ________

9. –5 – 6 ________ + ________ = ________

10. –2 – (–2) ________ + ________ = ________

11. $2\frac{1}{2} - 5\frac{1}{2}$ ________ + ________ = ________

12. $-8\frac{1}{3} - 2\frac{2}{3}$ ________ + ________ = ________

13. $9 - 10\frac{1}{4}$ ________ + ________ = ________

14. $7\frac{1}{4} - 6$ ________ + ________ = ________

Name: ______________________ Date: ______________

Reminder

The absolute value of a number is always positive.

Directions: For each problem, write a subtraction equation using the two points on the number line. Then, write the absolute value of the solution.

1. ________ – ________ = ________

Absolute value: ________

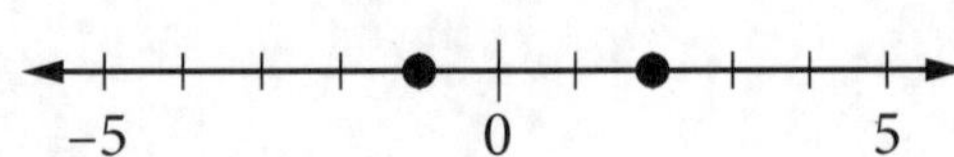

4. ________ – ________ = ________

Absolute value: ________

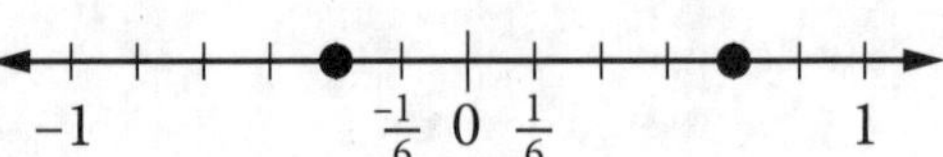

2. ________ – ________ = ________

Absolute value: ________

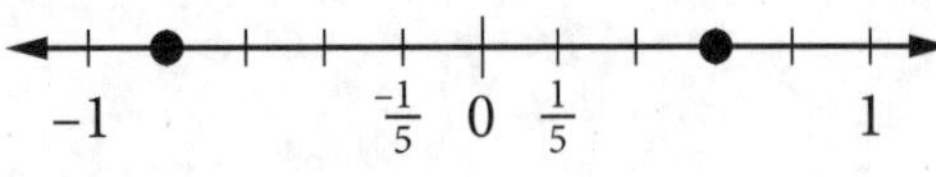

5. ________ – ________ = ________

Absolute value: ________

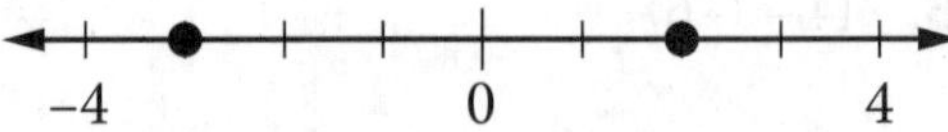

3. ________ – ________ = ________

Absolute value: ________

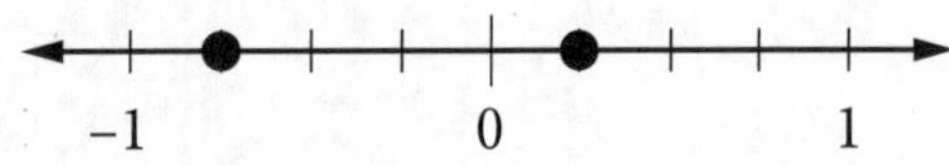

6. ________ – ________ = ________

Absolute value: ________

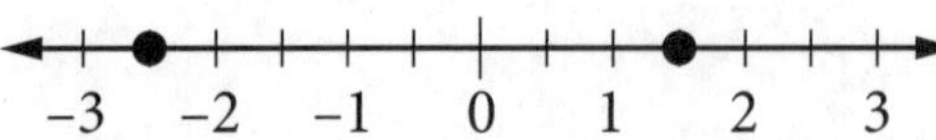

Name: ______________________ Date: ______________

Directions: Solve each problem.

1. $14\frac{1}{8} + 11\frac{1}{5} =$ ________

2. $-9.8 + 6.7 =$ ________

3. $-16 + 19 =$ ________

4. $-15 - (-4) =$ ________

5. $14.3 + (-20.6) =$ ________

6. $75\frac{1}{9} + (-15\frac{1}{3}) =$ ________

7. $26\frac{1}{3} - 16\frac{1}{4} =$ ________

8. $115.9 + (-120) =$ ________

9. $-10\frac{4}{5} - (-12\frac{1}{10}) =$ ________

10. $4\frac{5}{9} - 10\frac{7}{9} =$ ________

11. $-56.8 - (-13.2) =$ ________

12. $3\frac{5}{8} - 2\frac{1}{4} =$ ________

13. $-275 + 930 =$ ________

14. $150 + (-33) =$ ________

Name: ______________________ Date: ______________

Directions: Write and solve an addition or subtraction equation for each question.

1. On Monday, Mark picked $1\frac{1}{4}$ pounds of strawberries. On Tuesday, he picked $2\frac{1}{2}$ pounds of strawberries. How many total pounds of strawberries did Mark pick?

   ____

2. Kevin ran 8.2 miles on Saturday and 9.7 miles on Sunday. How many more miles did Kevin run on Sunday?

   ____

3. Seth has to drive 350 miles to his grandparents' house. On the first day, he drives 175.2 miles. On the second day, he drives 105.6 miles. How many more miles does Seth have to drive to get to his grandparents' house?

   ____

4. Penelope's goal is to swim 100 laps. So far, she swam $13\frac{1}{2}$ laps and $40\frac{2}{5}$ laps. How many more laps does Penelope have to swim?

   ____

5. Rocky works 40 hours every week. He worked $28\frac{4}{9}$ hours so far. How many more hours does Rocky have to work this week?

   ____

6. Ashley walked after school for four days. She walked 4.5 miles, 3.75 miles, $8\frac{1}{5}$ miles, and 3 miles. How many total miles did Ashley walk?

   ____

7. Ming and her two brothers were pulling weeds in their yard. Ming's brothers pulled $\frac{1}{5}$ and 0.75 of the weeds. How many of the weeds did Ming have left to pull?

   ____

8. Noah was working on his essay. He finished $\frac{3}{4}$ of it at school and 0.1 at his friend's house. How much of the essay did Noah have left to finish at home?

   ____

9. Ronnie likes to exercise for 60 minutes each day. One day, he ran for 23 minutes and used the rowing machine for 18 minutes. How many minutes of exercise did Ronnie have left that day?

   ____

10. Kimberly is using yarn to make a green, blue, and yellow blanket. She used green yarn on 0.8 of the blanket and blue yarn on $\frac{1}{10}$ of the blanket. How much of the blanket is made with yellow yarn?

    ____

Name: ______________________________ Date: ____________________

Directions: Use the diagrams to determine whether each answer will be positive or negative. Circle your answers.

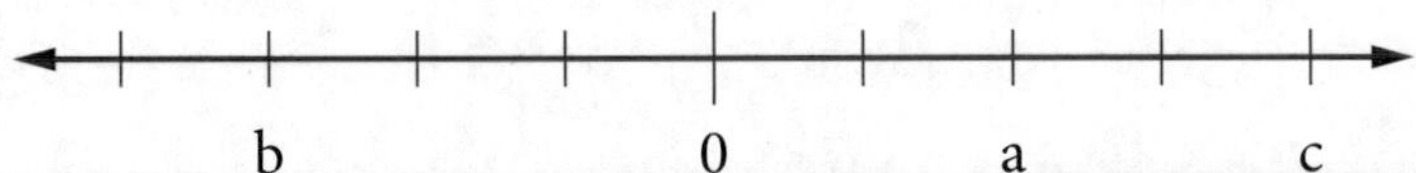

1. $a - b$ positive negative
2. $b - a$ positive negative
3. $a + b$ positive negative
4. $b + a$ positive negative
5. $c - b$ positive negative
6. $c + a$ positive negative
7. $b + c$ positive negative

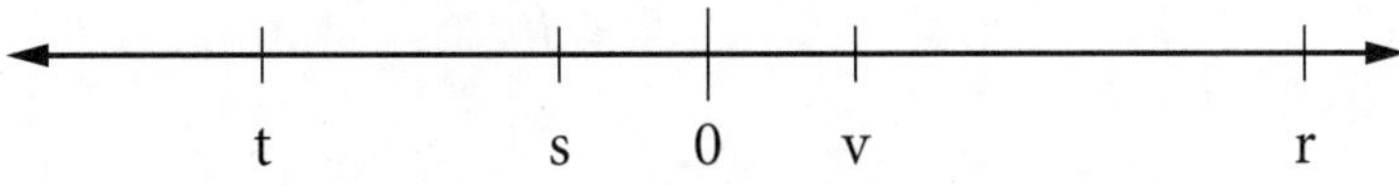

8. $t - r$ positive negative
9. $s - r$ positive negative
10. $r + t$ positive negative
11. $t - s$ positive negative
12. $t - v$ positive negative
13. $r - t$ positive negative
14. $v + t$ positive negative

Name: ____________________ Date: ____________

Directions: Solve each problem.

1. $-8.5 - \frac{12}{10} =$ ____________

2. $-1\frac{3}{10} + 0.1 + \frac{1}{5} =$ ____________

3. $6.5 - \frac{1}{2} + 8 =$ ____________

4. $4\frac{3}{5} - 6\frac{1}{5} =$ ____________

5. $-0.8 + \frac{25}{20} + 6 =$ ____________

6. $9\frac{2}{3} - \frac{1}{3} + 4 =$ ____________

7. $20.8 - 10\frac{1}{4} + 3.5 =$ ____________

8. $15.75 - 7\frac{1}{2} - 5.25 =$ ____________

9. $-0.8 + \frac{9}{10} =$ ____________

10. $-90 - (-20\frac{3}{4}) + 11 =$ ____________

11. $-3\frac{7}{8} - 2\frac{1}{4} + 1\frac{3}{8} =$ ____________

12. $28.8 - 10\frac{7}{10} =$ ____________

13. $45.08 - 30\frac{3}{100} + 3.01 =$ ____________

14. $19\frac{3}{5} - (-2\frac{1}{10}) + 3.2 =$ ____________

Name: ______________________ Date: ______________

Directions: Solve each problem.

1. Hadley picked $3\frac{3}{4}$ quarts of strawberries, 6.25 quarts of blueberries, and $8\frac{1}{2}$ quarts of raspberries. How many quarts of berries did Hadley pick in all?

____

2. Jerry deposited \$150 into his bank account. He went shopping and spent \$30.45 from his account on new clothes and \$12.43 on lunch. How much was left in his account?

____

3. Ralph works at the zoo and feeds the alligators. On Monday, he fed them $13\frac{3}{8}$ pounds of meat. On Tuesday, he fed them 12.65 pounds, and on Wednesday, he fed them 14.2 pounds. How many pounds of meat did Ralph feed the alligators over all three days?

____

4. Tricia ran $12\frac{1}{5}$ miles on Monday, 4.5 miles on Tuesday, and 9.07 miles on Wednesday. How many miles did she run in all?

____

5. Lacey was baking fruit pies. She peeled $2\frac{1}{2}$ pounds of apples and 5.3 pounds of peaches. How much fruit did Lacey peel in all?

____

6. Harley kept track of how many meters he swam over the last three weeks. In week 1, he swam $500\frac{1}{8}$ meters, in week 2, he swam 350.5 meters, and in week 3, he swam $498\frac{3}{4}$ meters. How many total meters did Harley swim?

____

7. Henry is a weightlifter. He is increasing the amount of weight he lifts every day. On day 1, he lifted 175.75 pounds, on day 2, he lifted $195\frac{1}{4}$ pounds, and on day 3, he lifted 201.85 pounds. How many pounds did Henry lift in all?

____

8. George walked $5\frac{5}{8}$ miles today and 7.85 miles yesterday. How many more miles did George walk yesterday than today?

____

9. Jenny ate $\frac{1}{3}$ of her birthday cake on Monday, another $\frac{1}{3}$ on Tuesday, and $\frac{1}{4}$ on Wednesday. How much of the cake was left?

____

10. Michael made \$126 mowing lawns, then spent \$82.50 at the mall and \$24 on gas. How much money did Michael have left?

____

Adding and Subtracting Rational Numbers

Learn about Multiplying and Dividing Rational Numbers

reciprocal—the inverse of a number

Example: The reciprocal of $\frac{1}{2}$ is $\frac{2}{1}$.

When multiplying or dividing fractions, make mixed numbers into improper fractions first.
When multiplying, multiply numerator × numerator and denominator × denominator.
When dividing fractions, multiply by the reciprocal of the fraction after the division sign.

Multiplication Rules

1. Positive × Positive = Positive
   Example: 4 × 2 = 8
2. Negative × Negative = Positive
   Example: –3 × –5 = 15
3. Positive × Negative = Negative
   Example: 8 × (–4) = –32
4. Negative × Positive = Negative
   Example: (–3) × 6 = –18

Division Rules

1. Positive ÷ Positive = Positive
   Example: 4 ÷ 2 = 2
2. Negative ÷ Negative = Positive
   Example: –6 ÷ (–2) = 3
3. Positive ÷ Negative = Negative
   Example: 14 ÷ (–7) = –2
4. Negative ÷ Positive = Negative
   Example: (–12) ÷ 2 = –6

Exponent Rules

1. When dividing exponents with the same base, subtract the exponent in the denominator from the exponent in the numerator.
   Example: $\frac{4^5}{4^3} = 4^2$
2. When multiplying exponents with the same base, add the exponents.
   Example: $5^2 \times 5^2 = 5^4$
3. When raising a power to a power, multiply exponents.
   Example: $(3^2)^3 = 3^6$
4. Anything to the 0 power = 1.
   Example: $4^0 = 1$
5. Any number to the first power is the same as the base of the number.
   Example: $5^1 = 5$

Example 1

15 × (–0.3) = ?

1. Multiply without the negative sign. 15 × 0.3 = ____________
2. Is a positive number × a negative number positive or negative? ____________________
3. So, 15 × (–0.3) = ____________

Example 2

$-9(3 + 4) = ?$

1. Using the Distributive Property, multiply –9 by each number inside the parentheses.
   $-9 \times 3 + (-9) \times 4$
   $-9 \times 3 = -27$
   $-9 \times 4 = -36$
2. Write the new expression, and solve.
   $-27 + (-36) =$ ____________

Example 3

$-4\frac{1}{5} \div \frac{7}{15} = ?$

1. Change $-4\frac{1}{5}$ to an improper fraction. What is the improper fraction? $-\frac{21}{5}$
2. Multiply by the reciprocal of $\frac{7}{15}$.
   $-\frac{21}{5} \times \frac{15}{7} =$ __________

Example 4

$81 \div (-9) = ?$

1. First, divide 81 by 9. $81 \div 9 =$ ____________
2. What is a positive number ÷ a negative number? ____________
3. So, what is the solution to $81 \div (-9)$? ____________

Example 5

When writing rational numbers, the fraction can be written in three ways.

$\frac{-3}{4} \quad \frac{3}{-4} \quad -\frac{3}{4}$

Write the fraction $-\frac{1}{5}$ in three ways.

1. ____________
2. ____________
3. ____________

Name: ______________________ Date: ______________

Reminder

Change mixed numbers to improper fractions before multiplying or dividing.

Directions: Solve each problem.

1. $3\frac{4}{5} \times 1\frac{2}{3} =$ ______________

2. $1\frac{7}{8} \div 1\frac{1}{2} =$ ______________

3. $15.4 \times 1.3 =$ ______________

4. $\frac{4}{9} \times \frac{18}{20} =$ ______________

5. $2\frac{2}{5} \div 3\frac{1}{7} =$ ______________

6. $3.75 \div 1.25 =$ ______________

7. $5\frac{1}{2} \times 2\frac{2}{3} =$ ______________

8. $4\frac{1}{5} \div \frac{1}{10} =$ ______________

9. $14.016 \times 2.3 =$ ______________

10. $\frac{12}{5} \times \frac{20}{24} =$ ______________

11. $9\frac{1}{4} \times \frac{5}{37} =$ ______________

12. $8.2 \times \frac{3}{8} =$ ______________

13. $6\frac{1}{5} \div 2\frac{2}{3} =$ ______________

14. $6\frac{4}{5} \div \frac{4}{10} =$ ______________

Name: ______________________________ Date: ____________________

Quick Tip

Remember to use the rules for multiplying and dividing rational numbers to help you.

Directions: Multiply or divide. Be sure to include a negative sign if the product or quotient is negative.

1. $8 \times (-4) =$ ____________

2. $-63 \div (-7) =$ ____________

3. $10 \times 3 =$ ____________

4. $42 \div (-7) =$ ____________

5. $-16 \div 8 =$ ____________

6. $-3 \times -8 =$ ____________

7. $72 \div 8 =$ ____________

8. $-4 \times (-4) =$ ____________

9. $-8 \times 0 =$ ____________

10. $-30 \div 5 =$ ____________

11. $-21 \div (-3) =$ ____________

12. $11 \times 2 =$ ____________

13. $1 \times (-12) =$ ____________

14. $-45 \div (-9) =$ ____________

Name: ______________________ Date: ______________

Hands-On Help

Use a multiplication chart for help with solving multiplication facts quickly.

Directions: Use the Distributive Property to multiply. The first problem is started for you.

1. $5(-8 + 3) =$ 5×-8 + 5×3 = $-40 + 15$ = ________

2. $-7(3 - 6) =$ ________ − ________ = ________ + ________ = ________

3. $-\frac{1}{5}[10 + (-5)] =$ ________ + ________ = ________ + ________ = ________

4. $1\frac{2}{3}(-6 + 3) =$ ________ + ________ = ________ + ________ = ________

5. $-1.5[2.8 + (-4)] =$ ________ + ________ = ________ + ________ = ________

6. $\frac{8}{9}(-27 + 18) =$ ________ + ________ = ________ + ________ = ________

7. $-6(\frac{1}{3} + 8) =$ ________ + ________ = ________ + ________ = ________

8. $-\frac{4}{5}(-10 + 20) =$ ________ + ________ = ________ + ________ = ________

9. $6.5(-2.1 + 4) =$ ________ + ________ = ________ + ________ = ________

10. $2(-2 + 5) =$ ________ + ________ = ________ + ________ = ________

11. $-\frac{3}{4}[24 + (-12)] =$ ________ + ________ = ________ + ________ = ________

12. $-7(5.4 + 2) =$ ________ + ________ = ________ + ________ = ________

13. $-2\frac{2}{3}(-9 + 12) =$ ________ + ________ = ________ + ________ = ________

14. $5(-8 - 4) =$ ________ + ________ = ________ + ________ = ________

Name: ______________________________ Date: ________________

Directions: Use the exponent rules to simplify each expression. Then, solve each problem. The first problem is done for you.

1. $\frac{8^3}{8^2} = 8^1 = 8$

2. $(4^2)^2$ = ________ = ________

3. $3^4 \times 3^2$ = ________ = ________

4. 9^0 = ________

5. 15^1 = ________

6. $\frac{6^3}{6^2}$ = ________ = ________

7. $5^3 \times 5^2$ = ________ = ________

8. $(2^2)^3$ = ________ = ________

9. $\frac{9^5}{9^3}$ = ________ = ________

10. 6^0 = ________

11. $(5^3)^2$ = ________ = ________

12. $7^2 \times 7^1$ = ________ = ________

13. $\frac{4^9}{4^6}$ = ________ = ________

14. $(5^1)^3$ = ________ = ________

Name: ______________________ Date: ______________

Directions: Multiply or divide to solve each problem.

1. John was running a 15-mile race. He ran $\frac{2}{3}$ of the race before he stopped for water. How far did he run before stopping for water?

______

2. Theresa swam $2\frac{1}{4}$ miles in the pool. Each lap is $\frac{1}{4}$ of a mile. How many laps did Theresa swim?

______

3. Riley mows 12 lawns each week. He is $\frac{1}{3}$ of the way finished mowing already. How many lawns did he mow?

______

4. Pete needs $10\frac{1}{2}$ pounds of dirt to fill the flower pots in his yard. The bags of dirt are sold in $3\frac{1}{2}$-pound bags. How many bags of dirt does Pete need?

______

5. Harry and Roger made cookies. Harry made $3\frac{1}{4}$ times as many cookies as Roger. If Roger made 20 cookies, how many did Harry make?

______

6. Janet can run a mile in 8.3 minutes. At that pace, how long will it take her to run 6 miles?

______

7. Reggie is baking bread. The recipe calls for $4\frac{1}{2}$ cups of flour. Reggie is measuring the flour with a $\frac{1}{2}$-cup measuring cup. How many $\frac{1}{2}$ cups will he need?

______

8. Mrs. Jones is grading papers. She has 120 papers to grade. She graded $\frac{2}{5}$ of the papers so far. How many papers did Mrs. Jones grade?

______

9. Marie is making muffins. The recipe calls for $\frac{1}{3}$ cup of sugar. How many batches of muffins can Marie make with 6 cups of sugar?

______

10. Warren rode his bike 6.5 miles in 30 minutes. At that pace, how many miles can Warren ride in 90 minutes?

______

Learn about Converting Rational Numbers to Decimals

To change a fraction to a decimal, divide the numerator by the denominator using long division.

numerator → 4
denominator → 5

$$\begin{array}{r} 0.8 \\ 5\overline{)4.0} \\ \underline{-40} \\ 0 \end{array}$$

Every rational number can be written as a **terminating** decimal or **repeating** decimal. In the example above, 0.8 is a terminating decimal.

In the following example, when converting $\frac{2}{3}$ to a decimal, the number 6 continues to repeat indefinitely. This is a repeating decimal. We can write the decimal using bar notation. Put a bar over the repeating digit(s). The decimal is written as $0.\overline{6}$.

$$\begin{array}{r} 0.666 \\ 3\overline{)2.000} \\ \underline{-18} \\ 20 \\ \underline{-18} \\ 20 \\ \underline{-18} \\ 2 \end{array}$$

Change a Percent to a Fraction and Decimal

Write 40% as a fraction and a decimal.

1. To write 40% as a fraction, put 40 in the numerator and 100 in the denominator.

   ____

2. To write 40% as a decimal, divide 40 by 100. What is 40 ÷ 100? ________

Name: ______________________ Date: ______________

Reminder

Terminating decimals end, or terminate, with no remainder.
Repeating decimals have one or more digits that repeat indefinitely.

Directions: Circle *terminating* or *repeating* to describe each decimal.

1. 0.4444444...
terminating repeating

8. 6.545
terminating repeating

2. 2.75
terminating repeating

9. 7.1111...
terminating repeating

3. 1.66666...
terminating repeating

10. 2.2
terminating repeating

4. 0.15151515...
terminating repeating

11. 8.45
terminating repeating

5. 0.2375
terminating repeating

12. 10.5
terminating repeating

6. 4.7777...
terminating repeating

13. 13.333...
terminating repeating

7. $7.\overline{8}$
terminating repeating

14. 0.875
terminating repeating

Name: ____________________ Date: ____________

Directions: Write each fraction as a decimal. Show your work. Then, circle *terminating* or *repeating* to describe the decimal.

1. $\frac{1}{3}$ decimal: __________
terminating repeating

6. $\frac{1}{9}$ decimal: __________
terminating repeating

2. $\frac{3}{8}$ decimal: __________
terminating repeating

7. $\frac{2}{3}$ decimal: __________
terminating repeating

3. $\frac{1}{5}$ decimal: __________
terminating repeating

8. $\frac{7}{8}$ decimal: __________
terminating repeating

4. $\frac{4}{9}$ decimal: __________
terminating repeating

9. $\frac{1}{4}$ decimal: __________
terminating repeating

5. $\frac{3}{5}$ decimal: __________
terminating repeating

10. $\frac{2}{5}$ decimal: __________
terminating repeating

Name: ______________________ Date: ____________

Quick Tip

When changing decimals to percents, multiply by 100. When changing percents to decimals, divide by 100. To write percents as fractions, put the percent in the numerator and 100 in the denominator because percents are out of 100.

Directions: Solve each problem.

1. Write 30% as a fraction. ____________

2. Write $\frac{1}{4}$ as a decimal. ____________

3. Write $\frac{10}{3}$ as a decimal. ____________

4. Write $\frac{4}{5}$ as a percent. ____________

5. Write 0.82 as a percent. ____________

6. Write $\frac{1}{2}$ as a percent. ____________

7. Write 45% as a decimal. ____________

8. Write 95% as a fraction. ____________

9. Write 1.5 as a percent. ____________

10. Write 0.35 as a fraction. ____________

11. Write 12% as a decimal. ____________

12. Write 50% as a fraction. ____________

13. Write $\frac{5}{8}$ as a percent. ____________

14. Write $\frac{3}{4}$ as a percent. ____________

Name: ______________________ Date: ______________

Directions: Write the missing numbers.

	Fraction	Decimal	Percent
1.	$\frac{3}{5}$		
2.		0.8	
3.			12%
4.	$\frac{7}{8}$		
5.		1.4	
6.			220%
7.	$\frac{3}{4}$		
8.		0.3	
9.			72%
10.	$2\frac{1}{4}$		
11.		3.5	
12.			38%
13.		0.90	
14.			1%

UNIT 2
DAY
20

Converting Rational Numbers to Decimals

Name: ______________________ Date: ______________

Directions: Solve each problem.

1. Martin scored $\frac{18}{20}$ on his math test.

a. What percent did Martin get correct? ________

b. What decimal did Martin get correct? ________

c. Is the decimal terminating or repeating? ________

2. Ryan completed 85% of his workout.

a. What is the decimal of the workout that he completed? ________

b. Is the decimal terminating or repeating? ________

c. What fraction of his workout did he complete? ________

3. Kevin ate $\frac{2}{3}$ of the bag of potato chips.

a. What is the decimal of the amount of the bag he ate? ________

b. Is the decimal terminating or repeating? ________

c. What percent of the bag of potato chips did he eat? ________

4. Each lap around the track is 0.4 of a mile.

a. Is the decimal terminating or repeating? ________

b. What fraction of a mile is one lap around the track? ________

c. What percent of a mile is one lap around the track? ________

5. Amy earned a perfect score on her quiz, and she also answered the bonus questions correctly. Her teacher wrote $\frac{22}{20}$ on her quiz.

a. What decimal is $\frac{22}{20}$? ________

b. Is the decimal terminating or repeating? ________

c. What percent did Amy score on her quiz? ________

6. Karen planted 55% of the garden.

a. What decimal of the garden did Karen plant? ________

b. Is the decimal terminating or repeating? ________

c. What fraction of the garden did Karen plant? ________

Learn about Solving Problems with Rational Numbers

rational number—any number that can be written as a fraction, where the numerator and denominator are integers; the denominator cannot be 0

Examples: 4, $\frac{1}{3}$, –8

integer—a whole number that can be positive, negative, or 0

Examples: –5, 0, 7

whole number—any positive number (or 0) that does not include a fraction or decimal part

Examples: 3, 10, 250

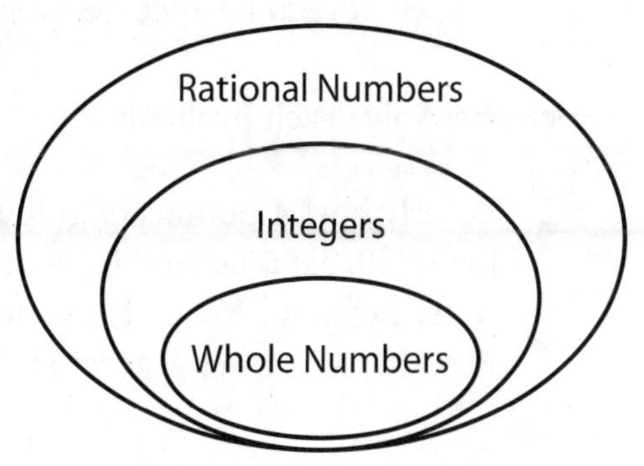

Example 1

Mariah's paycheck is \$550. Each month, she spends \$250 on her car payment, \$55 on her cell phone, and \$135 on other bills. The rest of her paycheck goes into her savings account. How much money is Mariah putting into her savings account each month?

1. Add Mariah's expenses.
   \$250 + \$55 + \$135 = \$________
2. Subtract the amount of her paycheck by your answer in Step 1.
   \$550 – \$________
3. The amount Mariah puts in her savings account each month is \$________.

Example 2

Ali earns \$300 each week. She spends $\frac{1}{8}$ of her pay on gas for her car. How much does Ali spend on gas?

1. Multiply \$300 × $\frac{1}{8}$ = \$________
2. Ali spends \$________ on gas.

Name: ______________________ Date: ______________

Quick Tip

Be sure to line decimal points up when adding or subtracting with decimals.

Directions: Solve each problem.

1. Beverly buys 4 pounds of grapes for \$2.50, bananas for \$0.54, and a watermelon for \$7.50. How much does Beverly pay for her groceries?

____

2. Makenzie has $\frac{1}{5}$ of her homework finished. Patrice has $\frac{3}{4}$ of her homework finished. How much more homework does Patrice have finished than Makenzie?

____

3. Tony ran $6\frac{1}{5}$ miles. Robert ran 2.05 miles. Miguel ran $4\frac{1}{10}$ miles. How many total miles did the three friends run?

____

4. James cleaned 25% of the garage. Michael cleaned 0.6 of the garage. Steven has to clean the rest of the garage. What fraction of the garage does Steven have left to clean?

____

5. The train traveled 356.25 miles. The Jones family drove $453\frac{3}{4}$ miles. How many more miles did the Jones family drive than the train traveled?

____

6. Ramon spent \$135.45 on groceries, \$64.25 on entertainment, and \$25 on a birthday gift for his friend. If Ramon had \$300, how much did he have left?

____

7. Angel ate $\frac{4}{5}$ of a pizza. Dominic ate $\frac{7}{8}$ of a pizza. How much more pizza did Dominic eat?

____

8. Amy rode her bicycle 9.5 miles on Monday and $14\frac{3}{4}$ miles on Tuesday. How many more miles did Amy ride on Tuesday compared to Monday?

____

9. Fatima bought $2\frac{3}{4}$ pounds of green grapes and $1\frac{4}{5}$ pounds of red grapes. How many total pounds of grapes did Fatima buy?

____

10. Evan picked $11\frac{1}{4}$ quarts of strawberries, 3.25 quarts of blueberries, and $\frac{4}{5}$ quarts of raspberries. How many total quarts of berries did Evan pick?

____

Name: ____________________ Date: ____________

Directions: Solve each problem.

1. Samantha earned $150 on her paycheck and wants to put $\frac{1}{3}$ of the money into her savings account. How much money will Samantha put into her savings account?

____

2. Charlie took $300 of his paycheck to make his car payment. The car payment was $\frac{1}{4}$ of Charlie's total paycheck. How much was Charlie's total paycheck?

____

3. Mrs. Smith hands out a worksheet to her math class that has 50 problems on it. She tells her students they should complete $\frac{3}{5}$ of the problems. How many problems should the students complete?

____

4. Jeffrey is planting seeds in the garden. The seeds should be planted $1\frac{1}{2}$ feet apart. If he is planting the seeds in rows that are 10.5 feet long, how many seeds can he plant in one row?

____

5. Sarah sent her grandmother a bouquet of 40 flowers. In the bouquet, $\frac{3}{8}$ of the flowers were daisies. How many of the flowers were daisies?

____

6. Diego and his family went camping. They spent $2\frac{1}{2}$ hours hiking and 4 times as long swimming. How many hours did Diego's family spend swimming?

____

7. Yaneli spent $3\frac{3}{5}$ hours studying for her test. Manny spent twice as long studying. How long did Manny spend studying for the test?

____

8. The walk to the library is 8 miles. Frank walked $\frac{3}{4}$ of the way to the library. How many miles did Frank walk?

____

9. There are 120 students in the seventh grade at East Middle School. Of the 120 students, $\frac{1}{3}$ of them made the honor roll. How many students made the honor roll?

____

10. Zander is running 26 miles. He already ran 10% of the distance. How many miles did Zander run already?

____

Name: ______________________ Date: ______________

Directions: Solve each problem.

1. Mickey's cell phone bill is $75 per month and $1.25 for every minute he goes over his allowed minutes. What is the cost of Mickey's cell phone bill if he goes over his plan by 12 minutes?

____

2. LeRoy is having friends over for dinner. He spends $35.80 on steaks, $15.50 on fresh produce, $9.60 on beverages, and $15.10 on dessert. If he pays with a $100 bill, how much change will he receive?

____

3. Marjorie pays $11 per month for a gym membership. For 3 months out of the year, she gets a $1.50 discount. How much does Marjorie pay for her membership for one year?

____

4. Li is paid a $150 bonus for working at the ice cream store. Every time he makes an incorrect ice cream order, $2.50 is subtracted from his bonus. If he makes 7 incorrect orders, how much will Li receive from his bonus?

____

5. Jefferson swam $12\frac{1}{2}$ miles each day for 3 days and ran $8\frac{1}{3}$ miles each day for 2 days. What is the total number of miles Jefferson swam and ran?

____

6. Geo has $500 and wants to buy 2 video games for $49.99 each, a pair of headphones for $299, and a new controller for $59. Then, he wants to buy trading cards that are $6.99 per pack. What is the greatest number of packs of cards Geo can buy with the money he has left?

____

7. Peppers are $1.50 per pound. Potatoes are $3.25 per pound. Marcella buys 3 pounds of peppers and 4 pounds of potatoes. How much does she spend in all?

____

8. Three friends went out to dinner. The total bill was $47.10, and the 3 friends split the bill equally. How much did each friend pay?

____

9. Kinley pays $225 each month for her car payment. If she pays it 5 days early, she gets a $25 discount. If Kinley made 6 payments early, what is the total amount she paid for all 12 months?

____

10. Tia bought 4 books for $7.99 each. She received a discount of $0.50 off each book because they were used books. How much did she pay for all 4 books?

____

Name: ______________________ Date: ______________

Quick Tip

Remember to follow the order of operations when completing multiple operations in a problem.

1. Complete all grouping symbols first. This includes parentheses ( ), brackets [ ], and absolute value | |.
2. Calculate any exponents, such as $3^2 = 9$.
3. Complete any multiplication or division, working from left to right.
4. Complete any addition or subtraction, working from left to right.

Directions: Solve each problem.

1. $(8^2 - 5^2) + 5(-3) =$ ________

2. $-16 + (9 - 10) + 4^2 =$ ________

3. $[4(6 - 5) + 9] =$ ________

4. $9^2 - [5 - (-4)] + 2^2 =$ ________

5. $14 + (6 - 7) + 3^3 =$ ________

6. $(\frac{1}{2})^2 + 2.25 - 1 =$ ________

7. $|-9| - 2^2 + (-4) =$ ________

8. $[(6 - (-5)] + 5^2 - (-2) =$ ________

9. $\frac{3}{4} + 4.5 - 1.6 =$ ________

10. $1\frac{1}{4} + \frac{7}{8} - (-4) =$ ________

11. $\frac{13}{5} \times \frac{20}{39} - 1 =$ ________

12. $(\frac{2}{5})^2 + 5\frac{1}{4} =$ ________

Name: ____________________ Date: ____________

Directions: Solve each problem.

1. Homer worked 8 hours, and he earns \$12.50 per hour. He has to pay $\frac{1}{8}$ of his paycheck for a new uniform shirt. How much of his paycheck will he have left after he pays for the shirt?

____

2. Camilla buys 4 ounces of onions at \$1.25 per ounce and 3 ounces of celery at \$0.99 per ounce. She is paying with a \$10 bill. How much change will Camilla receive?

____

3. Bo is running in a 26-mile race. He has already run $\frac{3}{4}$ of the race. How many miles does Bo still have left to run?

____

4. Sarah made one batch of 18 cups of lemonade. She is serving the lemonade at her party, and each serving is $\frac{3}{4}$ of a cup. How many $\frac{3}{4}$-cup servings can she make from two batches of lemonade?

____

5. Penelope cleaned her room, and it took her $1\frac{1}{2}$ hours. Her brother's room will take twice as long to clean. How many minutes will it take Penelope's brother to clean his room?

____

6. Ramone works at a restaurant and earns \$15 per hour plus tips. He has to give $\frac{1}{4}$ of his tips to the busboys. If Ramone works 8 hours and earns \$40 in tips, how much will he get to bring home after paying the busboys?

____

7. $9 - (-11) + 2 - (4^2) =$ ________

8. $5^2 + (-3)^3 - (-9) + 10 =$ ________

9. $[12 - (6 - 8)] + (\frac{4}{5})^2 =$ ________

10. $3(5 - 8) + 10^2 =$ ________

11. $6 - (10 - 12) + 4^2 - 9 =$ ________

12. $8^2 + (-15) - 7^2 =$ ________

Name: ______________________ Date: ______________

Directions: Solve each problem.

1. 75 dogs in 15 kennels

a. Write this as a rate. ________

b. What is the unit rate? ________

2. Myka runs 2 miles in $\frac{1}{2}$ of an hour. How many miles can she run in 1 hour?

____

3. What is the constant of proportionality from the table?

k = ________

x	y
9	13.5
10	15
11	16.5
12	18

4. $10 - (-3) =$ ________

5. Roger scored 60% on his science test.

a. What is 60% as a fraction?

____

b. What is 60% as a decimal?

____

6. $\frac{4^4}{4^2} =$ ________

7. How many seconds are in 5 days?

____

8. Paolo and his family went to dinner, and the bill was $65. They wanted to leave a 15% tip. What was the amount of the tip?

____

9. What is the additive inverse of –14.6?

____

10. $6\frac{1}{5} + 3\frac{2}{9} =$ ________

11. What is the constant of proportionality in the equation?

$y = 7x$

k = ________

12. Is the relationship proportional?

Circle yes no

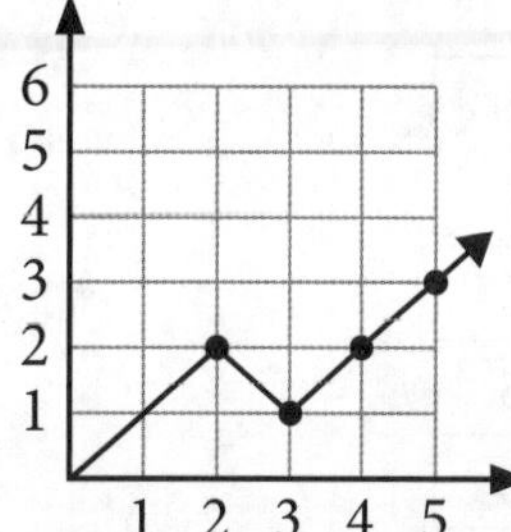

Spiral Review

Name: ____________________ Date: ____________

Directions: Solve each problem.

1. Write the equation modeled on the number line.

_______ + _______ = _______

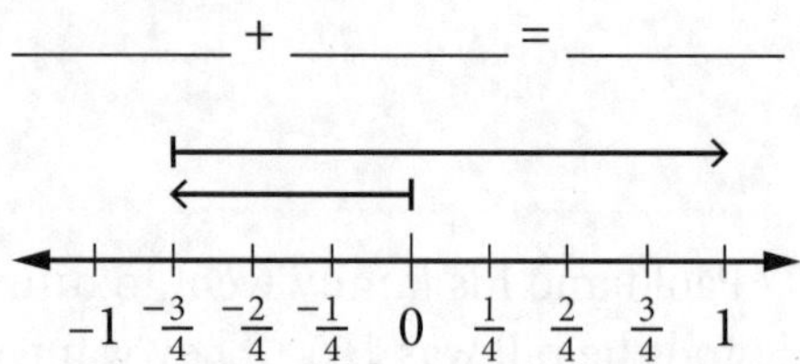

2. Find the constant of proportionality.

$k =$ _______

180
150
120
90
60
30
5 10 15 20 25

3. $5.65 - 3\frac{1}{4} =$ _______

4. Does the table show a proportional relationship?

Circle yes no

x	y
0	5
1	10
2	15
3	20

5. Find the constant of proportionality, and use it to complete the table.

Number of Plums	Cost
12	$5.40
14	
16	
18	

6. Nancy made 24 muffins in 2 hours. At this rate, how many muffins can Nancy make in 6 hours? _______

7. Does the graph show a proportional relationship?

Circle yes no

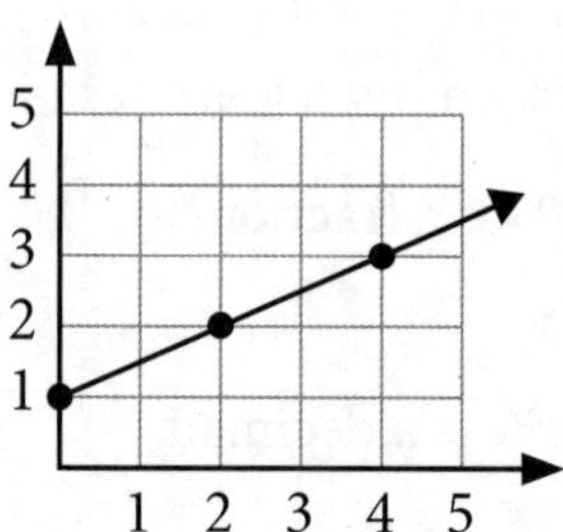

8. Solve the problem using the Distributive Property.

$3(-5 + 4) =$ _______ + _______ =

_______ + _______ = _______

Name: ______________________ Date: ______________

Directions: Solve each problem.

1. Rhonda made 35 cupcakes in $2\frac{1}{3}$ hours. At this rate, how many cupcakes does Rhonda make per hour?

____

5. If Sam builds 6 chairs in 2 hours, how many chairs can he build in 54 hours?

____

2. Write the equation modeled on the number line.

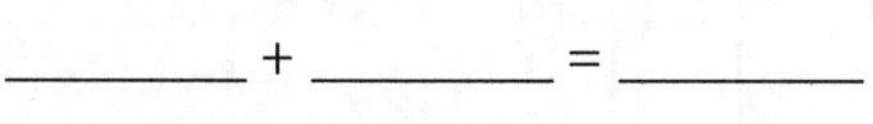

________ + ________ = ________

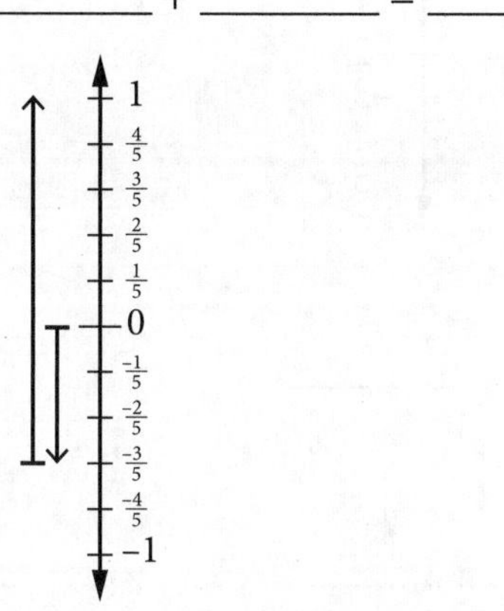

6. Write an equation for the proportional relationship shown on the graph.

$y =$ ________ x

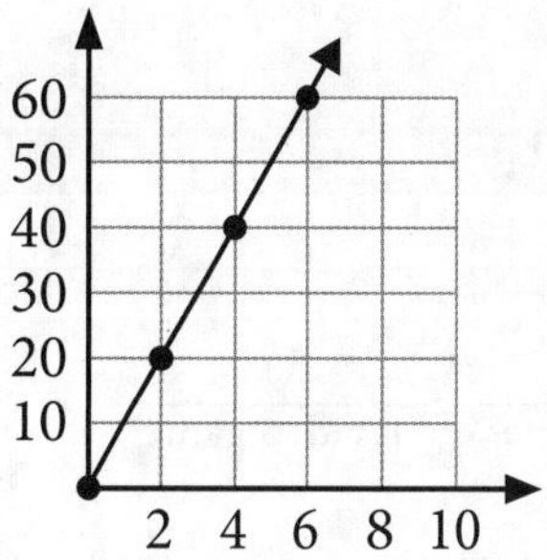

3. Solve the problem using the Distributive Property.

$-2(3 + 6)$ = ________ + ________ =

________ + ________ = ________

7. Use the diagram to determine whether the answer will be positive or negative.

Circle your response.

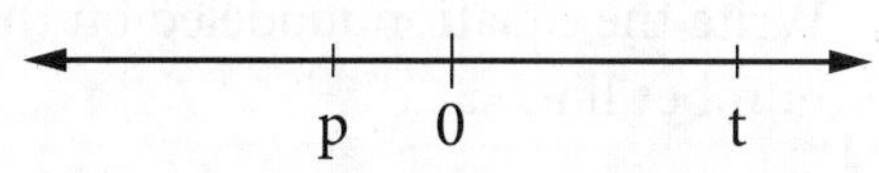

a. $t - p$ positive negative

b. $p + t$ positive negative

4. What is the constant of proportionality shown on the graph?

$k =$ ________

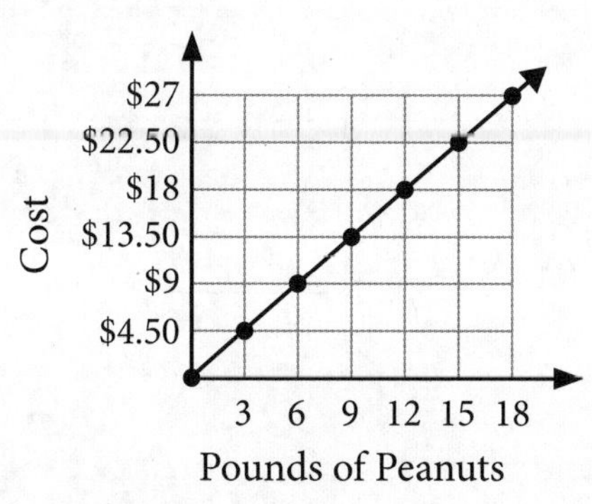

8. Mary babysat for 8 hours and earned $160. Write an equation to represent the proportional relationship.

$y =$ ________ x

Spiral Review

Name: ____________________ Date: ____________

Directions: Solve each problem.

1. Monroe plows 70 driveways in $17\frac{1}{2}$ hours. How many driveways can he plow in 1 hour?

____

2. $\frac{\$400}{5 \text{ video games}} = \frac{x}{1 \text{ video game}}$

$x =$ ________

3. $6^2 - 5^2 + 4 - (-2) =$ ________

4. Write the equation modeled on the number line.

________ + ________ = ________

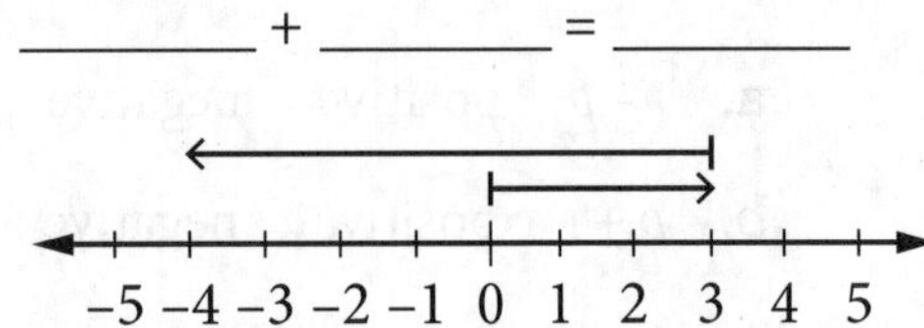

5. Li is buying a sweater that costs \$45. Last week, the sweater was \$60. What percent did the price decrease?

____

6. What is the additive inverse of –6?

____

7. Write the equation modeled on the number line.

________ + ________ = ________

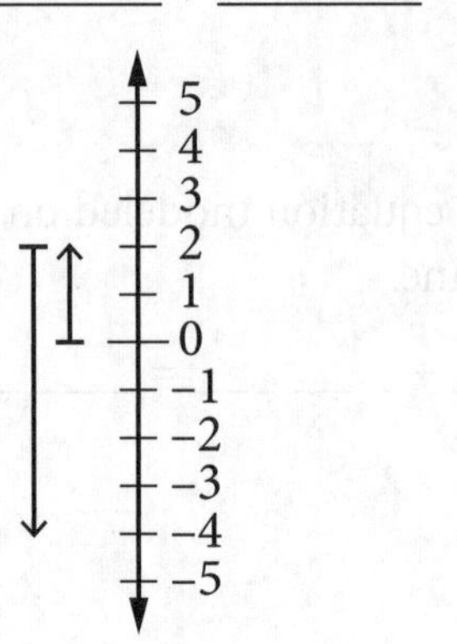

8. $(\frac{2}{5})^3 =$ ________

9. $7\frac{3}{4} - 2\frac{1}{6} =$ ________

10. Hakeem's tuition is \$12,000, but he gets 15% off. What is the price of the tuition with the discount?

____

11. $\frac{-40}{8} =$ ________

12. $9^3 - 8^2 + 4^2 =$ ________

Name: ______________________________ Date: ______________

Directions: Solve each problem.

1. The oatmeal cookie recipe calls for $\frac{1}{4}$ cup of sugar for $\frac{1}{2}$ of a recipe. How many cups of sugar would you need to make 3 batches of the recipe? ________

2. What is the constant of proportionality?

$k =$ ________

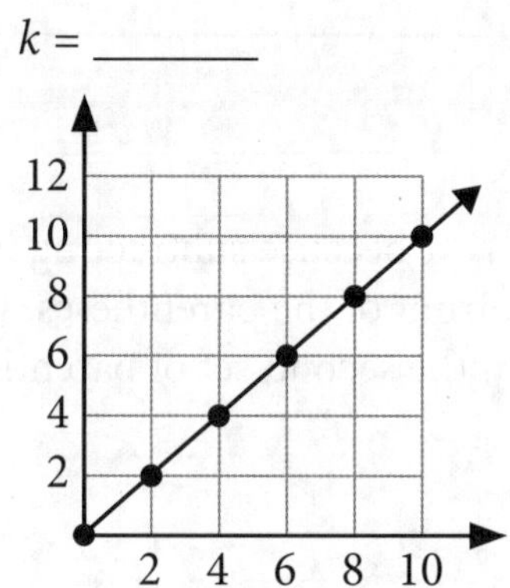

3. $\frac{\$50}{\text{12 pairs of socks}} = \frac{x}{\text{48 pairs of socks}}$

$x =$ ________

4. Write an equation for the proportional relationship in the table.

$y =$ ________ x

x	y
0	0
1	5
2	10
3	15

5. Beans are $1.99 per pound, and peppers are $1.25 per pound. Marvin buys 2 pounds of beans and 3 pounds of peppers. How much does Marvin spend?

____

6. $\frac{18}{48} = \frac{3}{x}$

$x =$ ________

7. $7^2 \times 7^2 =$ ________

8. Write the equation modeled on the number line.

________ + ________ = ________

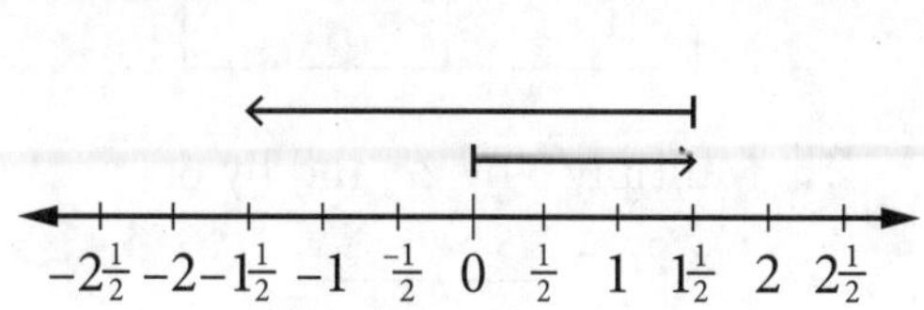

Learn about Equivalent Expressions

Distributive Property—multiplying the factor outside of the parentheses by every number inside the parentheses

Example: $3(2 + 7) = (3 \cdot 2) + (3 \cdot 7)$

equivalent—equal

like terms—terms that contain the same variable raised to the same power

Example: $4x$ and $2x$ are like terms because they both contain the variable x, and the x in both terms is raised to the first power.

You can add and subtract like terms, and you can multiply unlike terms.

Example: $3x \cdot 2 = 6x$

Example 1

Simplify the expression. $(8m - 5) - (4m + 2)$

1. Change the subtraction sign in front of the parentheses to + –1 because subtracting is the same as adding the opposite. When there is no number in front of the parentheses, we assume that there is a 1 there. Multiply –1 by everything in the second set of parentheses.

   $(8m - 5) + -(4m + 2)$

   $-1 \times 4m = -4m$

   $-1 \times 2 = -2$

   Write these numbers in the equation.

   $8m - 5 + (-4m) + (-2)$

2. Now, combine the like terms.
   Simplified expression: $4m - 7$

Example 2

Write an equivalent expression using the Distributive Property. Use the area model to help you. $3(2a + 6)$

1. Write the number outside the parentheses on the left side of the rectangle. Write each of the numbers in the parentheses above the rectangle.

	$2a$	6
3		

2. Multiply 3 by $2a$ and by 6.

   $3 \times 2a =$ ________

   $3 \times 6 =$ ________

3. Add the products to write an equivalent expression. ________ + ________

Example 3

Write an equivalent expression.

$18 + 3a$

1. Draw a rectangle and divide it into the same number of boxes as there are terms in the expression. Write each term in a separate box.

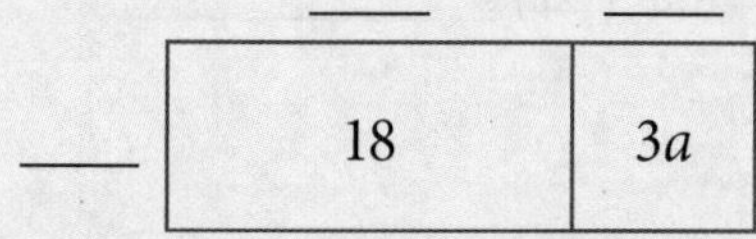

2. Find a common factor for both terms. When looking at 18 and $3a$, it can be determined that 3 is a common factor. Write 3 on the line on the left side of the rectangle.

3. Divide 18 and $3a$ by the 3. Write the answers on the lines on top of the 18 and $3a$.

4. Write the equivalent expression. Put the number on the left side of the box outside the parentheses. Inside the parentheses, write the terms left after dividing by 3.

3(________ + ________)

Example 4

Are the expressions equivalent?

$6(3x + 4)$ and $18x + 4$

1. Use the Distributive Property to rewrite the first expression.

$6 \cdot 3x =$ ________

$6 \cdot 4 =$ ________

________ + ________

2. Are the expressions equivalent? ________

Name: ______________________ Date: ______________

Quick Tip

If there is a subtraction sign in front of the parentheses, change it to + and write –1 in front of the parentheses. Then, multiply each number in the parentheses by –1.

Directions: Simplify each expression.

1. $(4b + 7) + (-8b - 6)$ ____________

7. $7c - (6a + 2c)$ ____________

2. $5v - 9w + 11v - 2w$ ____________

8. $21a - (-9a) + 15 - 2a$ ____________

3. $(3k + 9) - (5k + 6)$ ____________

9. $(5q - 6p + 3) - (2q - 4)$ ____________

4. $10a - 6b + 8 - 3a + 4b$ ____________

10. $-14f - 18 + 6f - 2 + 10f$ ____________

5. $(2x - 5y) - (4y + 8x)$ ____________

11. $11m - 4n + 10n - 6$ ____________

6. $18p - 9p + 4p + 5d - 8d$ ____________

12. $-12 + 3j - 15j + 8$ ____________

Name: ______________________ Date: ______________

Directions: Write equivalent expressions using the Distributive Property. Use the area models to help you.

1. $3(4x + 6)$ ______________

	$4x$	6
3		

2. $8(5m + 9)$ ______________

	$5m$	9
8		

3. $6(2a + 3b + 4)$ ______________

	$2a$	$3b$	4
6			

4. $2(3a + 9b + 9)$ ______________

	$3a$	$9b$	9
2			

5. $3(7m + 11)$ ______________

	$7m$	11
3		

6. $10(12a + 14)$ ______________

	$12a$	14
10		

7. $5(3x + 50)$ ______________

	$3x$	50
5		

8. $4(6p + 14)$ ______________

	$6p$	14
4		

Name: ______________________ Date: ______________

Directions: Write equivalent expressions using the Distributive Property.

1. $5(10x + 7)$ ______________

2. $-4(3a + 2b + 2)$ ______________

3. $2(a - 6b)$ ______________

4. $10(8b - 7c)$ ______________

5. $-8(a - 2b)$ ______________

6. $3(6a + 4b - 3c)$ ______________

7. $-10(2m - 20)$ ______________

8. $9(4k) - 5k + 7$ ______________

9. $11(2b - 11)$ ______________

10. $12(a - 2b)$ ______________

11. $4(3 - 4x)$ ______________

12. $-6(2x + 4)$ ______________

13. $3(3a - 2b + 6)$ ______________

14. $14(-3a - 7)$ ______________

Name: ______________________ Date: ______________

Directions: Write equivalent expressions. Label the area models to help you.

1. $2x + 10y + 30$

____ (____ + ____ + ____)

	$2x$	$10y$	30

2. $5p + 25 + 45q$

____ (____ + ____ + ____)

	$5p$	25	$45q$

3. $6q + 30$

____ (____ + ____)

	$6q$	30

4. $4n + 16 + 24m$

____ (____ + ____ + ____)

	$4n$	16	$24m$

5. $6m + 54$

____ (____ + ____)

	$6m$	54

6. $3a + 12b + 39$

____ (____ + ____ + ____)

	$3a$	$12b$	39

7. $16 + 32a + 40b$

____ (____ + ____ + ____)

	16	$32a$	$40b$

8. $3b + 12a + 6$

____ (____ + ____ + ____)

	$3b$	$12a$	6

Equivalent Expressions

Name:__________________________________ Date:_________________

Reminder

Remember, you can only add terms that have the same variables or terms that have no variable.

Directions: Determine whether the expressions are equivalent. Circle *yes* or *no.*

1. $15 - 4y$ and $3(5 - 2y)$

yes no

2. $8x + 10y + 20$ and $2(4x + 5y + 10)$

yes no

3. $6(\frac{1}{2} + 3x)$ and $3 + 18x$

yes no

4. $9(\frac{1}{3} - 2a)$ and $3 - 18a$

yes no

5. $7a + 4b + 4$ and $3a + 4a + 4b + 4$

yes no

6. $5k - 8$ and $5k + (-8)$

yes no

7. $8(\frac{1}{4} + 3m)$ and $8 + 24m$

yes no

8. $\frac{7}{8}(8 - 16p)$ and $7 + 12p$

yes no

9. $5(4y - 7)$ and $25y - 35$

yes no

10. $9m - 27$ and $9(m - 3)$

yes no

11. $7(3k + 9)$ and $24k + 64$

yes no

12. $6(3h - 2k)$ and $9h + 12k$

yes no

Learn about Multistep Problems with Rational Numbers

equation—a mathematical statement that shows two mathematical expressions are equal (Example: $x + 7 = 12$)

expression—a mathematical statement with at least two numbers or variables and at least one mathematical operation (Example: $3c + 7$)

inequality—comparison of two values, showing whether one is less than, greater than, equal to, or not equal to the other value (Example: $x + 3 < 14$)

Multistep Word Problem

Kiki is buying a new jacket priced at $75. She has a coupon for 30% off but then has to pay 8% sales tax. What is the price of her jacket after the discount, including tax?

1. Calculate 30% off of $75. Since 100% – 30% = 70%, Kiki is paying 70% of the original price. 70% as a decimal is 0.70.
2. Multiply $75 × 0.70 = ______________
   This is the new price with the discount.
3. Calculate the total with the sales tax. Kiki must pay 100% of the cost plus 8%. So, she must pay 108%. As a decimal, this is 1.08.
4. Multiply the discounted price ______________ × 1.08 = ______________
   This is the total price, with the discount, including tax.

Solutions to Inequalities

Is 3 a solution to the inequality? $2x + 4 > 9$

1. Substitute 3 in the inequality for x.
   $2 \times 3 + 4 =$ ______________
2. Is the answer in Step 1 greater than 9? ______________
   If the answer is *yes*, then 3 is a solution. If the answer is *no*, then 3 is not a solution.
   Is 3 a solution? ______________

Using Estimation

Gisselle is making pillow covers. Each cover uses 110 square inches of fabric. Gisselle has 1,200 square inches of fabric. Gisselle thinks she can make 15 pillows. Use estimation to determine whether Gisselle is correct. How do you know?

1. First, round 110 to 100. Next, multiply 100 × 15 = ______________
2. After finding the answer in Step 1, do you agree with Gisselle? ______________
3. Why or why not? ____

Name: ______________________ Date: ______________

Visual Support

Order of Operations

1. Parentheses and all grouping symbols
2. Exponents
3. Multiply or divide, from left to right
4. Add or subtract, from left to right

Directions: Solve each problem.

1. $(39.56 - 28.2) - 15.1 =$ __________

2. $-2[8 - (-4)] + 30 =$ __________

3. $-5\frac{4}{5} - 3\frac{1}{3} =$ __________

4. $18 - (4 - 9) \times 3.2 =$ __________

5. $6\frac{2}{3} \times 2\frac{1}{4} - 12 =$ __________

6. $90.5 + 20.3 - 8.6 + 4\frac{1}{3} =$ __________

7. $-3(\frac{1}{4} + \frac{7}{8}) =$ __________

8. $5(9 - 20) + (-10) \cdot 3 =$ __________

9. $3\frac{1}{8} \div \frac{5}{2} + 9\frac{1}{5} =$ __________

10. $5[9 - (-3 - 6)] + (-12) =$ __________

11. $-28.15 - 15.4 + (-19) - 6 =$ __________

12. $6\frac{3}{4} \cdot 3\frac{1}{3} + \frac{2}{5} =$ __________

Name: ________________________________ Date: ________________

Directions: Solve each problem. Show your work.

1. Michael is saving for a new set of golf clubs that costs $500 plus 8% tax. He has already saved up $190. His parents have agreed to pay $\frac{1}{4}$ of the total cost. What is the amount that Michael still has to earn to pay for the golf clubs?

____

2. Janie ordered a chicken tender meal at a restaurant for $10.99. She had a coupon for 10% off but wanted to leave a 20% tip. How much is the meal, including the discount and tip?

____

3. LeKeith and his friends were picking strawberries. LeKeith picked $4\frac{5}{8}$ pints, Marcel picked 3.04 pints, and Reginald picked 10% more pints than Marcel. How many pints of strawberries did the friends pick in all?

____

4. Katie is shopping for back-to-school clothes. She wants to buy 2 pairs of jeans that are $45 each, and she has a 20% off coupon on jeans. She also wants to buy 3 sweaters that are $34, and she has a 15% off coupon for the sweaters. What is the total of Katie's purchase with the discounts applied?

____

5. Ruiz earned $14 an hour and worked 25 hours. He put 15% of his paycheck in his savings account. He spent $45 on his cell phone and $35 on gas. How much money did he have left?

____

6. East Middle School is hosting a walkathon fundraiser. Each student receives a $5 donation per mile that they walk, and 30% of the total funds are donated to charity while the rest of the money is used for school repairs. If 185 students each walk 8 miles, how much money is donated to charity?

____

7. West Middle School received $4,500 from their school fundraiser. From the funds, 15% were used to purchase rulers and protractors, and 20% were used to purchase calculators. How much money was spent on calculators?

____

8. Tyrese spent $153.12 at the mall. Later that day, he went to dinner with his friends and spent $65.35. At the start of the day, he had $315. How much money does Tyrese have left?

____

Name: ______________________ Date: ______________

Directions: Determine whether the given number is a solution to each equation or inequality. Then, circle *yes* or *no*.

1. $5m - 8 \leq 12$
Is 4 a solution?
yes no

2. $7x - 8 = 22$
Is 4 a solution?
yes no

3. $2(y - 7) = 32$
Is 12 a solution?
yes no

4. $8z + 4 - 2z - 5 = 35$
Is 6 a solution?
yes no

5. $5p + 6 \geq 14$
Is 2 a solution?
yes no

6. $8(3x - 4) < 8$
Is 2 a solution?
yes no

7. $5(9 - 2x) > 65$
Is –2 a solution?
yes no

8. $9 - 14b + 5 = 12$
Is $\frac{1}{7}$ a solution?
yes no

9. $15p = 150$
Is 5 a solution?
yes no

10. $7m + 4 = 32$
Is 4 a solution?
yes no

Name: ______________________ Date: ______________

Directions: Solve each problem.

1. Maria earns $24 an hour, but her boss just told her she is getting a 10% raise.

a. How much more money will she make per hour? ________

b. How much will she make for a 6-hour shift after her raise? ________

2. Cam is buying new hockey equipment priced at $225. It is discounted by 15%, but he also has to pay 8% tax before the discount is taken.

a. What is the amount in dollars of the discount Cam gets? ________

b. What is the new price after the discount? ________

c. What is the amount of the sales tax? ________

d. How much does he pay for the equipment, including tax and the discount? ________

3. Marco is building a sandbox for his little brother. He needs 2 pieces of wood that are $6\frac{1}{2}$ feet long each and 2 pieces of wood that are $4\frac{1}{5}$ feet long each. He has 4 pieces that are 7 feet long each.

a. How much wood will be left over when he cuts one $6\frac{1}{2}$-foot piece of wood? ________

b. How much wood will be left over when he cuts one $4\frac{1}{5}$-foot piece of wood? ________

c. How much total wood will be left over after he cuts all 4 pieces of wood? ________

4. Niko is saving money for college. His last 3 paychecks were $356, $425, and $415.

a. If Niko saves 30% of his paychecks, how much will he put into his savings account? ________

b. If Niko spends 20% of what is left after taking out his savings account money, how much will he spend? ________

Multistep Problems with Rational Numbers

Name: ______________________ Date: ____________

Quick Tip

When rounding fractions, if the fraction is $\frac{1}{2}$ or larger, round up to the next whole number. If the fraction is less than $\frac{1}{2}$, round down to the nearest whole number.

Directions: Use estimation to determine the answers to the questions. Then, explain how you found your answers.

1. Dez is making bracelets and needs $7\frac{3}{4}$ inches of string for each bracelet. She wants to make 10 bracelets, and she has 60 inches of string.

a. Does Dez have enough string for 10 bracelets? ____________

b. How do you know? ____________

____

2. Tyrone runs $6\frac{1}{4}$ miles each day. After 8 days, he estimates that he ran slightly over 48 miles.

a. Do you agree with Tyrone?

____

b. Why or why not? ____________

____

3. Maya is baking strawberry pies. Each pie uses $3\frac{1}{5}$ pints of strawberries. Maya has 14 pints of strawberries. Maya thinks she can make 5 pies.

a. Do you agree with her? ________

b. Why or why not? ____________

____

4. Pablo loves to read. He read 6 books in 4 days. Pablo believes he could read 60 books in one 30-day month if he continues to read at the same rate.

a. Do you agree with Pablo?

____

b. Why or why not? ____________

____

5. Theresa has a bag of flour that has 18 cups. She is baking bread that uses $4\frac{1}{2}$ cups of flour per loaf. Theresa thinks she has enough flour to make 5 loaves of bread.

a. Do you agree with her? ________

b. Why or why not? ____________

____

6. Mila picked 8 pounds of cherries from the trees in her orchard. She is baking pies, and each pie takes 1.5 pounds of cherries. Mila believes she can make 4 pies.

a. Do you agree with her? ________

b. Why or why not? ____________

____

Learn about Using Variables

variable—a letter that represents an unknown number in an expression or equation

In the equation $y = mx + b$, m represents the slope of a line. The slope is also known as the **rate of change**. It shows how much the y-value increases each time the x-value increases by one. The b represents the y-intercept.

In the equation $y = 3x + 2$, the y-intercept is 2, and the slope (rate of change) is 3.

Example 1

Write an expression for *a number increased by 9.*

1. Choose a variable, and write it. ________
2. *Increasing* means addition, so now write the expression starting with the variable you chose in Step 1. ________ + 9

Example 2

Tyler and Greg work at an ice cream shop. Greg made 5 times as many milkshakes as Tyler. Write an expression to represent the number of milkshakes Greg made.

1. Let's use the variable m to represent the number of milkshakes Tyler made.
2. To represent the number of milkshakes Greg made, we can write the expression $5m$ because Greg made 5 times as many as Tyler.

Example 3

Write an equation based on the information in the table.

x	y
0	4
1	6
2	8
3	10

1. If you look in the x column for 0, the corresponding y value is the y-intercept. You can see that the y-intercept is 4.
2. We can see that each time an x-value increases by 1, the y-value increases by 2. This is the rate of change.
3. Write the equation in the form $y = mx + b$.
   $y = 2x + 4$

Example 4

Write a real-world problem to match the equation.
$2x + x = 60$

1. Think of a situation where the numbers 2 and 60 could be appropriate. Determine what the variable will represent. Then, write the problem.

   For example: Marcia has twice as many stamps in her collection as her friend. Together, they have 60 stamps. How many stamps does Marcia's friend have?
2. What does x represent in this problem? ________

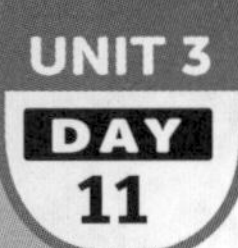

UNIT 3 DAY 11

Name: ______________________ Date: ______________

Quick Tip

The terms *sum*, *increased by*, and *plus* indicate addition. *Decreased by* and *difference* indicate subtraction. *Product*, *times*, or *multiplied by* indicate multiplication. *Quotient* indicates division.

Directions: Write an expression, equation, or inequality to represent each phrase.

1. six times a number is 12

2. the difference between k and 4

3. four times the sum of y and 2

4. nine times a number is 49

5. three times a number increased by 8 is 30

6. twice a number minus 9 is equal to 50

7. thirty times a number is equal to 270

8. eight times a number, decreased by 14, is equal to 30

9. eleven times a number is greater than 132

10. seven times a number, plus 18

11. ten times a number, increased by 6, is less than or equal to 40

12. ninety subtracted from 4 times a number is equal to 100

13. seventy times a number is greater than 350

14. a number increased by 15 is greater than or equal to 60

Using Variables

Name: ______________________________ Date: ________________

Directions: Write an equation or inequality with variables to represent each situation.

1. Diego spent some of his money at the mall. Jack spent three times as much money as Diego. Together, they spent \$200. Write an equation to model how much money each friend spent at the mall.

____

2. Lydia scored goals in her soccer game. Monique scored half as many goals as Lydia. Together, they scored 18 goals. Write an equation to model the number of goals each girl scored.

____

3. Johnny is saving up for new sports equipment. He earns \$50 per week and needs to save at least \$200. Write an equation to model the number of weeks Johnny has to save to have enough money to buy the sports equipment.

____

4. Lars needs twice as many cupcakes for his class than Mick needs for his class. Together, they need 45 cupcakes. Write an equation to model the number of cupcakes each friend needs.

____

5. To ride the ferris wheel at the fair, children must be at least 48 inches tall. Write an inequality to model how tall ferris wheel riders must be.

____

6. Germaine has at most \$75 to spend at the mall. He wants to buy a new hoodie for \$35 and spend the rest on shirts that cost \$7 each. Write an inequality to model the amount of money Germaine is spending at the mall.

____

7. Lola has 5 times as many stamps as Chris but less than 60. Write an inequality to model the number of stamps Lola has.

____

8. Roland feeds his dog 3.5 cups of dog food twice a day. Roland has 80 cups of dog food. Write an equation to model the number of days Roland can feed his dog from the 80 cups.

____

9. Gabriel's cell phone plan charges a \$65 monthly fee and an additional \$1 per text. Gabriel's last bill was \$95. Write an equation to model the number of texts Gabriel sent.

____

10. Lyla's gym membership is \$14 per month. She paid \$112 for the year. Write an equation to model the number of months Lyla had a gym membership.

____

Name: ______________________ Date: ______________

Example

Write an equation for the graph in the form $y = mx + b$.

1. b is the y-intercept, or the y value when x equals 0. Here, the y-intercept is 10.
2. m is the rate of change. Here, as x increases by 1, y increases by 10.
3. So, the equation is: $y = 10x + 10$.

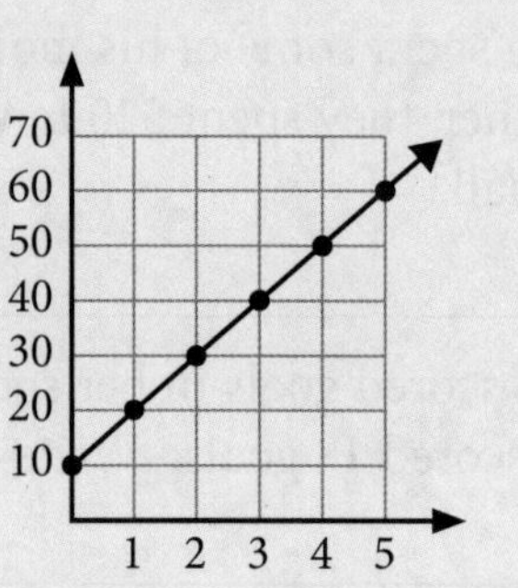

Directions: Write an equation for each graph.

1. $y =$ ________

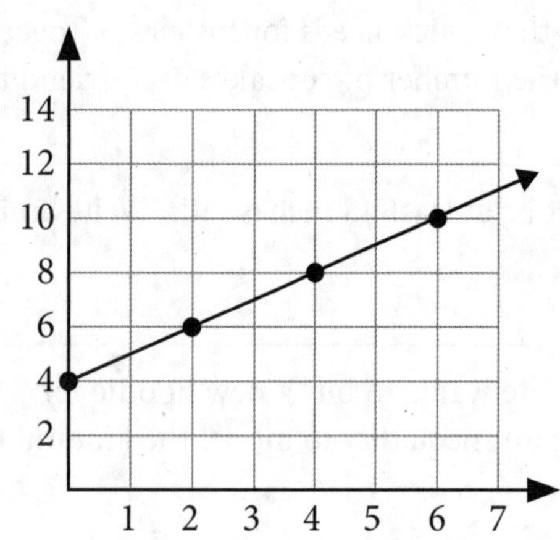

2. $y =$ ________

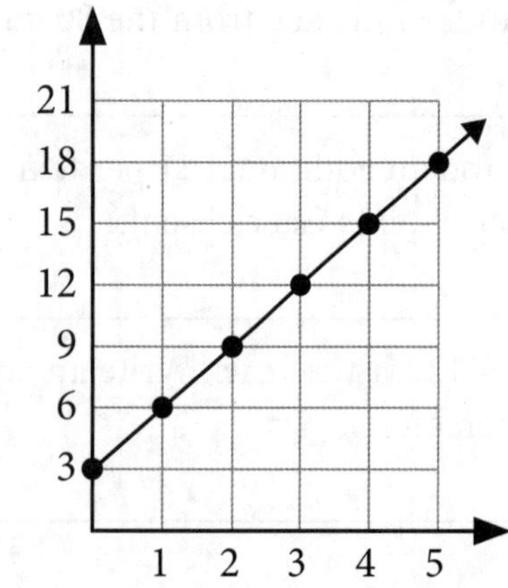

3. $y =$ ________

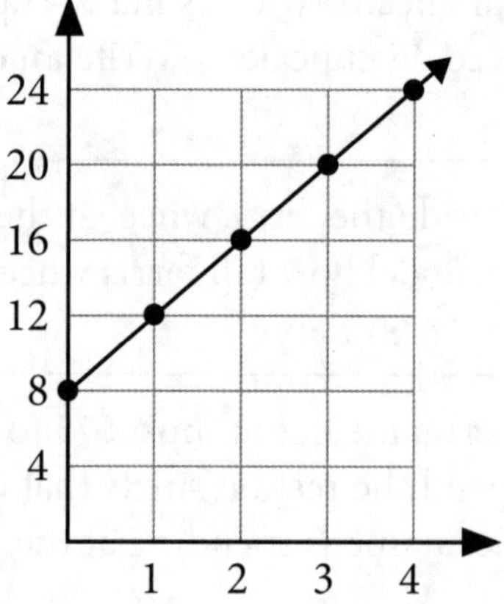

4. $y =$ ________

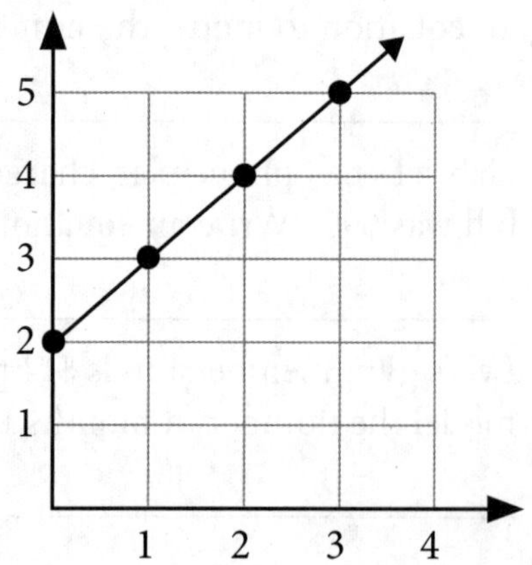

Name: ________________________ Date: ____________

Reminder

Remember, b represents the y-intercept, or the value of y when x equals 0.

Directions: Write an equation for each table in the form $y = mx + b$.

1. $y =$ ________

x	y
0	12
1	24
2	36

2. $y =$ ________

x	y
0	0.5
1	1.5
2	2.5

3. $y =$ ________

x	y
0	4
1	7
2	10

4. $y =$ ________

x	y
0	8
1	10
2	12
3	14

5. $y =$ ________

x	y
0	3
1	6
2	9

6. $y =$ ________

x	y
0	10
1	11
2	12

7. $y =$ ________

x	y
0	7
1	9
2	11

8. $y =$ ________

x	y
0	5
1	10
2	15
3	20

Name: ______________________ Date: ______________

Directions: Write a real-world situation to match each equation or inequality.

1. $2x + 3 = 13$

2. $5x > 40$

3. $6h = 60$

4. $4m + 2 = 6$

5. $9g \leq 50$

6. $2f < 100$

7. $5x = 30$

8. $3x = 120$

9. $25 + 2x > 75$

10. $7d + 1 = 15$

Learn about Solving Equations

Steps to Solve Equations

Follow the steps to solve $3(x + 1) = 12$.

1. Use the Distributive Property first. If you do not have anything to distribute, move on to Step 2.
   $3(x + 1) = 12$
   $3x + 3 = 12$

2. Undo (do the opposite of) addition or subtraction.
   In the example, there is addition in the equation. So, subtract on both sides of the equal sign.

$$\begin{array}{r} 3x + 3 = 12 \\ -3 \quad -3 \\ \hline 3x = 9 \end{array}$$

3. Undo (do the opposite of) multiplication or division.
   In the example, there is multiplication in the equation. So, divide on both sides of the equal sign.

$$\frac{3x}{3} = \frac{9}{3}$$

$$x = 3$$

Example 1

Solve the equation.

$3x + 7 = 46$

1. Subtract 7 from both sides of the equation.

$$\begin{array}{r} 3x + 7 = 46 \\ -7 \quad -7 \\ \hline 3x = 39 \end{array}$$

2. Divide both sides of the equation by 3.

$$\frac{3x}{3} = \frac{39}{3}$$

$x =$ ______

Example 2

Solve the equation. Represent the solution on a number line.

$4(2y - 6) = 40$

1. Distribute the 4.
   $(4 \cdot 2y) - (4 \cdot 6) = 40$
   _________ – _________ = 40
2. Add 24 to both sides of the equation.
   $8y - 24 = 40$
   $+24 \quad +24$
   $8y = 64$
3. Divide both sides of the equation by 8.
   $\frac{8y}{8} = \frac{64}{8}$
   $y =$ ____________
4. Graph it on the number line. Put a point on the number line for the solution that you found in Step 3.

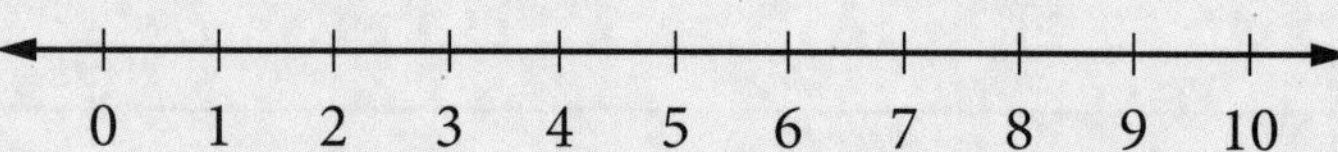

Example 3

Write and solve an equation to represent the problem.

Sal's lawn mowing business charges a flat fee of $15 plus $25 per lawn. Sal made $290 last week. How many lawns did he mow?

1. Identify the variable, or the unknown quantity. The variable is the number of lawns Sal mowed. We can use n to represent the number of lawns.
2. You know Sal charges $25 per lawn, so multiply 25 by n, and add the flat fee that Sal charges. This expression equals the total amount Sal earned last week.
   $\$25n + 15 = \$290$
3. To solve, subtract 15 from both sides first. Then, divide by 25.
   $25n + 15 = 290$
   $-15 \quad -15$
   $25n = 275$
   $\frac{25n}{25} = \frac{275}{25}$
   $n =$ ____________ lawns

Name: ______________________ Date: ______________

Directions: Solve each equation. Show your work.

1. $5m + 6 = 21$

7. $7 + 9w = 61$

2. $9 + 9b = 35$

8. $15q + 6 = 36$

3. $2y - 14 = 40$

9. $7 + 3x = 64$

4. $6p - 13 = 77$

10. $3p - 11 = 40$

5. $8x + 11 = 21$

11. $5 + 4x = 9$

6. $8 + 10m = 58$

12. $18 + 6r = 30$

Name: ____________________ Date: ____________

Reminder

Distribute (multiply) the number in front of the parentheses to each number inside the parentheses first. Then, add or subtract, and finally, multiply or divide.

Directions: Solve each equation. Show your work.

1. $4(c + 8) = 32$

2. $9(2x - 1) = 27$

3. $8(2m + 4) = 112$

4. $10(5 + w) = 80$

5. $6(x - 4) = 54$

6. $(4 + 2t)2 = 36$

7. $4(v - 9) = 20$

8. $7(3x - 2) = 91$

9. $(k - 9)3 = 3$

10. $2(b + 5) = 40$

11. $5(q - 3) = 20$

12. $2(x + 1) = 12$

Name: ______________________ Date: ______________

Directions: Write an equation with a variable for each problem. Solve for the unknown.

1. Marshawn wants to buy 5 concert tickets for himself and his friends. He has a coupon for $30 off his entire purchase. The tickets in total cost $275 after the discount. What is the original price of 1 ticket?

Equation: ______________________

Solution: ____________

2. Melinda works as a waitress. She earns $7 an hour plus tips. For the last two weeks, she earned $330, including $120 in tips. How many hours did she work over the last two weeks?

Equation: ______________________

Solution: ____________

3. Mrs. Jefferson bought 25 students each a box of pencils to start the school year. She had a coupon for $0.50 off each box of pencils. The total amount she spent was $87.25. How much was each box of pencils before the discount?

Equation: ______________________

Solution: ____________

4. Henry pays $40 per month for his gym membership plus a $15 one-time fee for his membership badge. This year, Henry paid $335. How many months did he pay for the membership?

Equation: ______________________

Solution: ____________

5. Enzo pays $75 per month for his cell phone plan, plus a one-time fee of $200 for access to his phone. He paid $425. How many months did he pay for?

Equation: ______________________

Solution: ____________

6. Cami makes pillow covers and sells them for $18 each. She paid a one-time fee of $60 for the material to make them but made a profit of $300 selling them over the summer. How many pillow covers did Cami make?

Equation: ______________________

Solution: ____________

Name: ______________________________ Date: ____________________

Directions: Solve each equation. Show your work, and circle the solution. Graph your solution on the number line.

1. $7x - 2 = 33$

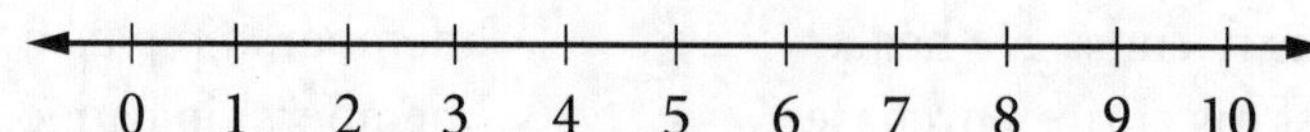

2. $6(n + 4) = 30$

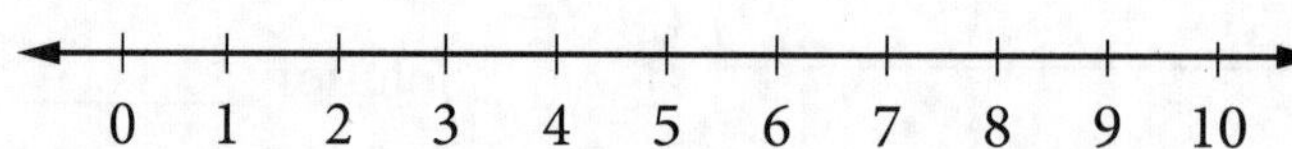

3. $10c - 4 = 16$

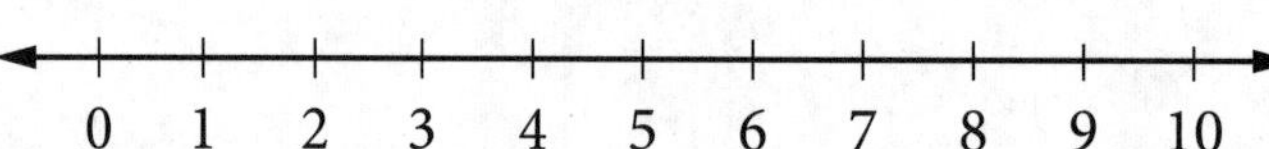

4. $5(2 + b) = 30$

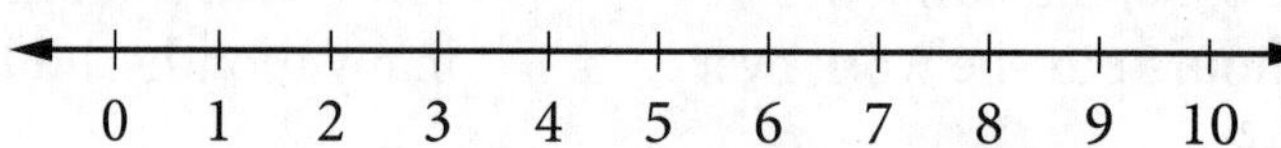

5. $7(w - 1) = 14$

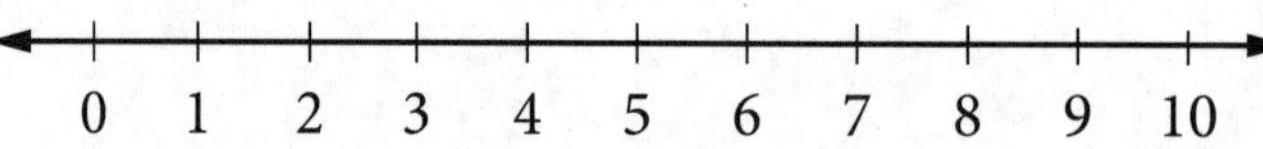

6. $2x - 4 = 16$

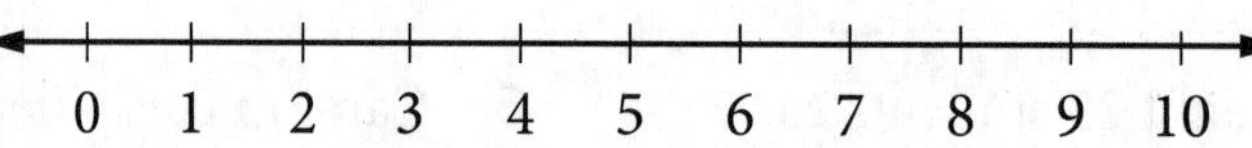

7. $3x + 3 = 36$

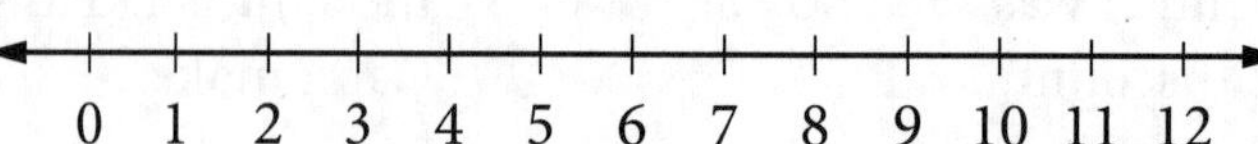

8. $-4f + 5 = 9$

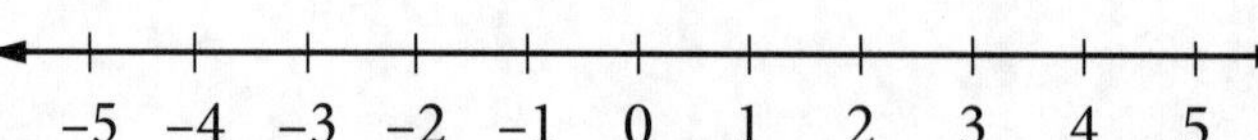

Name:______________________ Date:______________

Directions: Solve each equation. Show your work, and circle the solution. Graph your solution on the number line.

1. $3v + 4 = 10$

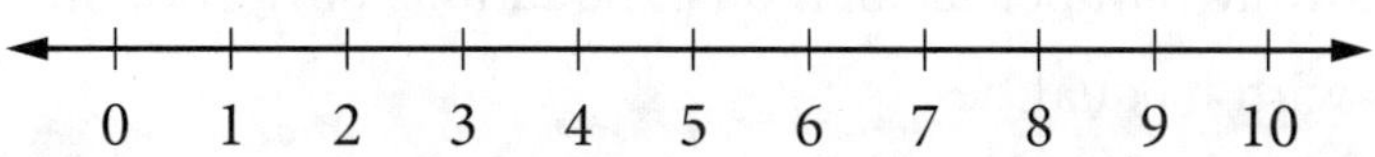

2. $4(4n + 4) = -48$

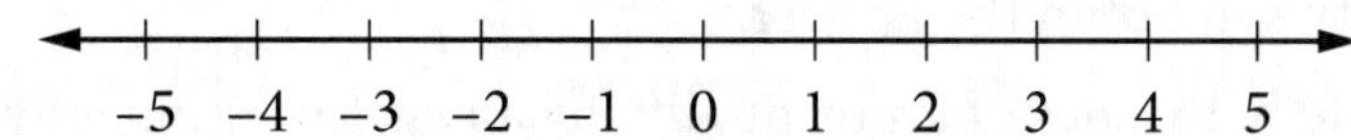

3. $(4 + b)2 = 18$

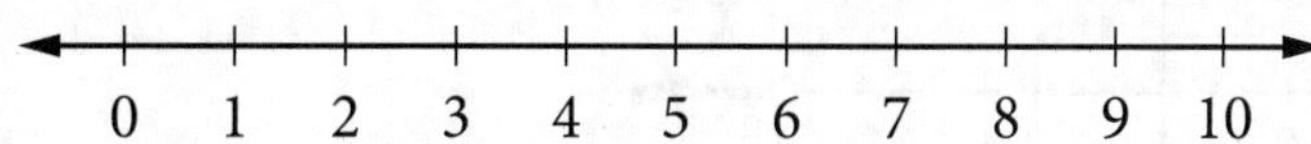

4. $6p - 2 = 22$

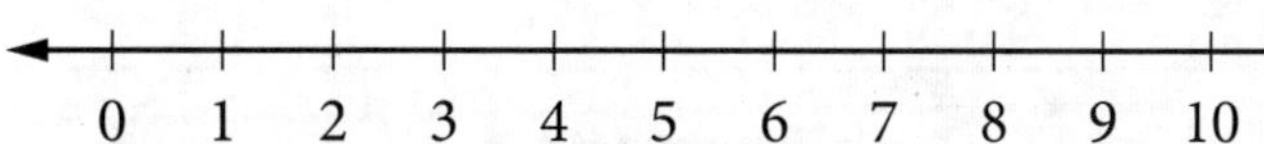

5. $3d + 4 = 31$

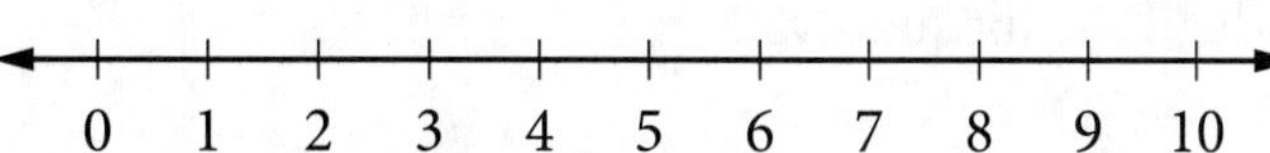

6. $4x + 3 = -9$

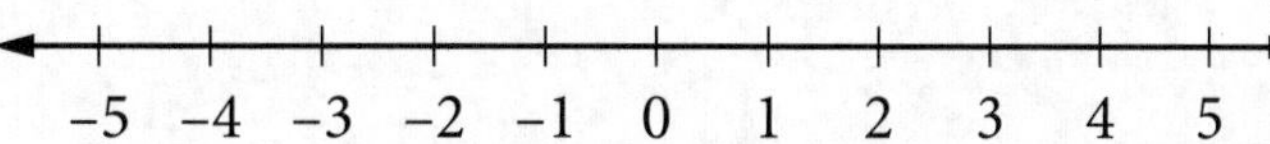

7. $2(x - 8) = 4$

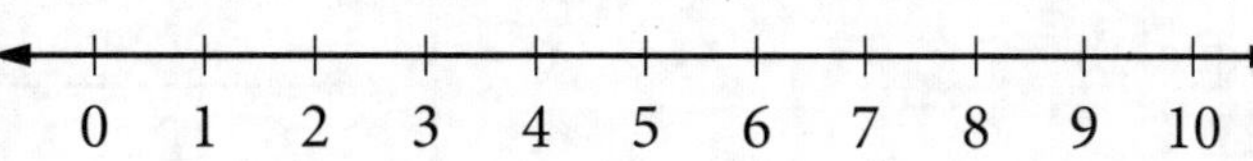

8. $7(c + 3) = 42$

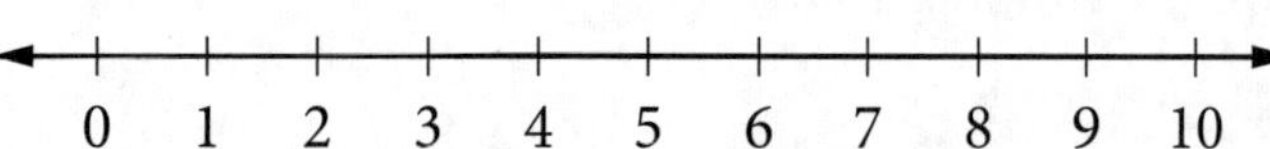

Learn about Solving Inequalities

inequality—a relationship between two values that are not equal

Inequalities have an infinite number of solutions. Equations only have one solution.

We use these symbols with inequalities:

< for *less than*	≤ for *less than or equal to*
> for *greater than*	≥ for *greater than or equal to*

To solve an inequality, follow the same steps as solving an equation. Instead of writing an equal sign, keep the inequality symbol in the answer.

If you multiply or divide both sides of an inequality by a negative number, you must flip the symbol in the final answer.

To plot the solution on a number line, shade the number line in the direction of the solution.

If the symbol is > or <, graph it with an open dot because the number is not part of the solution.

Example: $x > 4$
open dot

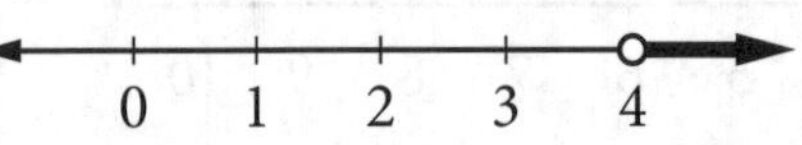

If the symbol is ≥ or ≤, graph it with a closed dot because the number is part of the solution.

Example: $x \leq 2$
closed dot

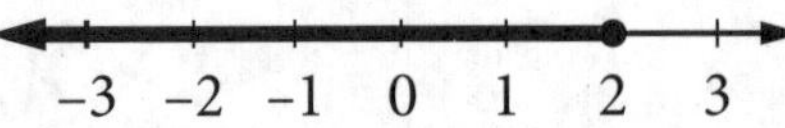

Example 1

Solve the inequality, and graph the solution on a number line.

$4g - 8 \geq 20$

1. Add 8 to each side of the inequality.

$$\begin{array}{r} 4g - 8 \geq 20 \\ +8 \quad +8 \\ \hline 4g \geq 28 \end{array}$$

2. Divide both sides of the inequality by 4.

$$\frac{4g}{4} \geq \frac{28}{4}$$

$g \geq$ ____________

3. Graph the solution. The symbol is ≥, which means it is a closed dot. Put a closed dot on the number line at 7. Then, shade the number line to the right of 7 to show all numbers greater than or equal to 7.

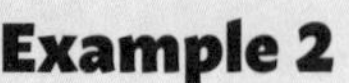

0 1 2 3 4 5 6 7 8 9 10

Example 2

Graph the inequality on the number line.

$x < 3$

1. < is the symbol used, so plot an open dot at 3 on the number line.
2. Shade to the left of the 3 to show numbers less than 3.

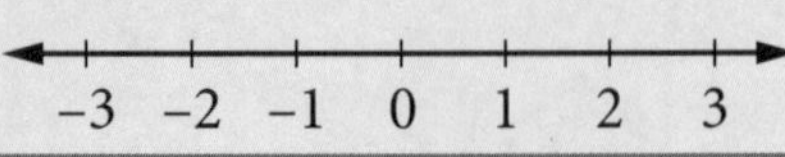

Name: ______________________________ Date: ____________________

Reminder

If you multiply or divide both sides of an inequality by a negative number, you must flip the sign. For example, to solve $-3x > 15$, you divide both sides of the inequality by -3, so you have to flip the sign. The final answer is $x < -5$.

Directions: Solve the inequalities. Show your work.

1. $4x - 9 > 15$

x __________

2. $6 + 8v \leq 22$

v __________

3. $51 > 3(x + 4)$

x __________

4. $-2x + 4 > 16$

x __________

5. $9 \geq 8d - 31$

d __________

6. $2(5 + j) < 40$

j __________

7. $-6f - 8 \leq 22$

f __________

8. $10k + 7 \geq 97$

k __________

9. $18 > 2y - 4$

y __________

10. $9g - 8 < 28$

g __________

11. $7 + 4n \leq 15$

n __________

12. $4(h - 4) > 40$

h __________

Name: ______________________ Date: ____________

Directions: Write and solve an inequality with a variable for each question. Show your work. Then, explain the meaning of the solution.

1. The soccer team is selling raffle tickets for \$6 each to raise money for a trip to play in a tournament. They need \$350 for the whole team to go. They already raised \$80 from a car wash. How many raffle tickets do they need to sell to raise at least \$350?

Inequality: ______________

Solution: ______________

Meaning of solution: ______________

____

2. The Ramirez family is going camping and needs a \$280 tent. The Ramirez children held a lemonade stand and earned \$40, and now they are selling bracelets for \$4 each to cover the rest of the cost of the tent. How many bracelets do they need to sell to make more than \$280?

Inequality: ______________

Solution: ______________

Meaning of solution: ______________

____

3. Gil needs \$300 for rent. Gil earns \$13 an hour at work, but he has to buy a work uniform for \$25. How many hours does Gil have to work to earn a profit of more than \$300?

Inequality: ______________

Solution: ______________

Meaning of solution: ______________

____

4. At the fair, a child must be at least 48 inches to ride the children's roller coaster. Mitchell has grown the same number of inches each of the last 4 years. Four years ago, Mitchell was 32 inches. How many inches did Mitchell have to grow each year to be able to ride the roller coaster?

Inequality: ______________

Solution: ______________

Meaning of solution: ______________

____

Name: ______________________ Date: ______________

Quick Tip

$<$ or $>$ are open dots on the number line.

$\le$ or $\ge$ are closed dots on the number line.

Directions: Graph each inequality on the number line.

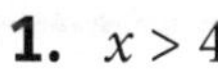

1. $x > 4$

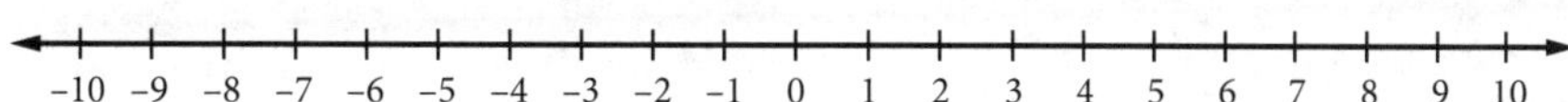

2. $v \ge -2$

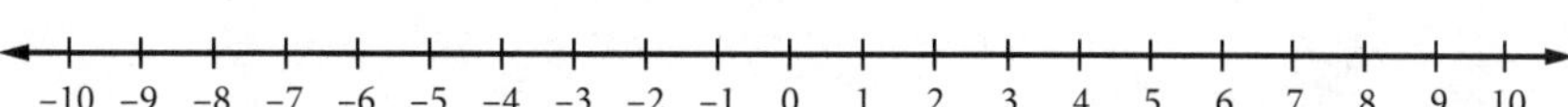

3. $b < 1.5$

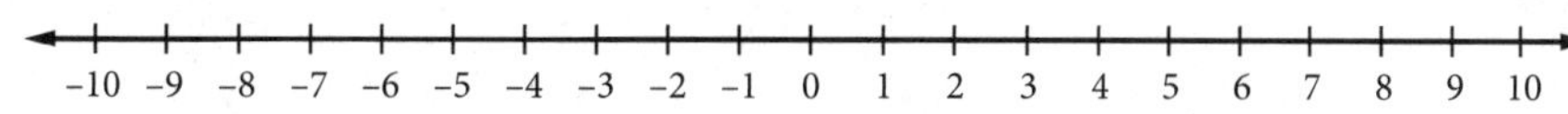

4. $w \ge -3$

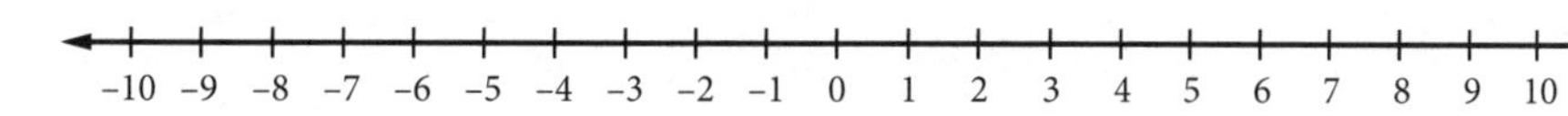

5. $6 > c$

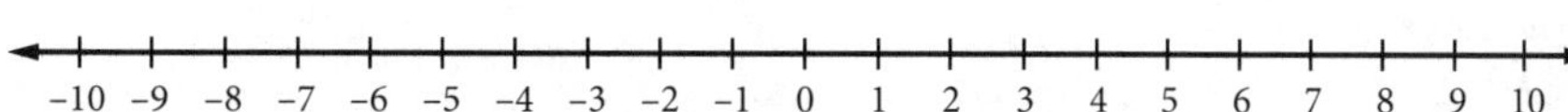

6. $-5 < d$

–10 –9 –8 –7 –6 –5 –4 –3 –2 –1 0 1 2 3 4 5 6 7 8 9 10

7. $q > 5$

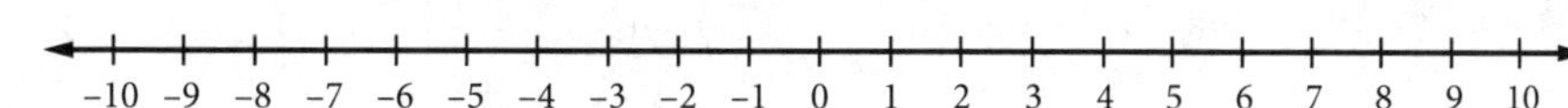

8. $7 \le y$

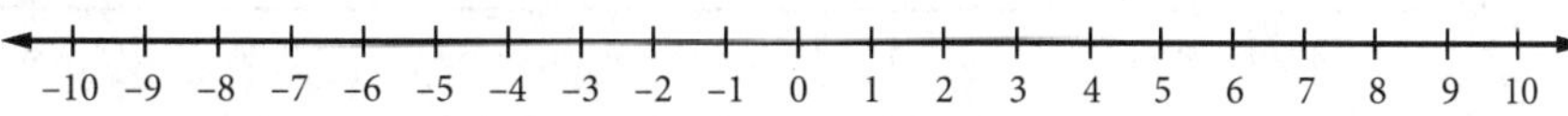

Name:________________________ Date:______________

Directions: Graph the solution to each inequality on the number line.

1. $5m + 4 < 14$

−10 −9 −8 −7 −6 −5 −4 −3 −2 −1 0 1 2 3 4 5 6 7 8 9 10

2. $8b - 6 \geq 26$

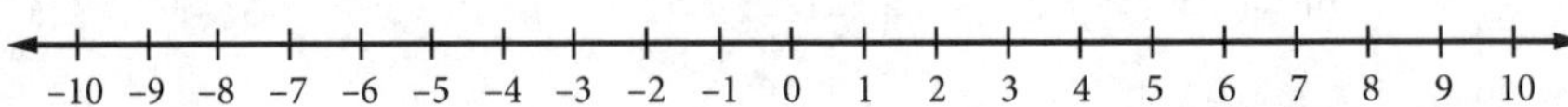

3. $5 > 4 + 2x$

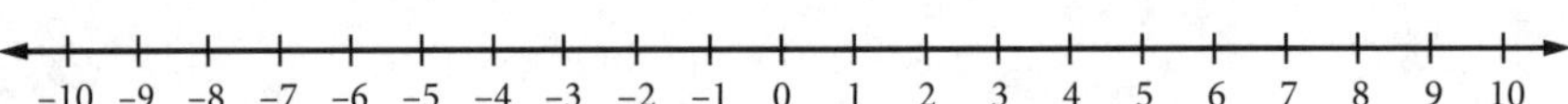

4. $6k + 1 \leq 19$

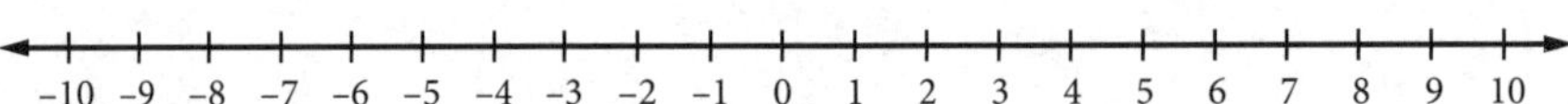

5. $7 + 3w > 22$

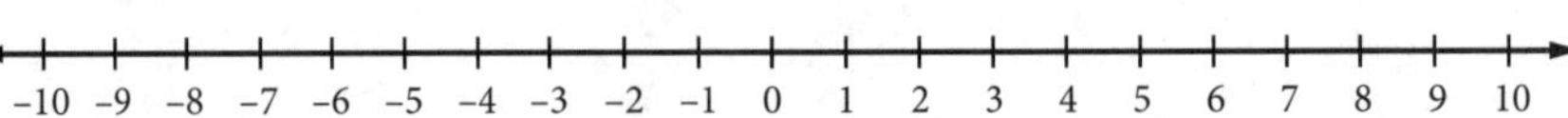

6. $20y + 3 < 123$

−10 −9 −8 −7 −6 −5 −4 −3 −2 −1 0 1 2 3 4 5 6 7 8 9 10

7. $11 > 4d - 1$

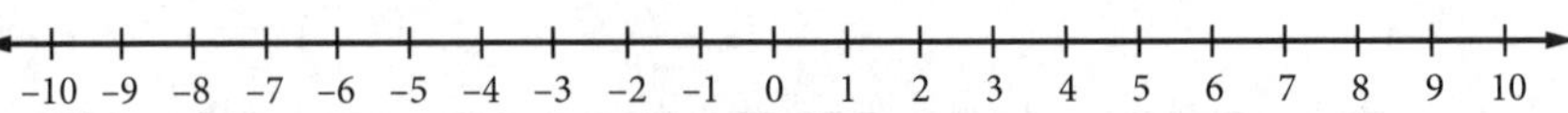

8. $9n + 12 \geq -51$

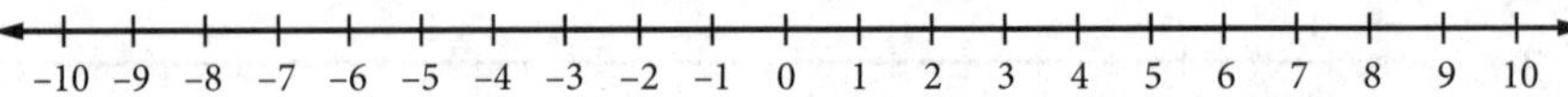

Name: ____________________ Date: __________

Directions: Write and solve an inequality for each problem. Graph your solution on the number line.

1. Mateo is saving to buy a new baseball mitt. He has $18 saved, and the mitt costs $48. Mateo snowplows driveways for $5 each. How many driveways does Mateo need to snowplow so he has at least $48 to purchase the new baseball mitt?

   Inequality with a variable: ____________

   Solution: ________

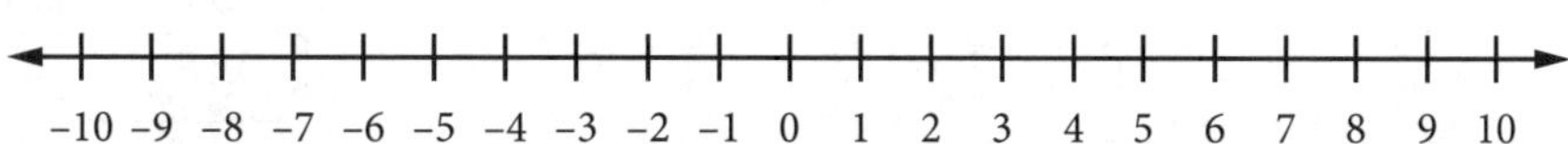

2. Pablo makes chairs and earns $25 per chair. He wants to grow his savings account to $400. He has $90 in his account now. How many chairs does Pablo need to sell to grow his balance to $400?

   Inequality with a variable: ____________

   Solution: ________

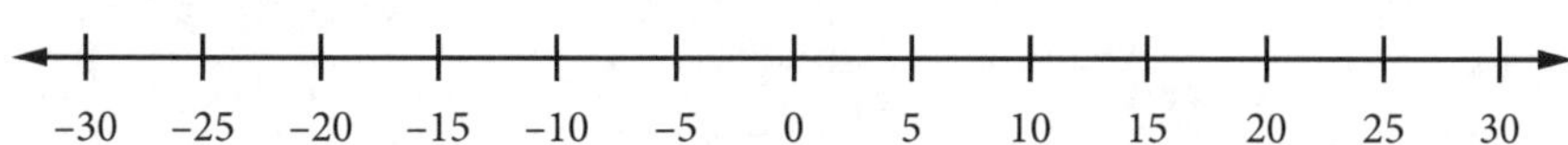

3. Eileen sells bracelets online for $5 each. She has to pay the sales app a fee of $10 to use the app. How many bracelets does she have to sell to make at least $105?

   Inequality with a variable: ____________

   Solution: ________

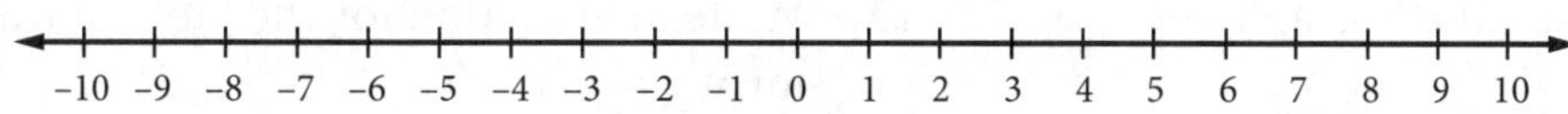

4. Marvin is saving his money to buy his mom a birthday present. He wants to save $75 for the gift, and he has $15. If he saves $5 each week, how many weeks does he need to save to have at least $75 for the gift?

   Inequality with a variable: ____________

   Solution: ________

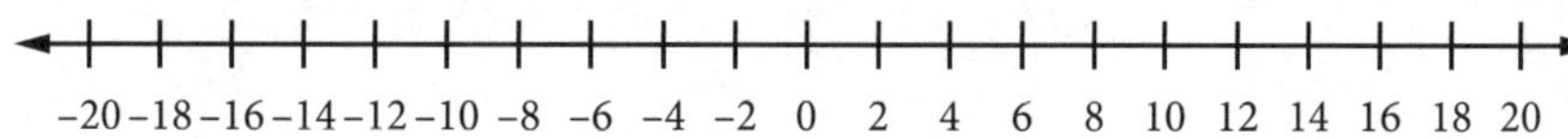

Name: ____________________ Date: ____________

Directions: Solve each problem.

1. $5m - 8 = 22$

$m =$ ________

2. $\frac{6}{15} = \frac{x}{45}$

$x =$ ________

3. Naomi makes 3 mugs in 2.5 hours. How many mugs can she make in 10 hours?

____

4. The Smith family drove 550 miles in 10 hours. How many miles did they drive in 1 hour?

____

5. Is the relationship on the graph proportional? ________

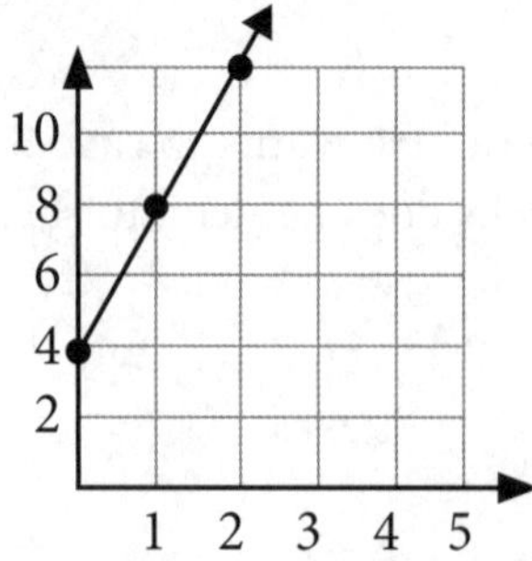

6. How many hours are in 4 days?

____

7. $-40 \div 5 =$ ________

8. What is the constant of proportionality?

$x =$ ________

x	y
5	12.5
6	15
7	17.5
8	20

9. Solve the inequality.

$3x - 6 > 12$

____

10. Write an expression for *three times the sum of a number increased by 8.*

____

11. Write an equation for the table in the form $y = mx + b$.

$y =$ ________

x	y
0	2
1	4
2	6
3	8

12. Write an equivalent expression.

$4(3x + 3) =$ ________

Spiral Review

Name: ______________________ Date: ____________

Directions: Solve each problem.

1. Yaneli has a discount of 20% at the shoe store.

a. What is 20% as a fraction?

____

b. What is 20% as a decimal?

____

2. Jackson earns $11 an hour walking the neighborhood dogs. Complete the table to show Jackson's earnings.

Number of Hours	Income
2	
4	
6	
8	

3. Lamar paid $80 for 4 T-shirts. Write an equation to represent the situation.

$y =$ ________ x

4. $6[4 - (10 - 12)] =$ ________

5. $y = 5x$

What is the constant of proportionality?

$k =$ ________

6. Ivory's college tuition is $18,000. She gets a discount of 10%. What is the cost of Ivory's tuition after the discount?

____

7. $100 - (-5) + 15 =$ ________

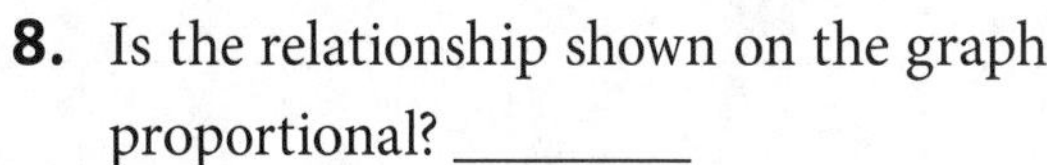

8. Is the relationship shown on the graph proportional? ________

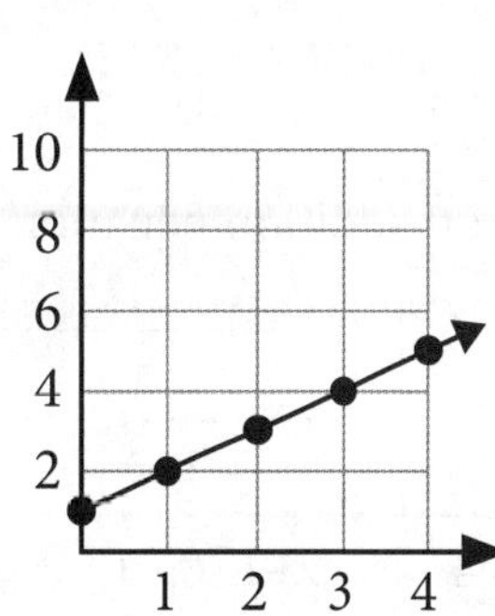

Name: ____________________ Date: ____________

Directions: Solve each problem.

1. Write an expression for *twice a number increased by 8.* __________

2. Write an equivalent expression using the Distributive Property.

$3x + 30$

______ (______ + ______)

3. Marshall earned $1,500. He put $\frac{2}{5}$ of his earnings into his savings account. How much money did Marshall put into his savings account? __________

4. A recipe calls for $3\frac{1}{2}$ cups of flour. How many recipes can be made with 20 cups of flour? __________

5. $8\frac{2}{5} \times 1\frac{3}{4} =$ __________

6. Write an addition equation to represent the diagram. __________

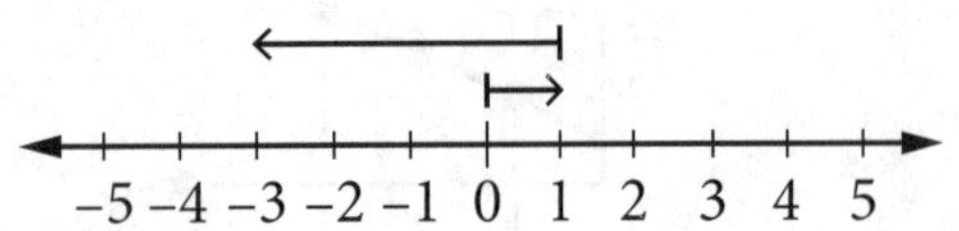

7. Write $\frac{5}{8}$ as a decimal. __________

8. What is the constant of proportionality from the table?

$y =$ ______

x	y
5	150
10	300
15	450

9. $(5^2)^3 =$ __________

10. Fred made $640 after working 40 hours. How much does Fred make per hour?

____

11. Sal is running a 24-mile race. He ran $\frac{3}{4}$ of the race so far. How many more miles does Sal have to run to finish the race?

____

12. Solve the inequality.

$6x - 3 < 9$

x __________

Spiral Review

Name: ____________________ Date: ____________

Directions: Solve each problem.

1. Write an equation for the graph.

$y =$ __________

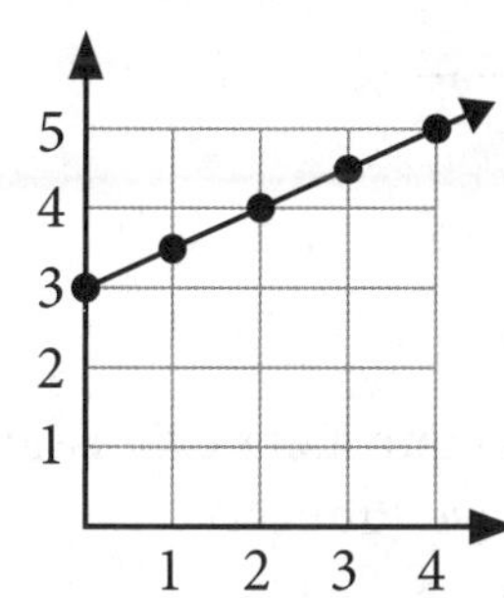

2. $-8 \times 6 =$ __________

3. Marty is buying a new jacket for $65. He has to pay 8% sales tax on the jacket. How much will Marty pay, including tax, for the jacket?

____

4. Write an equivalent expression using the Distributive Property.

$10x + 45 =$ __________

5. Write an equation modeled by the diagram. __________

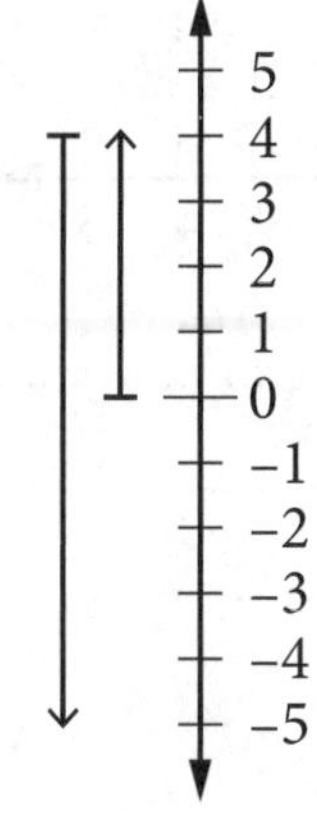

6. Dominick has a 35% off coupon.

   a. What is 35% as a decimal? __________

   b. What is 35% as a fraction?

   ____

7. Dimitri read 30 equally long books in 5 weeks. If he read at the same pace, how many books did Dimitri read in 1 week?

____

8. Nancy paid $55 for 5 cases of soda. What was the cost of 1 case of soda?

____

9. $-24 - (-6) =$ __________

10. $5\frac{3}{4} \times 4 =$ __________

Name: ______________________________ Date: ______________

Directions: Solve each problem.

1. Enrique went to dinner with his family. The bill was $75, but Enrique's family wanted to leave an 18% tip. What was the cost of the bill, including the tip?

____

2. Write $\frac{4}{5}$ as a decimal. ________

3. Write a subtraction equation to find the difference between the integers on the number line, and then solve the equation.

____

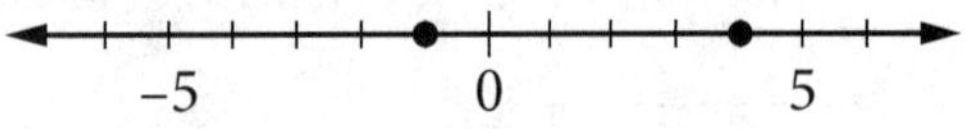

4. Kamal earned $202.50 for 15 hours of work. How much does Kamal earn per hour?

____

5. Does the equation show a proportional relationship?

$y = 6x + 5$

____

6. Solve.

$3x - 8 = 26$

$x =$ ________

7. Write an equivalent expression using the Distributive Property.

$9(4m + 10)$

____

8. $\frac{\$30}{6 \text{ hours}} = \frac{x}{30 \text{ hours}}$

$x =$ ________

9. Graph five points of the proportional relationship.

$y = 2x$

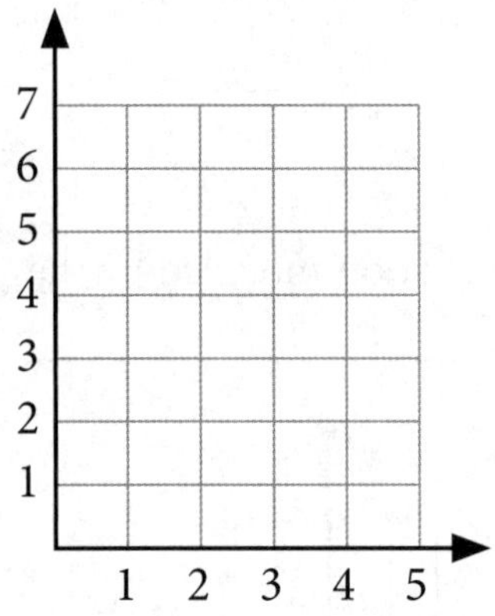

10. $64 \div (-8) =$ ______________

Learn about Scale Drawings

corresponding sides—sides that are in the same position on different two-dimensional shapes

scale factor—the numerical value that describes how much an object has been enlarged or reduced in size

If the scale factor is larger than 1, the scaled object will be larger than the original.

If the scale factor is smaller than 1, the scaled object will be smaller than the original.

If the scale factor is 1, the scaled object will be exactly the same size.

The perimeter and area of a scaled copy increases or decreases by the same amount as the scale factor.

Example: Scale factor is 2, so the perimeter is 2 times as large as the original figure's perimeter. The area is 2 × 2, or 4 times, as large as the original figure.

Example 1

What is the scale factor used to create the larger shape?

2 units by 3 units

4 units by 6 units

4

6

1. Match up corresponding sides. From the small rectangle, the side labeled 2 corresponds to the side on the large rectangle labeled 4. The side on the small rectangle labeled 3 corresponds to the side on the large rectangle labeled 6.
2. Divide the value of corresponding sides to find the scale factor.
   side length of new shape ÷ corresponding side length on the original shape
   4 ÷ 2 = ________
   6 ÷ 3 = ________
3. The number found by dividing is the scale factor. What is the scale factor? ________

Example 2

Draw a scaled copy of the figure using a scale factor of 2.

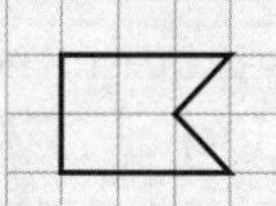

1. Count the length of each side, and label them on the diagram above.
2. Multiply each of the side lengths by 2.
   Draw the new shape on the grid.

Example 3

Find the missing side length.

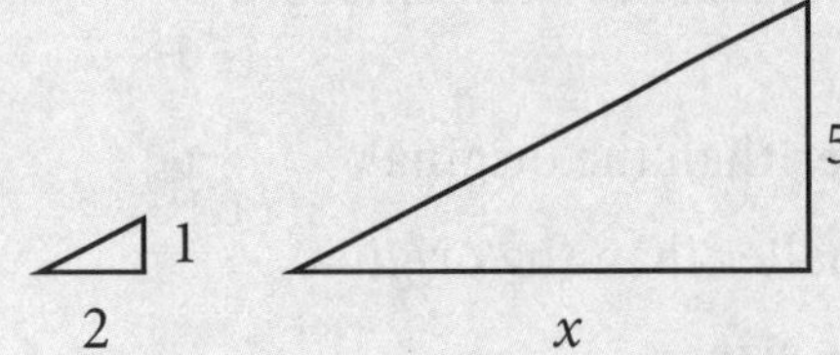

1. Find the scale factor by dividing the length of the new shape by the corresponding length of the original shape.

   5 ÷ 1 = __________

2. Next, multiply 2 by the answer from Step 1.

   2 × __________ = __________

   This is the length of the missing side. x = __________

Example 4

A new figure is created from the figure shown. If a scale factor of 3 is used to create the new image, what will be the area of the new image?

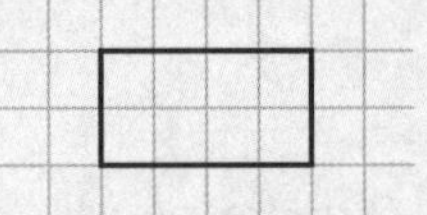

1. Find the area of the original figure. What is the area? __________
2. Multiply the scale factor by the scale factor to find the new area. What is 3 × 3?

   ____

3. Finally, multiply your answer in Step 1 (original area) by your answer in Step 2 (scale factor multiplied by itself). What is the area of the new figure with a scale factor of 3?

   ____

Example 5

Gary wants to give his grandmother his school picture so she can put it in a frame. Gary's picture is 4 inches by 6 inches. His grandmother has a frame with side lengths 2 times as long. What are the dimensions of an enlarged copy of the picture that will fit in the frame?

1. The scale factor is 2, so multiply each dimension of the original picture by 2.

   4 × 2 = __________

   6 × 2 = __________

2. The dimensions of the enlarged scaled copy that will fit in the frame are

   __________ inches by __________ inches.

Name: ______________________________ Date: ____________________

Directions: Find each scale factor from the original shape (on the left) to the new shape (on the right).

1. Scale factor: ______________

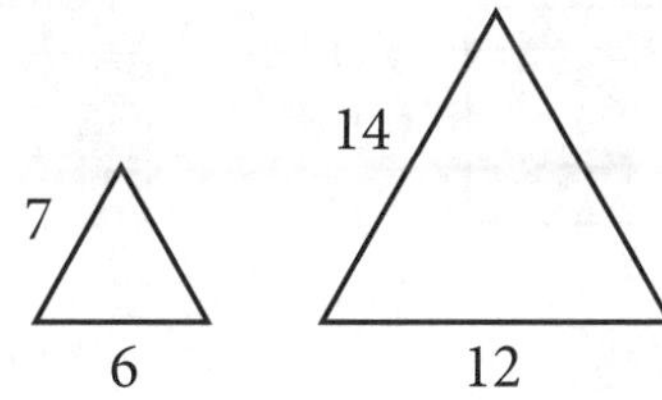

2. Scale factor: ______________

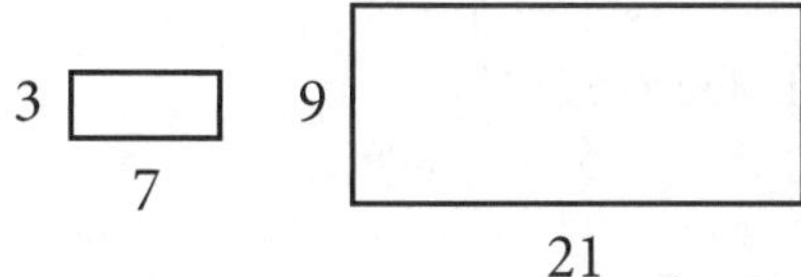

3. Scale factor: ______________

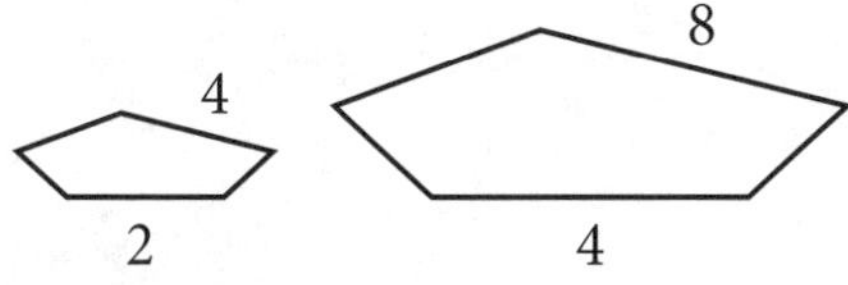

4. Scale factor: ______________

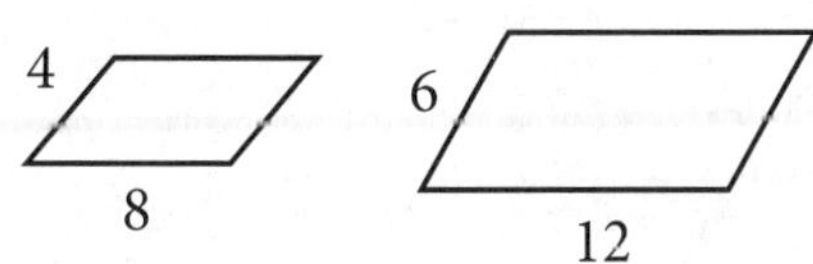

5. Scale factor: ______________

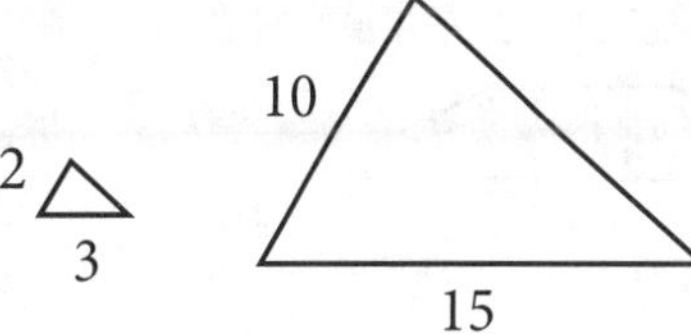

6. Scale factor: ______________

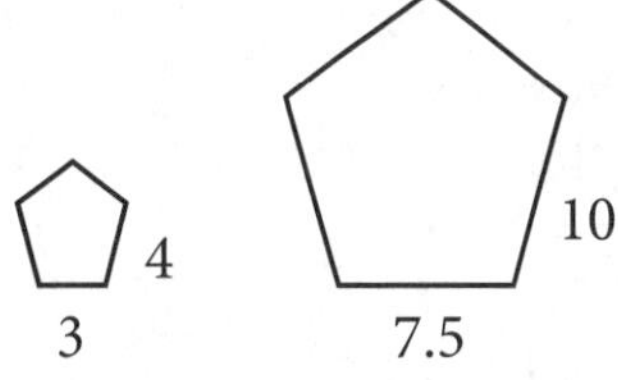

7. Scale factor: ______________

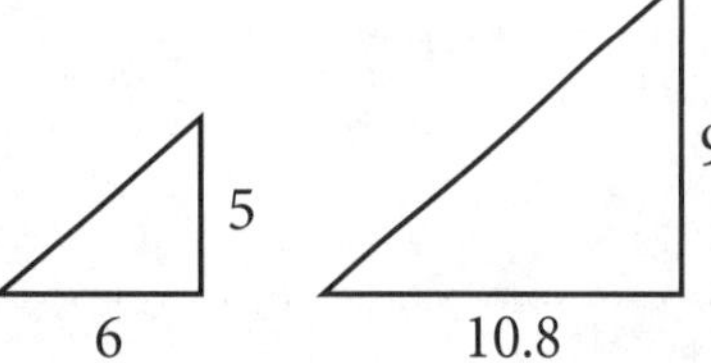

8. Scale factor: ______________

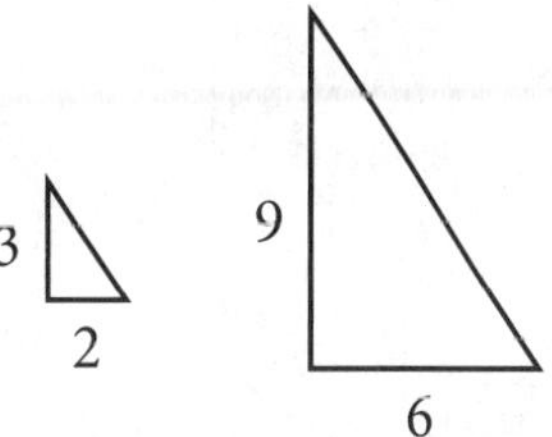

Name: ______________________________ Date: ______________

Directions: Draw a scaled copy of each figure with the given scale factor.

1. Scale factor: $\frac{1}{2}$

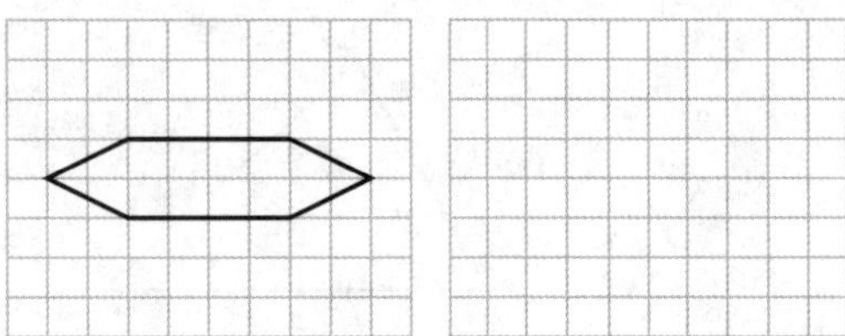

2. Scale factor: 0.5

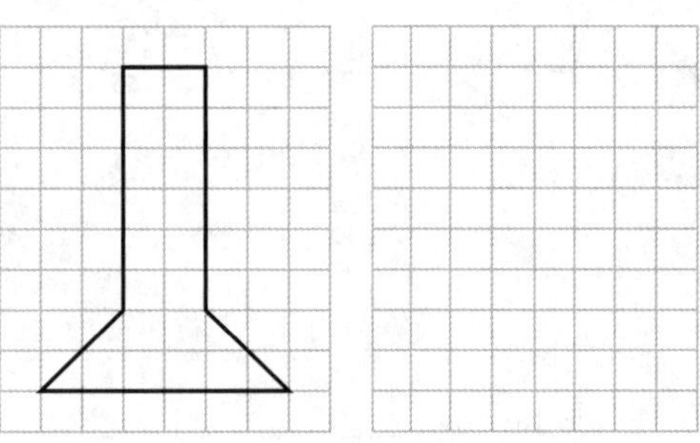

3. Scale factor: 3

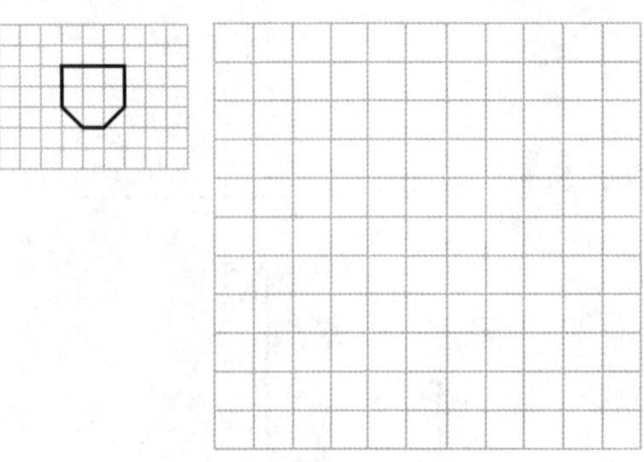

4. Scale factor: 1.5

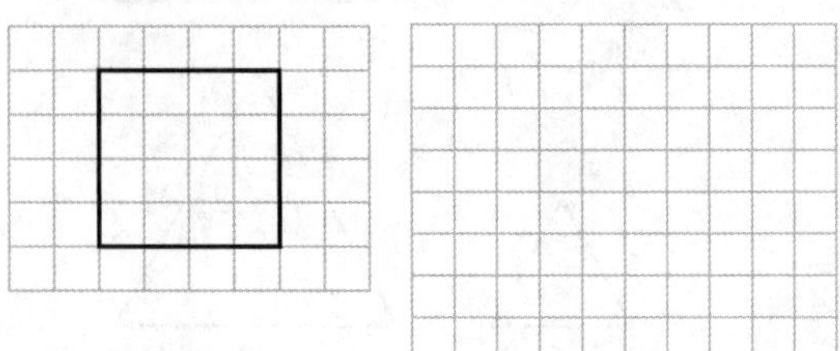

5. Scale factor: 5

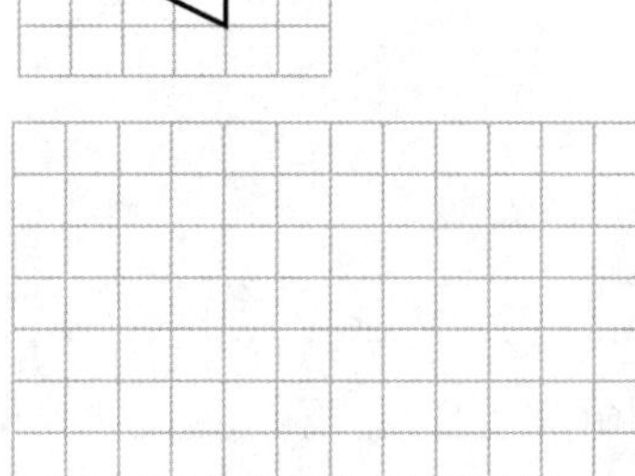

6. Scale factor: $\frac{1}{2}$

Name: ______________________________ Date: ____________________

Directions: Find the missing side length for each problem.

1. x = ____________

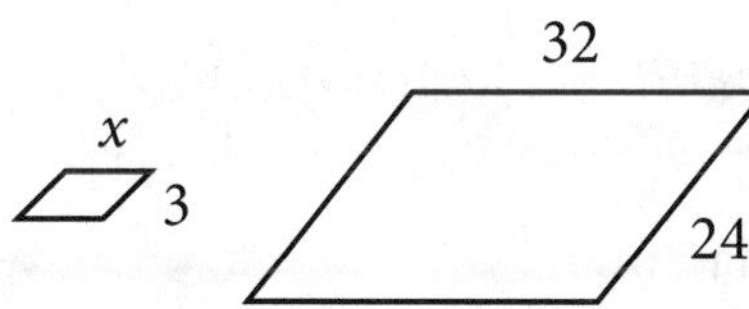

2. x = ____________

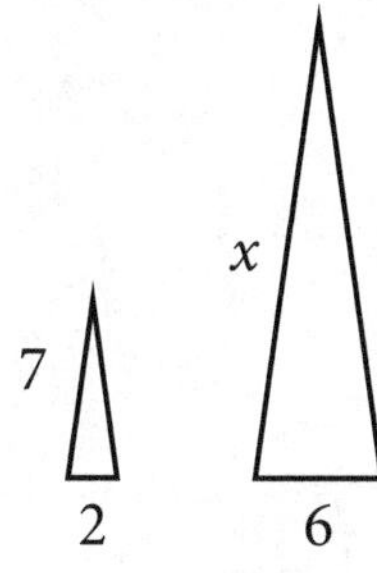

3. x = ____________

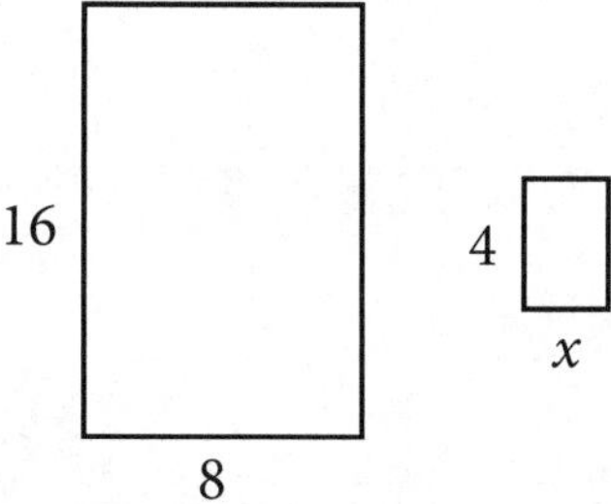

4. x = ____________

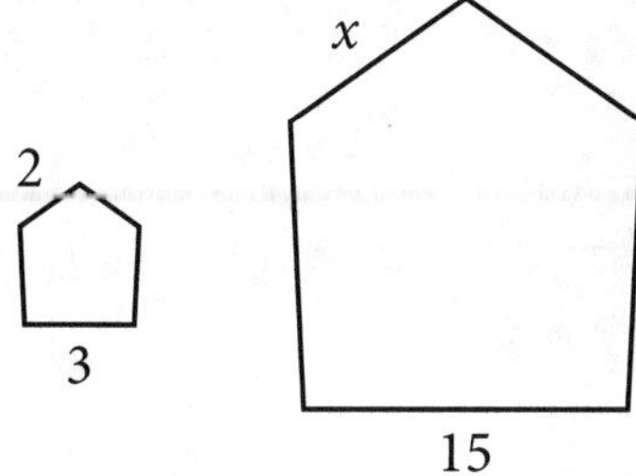

5. x = ____________

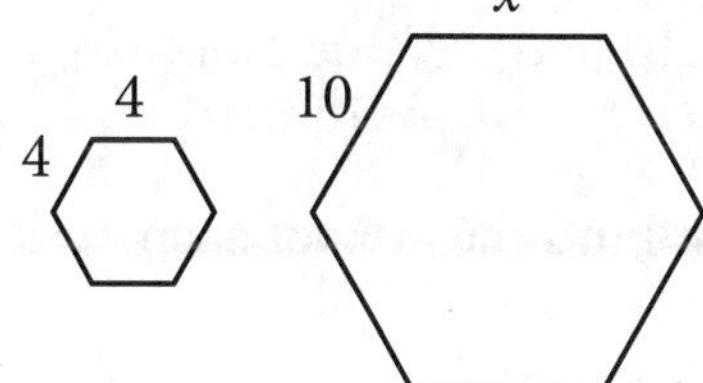

6. x = ____________

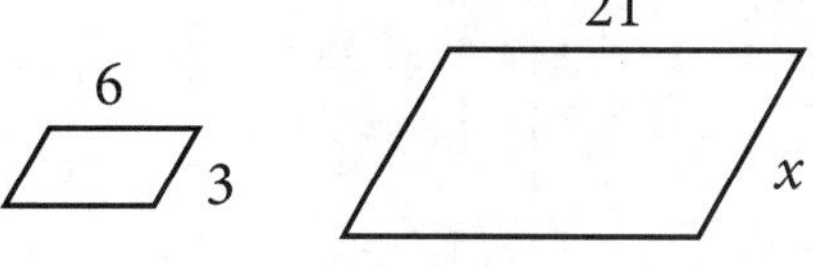

7. x = ____________

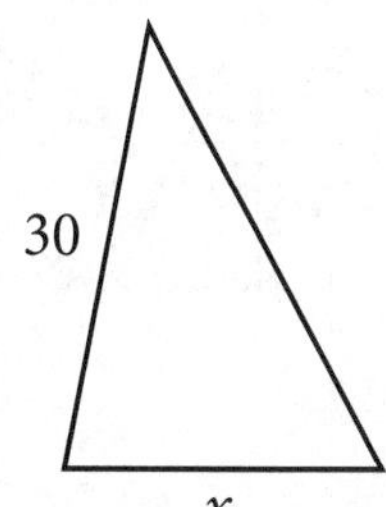

8. x = ____________

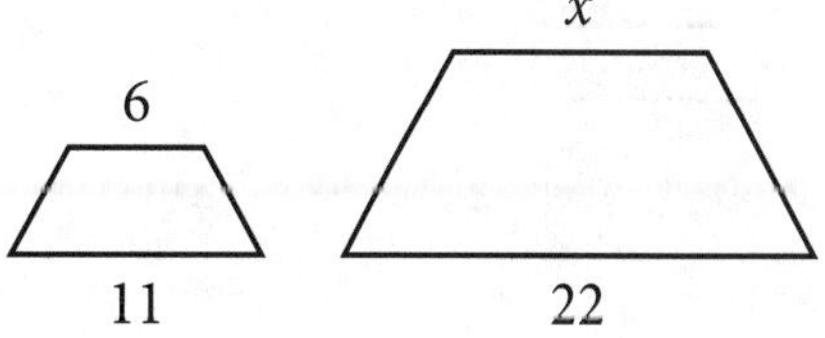

Name: ______________________ Date: ______________

Quick Tip

When finding the area of a scaled copy, square the scale factor (multiply it by itself), and multiply the answer by the original area.

To find the area of a triangle, multiply the base × height, and then divide by 2.

Directions: Find the area of each scaled copy using the scale factor.

1. Scale factor: 4

Area of scaled copy: ______________

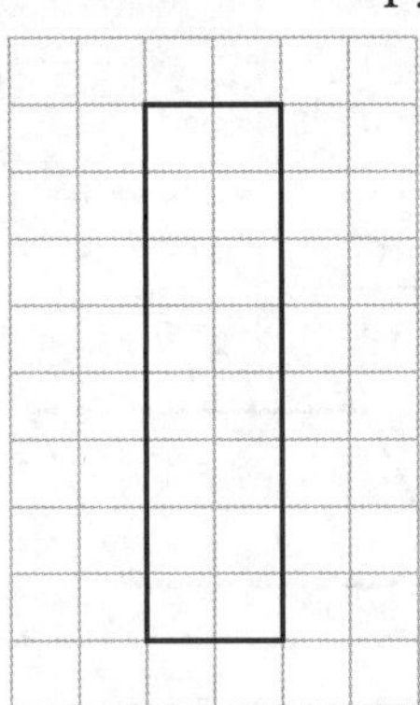

2. Scale factor: 3

Area of scaled copy: ______________

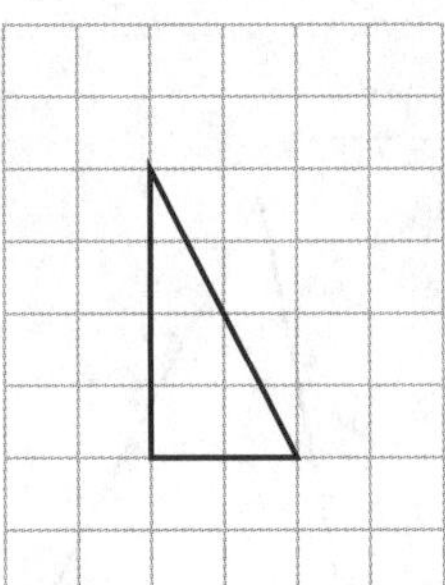

3. Scale factor: 6

Area of scaled copy: ______________

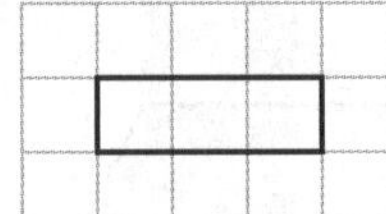

4. Scale factor: $\frac{1}{2}$

Area of scaled copy: ______________

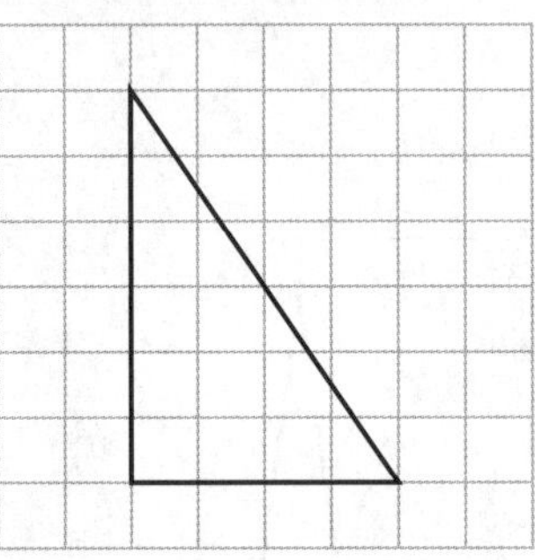

5. Scale factor: 5

Area of scaled copy: ______________

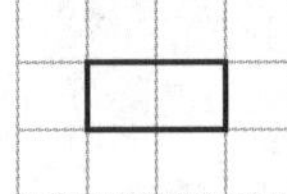

6. Scale factor: 2

Area of scaled copy: ______________

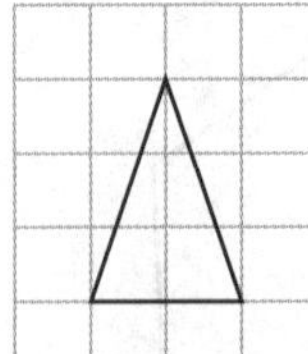

Name: ______________________________ Date: ______________

Directions: Solve each problem.

1. Randy made a drawing of a garden he is going to build. On the drawing, the length of the garden is 4 inches and the width is 5 inches. The sides of the actual garden are going to be 15 times as long. What are the dimensions of the actual garden?

________ by ________

2. Rachelle is reading a map. On the map, it states that 1 inch represents 150 miles. How many miles does 6 inches represent?

____

3. Kevin is building a picnic table. The rectangular benches on his drawing are 3 inches by 5 inches. He wants to make the actual benches 8 times as long. What are the dimensions of the actual benches?

________ by ________

4. Rayne is sewing square pillow cases. She has a pillow case that measures 8 inches by 8 inches, but she wants to make a larger pillow case with sides 3 times as long. What are the lengths of the larger pillow case sides?

________ by ________

5. Peter is drawing with chalk on his driveway. He draws a picture of his bike that is 6 inches tall. If the actual bike is 42 inches tall, what is the scale factor from his drawing to the actual bike?

____

6. Hank is making a mini version of a board game he loves to play. The actual board game measures 24 inches by 36 inches. If he wants to make the sides of the mini board $\frac{1}{2}$ as long, what should the dimensions be?

________ by ________

7. Farah has two dogs. Her large dog's bed is twice as large as her small dog's bed. The small bed is $2\frac{1}{2}$ feet long. How long is the large bed?

____

8. Stan has an area rug that measures 6 feet by 8 feet. He wants to buy a new rug that covers $\frac{1}{4}$ of the area of the original rug. What are the dimensions of the new rug?

________ by ________

Scale Drawings

Learn about 2D and 3D Shapes

There are mathematical rules to keep in mind when drawing different types of shapes.

Rectangles

Draw a rectangle with a length of 2 inches and a width of 1 inch.

1. Measure a length of 2 inches. Label the side length. 2 in.
2. Measure a 90° angle at the end of each side of the 2-inch length. Label each angle. 90° 90° 2 in.
3. Measure the 1-inch side lengths on each side and label them 1 inch each. 1 in. 1 in.
4. Connect the 2 side lengths to form the other side that measures 2 inches. 2 in.

Triangles

The three angles in any triangle add up to 180°. When drawing a triangle, the sum of the two smaller sides must be greater than the largest side. Example: 2, 3, 4
$2 + 3 > 4$, so the three given side lengths can form a triangle.

When drawing triangles:

- If you are given all three side lengths, only one triangle can be drawn.
- If you are given two side lengths and the angle between them, only one triangle can be drawn.
- If you are given two angles and the length of the side between them, only one triangle can be drawn.
- If you are given all three angle measures and no side lengths, different triangles can be drawn because the side lengths could vary.
- If you are given three angles that do not add up to 180°, no triangle can be drawn.

Example

Can you draw one unique triangle, many different triangles, or no triangle?
one 40° angle, one 120° angle, and side length between the angles measuring 4 cm

1. Because you know the measure of two angles and the side length between them, you can create ______ triangle(s). Finish drawing the shape. 40° 120° 4 cm

Cross-Sections

A **cross section** is the new face that you see when you slice through a three-dimensional figure.

Describe the two-dimensional shape (cross section) that is formed when the rectangular prism is sliced vertically.

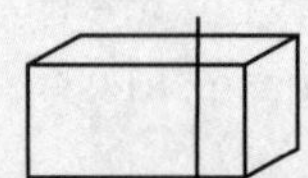

1. When the shape is sliced vertically, picture what shape you would see. It would look like the cross section shown to the right.

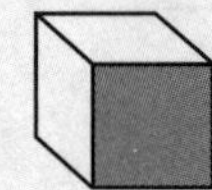

2. What two-dimensional shape is shown after the vertical slice? ________

Name: ______________________ Date: ______________

Hands-On Help

Use rulers and protractors to draw the shapes accurately.

Directions: Draw each diagram. Be sure to measure accurately and label each part that you measure.

1. Draw a right triangle with side lengths of 3 centimeters and 4 centimeters with a 90° angle between the 2 sides.

2. Draw a triangle with side lengths of 2 inches, 2 inches, and 1 inch.

3. Draw a square with side lengths of 1 inch.

4. Draw a triangle with an angle of 30°, an angle of 120°, and one side length of 5 centimeters.

5. Draw a parallelogram with a base of 3 centimeters and angles of 50° and 130° at each end of the base. Each slanted side should measure 2 centimeters.

6. Draw a rectangle with side lengths of 2.5 inches and 1.5 inches.

Name: ______________________ Date: ______________

Reminder

The two smallest sides of a triangle must add up to more than the largest side to be able to form a triangle.

Directions: Determine whether the three given sides form a triangle. Circle *yes* or *no*.

1. 6, 5, 10 yes no

2. 4, 6, 8 yes no

3. 2, 2, 2 yes no

4. 14, 15, 30 yes no

5. 13, 15, 19 yes no

6. 8, 9, 18 yes no

7. 24, 26, 50 yes no

8. 30, 60, 90 yes no

9. 11, 15, 20 yes no

10. 8, 8, 17 yes no

11. 9, 15, 23 yes no

12. 5, 5, 8 yes no

13. 9, 12, 20 yes no

14. 7, 7, 12 yes no

Name: ______________________ Date: ______________

Directions: Use the given information to determine whether you can draw one unique triangle, more than one triangle, or no triangle at all. If it is possible, draw a diagram of the triangle. Use a protractor for accuracy.

1. 50° angle, side length of 6 inches, angle of 75°

How many triangles can be formed?

____

2. side lengths of 15 mm, 18 mm, and 22 mm

How many triangles can be formed?

____

3. angles of 140°, 20°, and 20°

How many triangles can be formed?

____

4. angles of 10°, 80°, and 120°

How many triangles can be formed?

____

5. angle of 35°, angle of 80°, and the side length between the angles is 3 inches

How many triangles can be formed?

____

6. side length of 2 inches, side length of 4 inches, and angle of 50° between the two sides

How many triangles can be formed?

____

7. angles of 45°, 60°, and 75°

How many triangles can be formed?

____

8. angles of 110°, 40°, and 50°

How many triangles can be formed?

____

Name: ______________________________ Date: ______________

Quick Tip

Examples of two-dimensional shapes are triangles, squares, rectangles, and trapezoids.

Directions: Name each two-dimensional figure formed on the cross-section when the three-dimensional figure is sliced as shown.

1. ____________

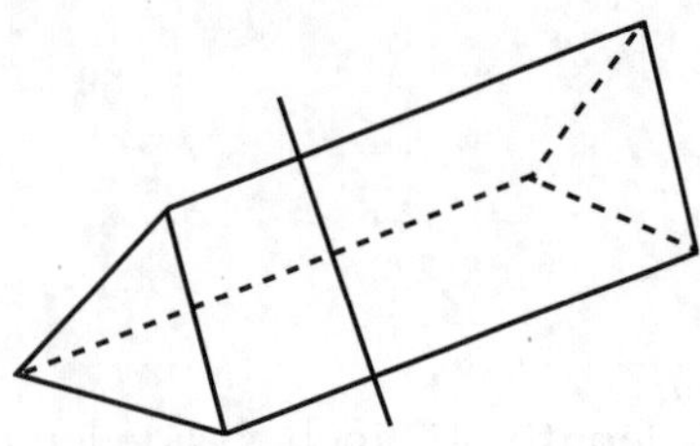

4. ____________

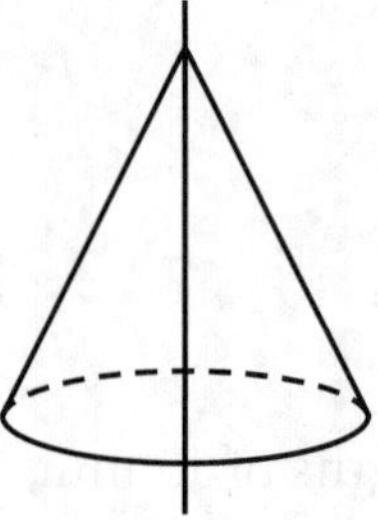

2. ____________

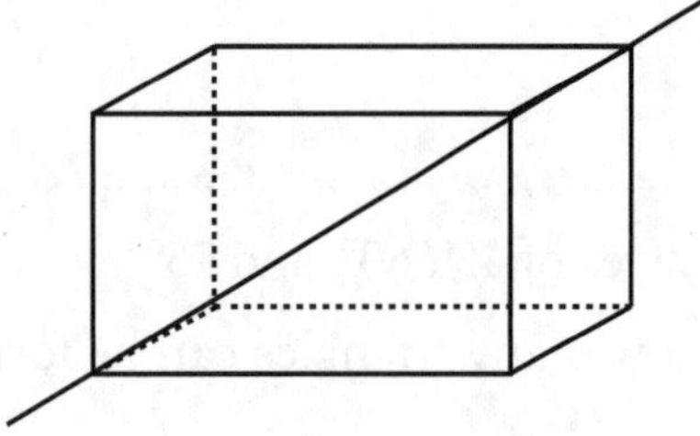

5. ____________

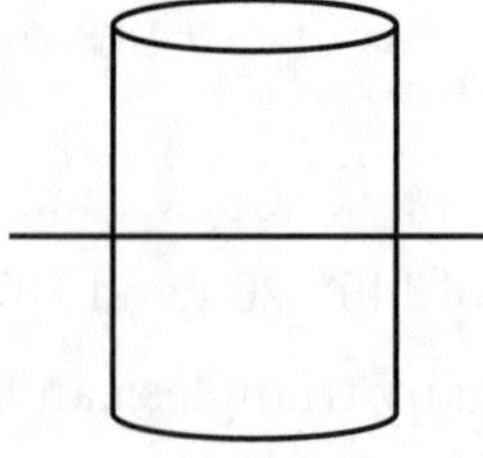

3. ____________

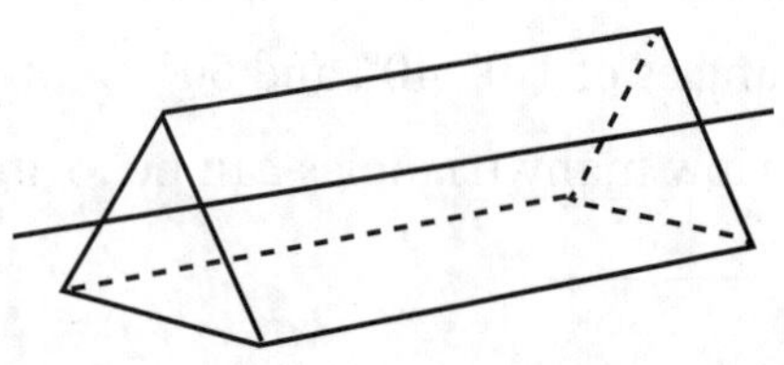

6. ____________

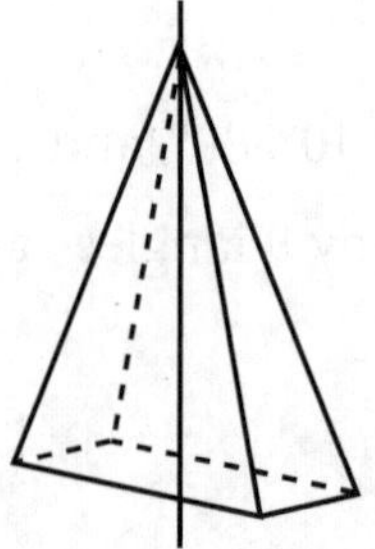

Name: ______________________________ Date: ________________

Directions: Solve each problem.

1. Can a triangle be drawn with angles measuring 70°, 40°, and 60°?

____

2. How many triangles can be drawn with sides of 4 inches and 3 inches and an angle of 75°? (One, more than one, or zero)

____

3. What do all three angles in every triangle always add up to?

____

4. Can a triangle be formed with side lengths of 2 centimeters, 2 centimeters, and 4 centimeters?

____

5. How many triangles can be drawn with angles of 20°, 40°, and 80°? (One, more than one, or zero)

____

6. Draw a triangle with angles of 130° and 30° and a side length of 3 centimeters between the two angles.

7. Draw a rectangle with side lengths of 1 inch and 3 inches.

8. What two-dimensional shape is formed when the cylinder is sliced vertically as shown here?

____

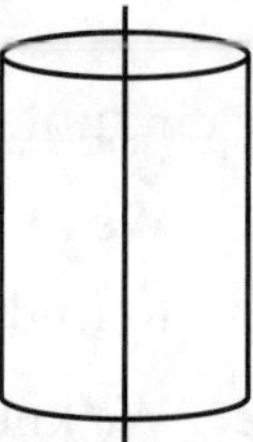

Learn about Circles

diameter—the distance across a circle, passing through the center

radius—the distance from the center to any point on the circle; the radius is one half of the diameter

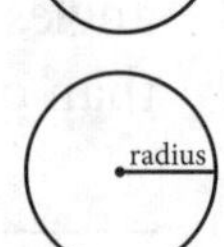

pi (π)—the ratio of the circumference of a circle divided by its diameter

We can use the decimal 3.14, or $\frac{22}{7}$, as an approximation for π.

circumference—the distance around a circle

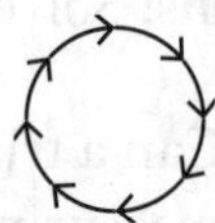

The circumference (C) is found by multiplying the diameter (d) of the circle by π, also known as *pi*. $C = \pi d$ (or $C = 2\pi r$)

area—the space inside a circle, measured in square units

The area (A) of a circle is found by multiplying pi by the radius (r) squared.

$A = \pi r^2$

Example 1

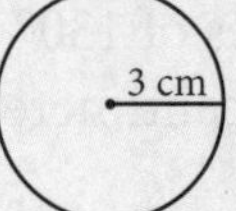

Find the circumference of the circle.

1. If the radius is 3, we can multiply 3 by 2 to find the diameter. What is the diameter? ________
2. Multiply the diameter by π, and label your answer. 6π cm
3. What is the decimal approximation for the circumference?
   $6 \times 3.14 =$ ________

Example 2

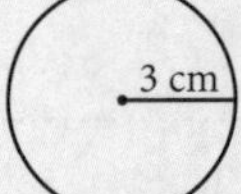

Find the area of the circle.

1. To find the area of the circle, we multiply $\pi \times r^2$. What is r^2?
   ______
2. Next, we multiply r^2 by π and label the answer. 9π cm^2
3. What is the decimal approximation for the area of the circle?
   $9 \times 3.14 =$ ________ cm^2

Example 3

Tamika wants to purchase a tablecloth to cover her round table. The table has a radius of 2 feet. How big should the tablecloth be to just cover the top of the table?

1. Because Tamika is covering the table, we can find the area. The formula for area is πr^2. $\pi(2)^2 = 4\pi$ ft.^{2}
2. What is the decimal approximation of the area of the table? $4 \times 3.14 =$ ________ ft.^{2}

Example 4

The circumference of a circle is 28π. What is the radius?

1. We know the formula for circumference is $C = \pi d$. We can divide the circumference by π to find the diameter. What is $28\pi \div \pi$? ________
2. We know the radius is half of the diameter. Divide your answer in Step 1 by 2. What is the radius? ________

Name: ______________________ Date: ______________

Directions: Find the circumference of each circle. Write your answers in terms of pi (using π) and as a decimal approximation. The first one has been modeled for you.

1. a. In terms of pi: 20π yd.
b. Approximated Decimal: 62.8 yd.

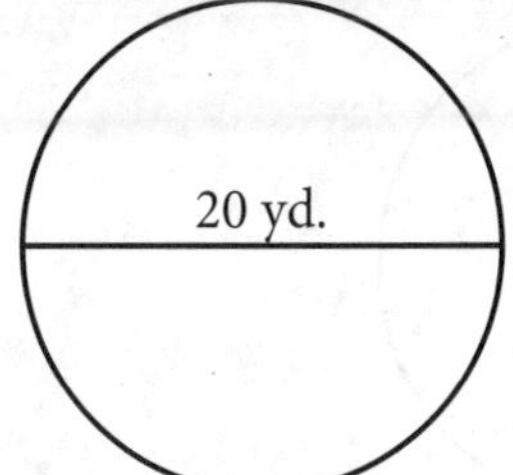

2. a. In terms of pi: ______
b. Approximated Decimal: ______

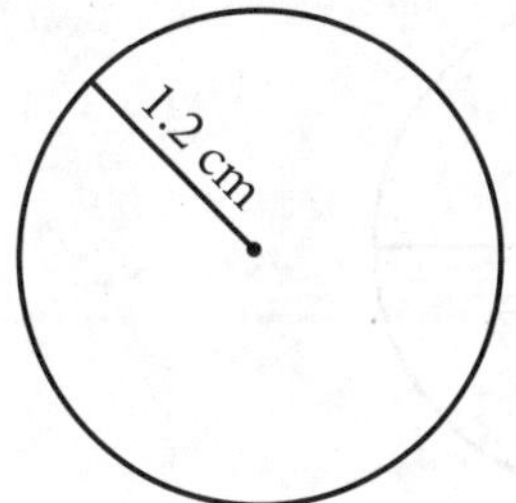

3. a. In terms of pi: ______
b. Approximated Decimal: ______

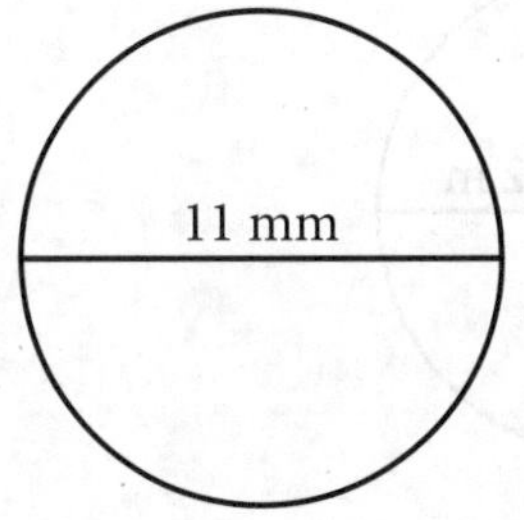

4. a. In terms of pi: ______
b. Approximated Decimal: ______

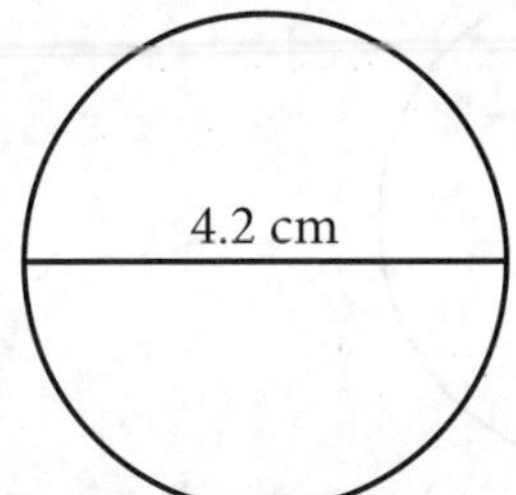

5. a. In terms of pi: ______
b. Approximated Decimal: ______

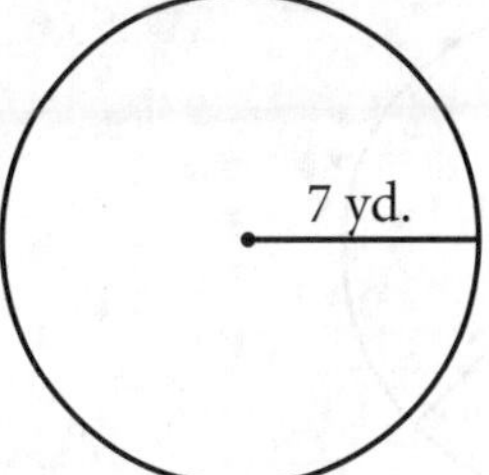

6. a. In terms of pi: ______
b. Approximated Decimal: ______

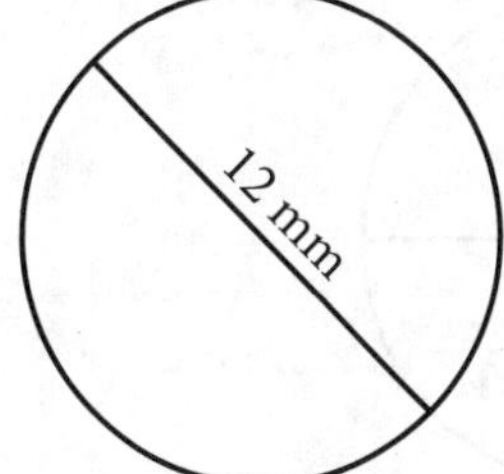

7. a. In terms of pi: ______
b. Approximated Decimal: ______

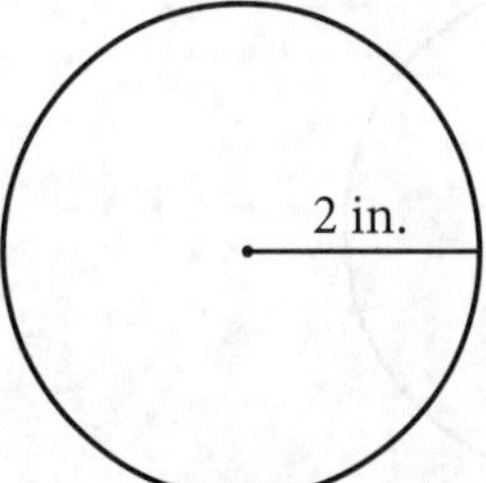

8. a. In terms of pi: ______
b. Approximated Decimal: ______

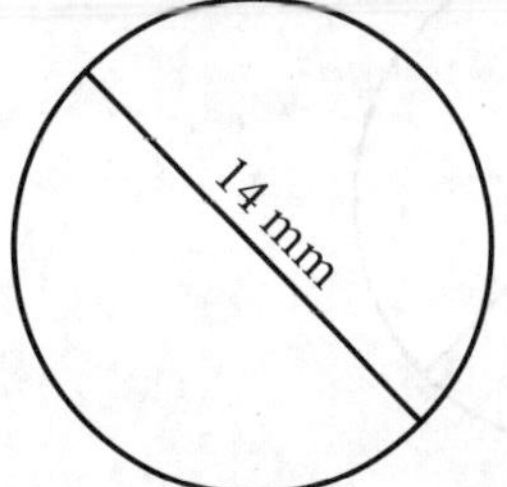

Name: ______________________ Date: ______________

Directions: Find the area of each circle. Write your answers in terms of pi (using π) and as a decimal approximation. The first one has been modeled for you.

1. a. In terms of pi: 36π mm²

b. Approximated Decimal: 113.04 mm²

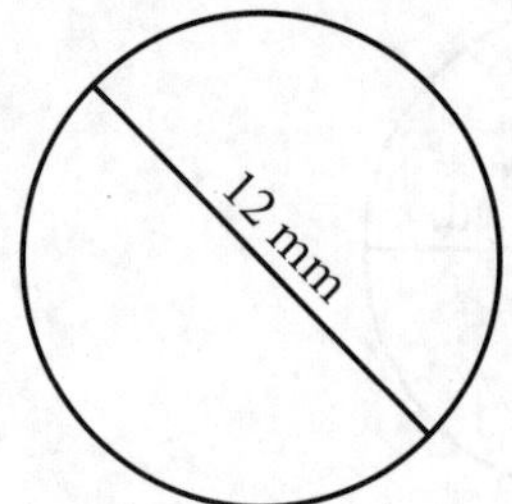

2. a. In terms of pi: ______

b. Approximated Decimal: ________

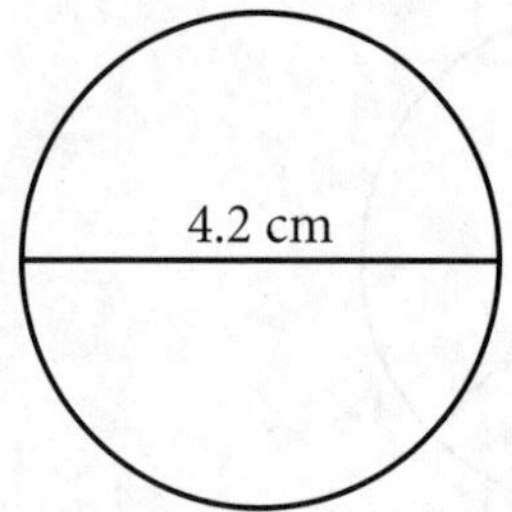

3. a. In terms of pi: ______

b. Approximated Decimal: ________

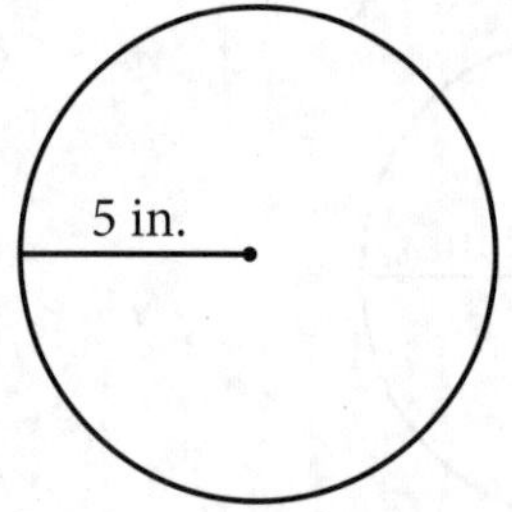

4. a. In terms of pi: ______

b. Approximated Decimal: ________

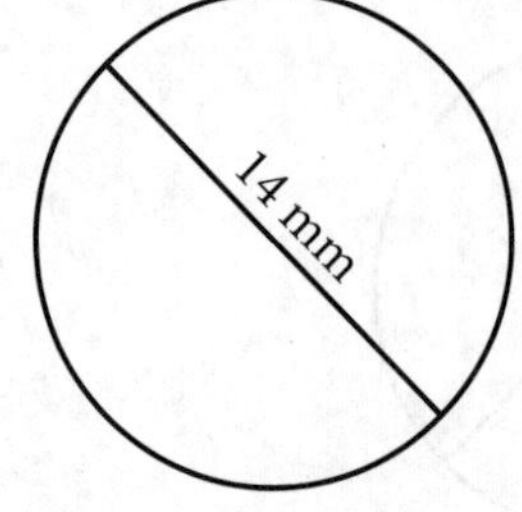

5. a. In terms of pi: ______

b. Approximated Decimal: ________

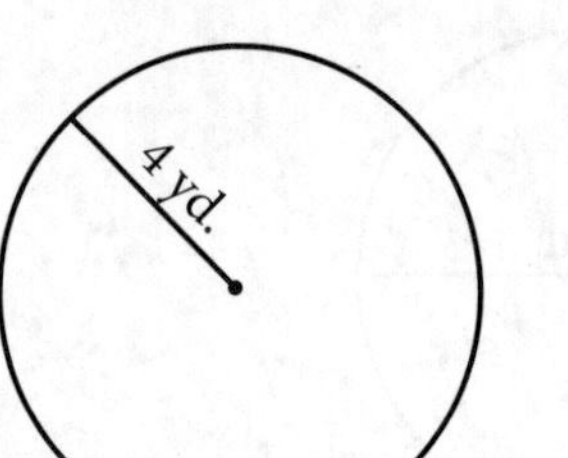

6. a. In terms of pi: ______

b. Approximated Decimal: ________

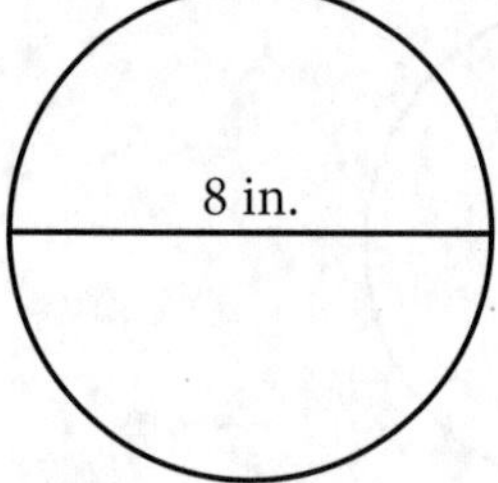

7. a. In terms of pi: ______

b. Approximated Decimal: ________

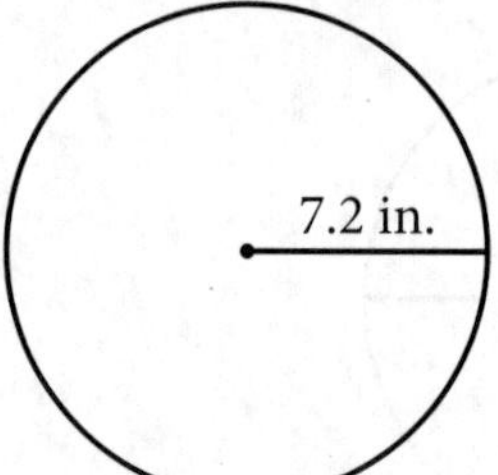

8. a. In terms of pi: ______

b. Approximated Decimal: ________

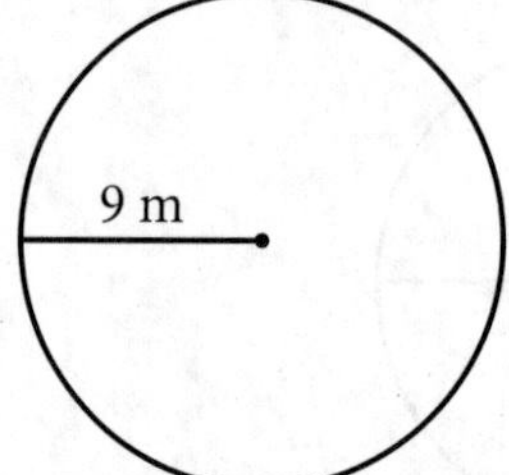

Name: ______________________ Date: ______________

Quick Tip

Remember, area is the space inside a circle. Circumference is the distance around a circle.

Directions: Circle whether you should find the area or circumference to solve each problem. Then, solve the problem.

1. Amarra is sewing a border around the edge of her lampshade. The diameter of the lampshade is 8 inches. How much border does Amarra need?
   area circumference
   ____

2. Farrah wants a round rug for her room. The place she wants to put the rug will cover a space with a radius of 2 feet. How much space will the rug cover?
   area circumference
   ____

3. Mikhail is buying a pool cover for his pool. The radius of the pool is 8 feet. How big should the pool cover be?
   area circumference
   ____

4. Sarah is making a pillow cover for a pillow with a radius of 6 inches. How much material does she need for the top of the cover?
   area circumference
   ____

5. Eva is stringing lights around her hula hoop. The hoop has a diameter of 28 inches. How long of a string of lights does Eva need?
   area circumference
   ____

6. Terrance wants to glue beads around the bottom of his birthday crown. The diameter of the crown is 7 inches. How many inches of beads does Terrance need?
   area circumference
   ____

7. The grounds crew at the baseball field is covering the pitcher's mound after the game. The mound has a radius of 4 feet. How big should the cover be?
   area circumference
   ____

8. Javier wants to decorate the edge of his mom's birthday cake with icing. The diameter of the cake is 4 inches. How much frosting does Javier need?
   area circumference
   ____

Circles

Name: ______________________ Date: ______________

Quick Tip

Remember, if you know the area, you can divide it by π or 3.14, which will give you the value of r^2. To find the radius, take the square root of r^2. If you need to find the diameter once you know the radius, multiply the radius by 2.

If you know the circumference, divide it by π to find the diameter. If you need to find the radius, divide the diameter by 2.

Directions: Answer the questions.

1. The area of a circle is 49π.

   What is the radius? __________

2. The circumference of a circle is 78π.

   What is the diameter? __________

3. The circumference of a circle is 18π.

   What is the radius? __________

4. The area of a circle is 81π.

   What is the diameter? __________

5. The circumference of a circle is 54π.

   What is the radius? __________

6. The area of a circle is 36π.

   What is the diameter? __________

7. The area of a circle is 25π.

   What is the radius? __________

8. The circumference of a circle is 100π.

   What is the diameter? __________

9. The area of a circle is 64π.

   What is the diameter? __________

10. The circumference of a circle is 92π.

    What is the radius? __________

Name: ____________________ Date: ____________

Directions: Solve each problem.

1. Find the circumference of the circle in terms of pi and as an approximated decimal.

a. In terms of pi: ________

b. Approximated decimal: ________

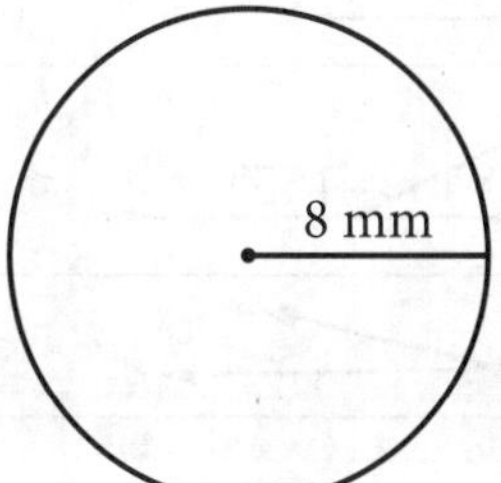

2. The circumference of a circle is 90π. What is the radius?

____

3. Henry is mowing around the outside of his circular yard. The diameter of his yard is 30 feet. What is the circumference of Henry's yard?

____

4. The area of a circle is 121π. What is the diameter?

____

5. Find the area of the circle in terms of pi and as an approximated decimal.

a. In terms of pi: ________

b. Approximated decimal: ________

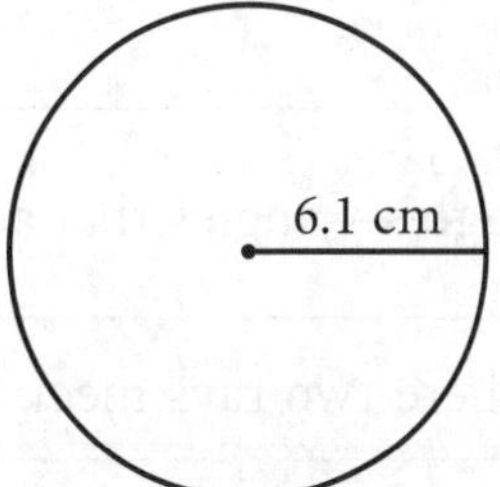

6. At the carnival, Ty is covering the outside of the kids ferris wheel with lights. The diameter of the ferris wheel is 10 feet. How many feet of lights will Ty need?

____

7. The circumference of a circle is 29π. What is the diameter?

____

8. The area of a circle is 144π. What is the radius?

____

Learn about Angles

adjacent angles—angles that have a common side and a common vertex	common side common vertex
complementary angles—angles that add up to 90°	30° 60°
supplementary angles—angles that add up to 180°	25° 155°
vertex—a point where two rays meet	vertex →
vertical angles—the pairs of opposite angles made by intersecting lines	1 2 3 4 In this diagram, angles 1 and 3 are vertical. Angles 2 and 4 are also vertical.

Example 1

What type of angles are Angles 1 and 2?

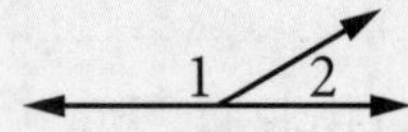

1. Angles 1 and 2 are next to each other, sharing a common side and a common vertex, so they are **adjacent** angles.
2. Angles 1 and 2 also add up to 180°, so they are **supplementary** angles.

Example 2

Write an equation to find the missing angle. Then, solve the equation.

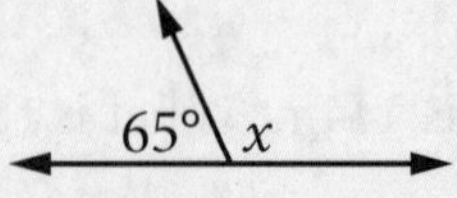

1. The angles are supplementary, so we know they add up to 180°.
   $x + 65 = 180$
2. To solve, subtract 65 from each side of the equation.
   $x =$ ________

Example 3

Write an equation to find the missing angle. Then, solve the equation.

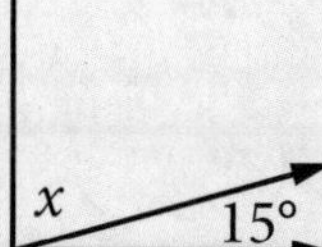

1. The angles are complementary, so we know they add up to 90°.
   $x + 15 = 90$
2. To solve, subtract 15 from each side of the equation.
   $x =$ ________

Example 4

Write an equation to find the missing angle. Then, solve the equation.

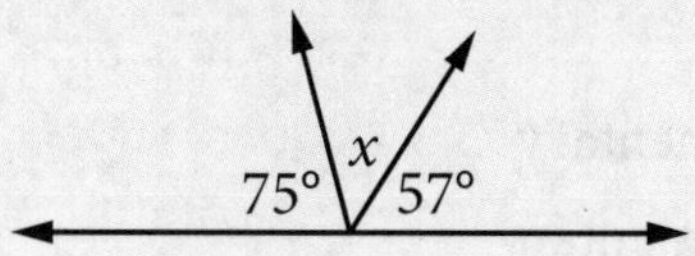

1. All three angles are supplementary, so they all add up to 180°.
   $75 + x + 57 = 180$
2. Add 75 + 57.
   $x + 132 = 180$
3. Subtract 132 from both sides of the equation.
   $x =$ ________

Example 5

Find the missing angle in the triangle.

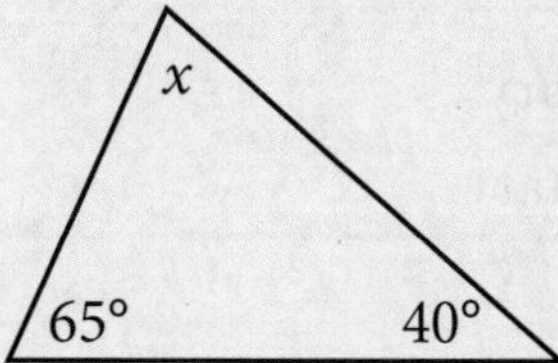

1. We know that the three angles in a triangle add up to 180°.
   $65 + x + 40 = 180$
2. Add 65 + 40.
   $x + 105 = 180$
3. Subtract 105 from both sides of the equation.
   $x =$ ________

Name: ______________________________ Date: ______________

Directions: Circle the word that describes Angles 1 and 2 in each diagram. If there is more than one answer, circle all answers.

1. **a.** supplementary
b. complementary
c. vertical
d. adjacent

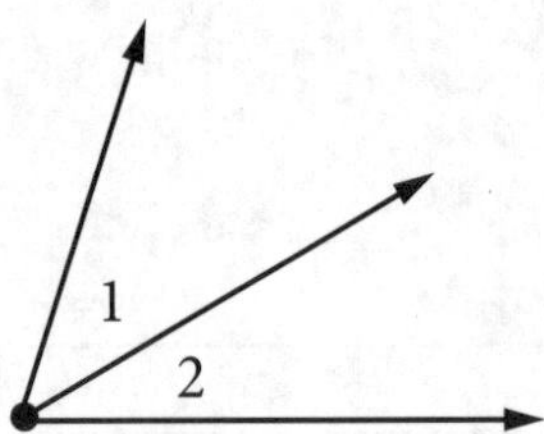

2. **a.** supplementary
b. complementary
c. vertical
d. adjacent

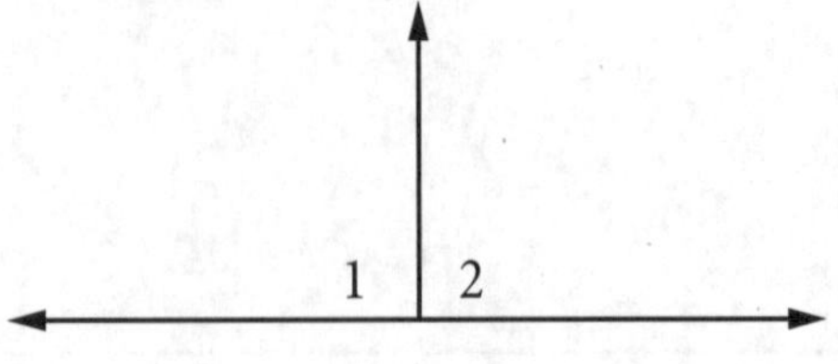

3. **a.** supplementary
b. complementary
c. vertical
d. adjacent

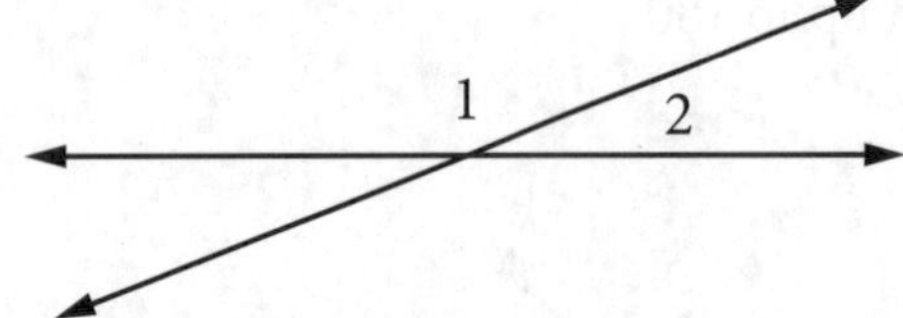

4. **a.** supplementary
b. complementary
c. vertical
d. adjacent

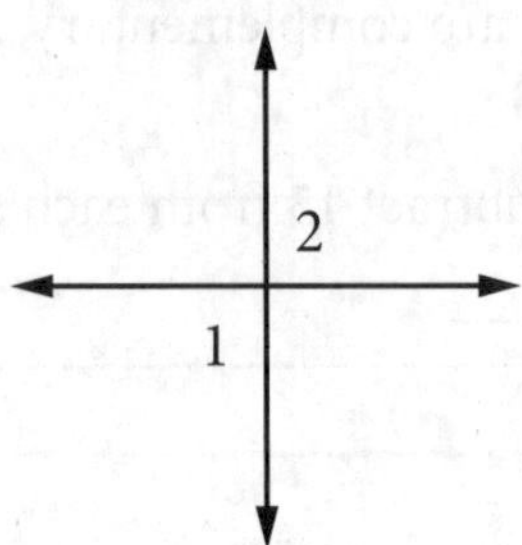

5. **a.** supplementary
b. complementary
c. vertical
d. adjacent

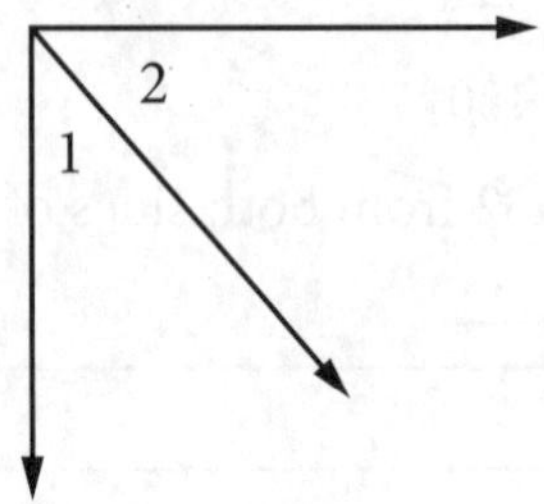

6. **a.** supplementary
b. complementary
c. vertical
d. adjacent

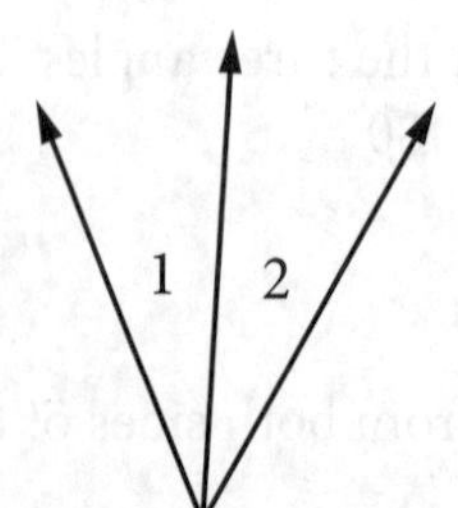

Name: ________________________________ Date: ________________

Directions: Write an equation to find each missing angle, and then solve the equation.

1. Equation with variable:

____

x = ________

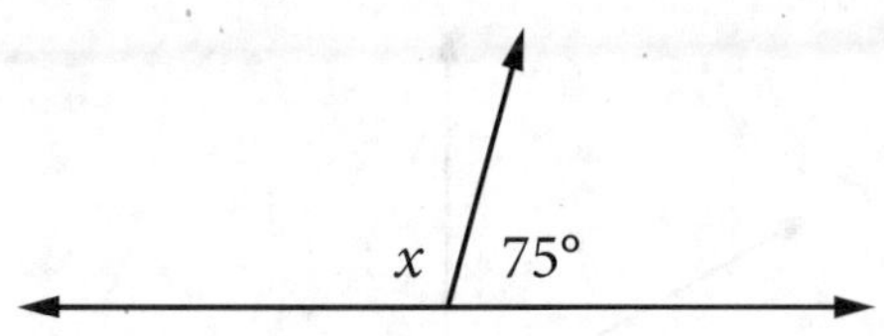

2. Equation with variable:

____

x = ________

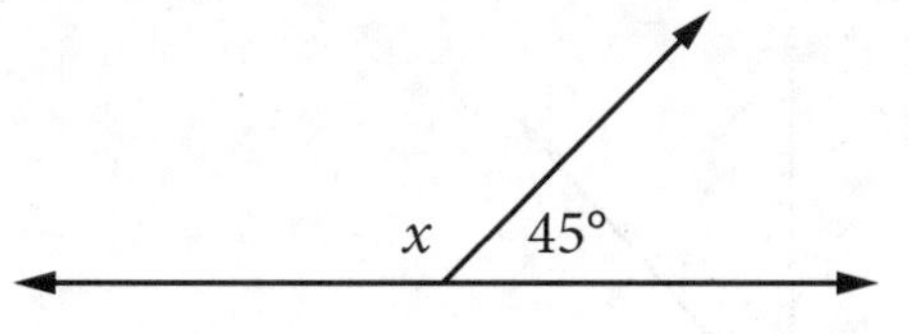

3. Equation with variable:

____

x = ________

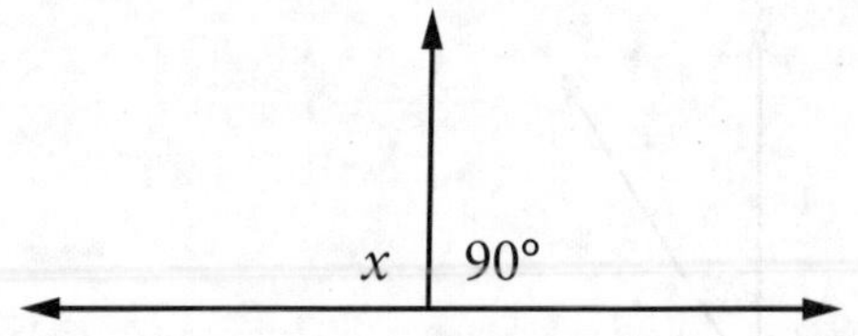

4. Equation with variable:

____

x = ________

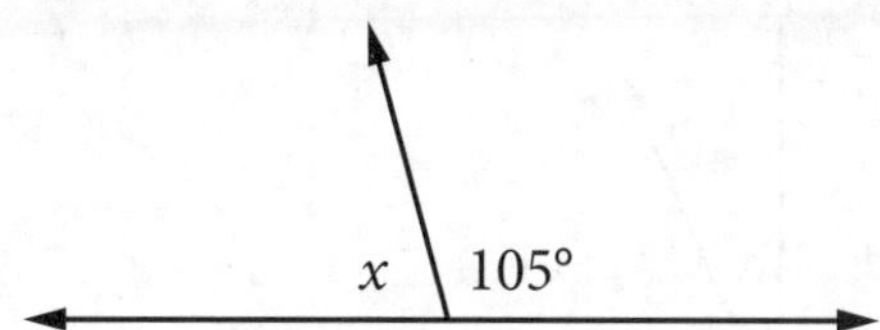

5. Equation with variable:

____

x = ________

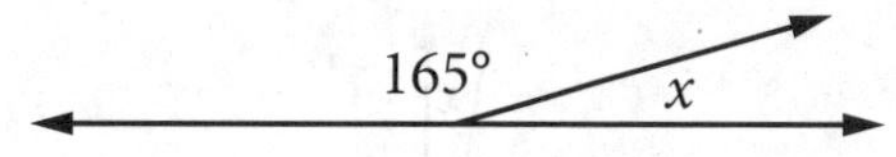

6. Equation with variable:

____

x = ________

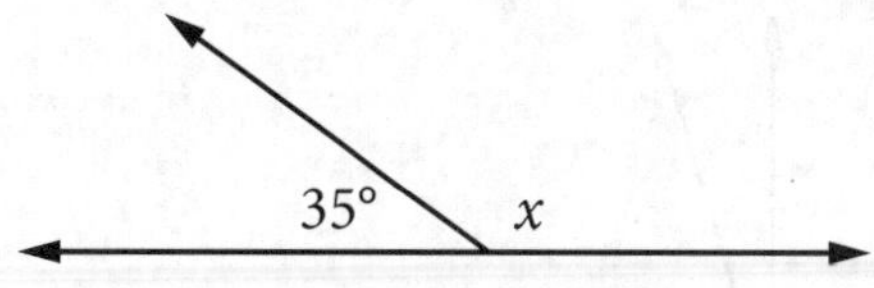

Angles

Name: ______________________ Date: ______________

Directions: Write an equation to find each missing angle, and then solve the equation.

1. Equation with variable:

____

$x =$ ________

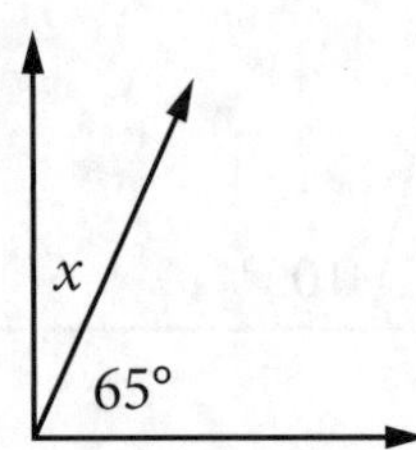

2. Equation with variable:

____

$x =$ ________

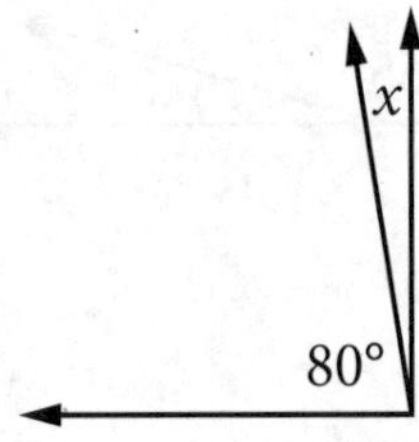

3. Equation with variable:

____

$x =$ ________

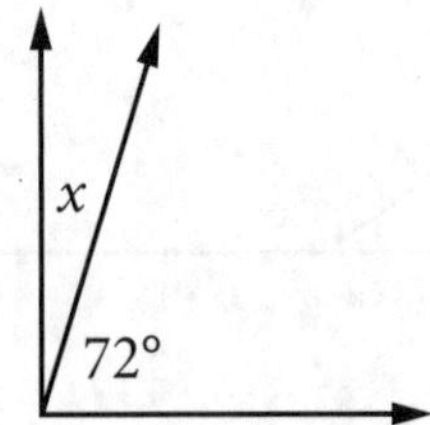

4. Equation with variable:

____

$x =$ ________

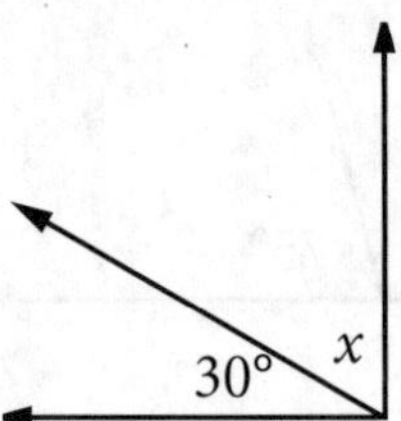

5. Equation with variable:

____

$x =$ ________

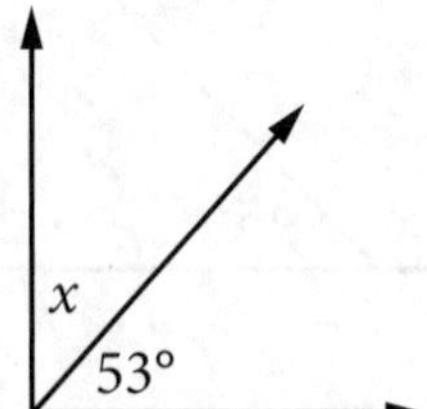

6. Equation with variable:

____

$x =$ ________

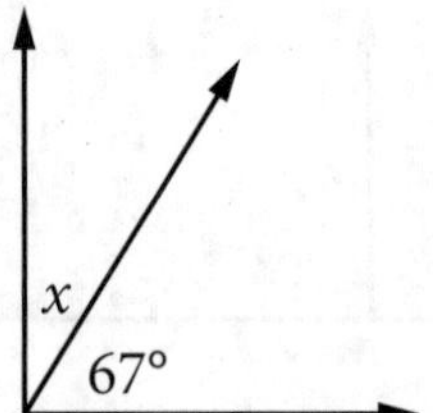

Name: ______________________ Date: ______________

Quick Tip

Remember, **supplementary** angles add up to 180°, and **complementary** angles add up to 90°.

Directions: Write an equation to find the missing angle, and then solve the equation.

1. Equation with variable:

____

$x =$ ________

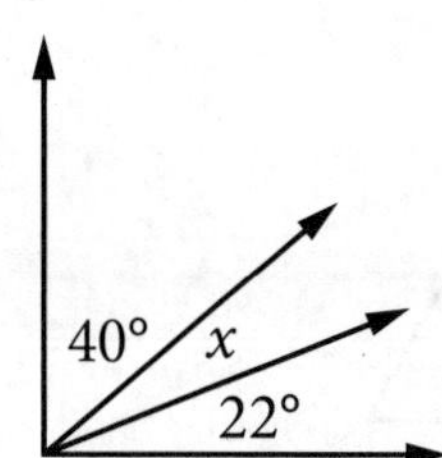

2. Equation with variable:

____

$x =$ ________

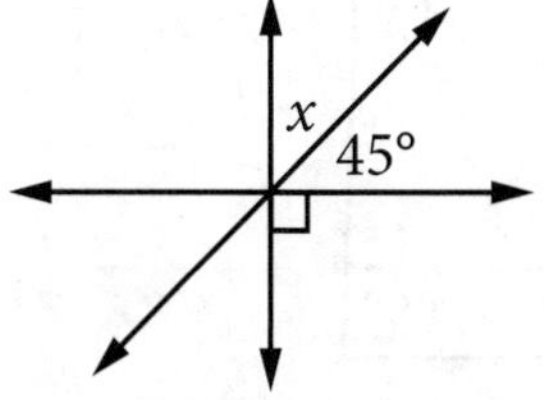

3. Equation with variable:

____

$x =$ ________

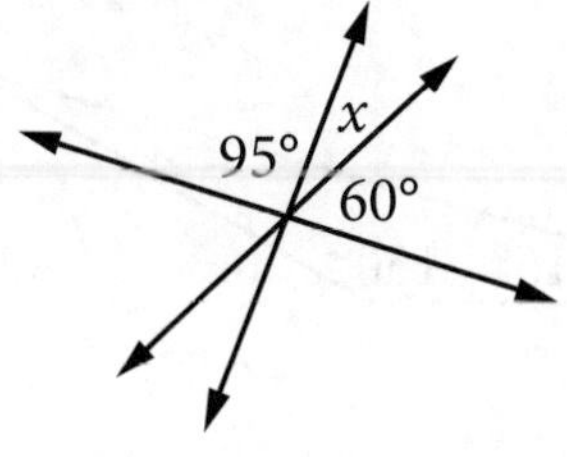

4. Equation with variable:

____

$x =$ ________

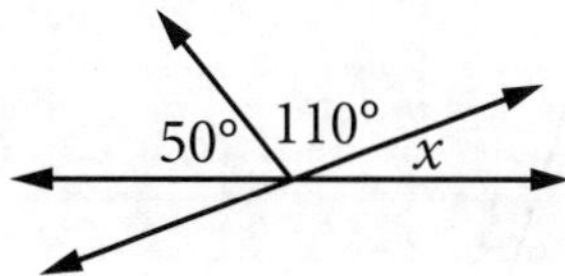

5. Equation with variable:

____

$x =$ ________

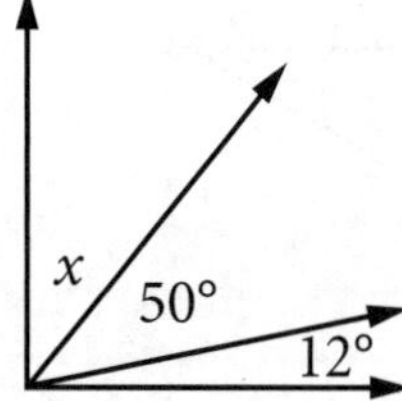

6. Equation with variable:

____

$x =$ ________

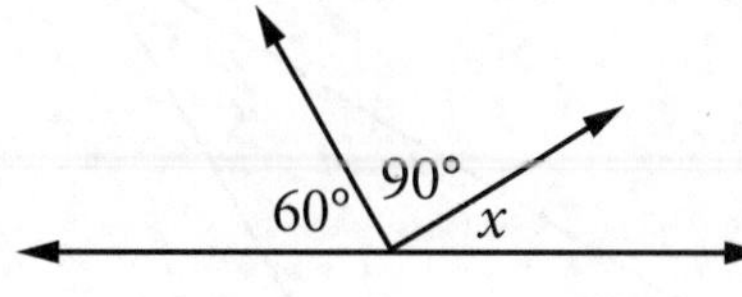

Angles

Name: ____________________ Date: ____________

Quick Tip

Remember, the three angles in a triangle add up to exactly 180°.

Directions: Write an equation to find the missing angle, and then solve the equation.

1. Equation with variable:

____

$x =$ ________

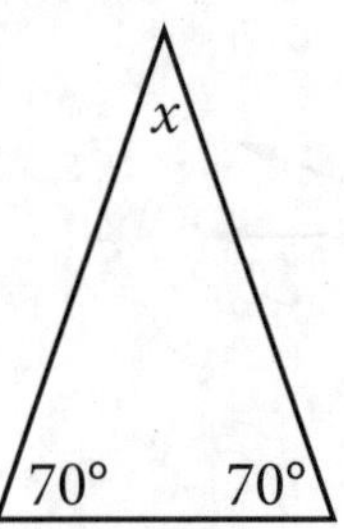

2. Equation with variable:

____

$x =$ ________

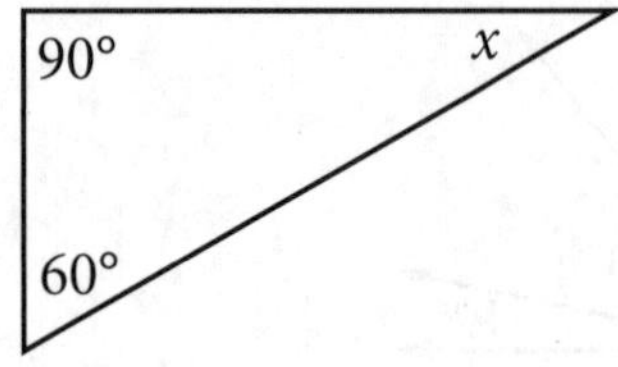

3. Equation with variable:

____

$x =$ ________

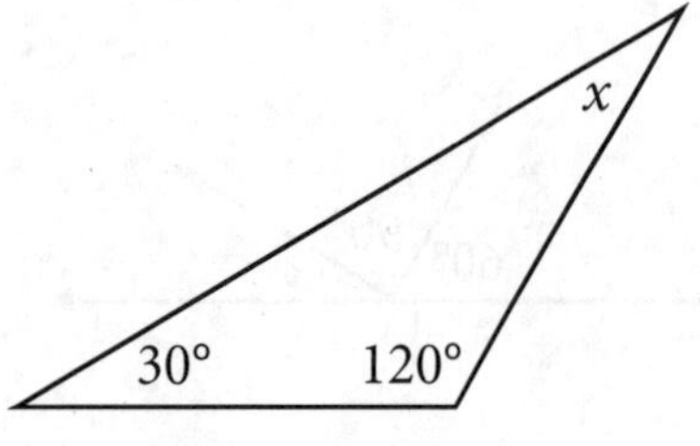

4. Equation with variable:

____

$x =$ ________

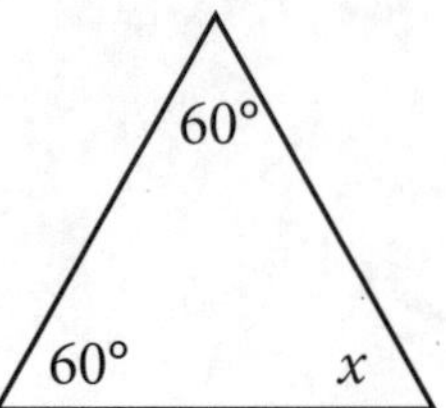

5. Equation with variable:

____

$x =$ ________

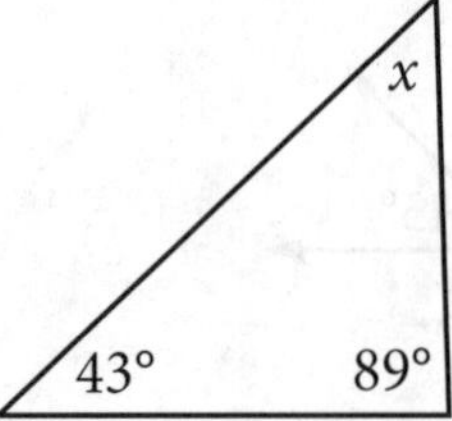

6. Equation with variable:

____

$x =$ ________

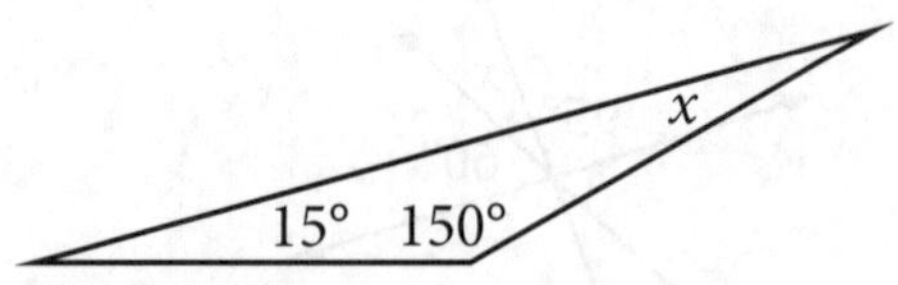

Learn about Area, Volume, and Surface Area

Area Formulas

area of a rectangle = length × width
area of a square = side × side
area of a triangle = $\frac{1}{2}$ × base × height
area of a parallelogram = base × height
area of a rhombus = base × height
area of a trapezoid = $\frac{(base_1 + base_2)}{2}$ × height

All area answers should be labeled in square units.

Surface Area

To find the surface area of any figure, find the area of each face, and add the areas together.

Surface area answers should be labeled in square units.

Volume

volume of a prism = area of the base × height
volume of a pyramid = area of the base × $\frac{height}{3}$. The volume of a pyramid is $\frac{1}{3}$ of the volume of a rectangular prism with the same dimensions.

Volume answers should be labeled in cubic units.

Example 1

Find the area of the trapezoid.

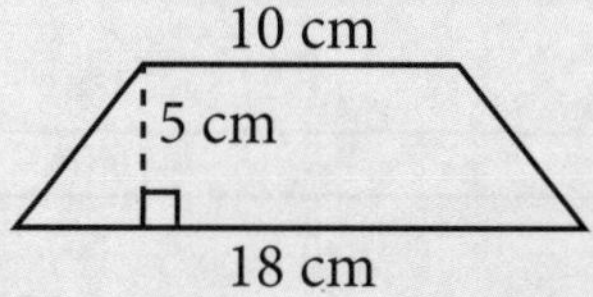

1. Follow the formula.
   $\frac{(base_1 + base_2)}{2}$ × height
   The bases are the parallel sides. Add the bases together.
   10 + 18 = 28
2. Divide by 2.
   28 ÷ 2 = ________
3. Now, multiply your answer from step 2 by the height.
   ________ × 5 = ________
   The area of the trapezoid is ________ cm^2.

Example 2

Find the volume of the pyramid.

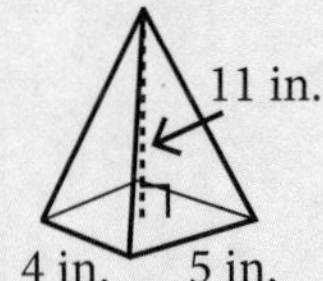

1. Follow the formula.
   area of the base × $\frac{\text{height}}{3}$
   (4 × 5 × 11) ÷ 3 = ________ cubic inches

Example 3

Find the surface area of the rectangular prism using the net.

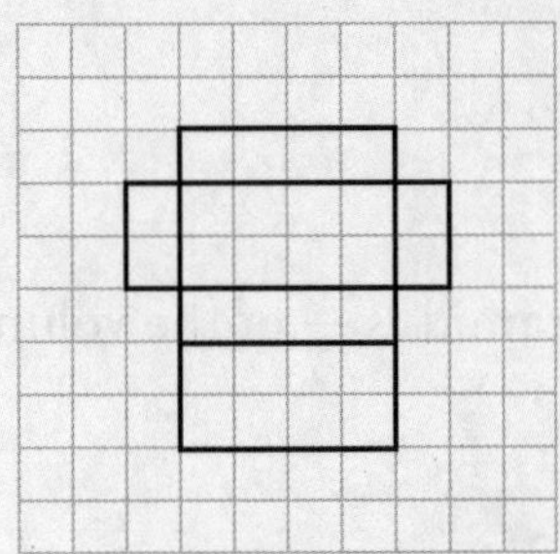

1. Find the area of each rectangle on the diagram, and record your answers on the diagram.
2. Add all of the areas that you found in Step 1.
   The surface area is ________ square units.

Example 4

Find the area of the figure.

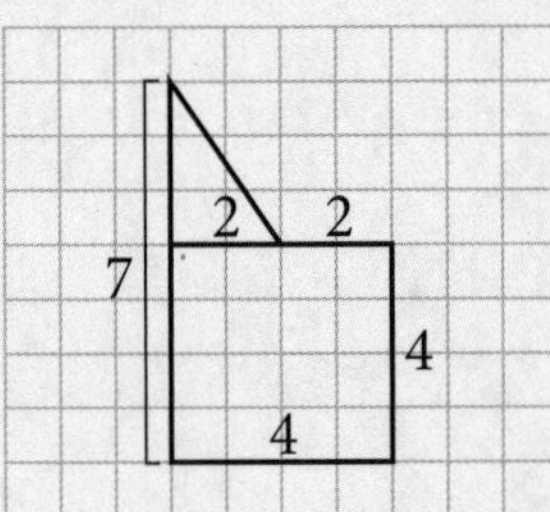

1. Decompose the diagram into a square and a triangle.
2. Find the area of each figure. Add the areas together.
   Area of square: ________
   Area of triangle: ________
3. The area of the figure is ________ square units.

Name: ______________________ Date: ______________

Directions: Find the area (*A*) of each figure. Label your answers in square units.

1. *A* = ______________

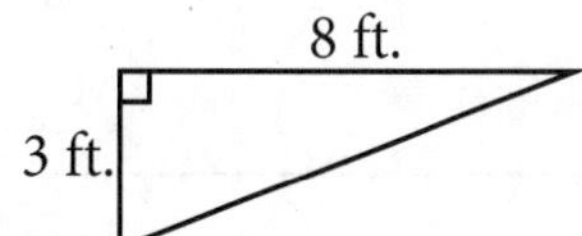

2. *A* = ______________

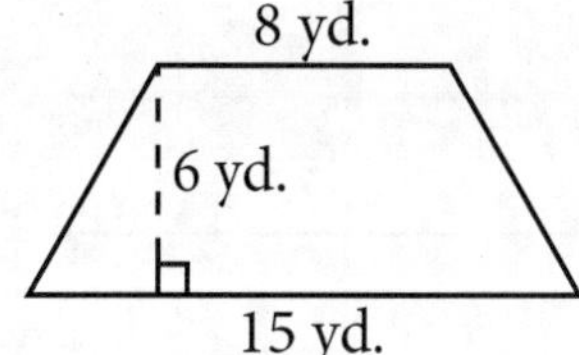

3. *A* = ______________

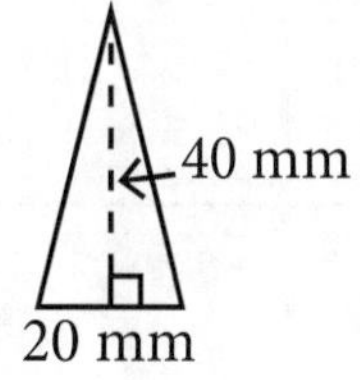

4. *A* = ______________

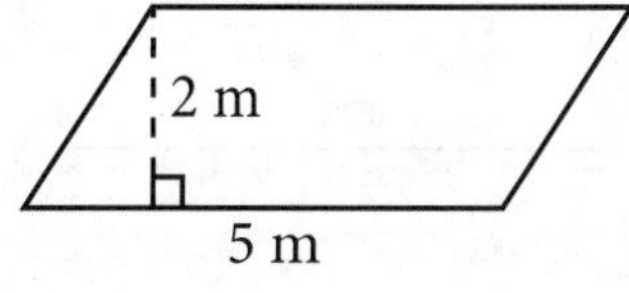

5. *A* = ______________

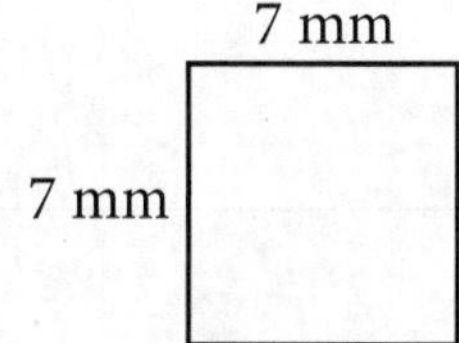

6. *A* = ______________

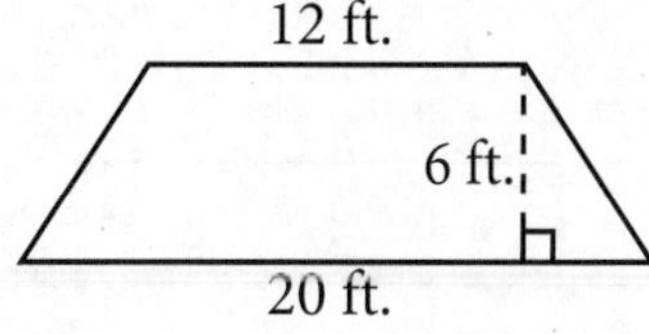

7. *A* = ______________

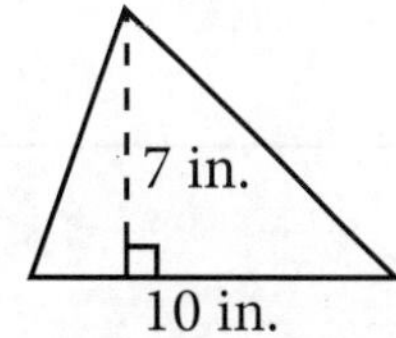

8. *A* = ______________

7 in.
10 in.

Name: ______________________ Date: ______________

Directions: Find the volume (*V*) of each figure. Be sure to label your answers in cubic units.

1. $V =$ ____________

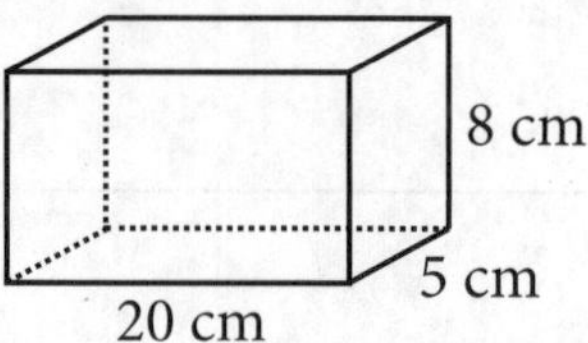

2. $V =$ ____________

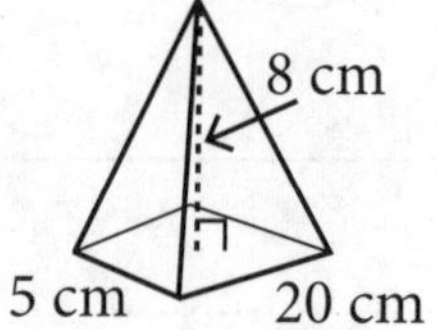

3. $V =$ ____________

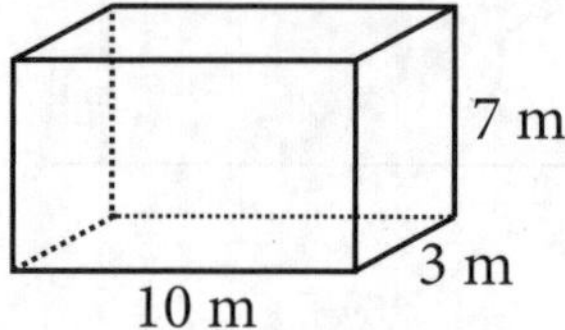

4. $V =$ ____________

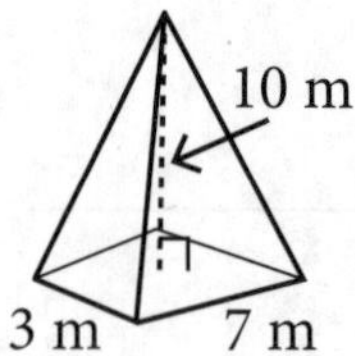

5. $V =$ ____________

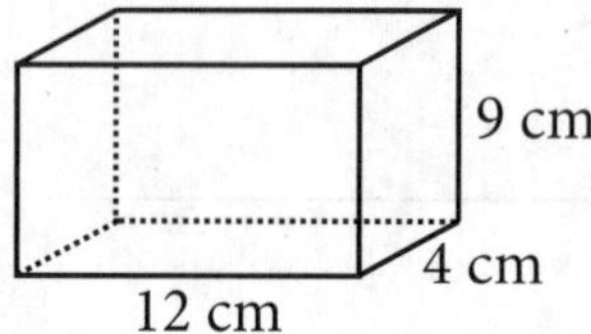

6. $V =$ ____________

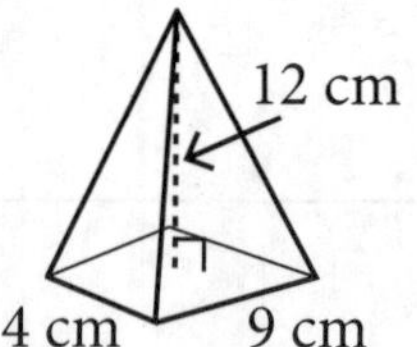

7. $V =$ ____________

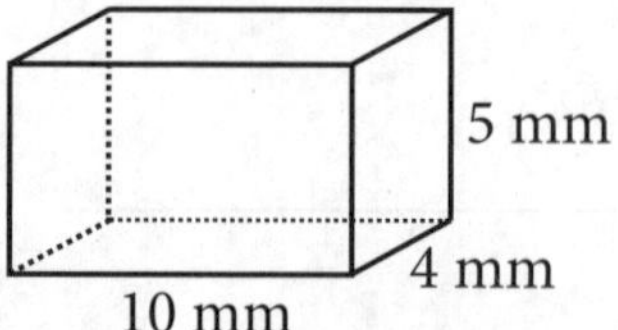

8. $V =$ ____________

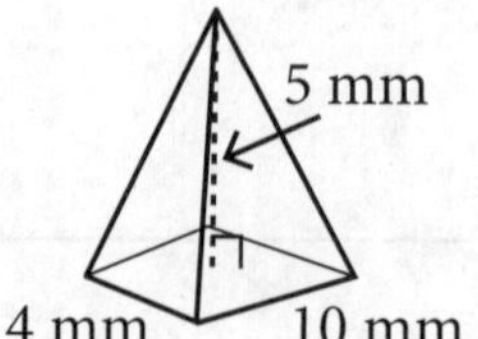

Name: ______________________________ Date: ____________________

Directions: Find the volume (V) of each figure. Be sure to label your answers in cubic units.

1. $V =$ ____________________

9 cm
6 cm
10 cm

2. $V =$ ____________________

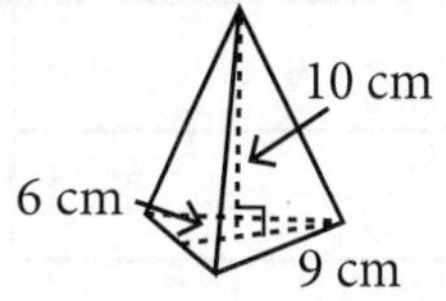

3. $V =$ ____________________

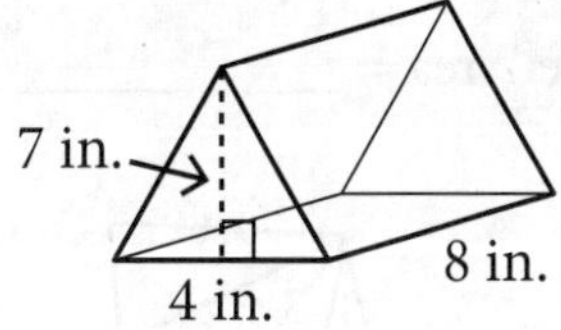

4. $V =$ ____________________

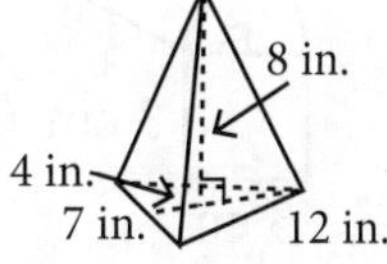

5. $V =$ ____________________

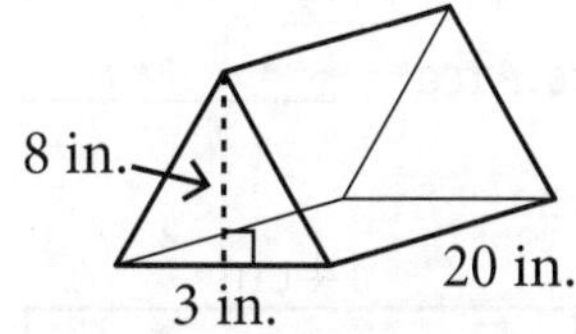

6. $V =$ ____________________

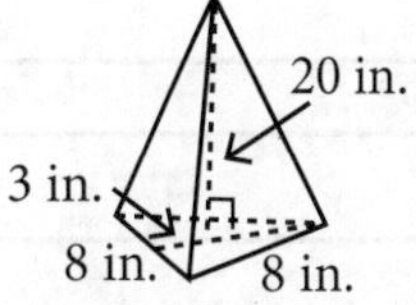

7. $V =$ ____________________

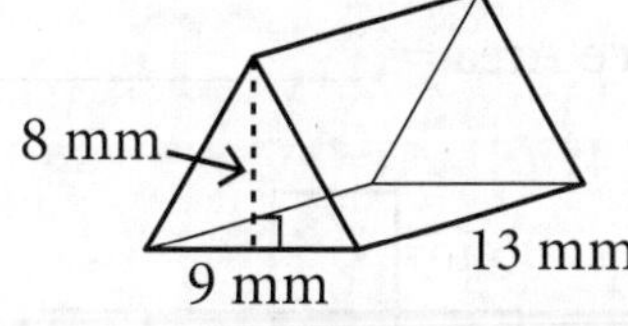

8. $V =$ ____________________

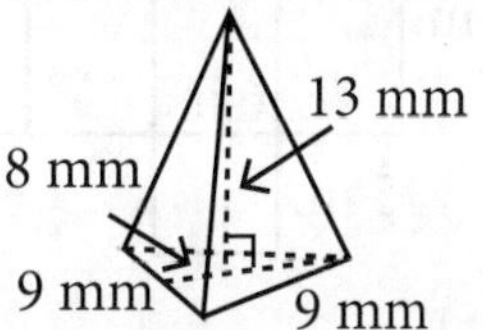

Name: ______________________ Date: ______________

Directions: Use the net to find the surface area of each figure. Label your answers in square units.

1. Surface Area = ______________

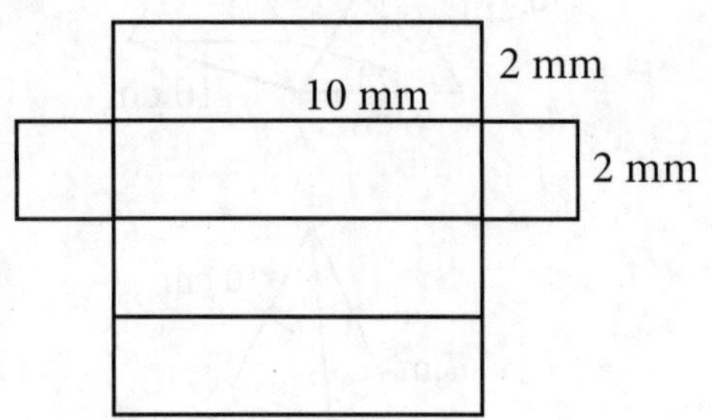

2. Surface Area = ______________

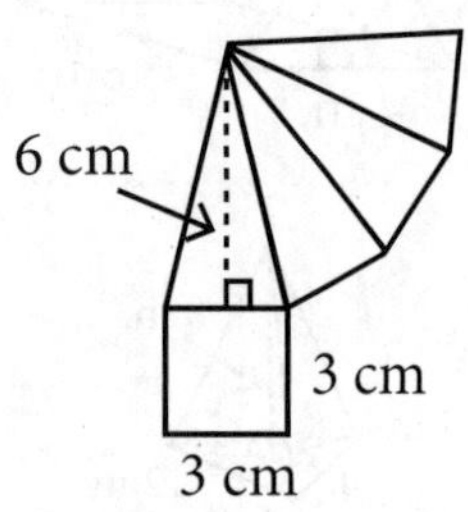

3. Surface Area = ______________

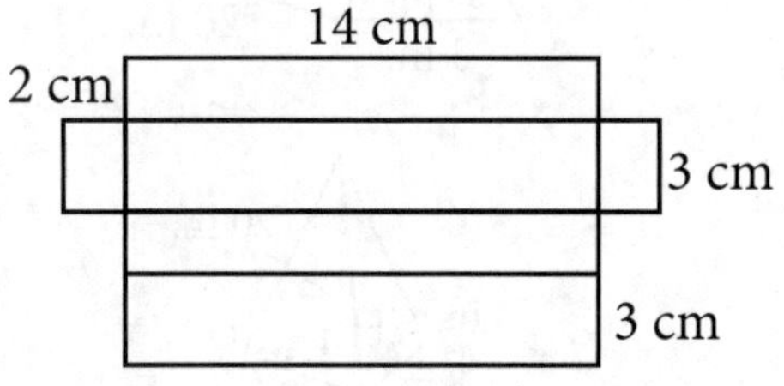

4. Surface Area = ______________

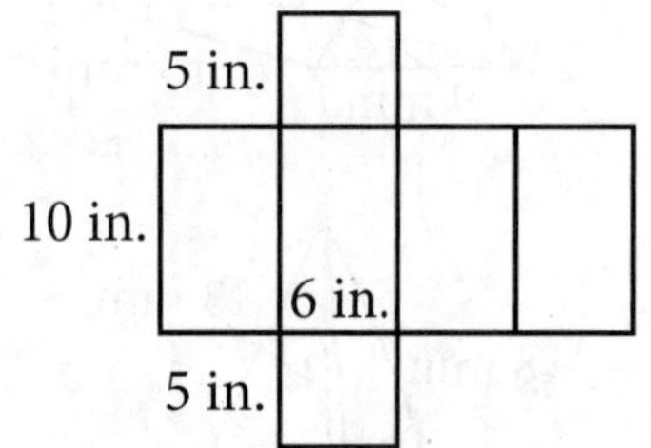

5. Surface Area = ______________

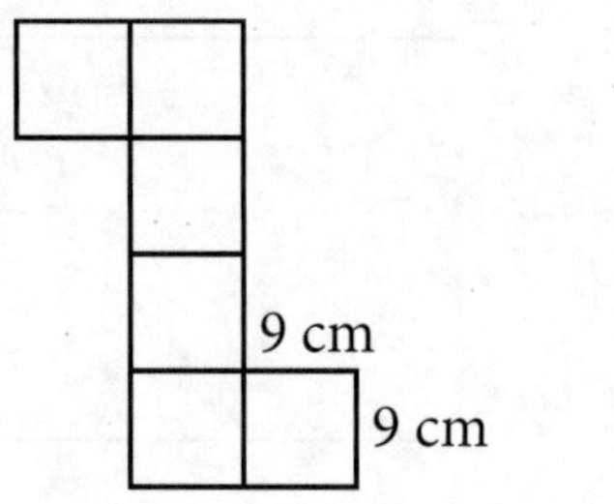

6. Surface Area = ______________

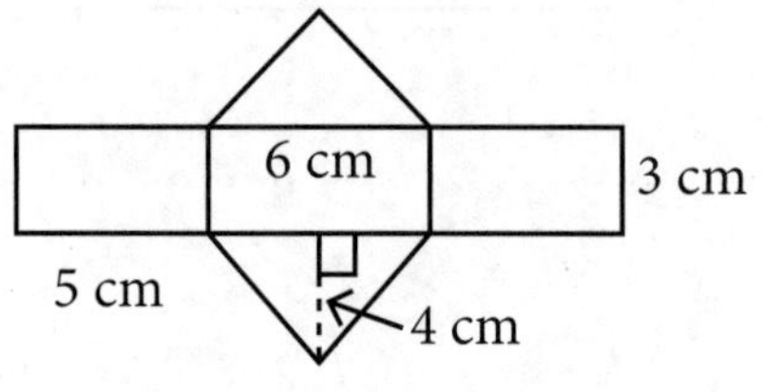

7. Surface Area = ______________

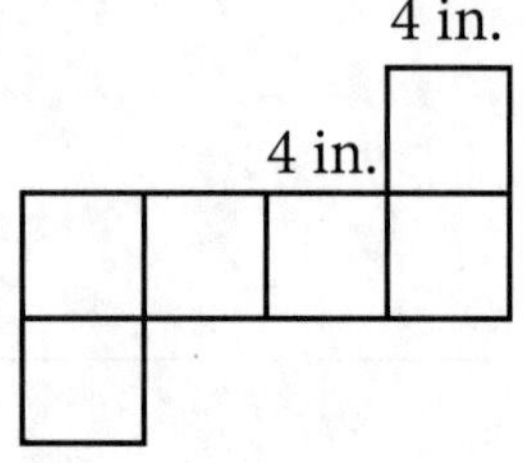

8. Surface Area = ______________

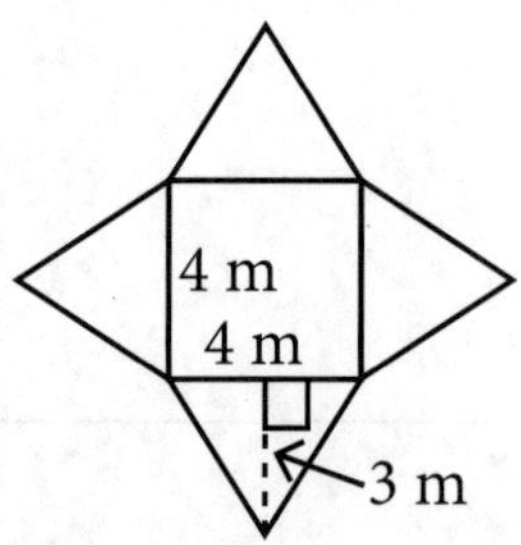

Name: ______________________________ Date: ________________

Directions: Find the area (*A*) of each figure. Be sure to label your answers in square units.

1. A = ________________

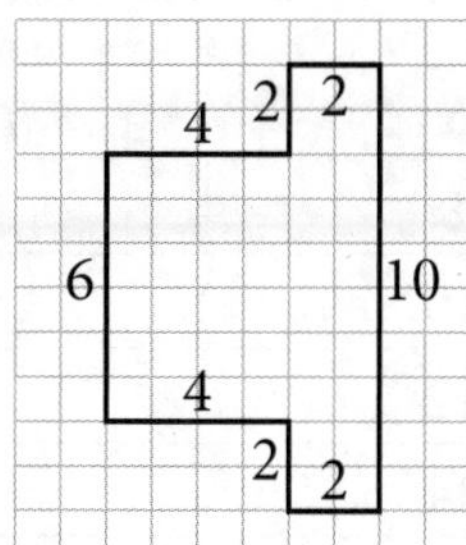

2. A = ________________

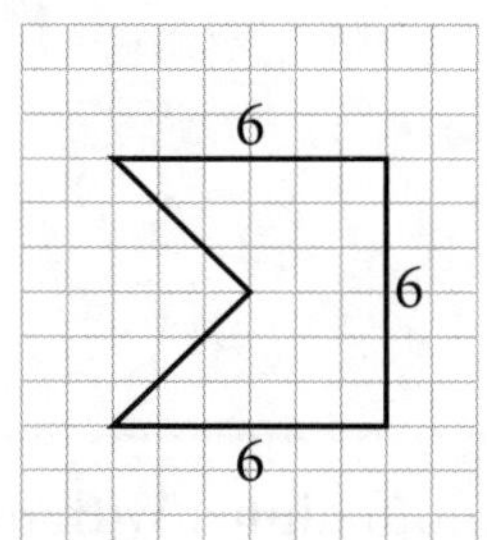

3. A = ________________

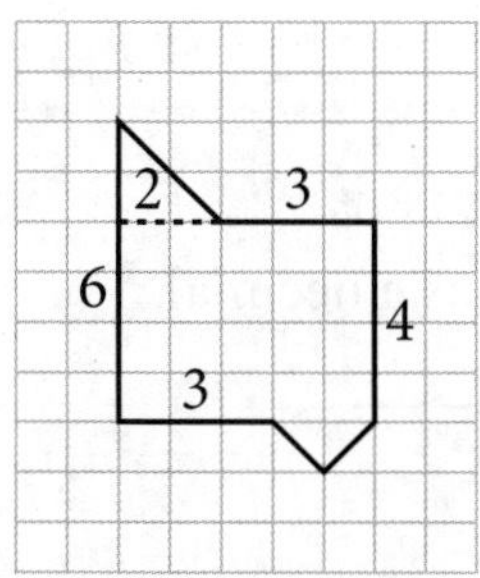

4. A = ________________

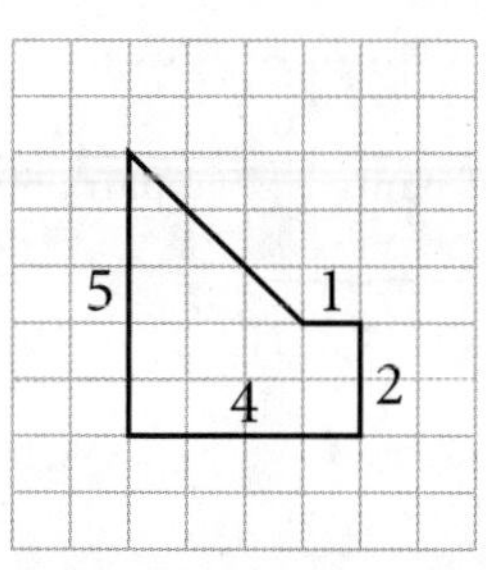

5. A = ________________

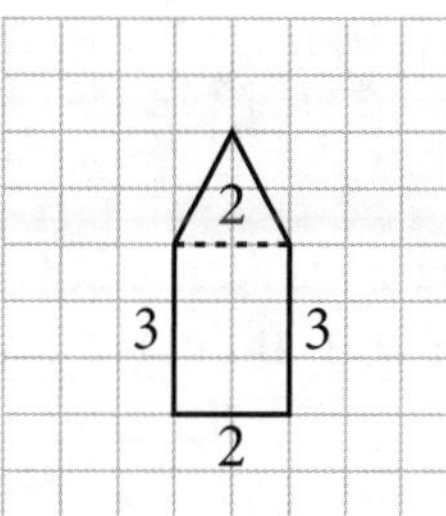

6. A = ________________

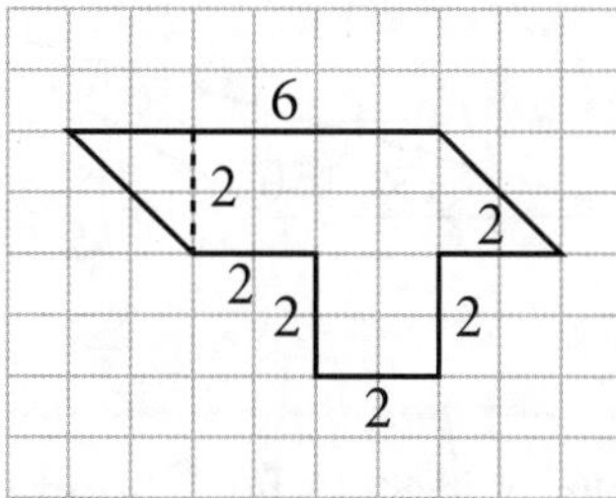

7. A = ________________

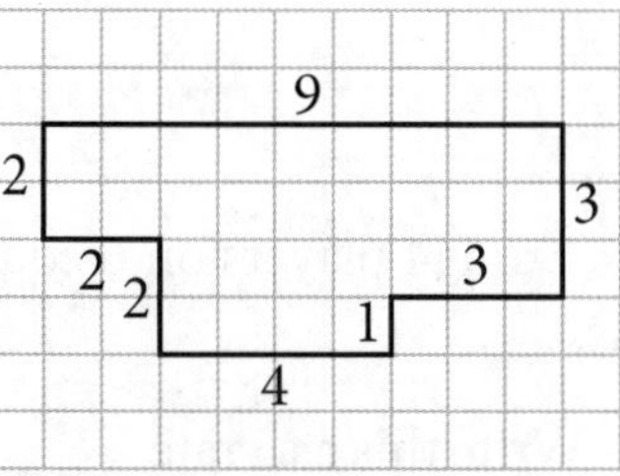

8. A = ________________

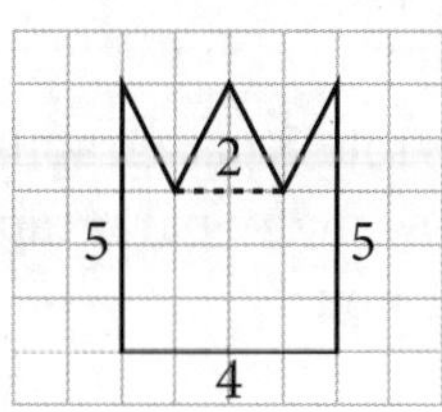

Area, Volume, and Surface Area

Name: ______________________ Date: ______________

Directions: Solve each problem.

1. Solve the inequality. Graph the solution to the inequality on the number line.

$6x - 7 \leq 17$

$x =$ __________

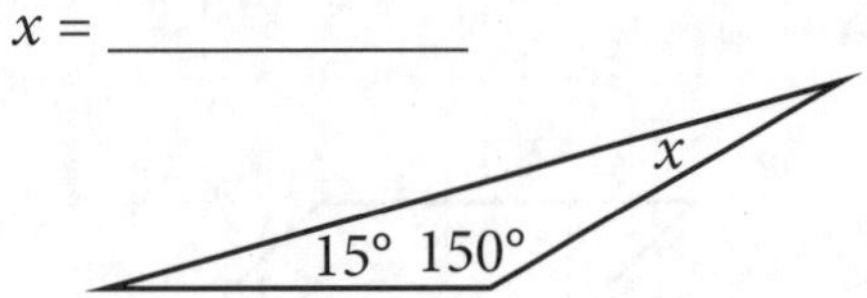

2. Solve for the unknown angle.

$x =$ __________

15° 150° x

3. Tameka paid $245 for 7 hoodies. How much did she pay for 1 hoodie?

____

4. There are 144 players on 6 equally sized teams.

a. Write this as a rate. ________

b. What is the unit rate? ________

5. Martha wrote 3 paragraphs in $\frac{3}{4}$ of an hour. How many paragraphs could she write in 1 hour?

____

6. Does the table show a proportional relationship? __________

x	y
8	24
10	40
12	60
14	84

7. $9 - (-8) =$ __________

8. Roger went to dinner with his friends. The bill was $55. Roger wanted to leave an 18% tip. How much was the bill, including the tip?

____

9. Write $\frac{5}{9}$ as a decimal.

____

10. $\frac{\$95}{\text{5 pairs of pants}} = \frac{x}{\text{20 pairs of pants}}$

$x =$ __________

Spiral Review

Name: ______________________ Date: ______________

Directions: Solve each problem.

1. Find the volume (V) of the rectangular prism.
   V = ____________

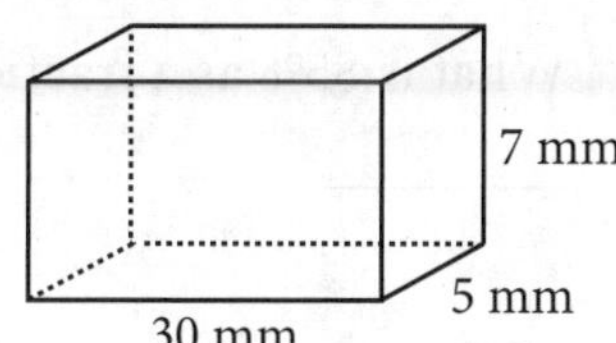

2. $6^3 \times 6^2$ = ____________

3. $9(7 - 11) + 4 - 0.5$ = ____________

4. What is the missing angle measure?
   x = ____________

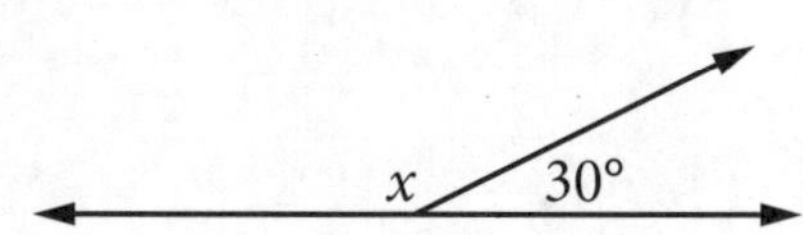

5. $\frac{4 \text{ dogs}}{3 \text{ cats}} = \frac{40 \text{ dogs}}{?}$
   ? = ____________

6. Kenny is buying a new car for $25,000. He has to pay sales tax of 8%. What is the amount of sales tax Kenny must pay?

   ____

7. What is the missing angle measure?
   x = ____________

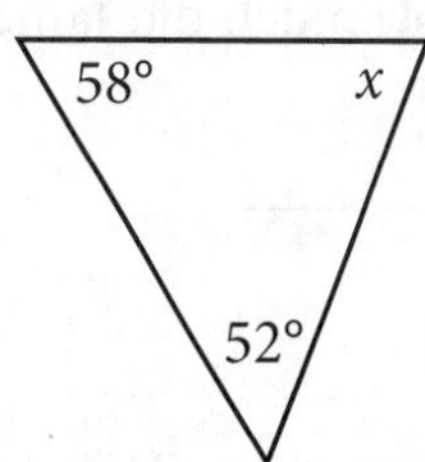

8. $4x + 5 = 23$
   x = ____________

9. $5\frac{3}{8} - 1\frac{2}{7}$ = ____________

10. What is the area of the scaled copy with a scale factor of 6 applied to the diagram?

    ____

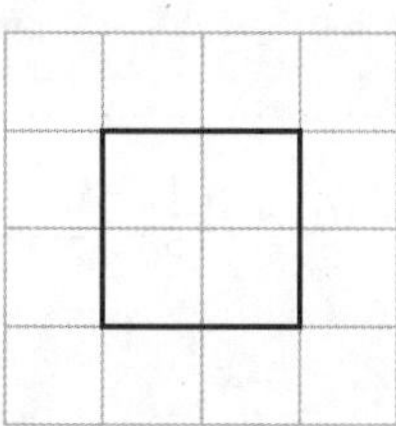

Spiral Review

Name: ____________________ Date: ____________

Directions: Solve each problem.

1. What kind of angles are Angles 1 and 2?

____

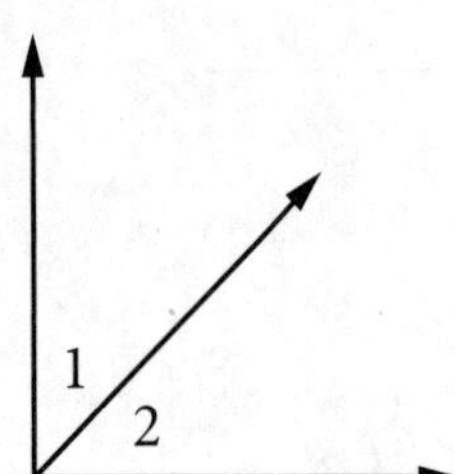

2. James earned \$231 for $10\frac{1}{2}$ hours of work. How much did James earn per hour?

____

3. What is the volume (V) of the rectangular prism?

$V =$ ________

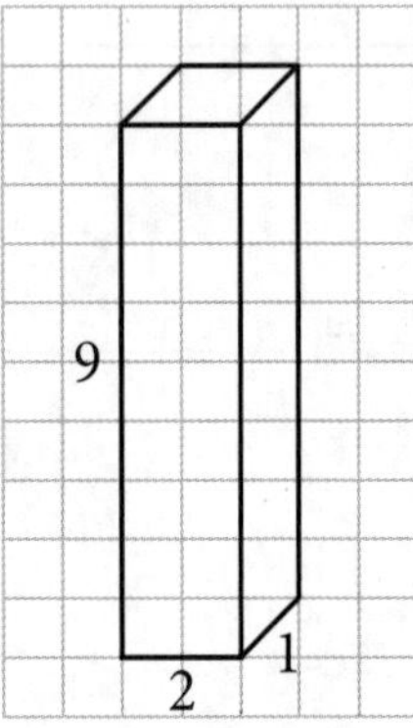

4. What is the additive inverse of –7?

____

5. $2(19.5 - 16) + 4\frac{1}{5} =$ ________

6. Marek scored an 85% on his math quiz.

a. What is 85% as a decimal?

____

b. What is 85% as a fraction?

____

7. Simplify the expression by combining like terms.

$4(3x + 2) - 5(x + 3) =$ ________

8. Solve the equation and graph the solution on the number line.

$9x - 8 = 28$

$x =$ ________

–8 –7 –6 –5 –4 –3 –2 –1 0 1 2 3 4 5 6 7 8

9. $5\frac{1}{4} \div 3\frac{1}{3} =$ ________

10. $-25 \div (-5) =$ ________

Name: ______________________ Date: ______________

Directions: Solve each problem.

1. Is the relationship shown on the graph a proportional relationship? __________

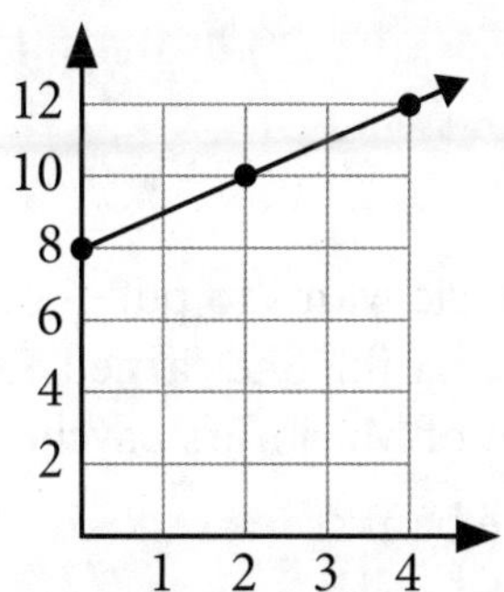

2. Write an equivalent expression using the Distributive Property.

$6(5x + 7) =$ __________

3. Look at the two scaled pentagons. What is the length of the missing side?

$x =$ __________

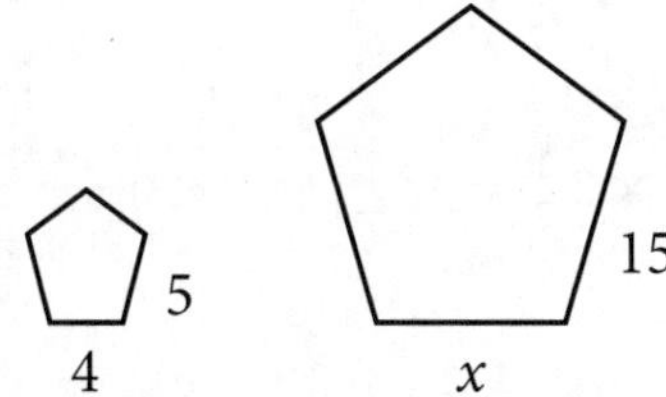

4. What is the constant of proportionality in the graph?

$k =$ __________

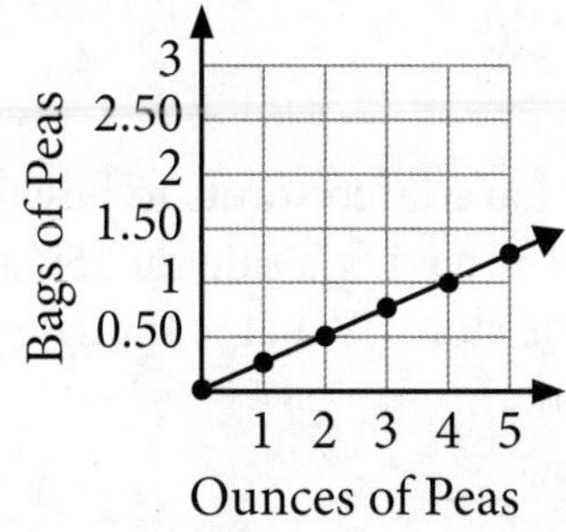

5. Write a subtraction equation to model the difference between the two numbers on the number line.

____

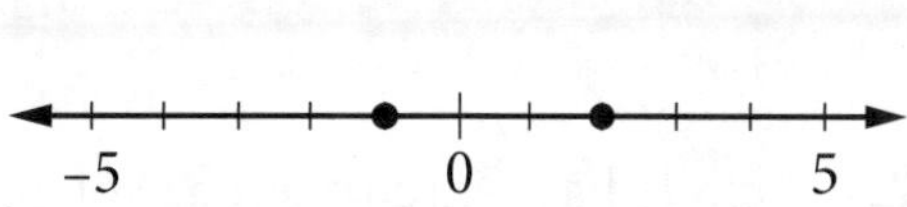

6. $-18 - (-5) =$ __________

7. What is the missing angle measure?

$x =$ __________

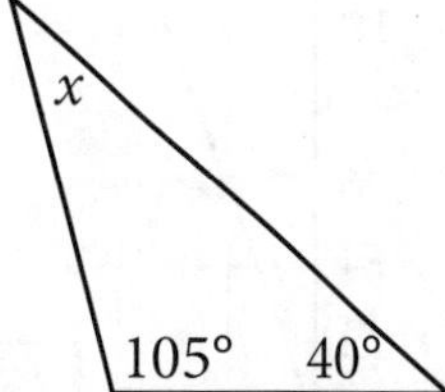

8. What two-dimensional shape is made on the face of the cross section when the triangular prism is sliced horizontally?

____

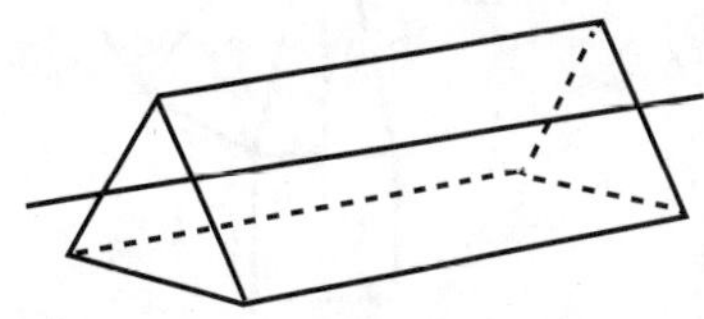

Spiral Review

Name: ______________________ Date: ______________

Directions: Solve each problem.

1. Write an equivalent expression using the Distributive Property.

$5a + 25 =$ ________

2. A circle has a circumference of 46π. What is the diameter?

____

3. Use the graph to answer the questions.

a. What is the constant of proportionality? $k =$ ________

b. Write an equation for the graph.

$y =$ ________

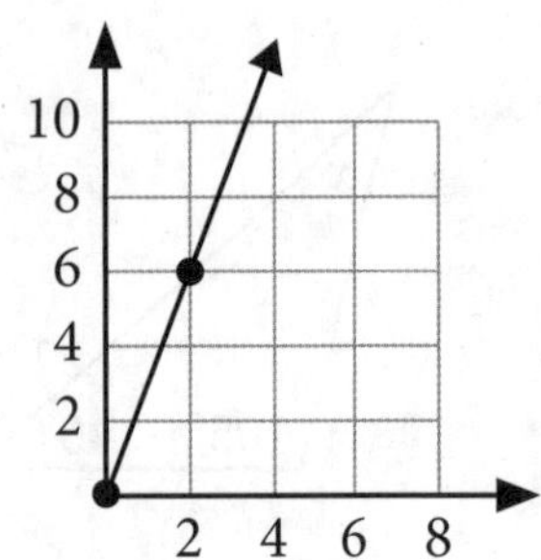

4. What is the surface area of the shape?

Surface Area = ________

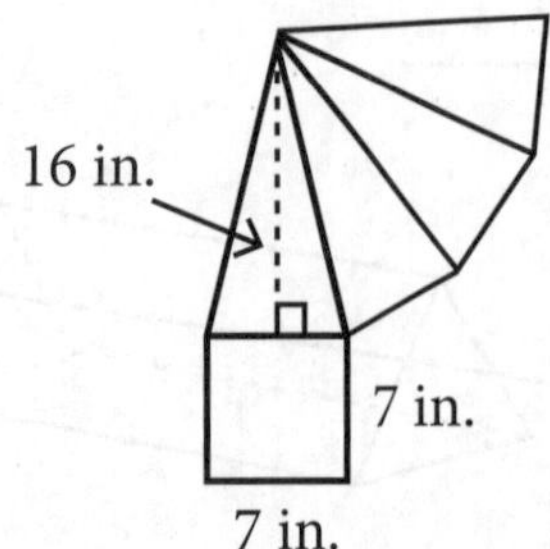

5. Can a triangle be formed with side lengths of 12, 13, and 26?

____

6. Marjorie wants to put $\frac{2}{3}$ of her paycheck in the bank. She earned $300. How much of Marjorie's paycheck will she put in the bank?

____

7. Complete the table.

Fraction	Decimal	Percent
$\frac{1}{5}$		
	0.9	
		18%

8. $7\frac{3}{5} \times 3\frac{1}{2} =$ ________

9. $\frac{2^3}{2^2} =$ ________

10. The hat Marco wants to buy is $45. The store is having a sale for 15% off anything in the store. What is the sale price of the hat?

____

Spiral Review

Learn about Sampling and Making Inferences

Words to Know

inference—an idea or conclusion that can be drawn based on evidence

population—a set of people or things to study

random sample—a sample where each person or item has an equal chance of being chosen

sample—a part of the population that is being studied; a sample should be fair, have enough people or items in it, and be selected randomly

Example 1

A seventh grade math teacher wants to find out if she is doing a good job. Which choice is the best population she can use?

- **a.** a group of 25 seventh graders
- **b.** the girls in seventh grade
- **c.** her first period math class
- **d.** all the seventh graders in all her classes

1. A population is the entire group of people who we want to collect data from. Smaller groups of the population are called **samples**.

2. Which choice includes all of the students? ______________________

Example 2

A computer company wants to know what features customers prefer on their laptops. They decided to collect information from a sample. Which choice represents the most reliable sample?

- **a.** people who have never owned a computer
- **b.** anyone who has purchased a computer from the store
- **c.** only people in the store on the weekend
- **d.** women with desktop or laptop computers

1. A sample is a small part of the population that you are collecting data from. In this case, the population would be everyone who owns a computer. We need a smaller group, or sample, of this population.

2. Which choice includes a smaller group of all the people who own computers?

____

Example 3

Evan is in charge of choosing a new student to dress up as the school mascot. He decides to write the names of everyone on slips of paper and put them in a hat. He will draw one name from the hat for each week of the school year. That student will dress up as the mascot for one week, and then another student will be chosen for the next week, and so on.

Will this method produce a random sample?

1. Evan is writing everyone's name and putting them in the hat. Does everyone have an equal chance of being chosen? ____________________

2. Will Evan's plan produce a random sample? ____________________

Example 4

Marcy wanted to know the favorite color of seventh graders in her school. During the seventh grade lunch period, she asked every 5th seventh grader who entered the cafeteria what their favorite color was. The results are shown in the table. What inference can you make from her results?

Color	Number of Students
blue	28
green	10
red	2

1. Looking at the data, you can see that the most popular color was blue.
   The inference that we can make is that blue is a very popular color, but red is not a popular color at all.

Example 5

Sydney was making charms to sell. She made 150 charms, but 5 were defective. If she makes 450 charms, predict how many charms will be defective.

1. Set up a proportion to solve the problem.
   $\frac{\text{5 defective charms}}{\text{150 total charms}} = \frac{x}{\text{450 total charms}}$

2. Divide 450 by 150 to find the scale factor. What is 450 ÷ 150? __________

3. Next, multiply 5 by the scale factor.
   5 × __________ = __________ defective charms

Name: ______________________ Date: ______________

Directions: Circle the answer that best describes a population for each problem.

1. The ice cream store wants to know what the most popular flavor of ice cream is for its customers. Which population should they use?

a. the first 50 customers on Monday

b. all the customers who purchase ice cream at the store

c. teenagers who purchase ice cream

d. Friday night customers

2. The soccer coach wants to know what color jerseys the team wants her to purchase. Which population should she use?

a. all the students in the school

b. all the students on the baseball team

c. all the students on the soccer team

d. the players who score the most goals on the team

3. The librarian wants to know what kind of books kindergarteners enjoy. Which population should he use?

a. all the students in the school

b. the middle school students in the district

c. the 25 kindergarteners in Mrs. Smith's class

d. all the kindergarteners in the school

4. The cafeteria cook wants to know what meals middle school students prefer for lunch. Which population should he use?

a. only students who bought lunch on Friday

b. all middle school students

c. all the students who pack their lunch

d. students who don't like hamburgers

5. A cell phone company wants to know how many texts teenagers send in a week. Which population should they use?

a. anyone who pays for a cell phone from that company

b. parents who have cell phones for their children

c. all teenagers with cell phones

d. anyone ages 5–12 with cell phones

6. A bakery wants to know what muffin flavors are the customers' favorites. Which population should they use?

a. teenagers who buy the muffins

b. all the customers from the bakery

c. people who love chocolate

d. new customers

Name: ______________________________ Date: ______________

Directions: Circle the answer that describes the most reliable sample for each problem.

1. The principal wants to know how long, on average, it takes middle school students to get to school. Which sample should he use?

a. every 20th student who walks through the front door of the school
b. all the eighth grade students
c. students in classes on the first floor
d. only students who ride the bus

2. A potato chip company wants to see if people in the United States like the new flavor of potato chips they are selling. Which sample should they use?

a. a selection of people from every state
b. teenagers in the southern states
c. only people from the west coast
d. a selection of adult women

3. A poll worker wants to know how people feel about current events in their town. Which sample should they use?

a. women voters from the town
b. adults ages 18–25 in the town
c. a selection of people of various ages over the voting age in the town
d. only elderly voters from the town

4. One student wants to know the most popular pet of eighth grade students. Which sample should he use?

a. all middle school students
b. 10 students from every eighth grade class
c. all eighth grade students
d. only students who do not like cats

5. Garrett wants to know how much people charge for babysitting. Which sample should he use?

a. 30 students with siblings
b. only students who have dogs
c. 25 students who babysit on the weekends
d. students ages 5–10

6. A restaurant wants to know if they should offer different flavors of iced tea. Which sample should they use?

a. all female customers
b. every third table in the restaurant each day for a week
c. calling random telephone numbers and asking the opinions of people who answer
d. every person who orders coffee

Name: ______________________________ Date: ______________

Directions: Determine whether the sample will be a random sample. Circle *yes* or *no*. If the answer is no, explain why the sample is not a random sample.

1. Mira, a seventh grader, wants to know what eighth graders do in their free time after school. She decides to ask the students in her homeroom.

yes no

____

2. Simeon wants to know what the most popular cake flavor is at the bakery. He surveys every fifth customer who enters the bakery for a week.

yes no

____

3. The post office wants to know, on average, what time the mail is delivered. They decide to ask the people who live on the same street as the post office.

yes no

____

4. The student council at the middle school wants to know what students would like to do for spirit week. They decide to put together a survey and pass it out to five students in every homeroom who were chosen through a lottery by the teacher.

yes no

____

5. The principal of the middle school wants to choose 25 students to attend a leadership conference. He chooses 25 students with the highest grade point average.

yes no

____

6. Mrs. Jackson wants to choose 5 classroom helpers. She places all the students' identification numbers on slips of paper in a bowl and chooses 5 numbers. Those students become the classroom helpers.

yes no

____

7. A cell phone company wants to know what color to make the next new cell phones. They decide to survey 30 people at the mall on Saturday morning.

yes no

____

8. The math teacher wants to know about how many minutes are spent on math homework. She assigns each student in seventh grade a number and then uses a number generator program to select 40 numbers. These are the students she collects data from.

yes no

____

Name: ______________________ Date: ______________

Quick Tip

Remember, an **inference** is a conclusion that is made based on data or evidence collected.

Directions: Write an inference you could make based on the data collected.

1. Ryan wanted to know what pets the students in his class have. He collected the data in the table.

____

Pet	Number of Students
dog	14
cat	11
bird	3
fish	2

2. Ruiz asked every 10th student who entered the school what their favorite subject was when given three options. The results are in the table.

____

Subject	Number of Students
art	30
physical education	18
music	11

3. A grocery store wanted to know which day of the weekend had the most customers so they could have enough employees working. An employee marked a tally for every customer who walked into the store on each of the three days. The results are in the table.

____

Day of the Week	Number of Customers
Friday	145
Saturday	275
Sunday	128

4. Mrs. Smith collected test scores from her first period class and recorded them in the table.

____

Grade	Number of Students
A	4
B	5
C	6
D	10

5. A radio station wanted to know their listeners' favorite types of music. They asked listeners to call in, and they recorded every 5th caller's response. The results are shown in the table.

____

Type of Music	Number of Votes
country	110
rap	98
rock	45

6. The student council was choosing a theme for the school dance. They decided to poll the students, so they randomly chose 10 students from each homeroom and recorded their responses. The results are shown in the table.

____

Theme	Number of Votes
beach	32
winter wonderland	24
patriotic	8

Name: ______________________________ Date: ________________

Directions: Solve each problem.

1. The middle school polled students, asking whether they prefer to have the school dance on Friday night or Saturday night. Of the 75 students polled, 25% said they prefer the dance on Friday night. If all 440 students were polled, how many do you predict would prefer the dance on Friday night?

____

2. The mayor polled residents, asking if they would like the curbs in front of their houses painted. Of the 200 residents polled, 65% said they would like the curb painted. If the mayor polled all 3,000 residents, how many do you predict would like the curbs in front of their houses painted?

____

3. The soccer coach polled parents, asking how far they would be willing to travel for soccer games. They polled 50 parents, and 20% of them said they would be willing to drive up to 40 miles away. If they polled 250 parents, how many do you predict would say they would be willing to travel up to 40 miles away?

____

4. The concession stand workers wanted to know whether customers thought they should sell popcorn. Of the 80 customers surveyed, 85% of them said the stand should sell popcorn. If 1,500 customers were surveyed, how many of them do you predict would say the stand should sell popcorn?

____

5. A newspaper employee wanted to know how many people still get a newspaper. Of the 200 people polled, 80 of them stated that they still get the newspaper. If the employee polled 4,000 people, how many do you predict would say they still get a newspaper?

____

6. A high school student was asking her classmates if they work part-time jobs. Of the 60 students asked, 18 of them replied that they do work part-time jobs. If she asked 300 students, how many do you predict work part-time jobs?

____

Learn about Data and Graphs

Words to Know

box plot—a way to display data using a five-number summary

distribution—a representation of data

measure of center—a single number used to summarize a set of numerical data; measures of center are mean, median, and mode

measure of variability—how the data in a distribution is spread out; measures of variability are the range and the interquartile range

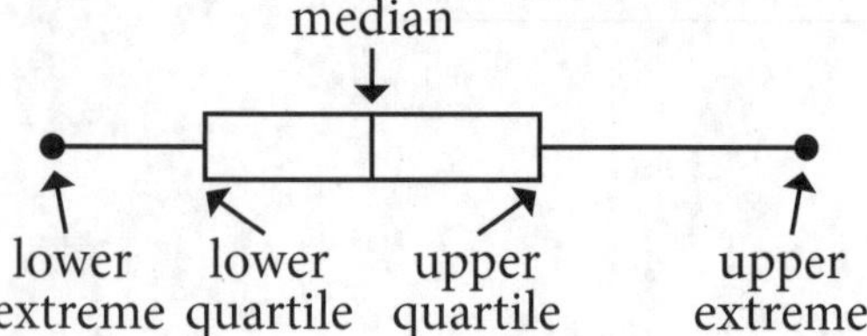

The **upper** and **lower extremes** are the highest and lowest data points in the set.

The **range** is the difference between the upper extreme and the lower extreme.

The **median** is the middle number, when the data are arranged from least to greatest.

The **lower quartile** is the median of the lower half of the data, while the **upper quartile** is the median of the upper half of the data.

The **interquartile range (IQR)** is found by subtracting the upper quartile and the lower quartile. The IQR includes 50% of the total data.

Example 1

According to the box plots, which team had more average wins per season?

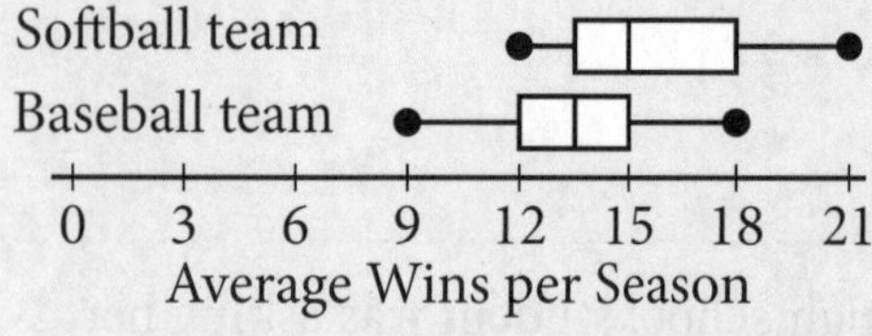

1. You can look at different measures to compare them. Complete the table, comparing the measures.

	Median	Range
softball team		
baseball team		

2. If we are looking at the measure of center, or the median, we can conclude that the ________________ team has a higher median.

3. If we are looking at the measure of variability, or the range, we can conclude that ________________________.

4. We can conclude that the ________________ team had more average wins per season.

Name: ________________________ Date: ________________

Directions: Use the data to answer the questions.

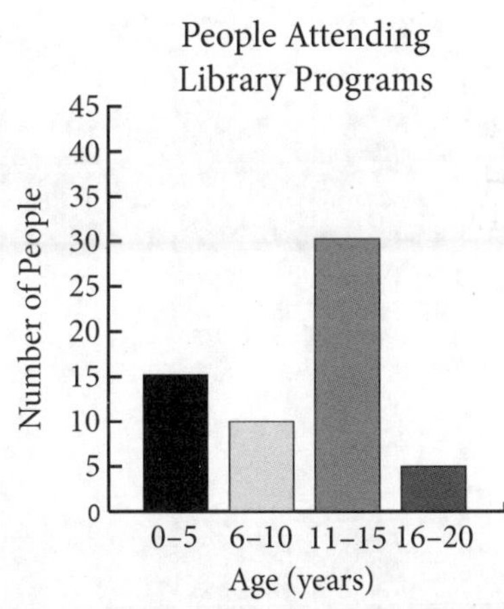

1. How many total people attended the library programs? ________________

2. What is the most popular age group to attend library programs? ________________

3. Which age group attended library programs the least?

____

Marvin's Money

Savings 33%

College 50%

17%

Spending

4. If Marvin earns $500, how much of his earnings will go into his savings account? ________________

5. How much of Marvin's $500 will go toward college?

____

6. How much of Marvin's money is left for spending?

____

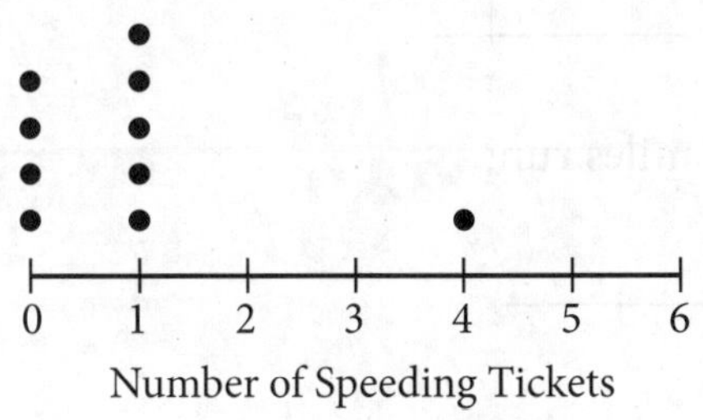

7. How many people were asked how many speeding tickets they had received? ________________

8. What is the range of the number of speeding tickets?

____

9. What is the median number of speeding tickets received? ________________

Name:______________________________ Date:______________

Directions: Use the line plots to answer the questions.

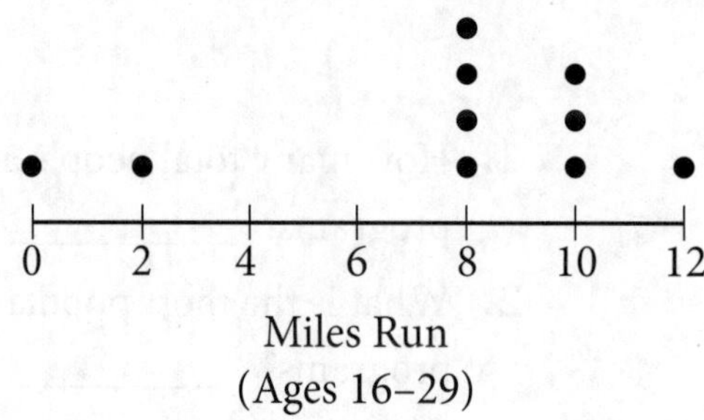

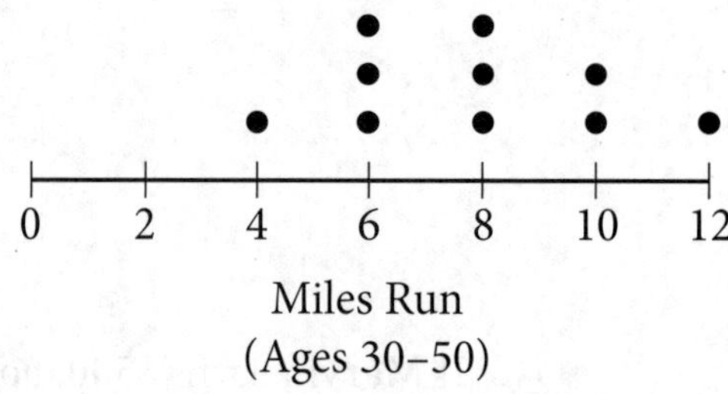

1. What is the range of miles run for ages 16–29? __________

2. What is the range of miles run for ages 30–50? __________________

3. Which age group has more variability in the number of miles run? __________________

4. What is the median number of miles run for ages 16–29? __________

5. What is the median number of miles run for ages 30–50? __________

6. What can you conclude about the medians for number of miles run?

____

7. Based on the data, which age group would you say runs more miles? __________

Name: ______________________________ Date: ________________

Directions: Use the data to answer the questions.

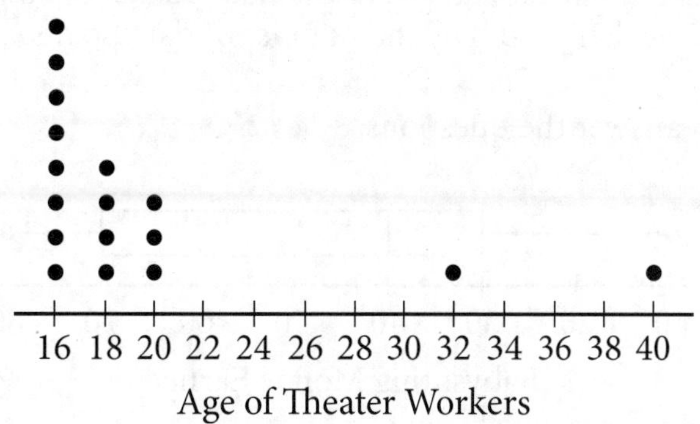

Age of Theater Workers

1. How many theater workers are represented on the dot plot? __________

2. What is the age range of theater workers, according to the data? __________

3. What is the median age of the theater workers, according to the data? __________

4. Looking at the data, what would you estimate is a typical age for a theater worker?

____

5 10 15 20 25 30 35 40 45

Number of Times Teenagers Went to the Pool

5. What is the range of the data? __________

6. What is the interquartile range of the data? __________

7. What is the median of the data? __________

8. What is the fewest number of times anyone went to the pool, according to the data?

____

9. Based on the data, what is a typical number of times a teenager would go to the pool?

____

Name: ______________________ Date: ______________

Quick Tip

To find the mean, add all of the data points together, and divide the sum by the number of data points.

Directions: Use the data to answer the questions.

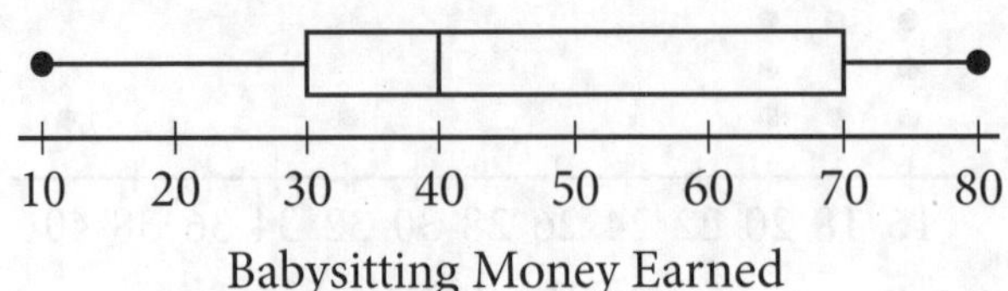

1. What is the IQR of the box plot? ____________
2. What is the range of the box plot? ____________
3. Does the data represented in the box plot have a lot of variability? Explain your answer.

   ____

4. According to the data, what is the typical amount of money earned babysitting? Explain your answer. ______________________________

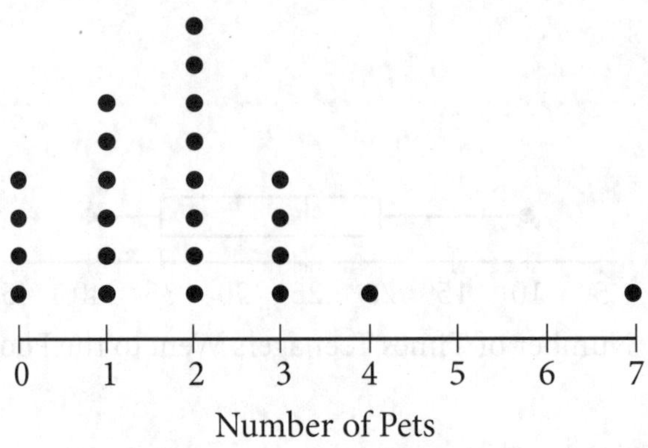

5. What is the range of number of pets? ____________
6. Does the data represented on the dot plot have a lot of variability? Explain your answer.

   ____

7. What is the median number of pets that people reported having? ____________
8. What is the mean number of pets that people reported having? ____________
9. Based on the data, what is the typical number of pets that people have? Explain your answer.

   ____

Name: ________________________ Date: ______________

Quick Tip

A large range or large IQR means there is a large amount of variability. If there is a great deal of variability, we can say the data are not as reliable. Variability makes it difficult to make predictions because the data are not as consistent.

Directions: A math teacher is comparing test scores for her first two classes. The data are displayed on the box plots. Use the data to answer the questions.

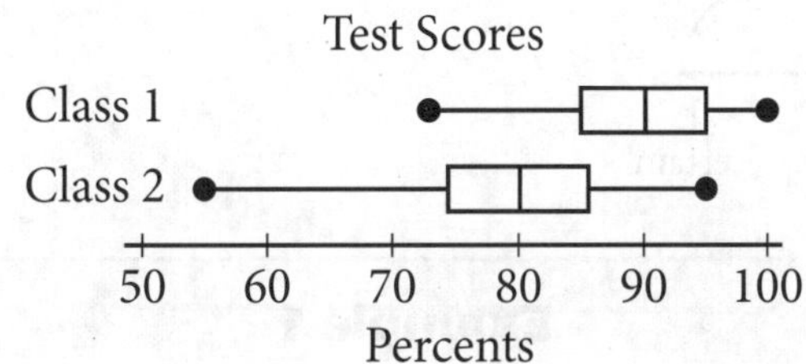

1. Which class has a higher median? ____________
2. Which class has a higher range? ____________
3. Which class has a higher IQR? ____________
4. Which class has more variability in their scores? ____________
5. According to the data, which class scored higher on their tests? ____________

Directions: Enrique is comparing the average monthly car payment in 2020 with 2022. The data are displayed on the box plots. Use the data to answer the questions.

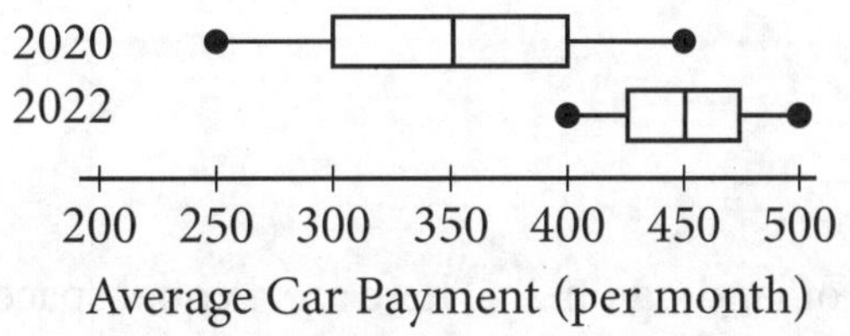

6. Which year has a higher median? ____________
7. Which year has a higher range? ____________
8. Which year has a higher IQR? ____________
9. Which year has more variability in the monthly car payment? ____________
10. According to the data, which year has higher average car payments? ____________

Learn about Probability

Probability is the likelihood of an event occurring. Probability must be a value between 0 and 1. There are two types of probability.

Experimental probability is found by collecting data through an experiment and using the results to find the probability.

Theoretical probability is finding the probability by analyzing all the possible outcomes.

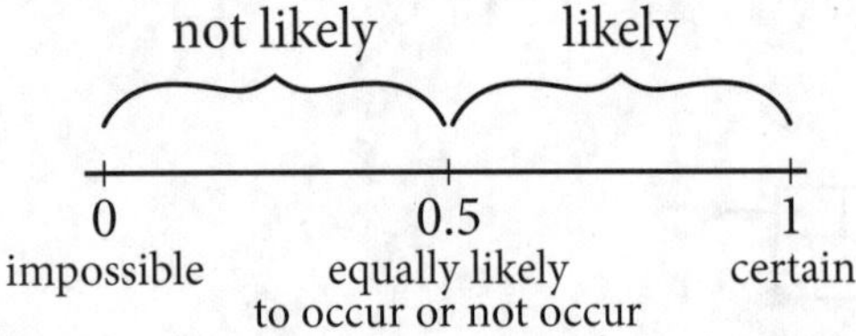

Example 1

What is the probability that the sun will rise tomorrow?

1. The sun rises every day. This is certain to happen, so the probability written as a decimal is 1.
2. We can also write probability as a fraction or percent. The probability that the sun will rise tomorrow, written as a fraction, is $\frac{1}{1}$. Written as a percent, it is 100%.

Example 2

If you spin the spinner 200 times, how many times would you expect to land on number 2?

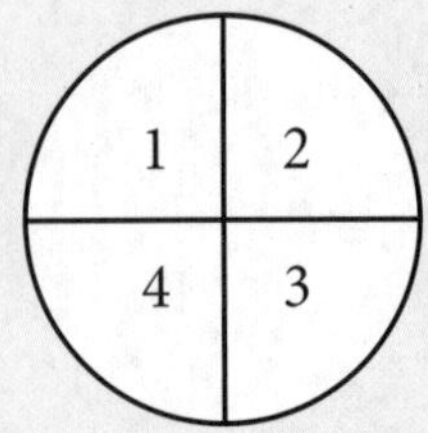

1. Find the probability of landing on 2. There are 4 equal spaces, and 1 of the spaces has a 2, so the probability of spinning a 2 is $\frac{1}{4}$ or 0.25.
2. Now, we can multiply the probability we found in Step 1 by the number of times we are spinning the spinner.

   ____________ × 200 = ____________ times

Name: ______________________________ Date: ________________

Directions: Write an estimated probability for each event occurring. Your answer can be a decimal, a fraction, or a percent.

1. flipping tails on a coin ____________
2. driving a car as a seventh grader ____________
3. snow in California in July ____________
4. eating your shoe ____________
5. guessing the right answer on a multiple-choice question with 4 options ____________
6. picking a card with hearts from a deck of cards ____________
7. rolling a 5 on a number cube ____________
8. blinking your eyes ____________
9. a pig flying over your house ____________
10. you eating a slice of pizza this week ____________
11. raining at least one day this week ____________
12. choosing a green block out of a bag with 4 green blocks and 1 red block ____________
13. rolling an even number on a number cube ____________
14. you being absent from school at least 1 day this year ____________

Name: ______________________ Date: ______________

Quick Tip

The sum of all probabilities for any event is always 1.

For example, the probability of rolling a 3 on a number cube is $\frac{1}{6}$. The probability of not rolling a 3 on the number cube is $\frac{5}{6}$ because $1 - \frac{1}{6} = \frac{5}{6}$, and $\frac{5}{6} + \frac{1}{6} = \frac{6}{6} = 1$.
The **probability** is the desired event, while the remaining probability is called the **complement**.

Directions: In a bag, there are 4 red balls and 6 yellow balls. Use the bag to answer the questions.

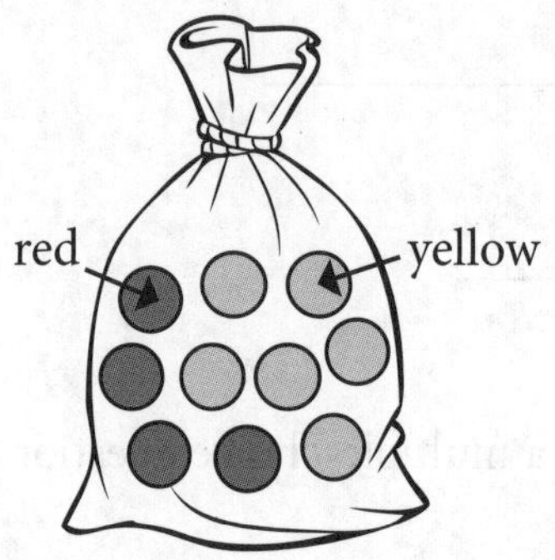

1. What is the probability of picking a yellow ball from the bag? ____________
2. What is the complement to the probability in problem 1? ____________
3. What is the probability of picking a red ball from the bag? ____________
4. What is the complement to the probability in problem 3? ____________

Directions: Use the spinner to answer the questions.

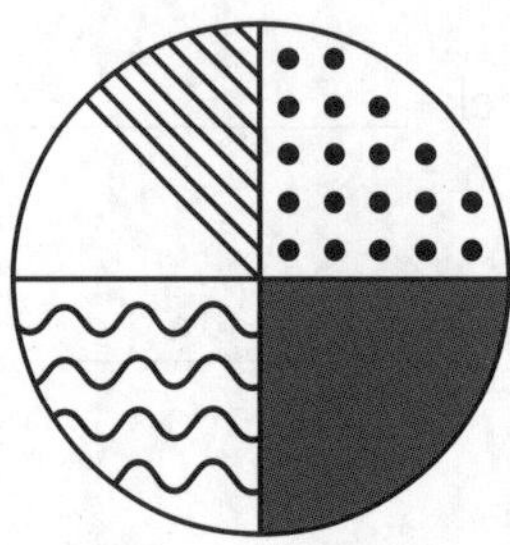

5. What is the probability of the spinner landing on the shaded space? ____________
6. What is the complement to the probability in problem 5? ____________
7. What is the probability of the spinner landing on the striped space? ____________
8. What is the complement to the probability in problem 7? ____________

Name: ______________________ Date: ____________

Directions: Use the spinners to answer the questions.

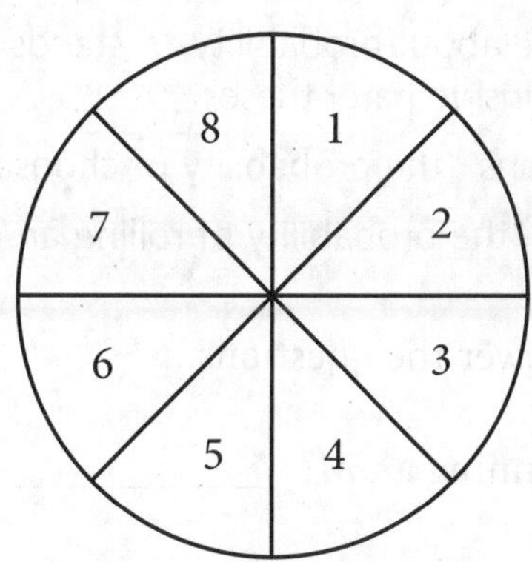

1. If you spin the spinner 400 times, how many times would you expect to spin an 8? ____________

2. If you spin the spinner 400 times, how many times would you expect to spin a number greater than 6? ____________

3. If you spin the spinner 400 times, how many times would you expect to spin an odd number? ____________

4. If you spin the spinner 400 times, how many times would you expect to spin a 2 or lower? ____________

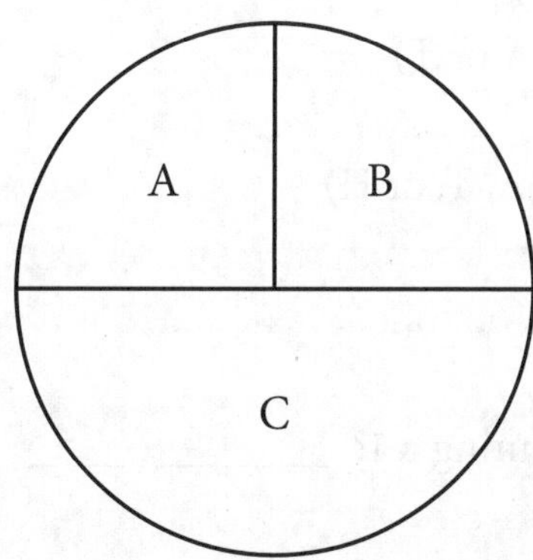

5. If you spin the spinner 200 times, how many times would you expect to spin a vowel? ____________

6. If you spin the spinner 200 times, how many times would you expect to spin a *C*? ____________

7. If you spin the spinner 200 times, how many times would you expect to spin a *B* or *C*? ____________

8. If you spin the spinner 200 times, how many times would you expect to spin a letter in the word *bat*? ____________

Name: ______________________________ Date: ____________________

Quick Tip

We use notation to write about probability. *P* stands for probability, and the desired event is written inside parentheses.

For example: P(red) means "the probability of choosing red."

P(even number) means "the probability of rolling an even number."

Directions: Use the spinners to answer the questions.

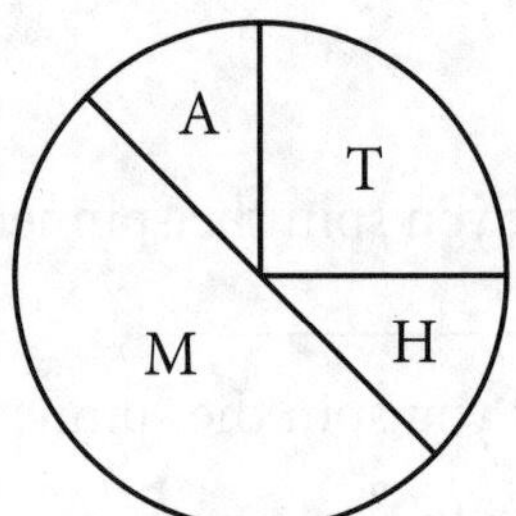

1. What is the probability of spinning an *M*? ____________
2. What is the probability of spinning an *A*? ____________
3. What is the probability of spinning a *T*? ____________
4. What is the probability of spinning an *H*? ____________
5. Use <, >, or = to compare the probabilities.
   a. P(A) ____________ P(M)
   b. P(T) ____________ P(H)
   c. P(H) ____________ P(A or T)
   d. P(M) ____________ P(A, T, or H)

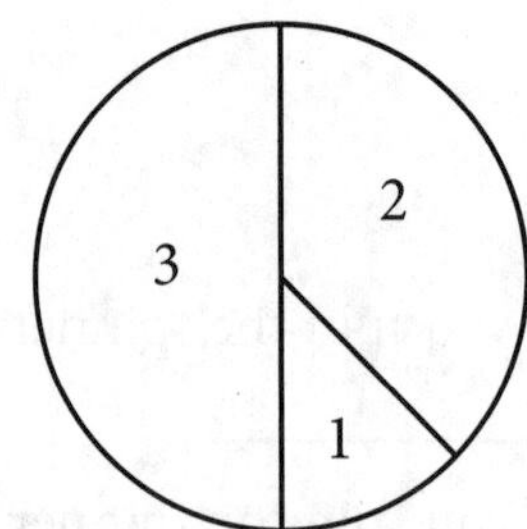

6. What is the probability of spinning a 1? ____________
7. What is the probability of spinning a 2? ____________
8. What is the probability of spinning a 3? ____________
9. Use <, >, or = to compare the probabilities.
   a. P(3) ____________ P(1)
   b. P(1 or 2) ____________ P(3)
   c. P(2) ____________ P(1)

Probability

Name: ______________________________ Date: ________________

Quick Tip

The **relative frequency** can be found by counting how often an event occurs and writing the number as a fraction. The denominator is the total number of events.

Example: Dario played tennis 13 days in August. There are 31 days in August, so the relative frequency of Dario playing tennis in August is $\frac{13}{31}$.

Directions: Answer the questions.

1. Jamal rode his bike to the park and passed through 8 intersections, 5 of which had stop signs. What is the relative frequency of Jamal riding his bike through an intersection with a stop sign? ____________

2. Marquita took 12 quizzes and scored As on 10 of them. What is the relative frequency of Marquita scoring As on her quizzes? ____________

3. Sven watched 30 movies, 25 of which were comedies. What is the relative frequency that Sven watched a movie that was a comedy? ____________

4. Van played 24 baseball games. His team won 19 games. What is the relative frequency of Van's team winning baseball games? ____________

5. Margie rolled a number cube 60 times. How many times would you expect her to roll a 5?

   ____

6. Jin flipped a coin 70 times. How many times would you expect Jin to flip tails?

   ____

7. Compare using >, <, or =.
   a. On a fair coin P(heads) _______ P(tails)
   b. On a number cube P(odd) _______ P(number greater than 5)
   c. On a spinner divided into 4 equal sections numbered 1 through 4 P(1) _______ P(4)

8. Estimate the probability.
   a. snow falling in the rainforest ____________
   b. rolling a 2 or 4 on a number cube ____________
   c. your birthday falling on the same date every year ____________

Probability

Learn about Probability Models

A **probability model** shows all the possible outcomes of an event and helps you find the probability.

An **area model** uses the entire area of a figure to show all the possible outcomes of an event.

A **frequency table** lists all the possible outcomes along with how many times each one occurred.

The **sample space** is all of the possible outcomes of an event.

A **tree diagram** is another way to show all the possible outcomes of an event.

Example 1

You are spinning a spinner with 4 equal spaces, numbered 1 through 4.

1. What is the sample space? What are the possible outcomes on the spinner? *1, 2, 3, and 4*
2. What is P(3)?
   Of the four numbers on the spinner, only one of them is 3.
   The probability can be written as a fraction: the number of possible desired coutcomes over the total number of possible outcomes. So, the probability of landing on a 3 is $\frac{1}{4}$.

Example 2

Jalel rolled a number cube 20 times. His results are listed in the frequency table. Based on Jalel's experimental data, if he rolls again, what is the probability that he will roll a 3?

Number	Frequency
1	3
2	2
3	4
4	2
5	6
6	3

1. Calculate the probability of Jalel rolling a 3 from his data. The probability is $\frac{4}{20}$.
2. Now, if Jalel rolls again, the probability of him rolling a 3 should be the same as his experimental data. What is P(3)? ________

Example 3

Ayanna works at a shop making sub sandwiches. They are doing a promotion where you spin two spinners and get the items that you land on. Make a tree diagram showing all the possible outcomes.

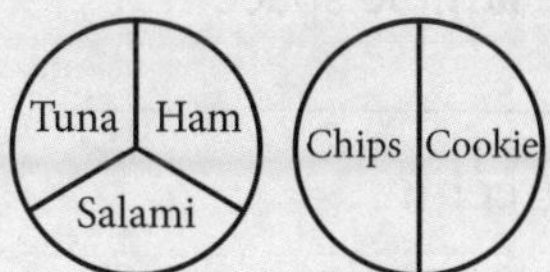

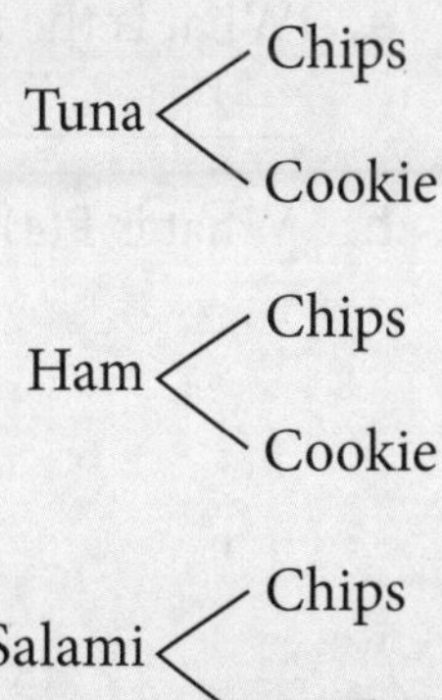

1. Start with the three options on the first spinner. Make two branches for the items on the second spinner off each type of sandwich. The first branches are filled in. Complete the tree diagram to show all the possible outcomes.
2. There are six possible outcomes.

Example 4

Frannie is spinning the spinner and then flipping a coin. Make an area model showing all the possible outcomes.

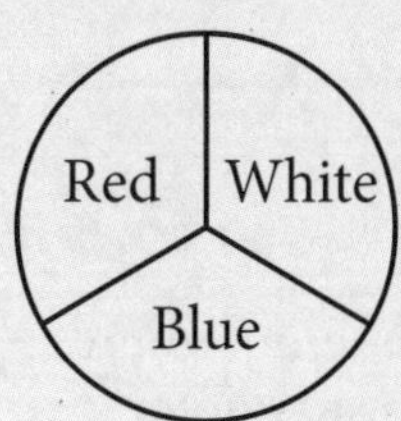

1. First, start with a square. Divide it into three equal rows because there are three equal spaces on the spinner. Label each row with a color from the spinner.

Red	
White	
Blue	

2. Next, divide the area model vertically into two columns, one representing heads and the other representing tails. Label heads and tails at the top of each column, and complete the area model. The first row is modeled for you. R stands for "red," H stands for "heads," and T stands for "tails".

	Heads	Tails
Red	RH	RT
Blue		
White		

3. How many total outcomes are there? ____________

Name: ____________________ Date: ____________

Directions: List the sample space, and find the probability of each event.

1. You have a stack of cards numbered 1 through 5.
   a. What is the sample space?
   ____
   b. What is P(4)? ____________

2. You have a bag of 5 marbles, where 3 are green and 2 are blue.
   a. What is the sample space?
   ____
   b. What is P(blue)? ____________

3. You have a spinner with equal spaces that spells the word *PARTY.*
   a. What is the sample space?
   ____
   b. What is P(T)? ____________

4. You have a standard 6-sided number cube.
   a. What is the sample space?
   ____
   b. What is P(odd number)?
   ____

5. In a bag, you have 5 yellow blocks, 3 red blocks, and 1 green block.
   a. What is the sample space?
   ____
   b. What is P(green)?
   ____

6. On a spinner, there are 8 equal sections numbered 1 through 8.
   a. What is the sample space?
   ____
   b. What is P(1)? ____________

7. You have a 12-sided number cube.
   a. What is the sample space?
   ____
   b. What is P(factor of 12)?
   ____

8. You have a coin for flipping.
   a. What is the sample space?
   ____
   b. What is P(tails)? ____________

Name: ____________________ Date: ____________

Directions: Use the frequency tables of experimental data to answer the questions.

Gabriella works at a cupcake shop that sells different cupcake flavors. She kept track of how many cupcakes of each flavor were sold. The frequency table shows her results.

Cupcake Flavor	Frequency
vanilla	22
chocolate	28
red velvet	15
cookie dough	35

1. Based on Gabriella's data, what is the probability that the next customer will buy a chocolate cupcake? ____________
2. Based on Gabriella's data, what is the probability that the next customer will buy a cupcake that is NOT cookie dough? ____________
3. Based on Gabriella's data, what is the probability that the next customer will buy a cupcake that is either chocolate or vanilla? ____________

Ms. Jackson wanted to know how well students in her classes did on their math test. She recorded her students' test scores in the frequency table.

Percent	Frequency
90–100	21
80–89	25
70–79	18
60–69	9
50–59	2

4. Based on Ms. Jackson's data, what is the probability that a student scores 80–89% on the next test? ____________
5. Based on Ms. Jackson's data, what is the probability that a student scores 70% or higher on the next test? ____________
6. Based on Ms. Jackson's data, what is the probability that a student scores below 60% on the next test? ____________

Remi drew blocks from a bag and recorded her results in the frequency table.

Color	Frequency
blue	15
green	5
yellow	30

7. Based on Remi's data, what is the probability that the next block she draws is blue?

   ____

8. Based on Remi's data, what is the probability that the next block she draws is NOT yellow?

   ____

9. Based on Remi's data, what is the probability that the next block she draws is green or blue?

   ____

Name: ______________________ Date: ______________

Directions: Make a tree diagram showing all the outcomes for each problem. Then, write the total possible outcomes.

1. Ming sells animal stickers online. Her customers get one animal—elephant, lion, tiger, or penguin—chosen at random. She wants to reward her customers with an extra sticker of either a smiley face or a heart chosen at random.

__________ total possible outcomes

2. Jerry and his friends are trying to decide which activity to do. They make a spinner with 4 equal sections labeled *kickball*, *tennis*, *laser tag*, and *basketball* and take one spin. Afterward, they are going out for a treat, so they have a second spinner with *ice cream* and *snow cone* in two equal sections.

__________ total possible outcomes

3. Gary's mom is preparing a surprise dinner. She said Gary can pick one entrée and one vegetable out of two separate bags. The options for entrées are pizza, steak, pork chops, or pasta, and the vegetables are broccoli, asparagus, or peas.

__________ total possible outcomes

4. Milo is using a number cube, marked from 1 to 6, to determine how many miles he will run today. Then, he is flipping a coin to see if he will practice shooting baskets (heads) or walk the dog (tails).

__________ total possible outcomes

Name: ______________________________ Date: ________________

Directions: Make an area model for each problem. Then, write the total possible outcomes.

1. Max is spinning a spinner with 4 equal spaces numbered 1 through 4. Then, he is spinning a second spinner with 3 equal spaces marked A, B, and C.

__________ total possible outcomes

2. Margaret is choosing a theme and a cake flavor for her mother's birthday party. The themes she is considering are carnival, fantasy, beach, and spa. The cake flavors are lemon, strawberry, and blueberry.

__________ total possible outcomes

3. Riley is choosing his outfit for the football game this weekend. He is choosing from jeans, shorts, or sweat pants, and a tank top, T-shirt, or hoodie.

__________ total possible outcomes

4. Marissa is making an exercise plan for the weekend. She can jog, swim, ride a bike, or play volleyball. She also has to decide on the time of day she will exercise—morning, afternoon, or evening.

__________ total possible outcomes

Name: ______________________________ Date: ____________

Directions: Make graphical representations of the given data.

1. Peter asked how many pets everyone in his class had and recorded the data in a table. Make a dot plot representing the data.

Number of Pets	Frequency
0	卌
1	||||
2	卌 卌
3	||

2. A radio station polled callers and asked what type of music they listened to. The results are in the table. Make a circle graph to represent the data.

Type of Music	Percent of Callers
classical	30%
country	20%
pop/rock	25%
rap	25%

3. Theresa surveyed customers at the donut shop about their favorite donut. Her results are in the table. Make a bar graph representing Theresa's data.

Type of Donut	Number of Customers
sprinkles	20
jelly	5
cream-filled	10
glazed	15

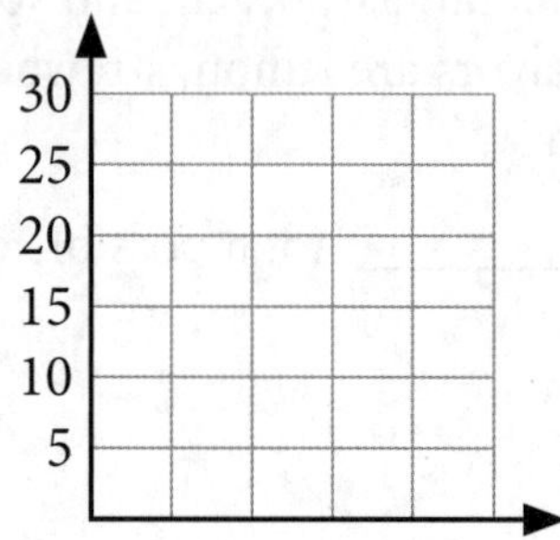

4. Yari asked his classmates how many books they read over the summer and recorded his results in the table. Make a line plot representing Yari's data.

Books Read	Frequency
3 books	6
4 books	3
5 books	3
6 books	1

Learn about Finding Probability

A **compound event** is the likelihood of two independent events occurring; for example, spinning a spinner and then flipping a coin would be a compound event.

An **independent event** is an event whose occurrence does not depend on any other event.

A **simulation** is used to re-create a probability model to collect data and make predictions.

Example 1

Find the probability of spinning a 2 on the spinner and flipping heads on a coin.

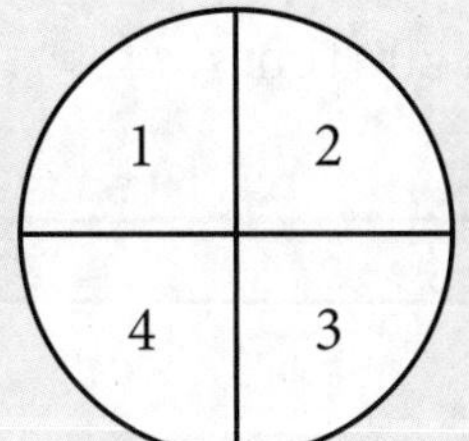

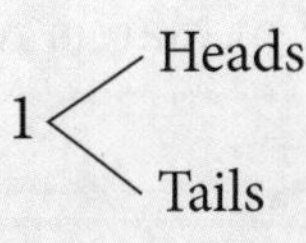

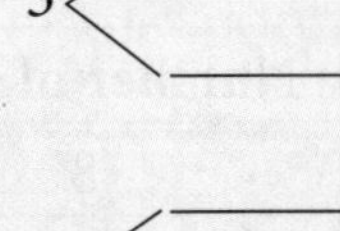

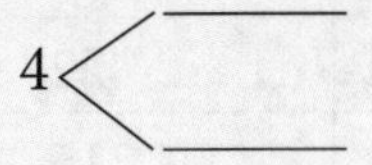

1. To show all the outcomes, or the sample space, make an organized list, a tree diagram, or an area model to represent the sample space. Once the probability model is made, use the model to find the probability. You might choose a tree diagram. Complete the tree diagram to show all the possible outcomes.
2. Using the tree diagram we can see that the probability of spinning a 2 and then flipping heads on the coin is $\frac{1}{8}$.

Example 2

Monte noticed 25% of customers order a cake when they come to the bakery, while the rest of the customers order a different dessert. Design a simulation to model the probability of the next customer at the bakery ordering a cake.

1. Use something that would simulate 25%, such as a spinner or different colored blocks in a bag.
2. If you used a bag of different colored blocks, how many total blocks should go in the bag?

   ____
3. If you use white blocks to represent cake and yellow blocks to represent other desserts, how many white blocks should go in the bag? ____________

   How many yellow blocks should go in the bag? ____________
4. To collect data, you could draw blocks from the bag and record the results.

Example 3

If Marcia rolled a 10-sided number cube, what is the probability that she would roll an 8? If she rolled the number cube 200 times, how many times do you expect her to roll an 8?

1. Find the theoretical probability by analyzing the outcomes. There are 10 sides on the number cube, so the denominator is 10. There is only one side on the number cube with an 8, so the numerator is 1. The probability of rolling an 8 is ______________.
2. Next, using the probability found in Step 1, multiply by 200 to predict how many out of 200 times Marcia would roll an 8.
   $\frac{1}{10} \times 200 =$ ______________
3. The probability of Marcia rolling an 8 after rolling the number cube 200 times is ______________.

Example 4

Henry kept a frequency table of the breeds of dogs people walked down his street last week. Using Henry's experimental data, what is the probability that the next dog walking down his street will be a beagle?

Type of Dog	Number of Dogs
beagle	8
German shepherd	22
golden retriever	15
dachshund	5

1. There are 8 beagles, and 50 total dogs, so we can write the probability as $\frac{8}{50}$. If 100 more dogs walked down the street, how many of them would you expect to be beagles?
2. Find the probability of the dog being a dachshund, which is __________, and multiply that probability by 100. How many dogs will be dachshunds? ______________

Name: ______________________________ Date: ____________________

Directions: Solve each problem.

1. Mack wants to use a spinner to decide which workout he should do. He has the following spinner and a number cube. He is going to spin the spinner once and then roll the number cube. The spinner will tell him the workout and the number cube will tell him how many miles he should complete in his workout. Make a tree diagram to show all the possible outcomes.

What is the probability that Mack will bike for 6 miles?

____

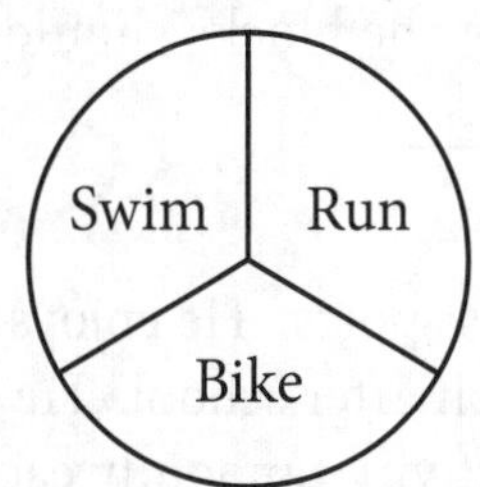

3. Kiki is trying to decide which cereal to have for breakfast and who has to wash the dishes. She makes the following spinner and spins it to decide which cereal to have. Then, she flips a coin to decide who washes the dishes. If she flips heads, she does the dishes, and tails means her brother does the dishes. Make an organized list of all the outcomes.

What is the probability Kiki will eat Yum Yum Puffs and have to wash the dishes?

____

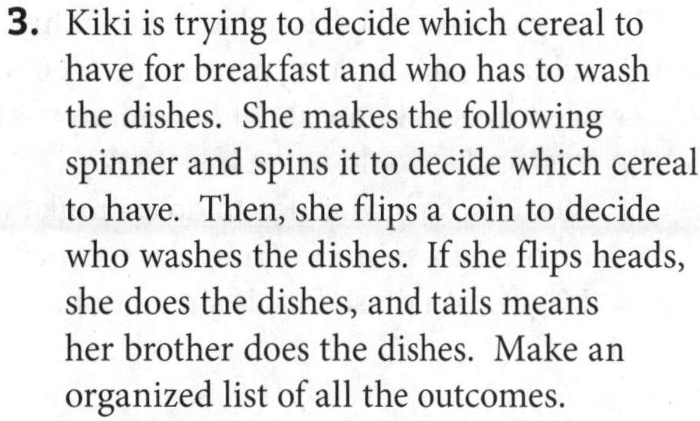

2. Shun is playing a game with his sister. She rolls two number cubes. If the sum is greater than 6, Shun wins. If the sum is 6 or less, his sister wins. Make an area model showing all the possible outcomes.

What is the probability that Shun wins?

____

What is the probability that Shun's sister wins?

____

4. Myka is trying to decide what color to paint her room, so she puts 3 blocks in a bag. One block is green, one block is purple, and one block is pink. She also designs a spinner to decide on the theme of her room. Make a tree diagram or an area model to show all the possible outcomes.

What is the probability that Myka will choose a purple block with a butterfly theme?

____

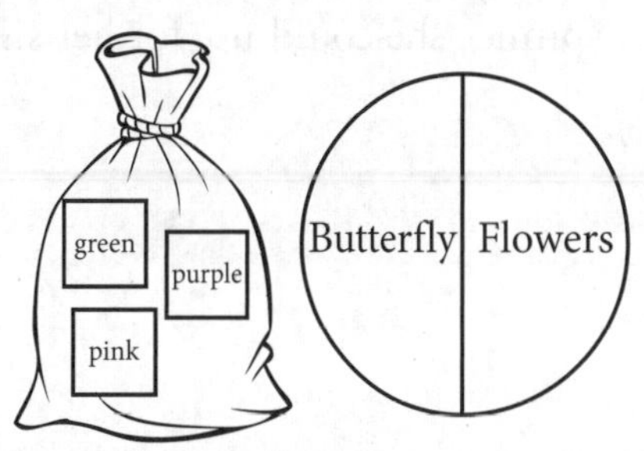

Name: ______________________________ Date: ________________

Directions: Solve each problem.

1. Miguel is on the basketball team at his school. His shooting percentage is 60%. He wants to know about how many baskets he would make if he took 50 shots, so he decided to do a simulation involving a spinner. Draw the spinner Miguel could use for his simulation.

2. Nora's teacher chooses a volunteer each day for her classroom. There are 25 students in the class: 16 boys and 9 girls. Nora wants to know after 30 days about how many girls were picked as volunteers. Nora wants to run a simulation. How should she design the simulation?

____

____

3. Simone is planning an outdoor party, but she is worried about rain. There is a 75% chance of rain the day of the party. Simone wants to simulate the chance of rain by spinning a spinner. Draw the spinner she could use for her simulation.

4. Tyrese calculated his batting average and found that it is 0.250. The playoffs are coming up, and Tyrese wants to know about how many hits he will get in 45 at bats. He decides to draw a block from a bag with blocks. He wants to use blue blocks to simulate getting a hit and red blocks to simulate not getting a hit.

How many blocks should he put in the bag? ____________

How many of the blocks should be blue?

____

How many of the blocks should be red?

____

5. Ramone loves sports. He enjoys playing tennis and golf after school. He wants to choose his activity randomly each day. He wonders how many times he would play tennis after 40 days. How could he use a coin to design a simulation?

____

____

6. Every weekend, Malone does one chore chosen randomly. He either mows the lawn, cleans the hamster cage, or walks the dog. After 30 weekends, he wonders about how many times he will have to clean the hamster cage. How could he use a 6-sided number cube to design a simulation for this question?

____

____

Finding Probability

Name: ______________________ Date: ______________

Directions: Solve each problem.

Reggie and Theo are playing a game. They roll two number cubes and add the numbers together. Complete an area model to find the sample space. Then, use the model to answer the questions.

	1	2	3	4	5	6
1						
2						
3						
4						
5						
6						

1. If Reggie wins with a sum of 7 or greater, what is the probability that Reggie wins?

____

2. If Theo wins with a sum of 6 or less, what is the probability that Theo wins?

____

3. If Theo wins with an odd-numbered sum, what is the probability that Theo wins?

____

Reese and Tiana are playing a game. They roll two number cubes and multiply the numbers together. Complete an area model to find the sample space. Then, use the model to answer the questions.

	1	2	3	4	5	6
1						
2						
3						
4						
5						
6						

4. If Reese wins with a product of 12 or greater, what is the probability that Reese wins?

____

5. If Tiana wins with a product of less than 12, what is the probability that Tiana wins?

____

6. If Reese wins with an even-numbered product, what is the probability that Reese wins?

____

Name: ______________________ Date: ______________

Directions: Solve each problem.

Eliana spun the spinner 50 times, as shown. Her results are in the table. Use Eliana's data to answer the questions.

Number	Frequency
1	8
2	19
3	23

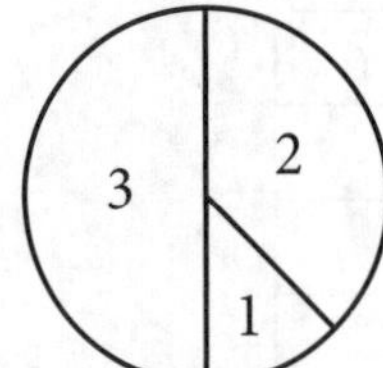

1. What is the probability that Eliana spun a 1? ____________

2. What is the probability that Eliana spun a 2? ____________

3. What is the probability that Eliana spun a 3? ____________

4. What is the probability that Eliana spun a number greater than 1? ____________

Mira flipped two coins 40 times and recorded her results in the table.

Results	Frequency
HH	4
HT	19
TH	11
TT	6

5. What is the probability that Mira flipped two coins that matched? ____________

6. What is the probability that Mira flipped two coins that did NOT match? ____________

7. What is the probability that Mira flipped *at least* one coin with heads? ____________

8. What is the probability that Mira flipped *at least* one coin with tails? ____________

Yara used a random number generator 60 times to generate numbers from 1 through 6. Her results are listed in the table.

Number	Frequency
1	8
2	12
3	12
4	12
5	11
6	5

9. What is the probability that the number 4 or a number greater than 4 was generated? ____________

10. What is the probability that the number 3 or a number less than 3 was generated? ____________

11. What is the probability that the number 6 was generated? ____________

12. What is the probability that the number 1 was generated? ____________

Finding Probability

Name: ______________________ Date: ______________

Directions: Solve each problem.

Javier flipped 3 coins. Complete the tree diagram of all the possible outcomes. Then, list the sample space, and use the information to answer the questions.

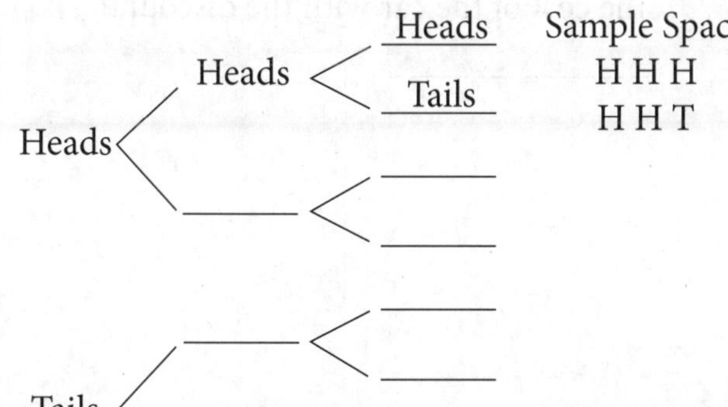

1. How many total outcomes are there? ______________

2. What is the probability that Javier flips all heads or all tails? ______________

3. What is the probability that Javier flips *exactly* two heads? ______________

4. What is the probability that Javier flips *exactly* two tails? ______________

Giovanni spun the spinner 40 times and recorded his results in the table.

Results	Frequency
A	8
B	11
C	8
D	13

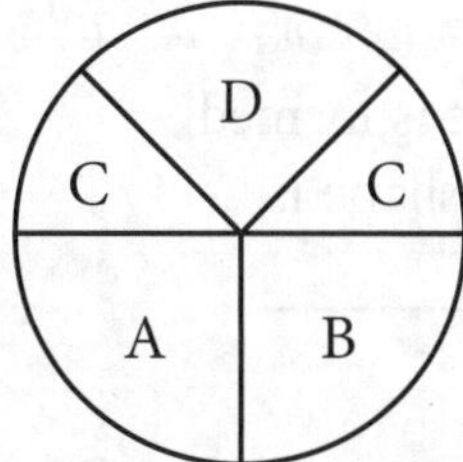

5. What is the probability that Giovanni spun a C? ______________

6. What is the probability that Giovanni spun any letter other than A? ______________

7. What is the probability that Giovanni spun a B? ______________

8. What is the probability that Giovanni did NOT spin a D? ______________

Name: ______________________ Date: ____________

Directions: Solve each problem.

1. What is the circumference of the circle in terms of pi? ____________

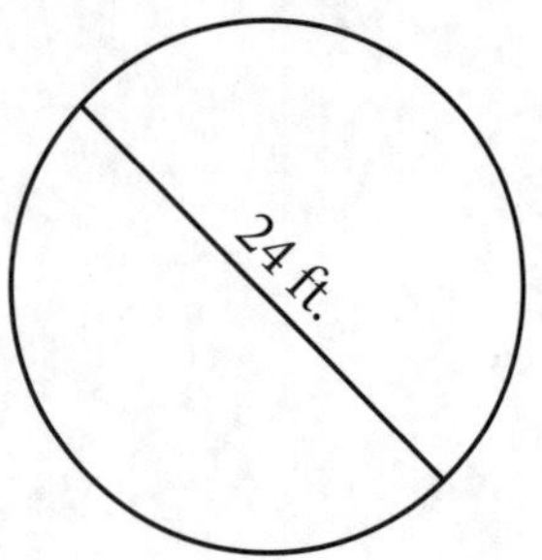

2. What is the surface area of the net?

Surface Area = ____________

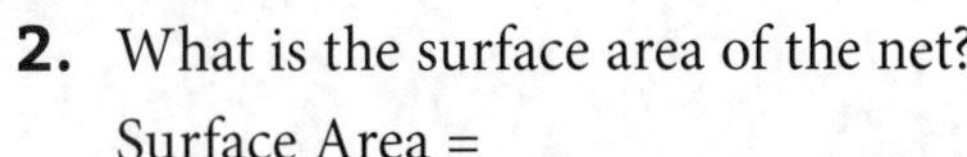

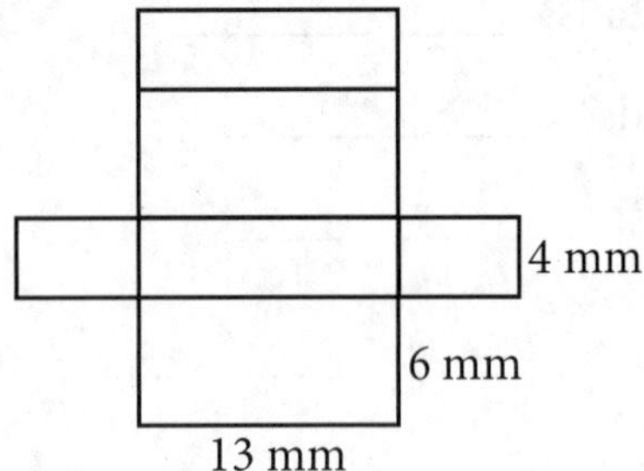

3. What two-dimensional shape is formed when the three-dimensional shape is sliced as indicated? ____________

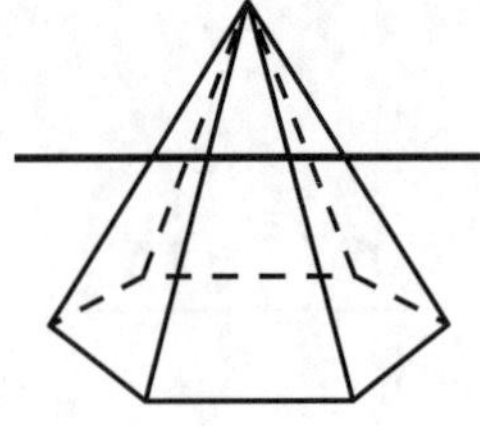

4. What is the additive inverse of –16.2?

____

5. Marni's new car is $25,000, but she gets a loyalty discount of 15%. What is the cost of the car with the discount?

____

6. Is the relationship shown in the table proportional? ____________

x	y
5	40
10	80
15	120
20	160

7. Solve the inequality, and graph the solution on the number line.

$3x - 7 < 17$

x ____________

–8 –7 –6 –5 –4 –3 –2 –1 0 1 2 3 4 5 6 7 8

8. $\frac{40 \text{ sandwiches}}{35 \text{ people}} = \frac{8 \text{ sandwiches}}{x}$

$x =$ ____________

Cumulative Review

Name: ______________________________ Date: ________________

Directions: Solve each problem.

1. What is the constant of proportionality?

$y = 8x$

$k =$ __________

2. What is the scale factor from the first shape to the second shape?

____

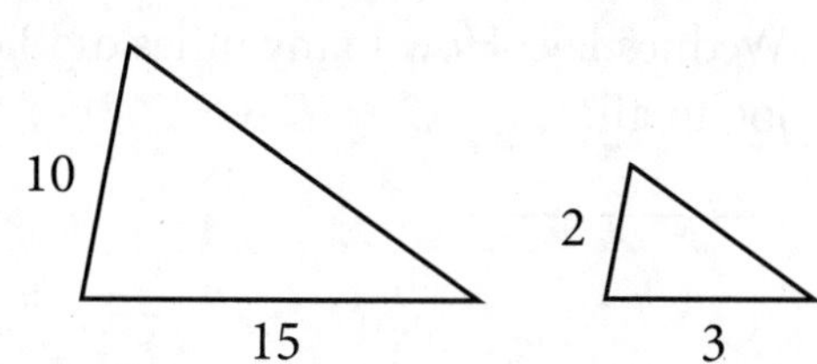

3. What is the area of the figure?

____

8
5
7
4
2

4. Answer the questions as if you were to apply a scale factor of 3 to the triangle.

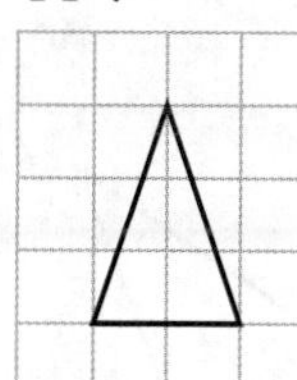

a. What is the base of the scaled copy?

____

b. What is the height of the scaled copy?

____

c. How many times larger is the area of the scaled copy?

____

5. Write an equivalent expression using the Distributive Property.

$4(7 - 3) =$ __________

6. $8.5 - (9 - 7.65) + 6\frac{1}{2} =$ __________

7. Write $\frac{4}{5}$ as a decimal.

____

8. Can a triangle be drawn with side lengths of 21, 23, and 40?

____

Cumulative Review

Name: ____________________ Date: ____________

Directions: Solve each problem.

1. What is the missing side length of the scaled triangle?

$x =$ __________

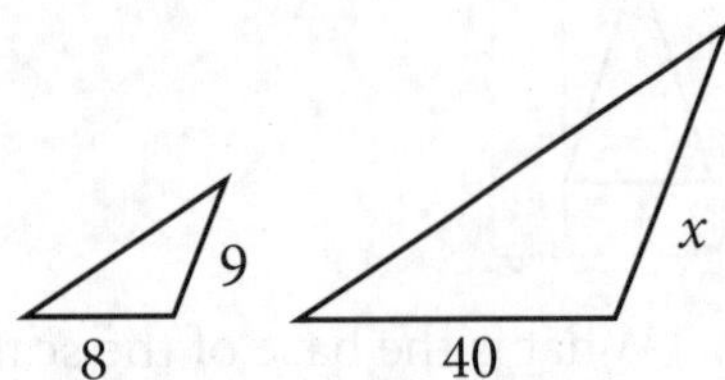

2. What is the measure of the missing angle?

$x =$ __________

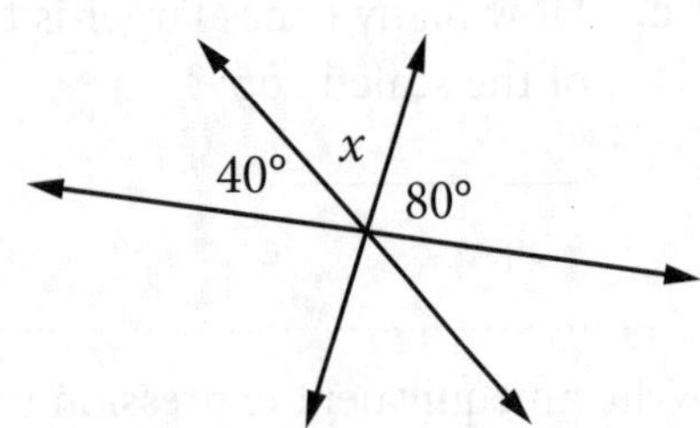

3. Use the graph to answer the questions.

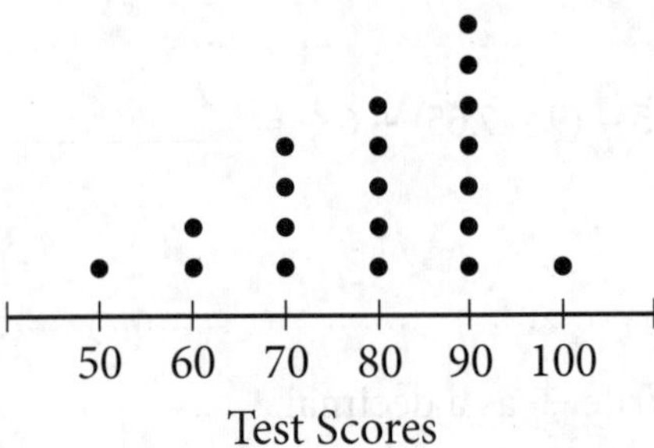

a. How many test scores are represented on the line plot?

____

b. What is the range of test scores?

____

c. What is the median of the test scores?

____

4. Is 5 a solution of $3x + 6 = 21$?

____

5. James jogged $9\frac{1}{2}$ miles on Monday, 6.75 miles on Tuesday, and $8\frac{3}{4}$ miles on Wednesday. How many miles did James jog in all?

____

6. What is the measure of the missing angle?

$x =$ __________

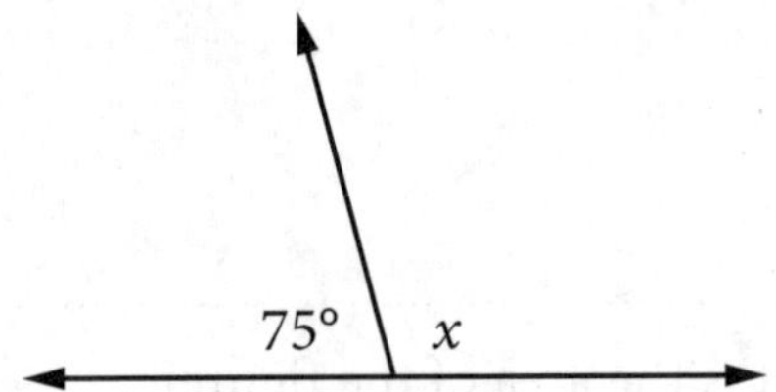

7. $6\frac{2}{5} \div 1\frac{3}{5} =$ __________

8. Write 14% as a decimal. __________

Cumulative Review

Name: ______________________________ Date: ________________

Directions: Solve each problem.

1. Use the phrase to answer the questions.
81 pencils for 27 students

a. What is the rate?

____

b. What is the unit rate?

____

5. What is the missing angle of the triangle?

$x =$ __________

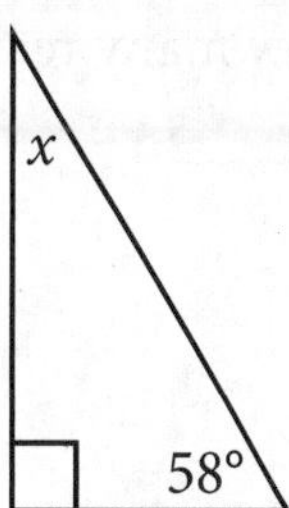

2. Are the expressions equal?

Circle *yes* or *no*

$4(x + 3)$ and $4x + 12$

6. Rafael spent 30% of his 90-day summer at work. How many days did Rafael work?

____

3. $3(3 - 8) + (-7) - 4^2 =$ __________

7. What is the area of the circle in terms of pi? __________

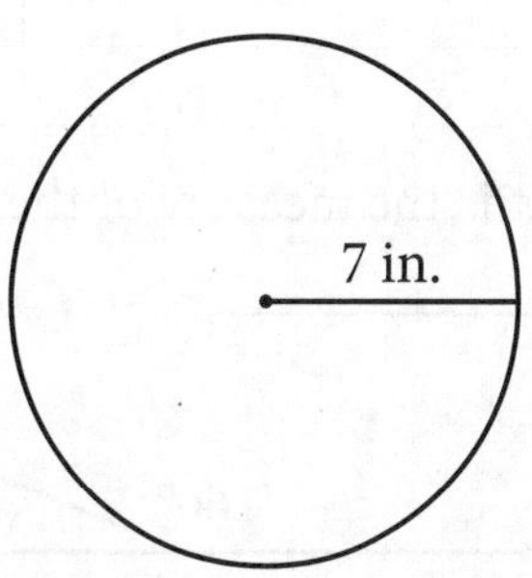

4. What is the measure of the missing angle?

$x =$ __________

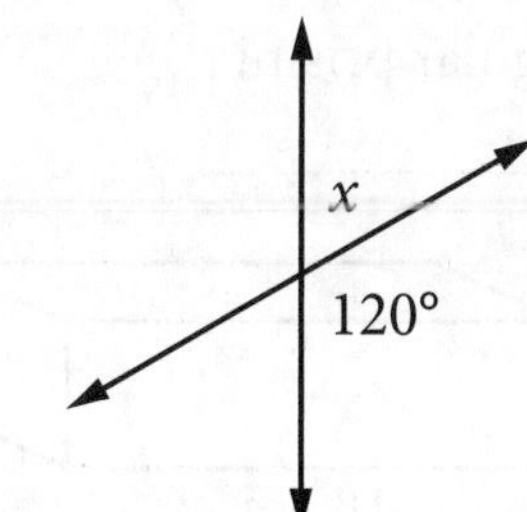

8. Write an equation for *seven times a number, increased by 4, is equal to 14.*

____

Cumulative Review

Name: ______________________ Date: ______________

Directions: Solve each problem.

1. Yani has $6\frac{3}{4}$ cups of sugar in a three-pound bag. Yani is making a cookie recipe that calls for $2\frac{1}{2}$ cups of sugar. How many recipes can Yani make?

____

2. Complete the table.

Fraction	Decimal	Percent
$\frac{1}{5}$		
	0.55	
		84%

3. What is the measure of the missing angle?

x = __________

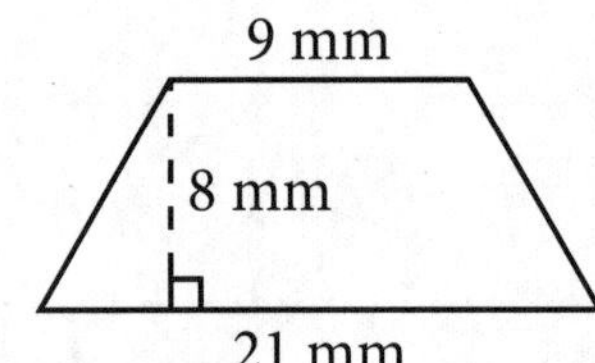

4. What is the missing side length in the scaled figures?

Scale factor __________

x = __________

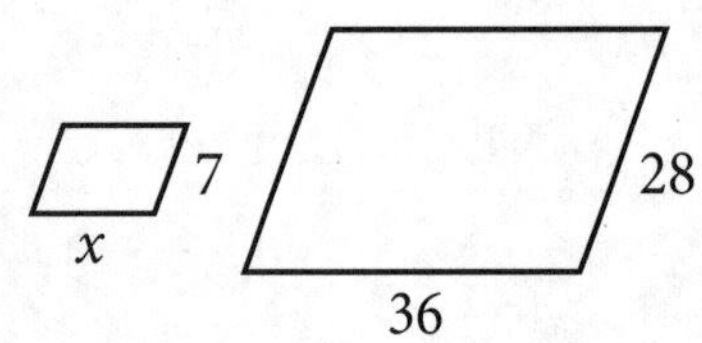

5. Use the graph to answer the questions.

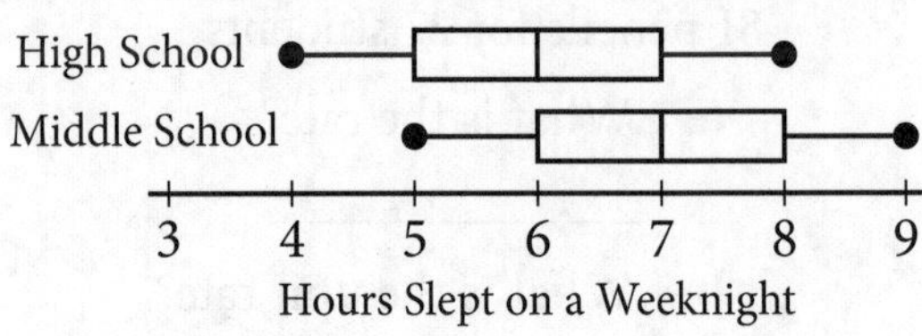

a. Which group of students gets more sleep, on average, on a weeknight?

____

b. Which group of students has a higher median?

____

6. What percent of Malik's expenses are his car and house together? __________

Expenses

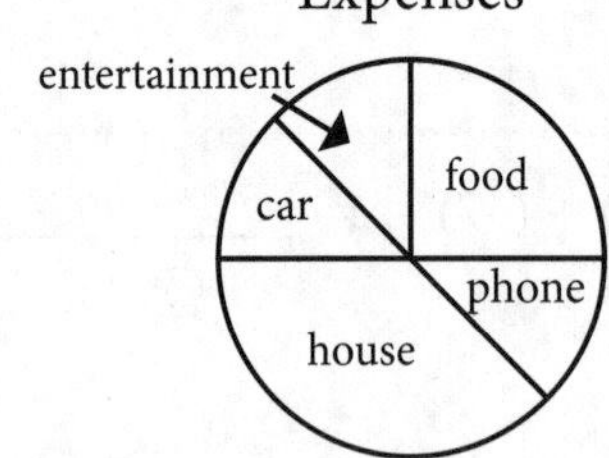

7. What is the area (A) of the trapezoid?

A = __________

9 mm

8 mm

21 mm

8. What is the volume (V) of the rectangular prism?

V = __________

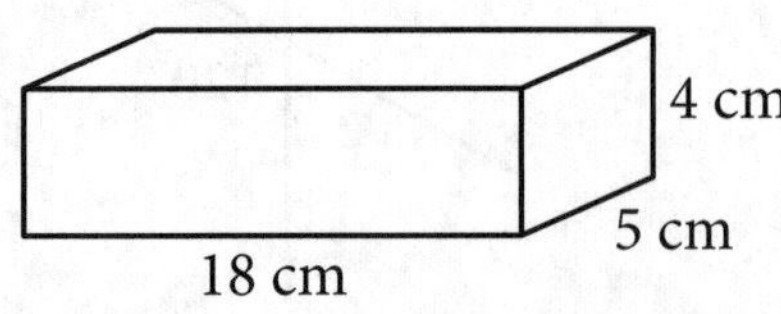

Cumulative Review

Name: ________________________________ Date: ________________

Directions: Solve each problem.

1. If the circumference of a circle is 72π, what is the diameter? ______________

2. What is the area (A) of the shape?

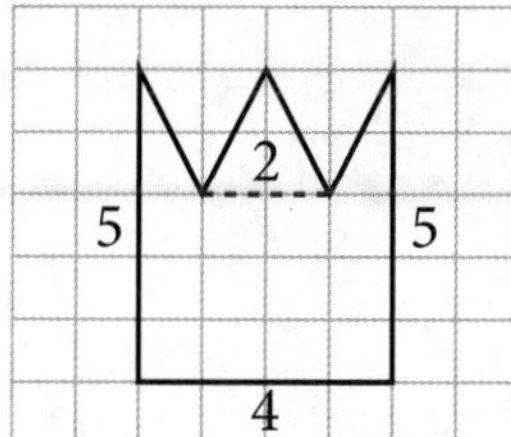

$A =$ ______________

3. What is the measure of the missing angle?

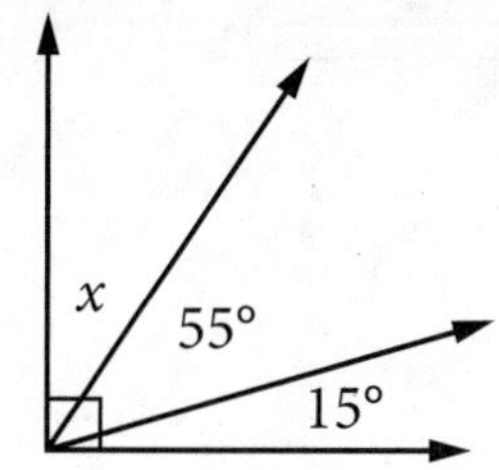

$x =$ ______________

4. Solve the inequality, and graph the solution on the number line.

$5x - 12 \geq 8$

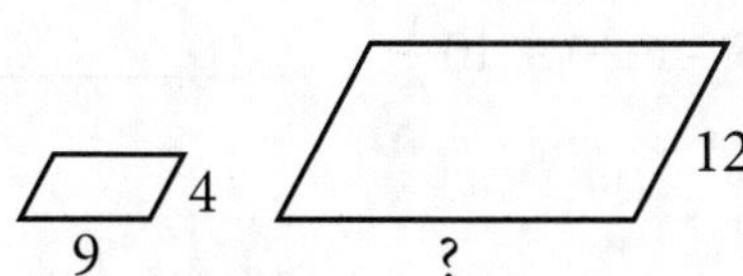

$x =$ ______________

5. What is the missing side length?

? = ______________

6. Is 6 a solution to $2x + 4 < 15$? ______________

7. Answer the questions if the shape had a scale factor of 6.

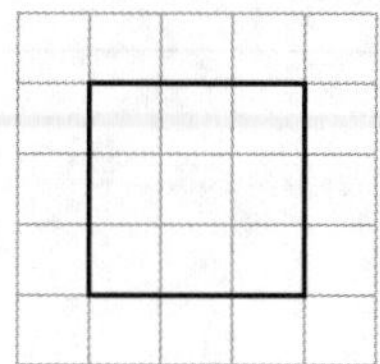

a. What is the new side length? ______________

b. What is the area of the scaled copy? ______________

REVIEW DAY 7

Name: ____________________ Date: ____________

Directions: Solve each problem.

1. Use the box plot to answer the questions.

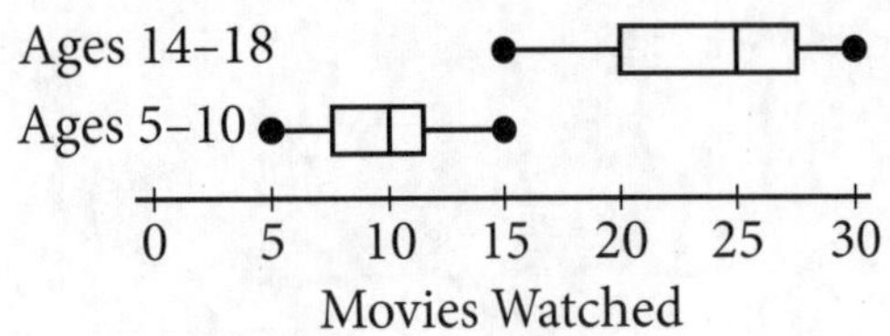

a. Which age group watched more movies?

____

b. Which age group has more variability in their data?

____

c. Which group has a higher median?

____

2. Write an equivalent expression using the Distributive Property.

____________ $= 11x + 55$

3. Use the spinner to answer the questions.

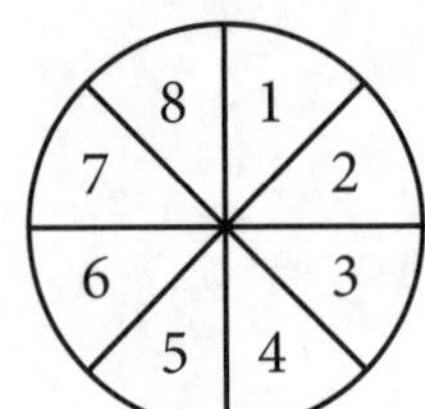

a. What is the probability of spinning a 7?

____

b. What is the probability of spinning an even number?

____

c. What is the probability of spinning a number greater than 5?

____

4. If a circle has an area of 144π, what is the radius? ____________

5. $3(x + 4) = 21$

$x =$ ____________

6. Write an equation for *three times a number plus 6 is equal to 32.*

____

7. $(15.25 - 6\frac{3}{4}) + 10\frac{1}{4} =$ ____________

8. $6^2 - 5 + 3^2 - 20 =$ ____________

Cumulative Review

Name: ______________________ Date: ______________

Directions: Solve each problem.

1. What is the circumference of the circle in terms of pi? ____________

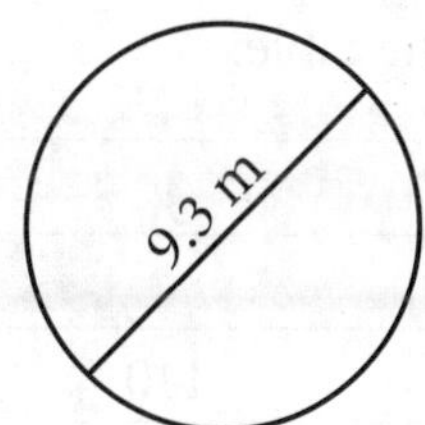

2. How many triangles can be drawn with angles of 35°, 55°, and a side length of 1 inch? One, more than one, or zero? ____________

3. If the area of a circle is 16π, what is the radius? ____________

4. What is the area (A) of the trapezoid?

$A =$ ____________

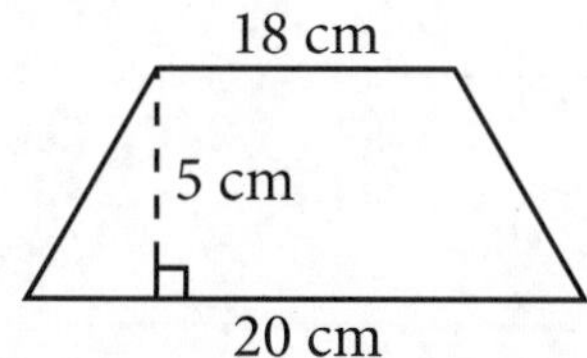

5. What is the surface area of the net? Surface Area = ____________

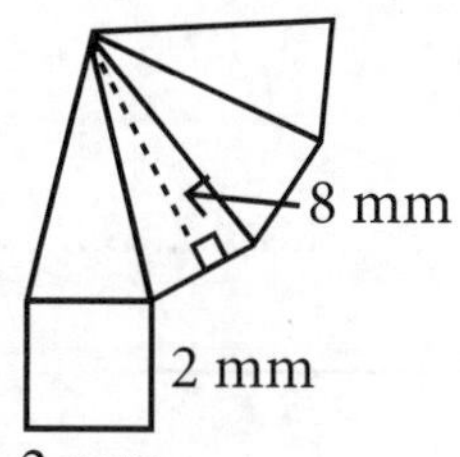

6. $\frac{50 \text{ tables}}{250 \text{ people}} = \frac{x \text{ tables}}{1{,}000 \text{ people}}$

$x =$ ____________

7. What is the volume (V) of the triangular prism?

$V =$ ____________

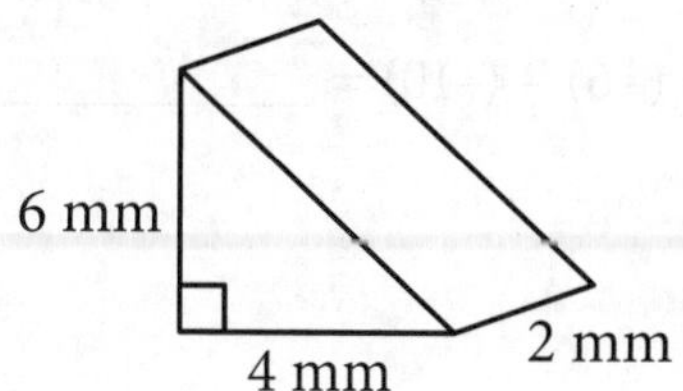

8. $-8(-3) =$ ____________

Name: ______________________ Date: ______________

Directions: Solve each problem.

1. What is the volume (V) of the figure?

$V =$ ____________

6 cm

4 cm

12 cm

2. What is the measure of the missing angle?

$x =$ ____________

x

73°

3. Write an equivalent expression using the Distributive Property.

$8(3a + 6) =$ ____________

4. Solve the inequality, and graph the solution on the number line.

$9x + 3 < 12$

____

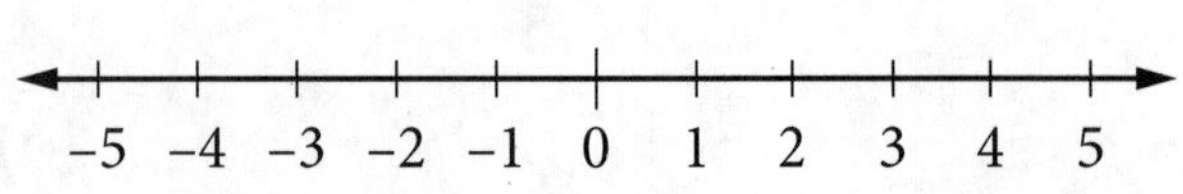

5. Find the constant of proportionality, and use it to complete the table.

x	y
1	
20	140
50	
	560

6. Can a triangle have three angles measuring 80°, 85°, and 90°?

____

7. $7\frac{1}{5} \cdot 4\frac{2}{9} =$ ____________

8. $-8 + 9 + (-6) - (-10) =$ ____________

Cumulative Review

Name: ______________________ Date: ______________

Directions: Solve each problem.

1. What is the measure of the missing angle?

x = __________

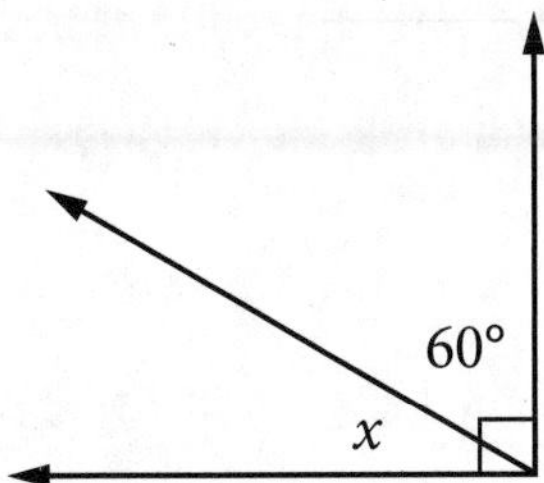

2. Use the Distributive Property to write an equivalent expression.

$3(5x + 7y + 9)$ = __________

3. $-5 - 9$ = __________

4. If a slice is made horizontally through the cube, what two-dimensional shape is formed on the face of the cross section?

____

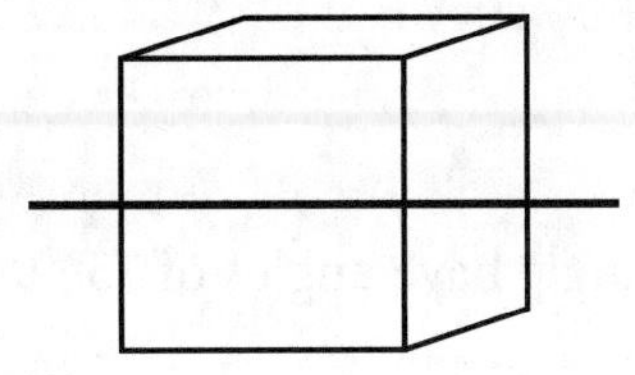

5. What is the area of the circle?

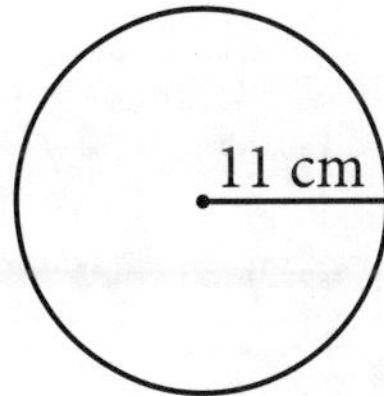

a. In terms of pi: __________

b. As a decimal approximation:

____

6. What is the additive inverse of -6.3?

____

7. Can a triangle have side lengths of 3, 3, and 7 units? __________

8. $-48 \div (-8)$ = __________

Name: ________________________ Date: ____________

Directions: Solve each problem.

1. $-72 \div (-8) =$ ____________

2. What is the area (A) of the figure?

$A =$ ____________

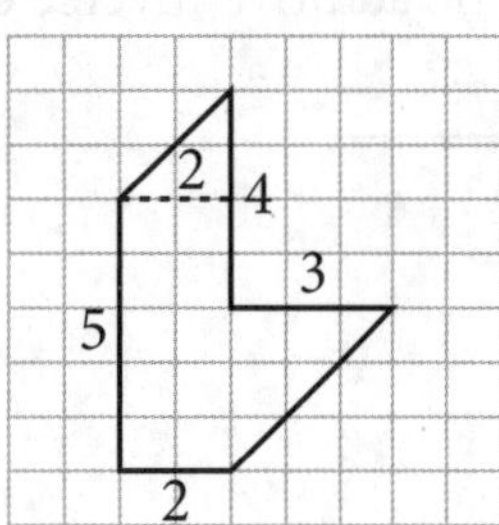

3. Use the dot plot to answer the questions.

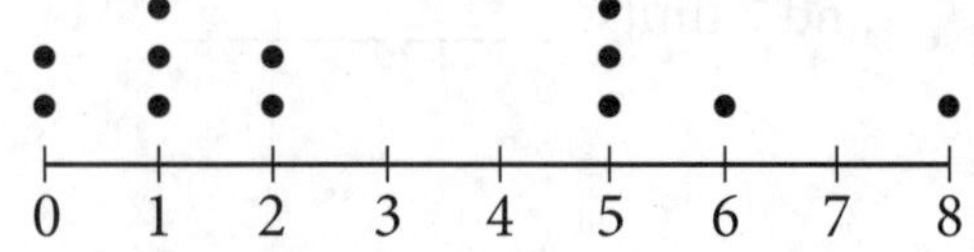

a. How many total data points are represented? ____________

b. What is the range of the data?

____

c. What is the median of the data?

____

4. $\frac{168 \text{ football players}}{6 \text{ teams}} = \frac{x}{15 \text{ teams}}$

$x =$ ____________

5. What is the constant of proportionality in the equation $y = 8x$?

$k =$ ____________

6. $5\frac{3}{4} \times 1\frac{1}{5} =$ ____________

7. $54 \div (-9) =$ ____________

8. Can a triangle have angles of 75°, 90°, and 25°? ____________

Name: ______________________ Date: ______________

Directions: Solve each problem.

1. If the area of a circle is 25π square units, what is the radius? ______________

2. $8\frac{1}{4} \times 2\frac{1}{11} =$ ______________

3. $8 + (-10) =$ ______________

4. What is the absolute value of $(-7) - 15$?

____

5. What is the missing angle measure?

$x =$ ______________

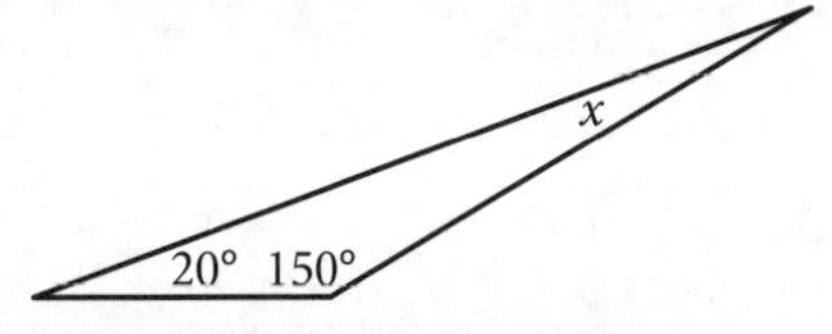

6. Is the relationship shown on the graph proportional? ______________

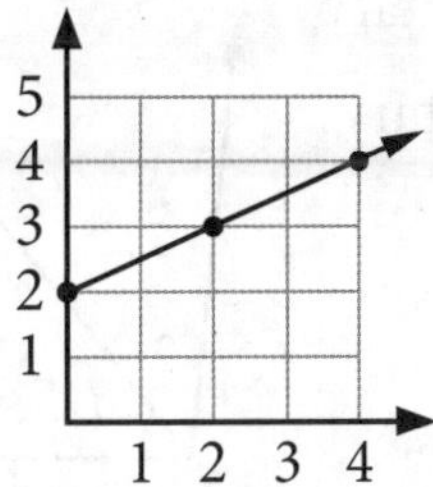

7. What is the volume (V) of the triangular prism?

$V =$ ______________

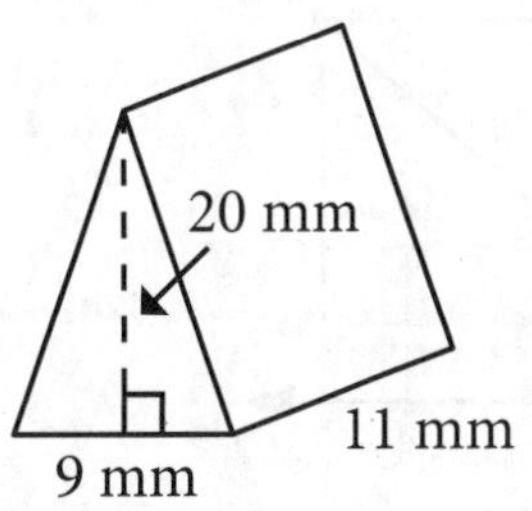

8. Geoffrey wants to buy a new set of skis for \$450. He has a 15% off coupon. What is the price of the skis with the discount?

____

9. Write an equivalent expression using the Distributive Property.

$9(v + 8) =$ ______________

10. What is the constant of proportionality?

$k =$ ______________

x	y
5	15
6	18
7	21

Name: ______________________ Date: ______________

Directions: Solve each problem.

1. What type of angles are angles 1 and 2? Circle the correct answer.

a. complementary

b. supplementary

c. vertical

d. adjacent

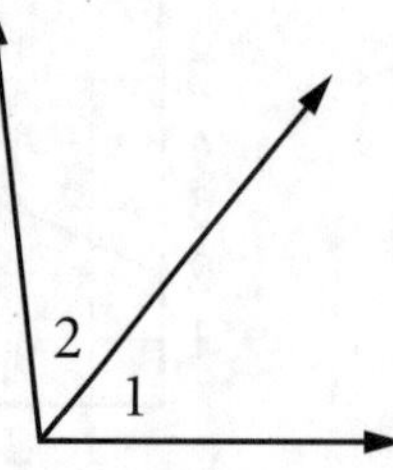

2. Is the relationship shown on the graph proportional? ______________

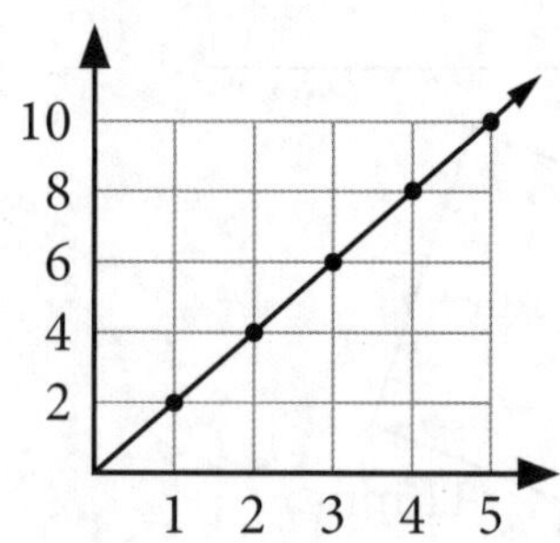

3. The circumference of a circle is 4π units.

a. What is the diameter?

____

b. What is the radius?

____

4. What is the area (A) of the trapezoid?

$A =$ ______________

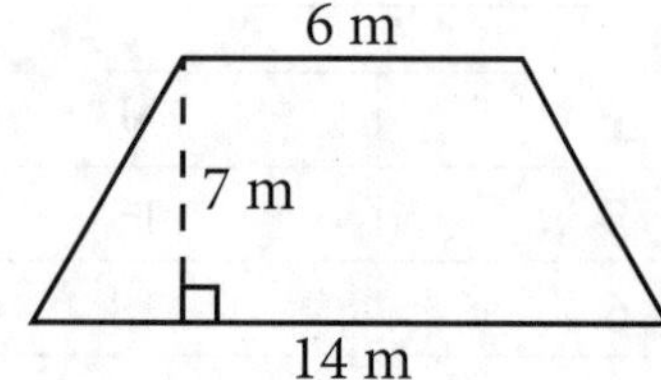

5. In a game, Jackson scored 25% more points than Shae. Shae scored 1,000 points. How many points did Jackson score?

____

6. $\frac{6}{4} = \frac{x}{2}$

$x =$ ______________

7. What is the volume (V) of the figure?

$V =$ ______________

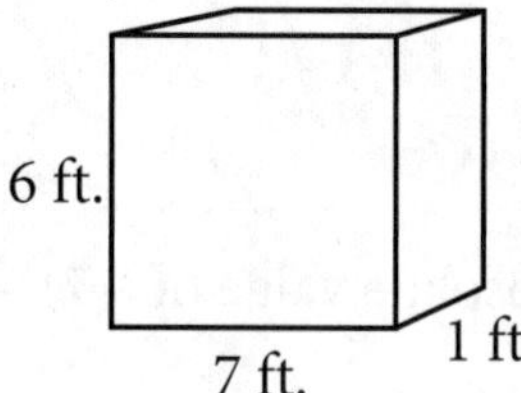

8. $19 - (-8) =$ ______________

Cumulative Review

Name: ______________________________ Date: ______________

Directions: Solve each problem.

1. What is the surface area of the net?

Surface Area = ____________

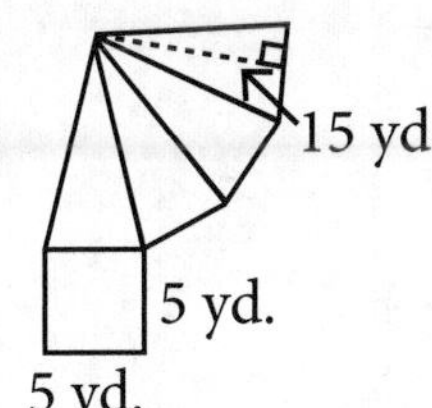

2. What is the volume (V) of the triangular prism?

V = ____________

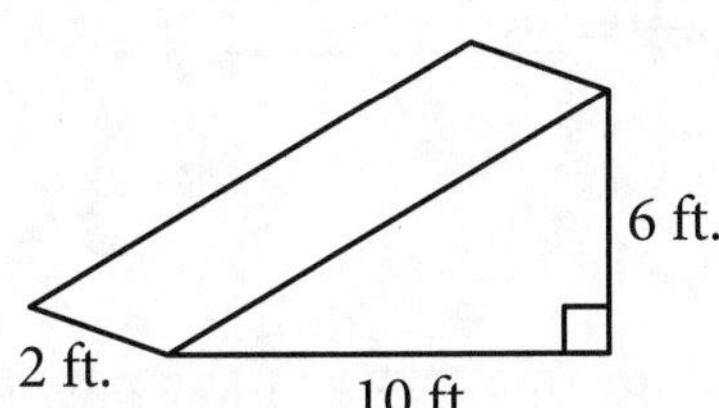

3. What is the area (A) of the triangle?

A = ____________

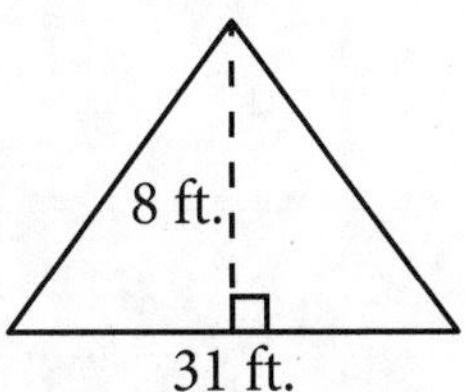

4. Write an equation for the proportional relationship on the graph.

y = ____________

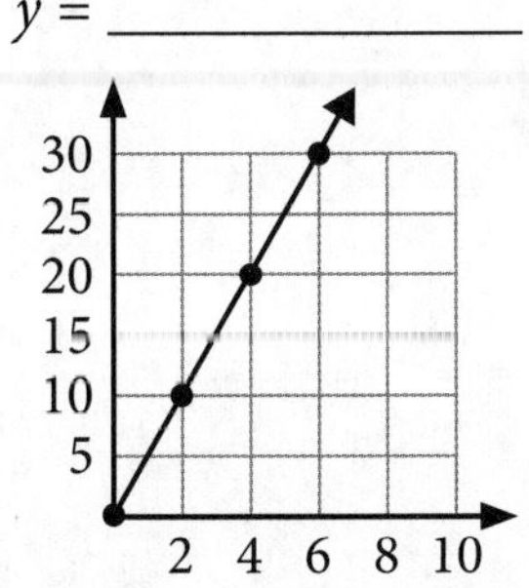

5. $-\frac{1}{8} \times \frac{16}{6} =$ ____________

6. What is the missing angle measure?

x = ____________

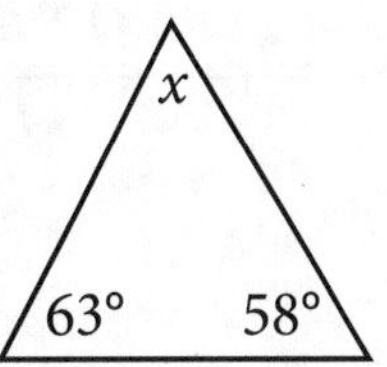

7. What is the area of the circle in terms of pi? ____________

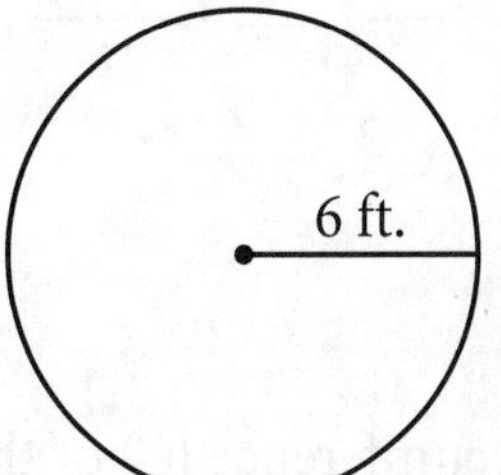

8. $-10 \div 5 =$ ____________

Cumulative Review

Name: ______________________ Date: ______________

Directions: Solve each problem.

1. What is the volume (V) of the rectangular prism?

$V =$ __________

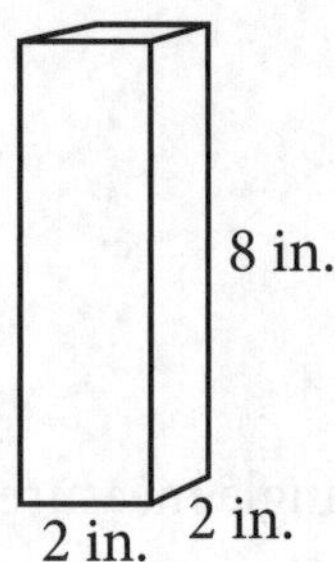

2. $(-9 \div 3) + (-2.5) =$ __________

3. What is the missing side length?

$x =$ __________

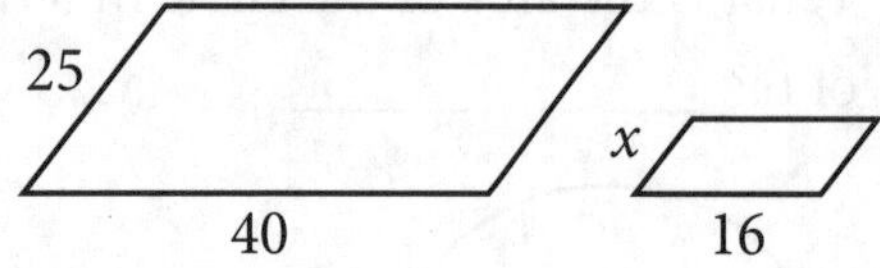

4. What is the circumference (C) of the circle in terms of pi?

$C =$ __________

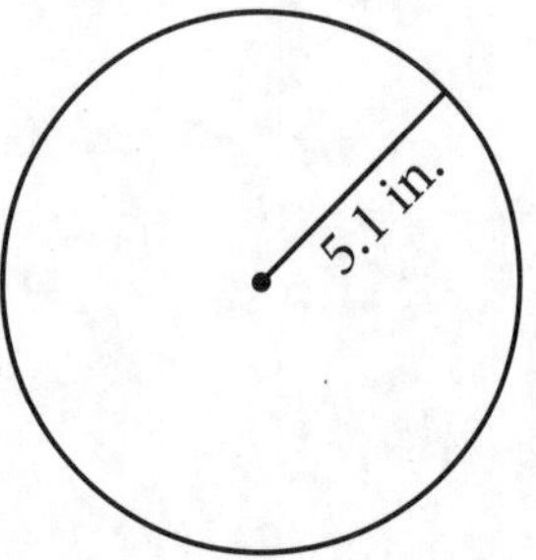

5. Write an equation for the proportional relationship shown on the graph.

$y =$ __________

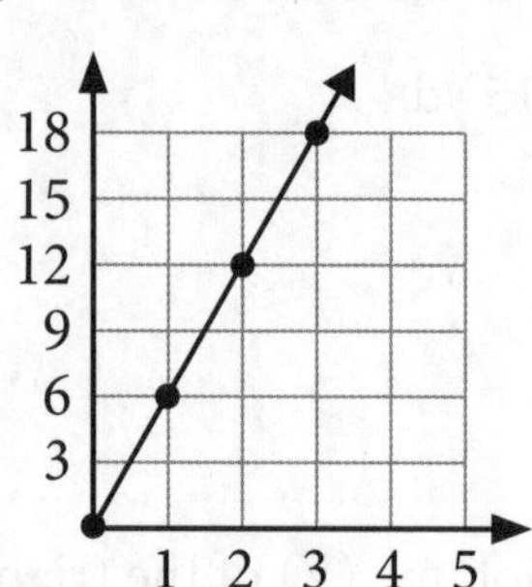

6. $7\frac{1}{5} \div 2\frac{1}{4} =$ __________

7. $-8 \cdot (-6) =$ __________

8. $7(4 - 8) + (-6) - 5 =$ __________

Name: ______________________ Date: ______________

Directions: Solve each problem.

1. What is the missing angle measure?

x = __________

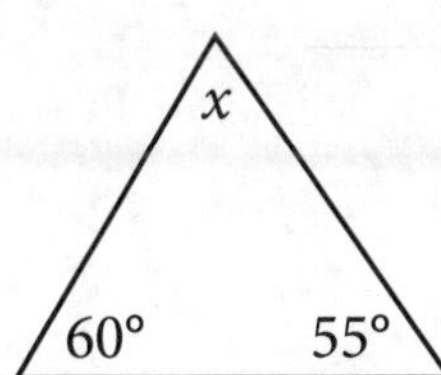

2. What is the probability of spinning a B on the spinner? __________

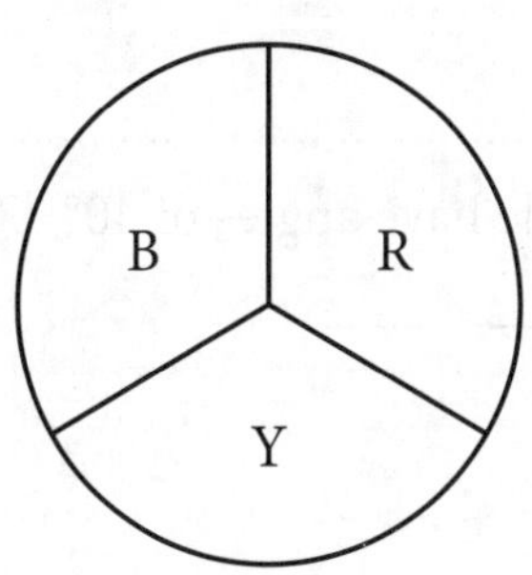

3. Write and solve an equation for the addition problem shown on the number line.

________ + ________ = ________

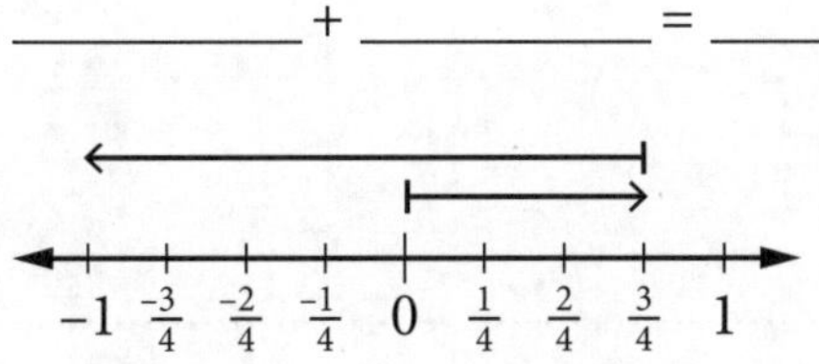

4. What is the missing angle measure?

x = __________

5. Use the Distributive Property to write an equivalent expression.

$36 + 4c$ = __________

6. Can a triangle have side lengths of 1, 3, and 5? __________

7. Jarrod is buying a new pair of shoes priced at $38. He has a coupon for 30% off. What is the sale price of his new shoes?

____

8. $10(x - 4) = 100$

x = __________

Cumulative Review

Name: ______________________ Date: ______________

Directions: Solve each problem.

1. What type of angles are angles 1 and 2? Circle all the correct answers.

a. complementary

b. supplementary

c. vertical

d. adjacent

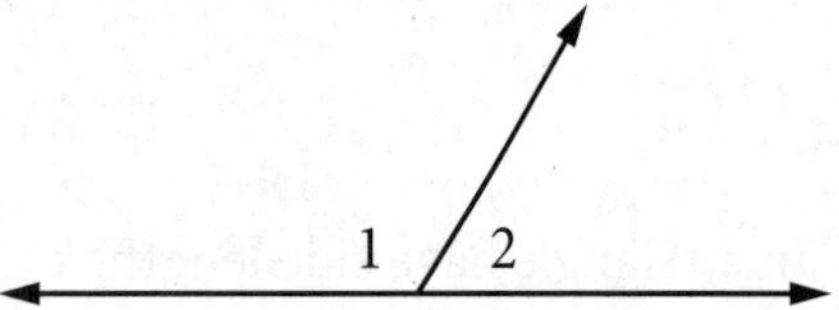

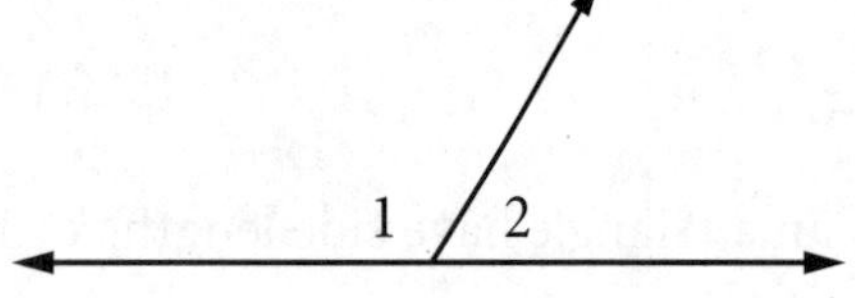

2. Write an equation for the graph.

$y =$ __________

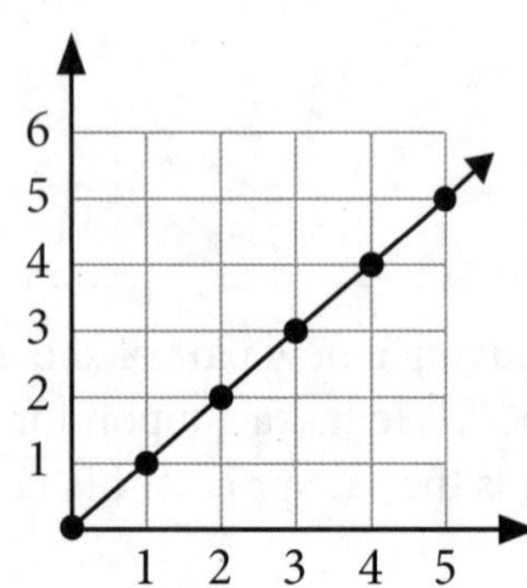

3. What is the area (A) of the trapezoid?

$A =$ __________

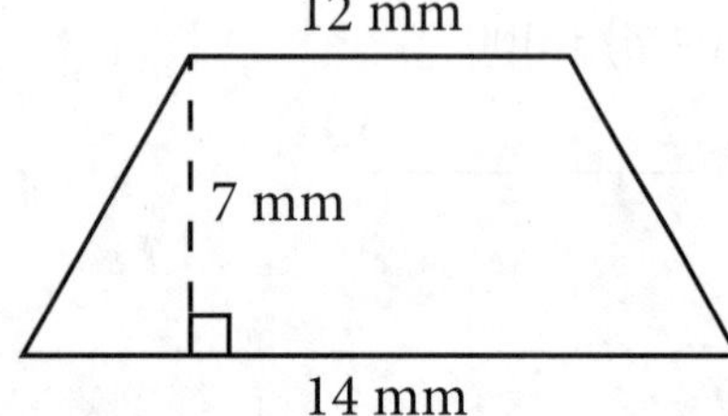

4. Write an equivalent expression using the Distributive Property.

$3(x + 8) =$ __________

5. Write 95% as a fraction.

____

6. Can a triangle have angles of 40°, 60°, and 90°? __________

7. $\frac{60 \text{ shoes}}{30 \text{ people}} = \frac{180 \text{ shoes}}{x}$

$x =$ __________

8. $9.6 - 5\frac{3}{5} =$ __________

Name: ______________________ Date: ______________

Directions: Solve each problem.

1. Write and solve an equation for the addition problem shown on the number line.

______ + ______ = ______

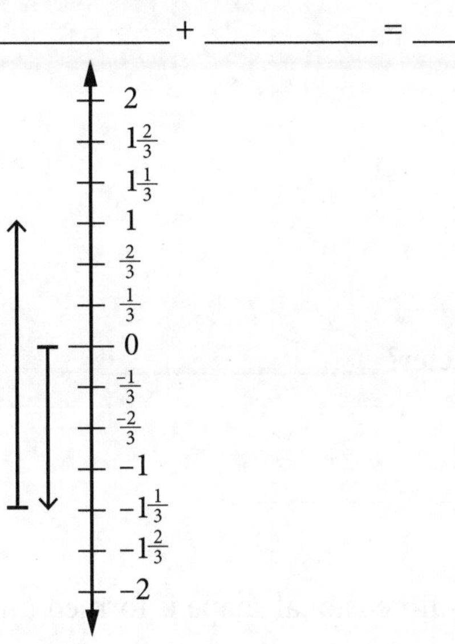

2. What is the missing angle measure?

______

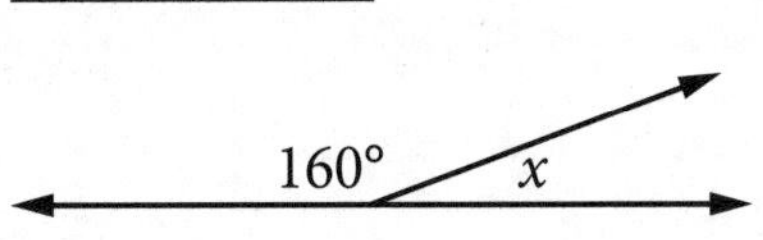

3. Kevin and his friends went to dinner. The bill was $55, and they decided to leave an 18% tip. How much was the bill, including the tip?

______

4. What is the surface area of the net?

Surface Area = ______

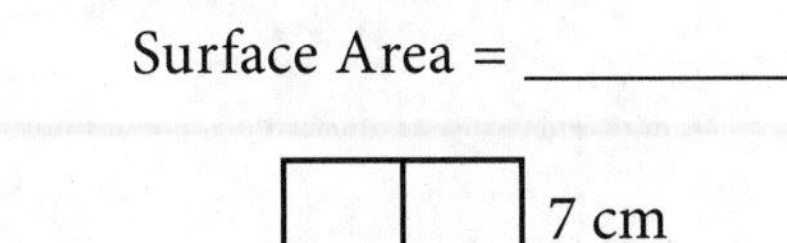

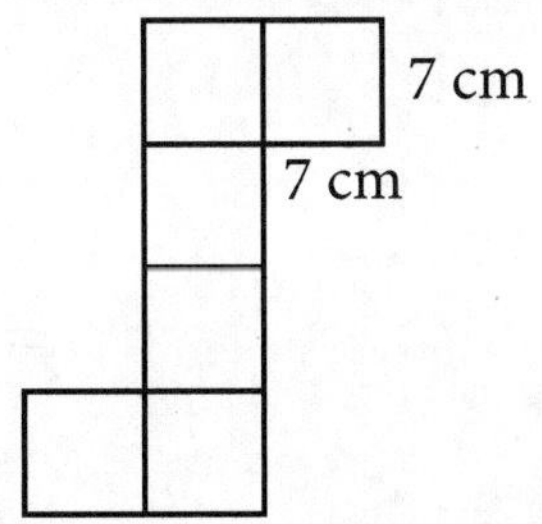

5. Is the relationship on the graph proportional? ______

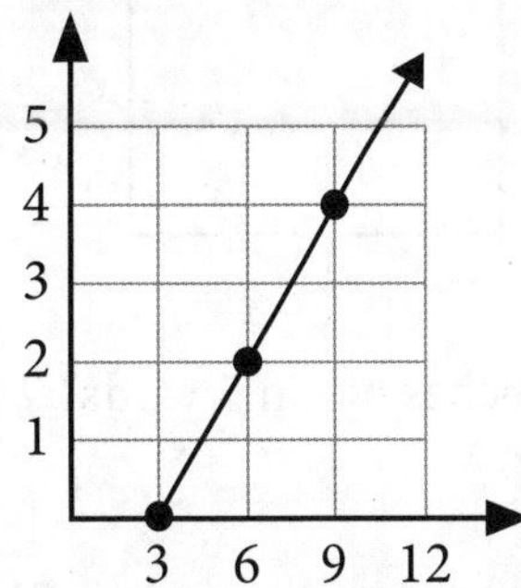

6. What is the circumference of the circle?

a. In terms of pi:

______

b. As a decimal approximation:

______

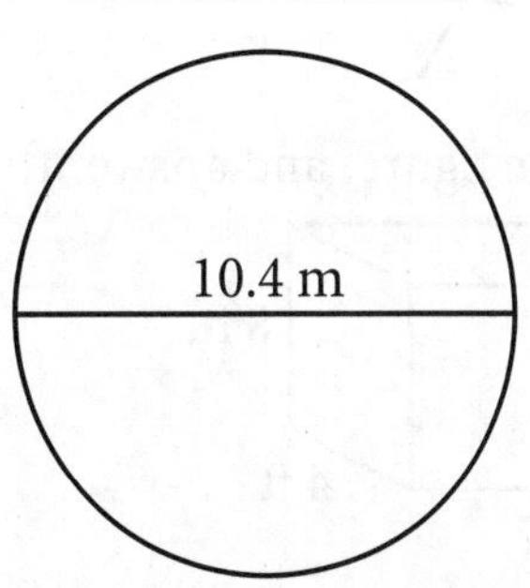

7. What is the missing side length in the similar figures?

x = ______

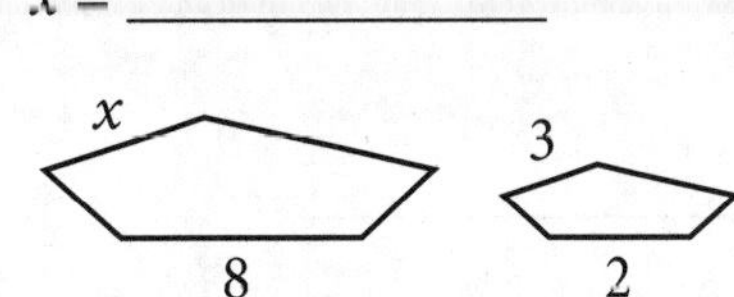

8. $42 \div (-7) =$ ______

Name: ______________________ Date: ______________

Directions: Solve each problem.

1. What is the missing side length?

   x = ______________

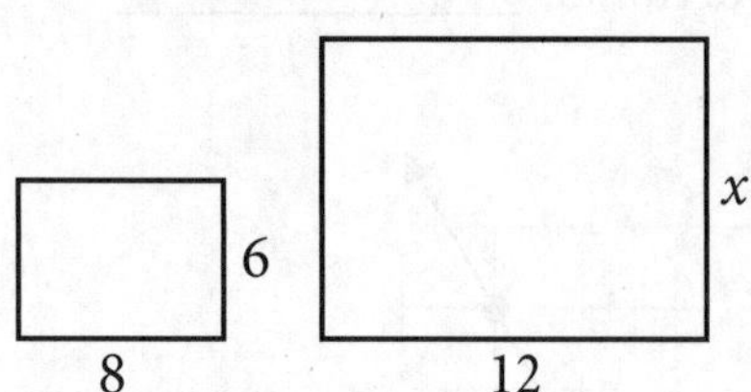

2. How many inches are in 5 yards? ______________

3. If the circumference of a circle is 51π, what is the diameter? ______________

4. Can a triangle have sides of 15, 16, and 35 units? ______________

5. If the triangular prism is sliced as indicated, what two-dimensional shape is formed on the face of the cross section? ______________

6. Look at the figure, and answer the questions.

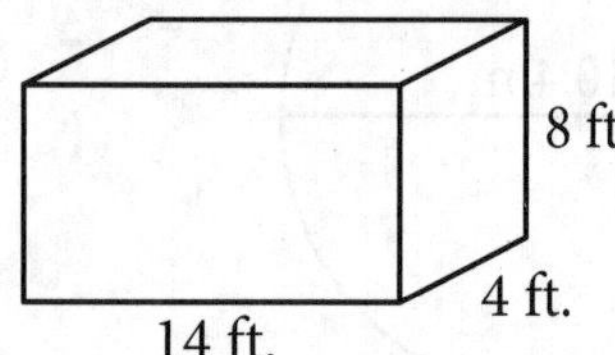

   a. What is the volume (V) of the rectangular prism?

   V = ______________

   b. What is the surface area of the rectangular prism?

   Surface Area = ______________

7. 35 – (–4) = ______________

8. $\frac{5^3}{5^2}$ = ______________

Cumulative Review

Name: ______________________ Date: ______________

Directions: Solve each problem.

1. What is the area of the circle?

a. In terms of pi: ______________

b. As an approximated decimal rounded to hundredths: ______________

2. What is the measure of the missing angle?

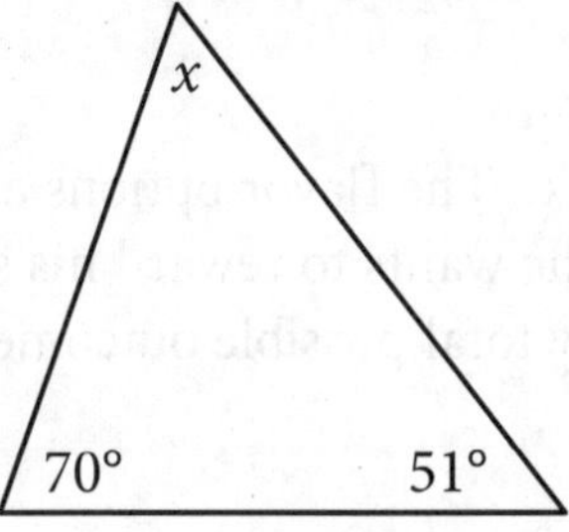

$x =$ ______________

3. The Thomas family drove 2,600 miles in 40 hours. How many miles did they drive in 1 hour?

____

4. Write an equivalent expression using the Distributive Property.

$4(3a + 2b + 5) =$ ______________

5. Wren has a 35% off coupon.

a. What is 35% as a decimal? ______________

b. What is 35% as a fraction? ______________

6. $25 - (-6) =$ ______________

7. $-9 + (-5) =$ ______________

8. $-18 \div (-6) =$ ______________

Cumulative Review

Name: ____________________ Date: ____________

Directions: Solve each problem.

1. Write the missing number for the unit rate.

$\frac{260 \text{ miles}}{4 \text{ hours}} = \frac{\_\_\_\_}{1 \text{ hour}}$

2. Simplify the expression.

$77a - (-4a) + 15 - 8a$

____

3. What is the probability of spinning a B on the spinner? ____________

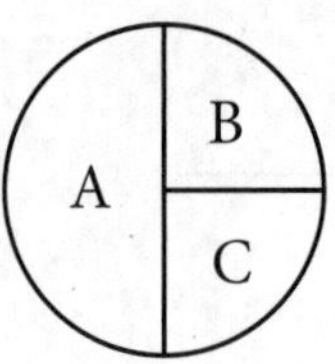

4. Mr. Bart gives each of his students a candy at the end of the week. The flavor options are chocolate, caramel, mint, or coconut. At the end of the month, he wants to reward his students with an extra candy of either cherry or lemon flavor. How many total possible outcomes of candy flavors are there?

____________ total possible outcomes

5. At the carnival, David bought 5 buckets of popcorn for $47.25. How much is one bucket of popcorn? ____________

6. Write the equation for the problem represented on the vertical number line.

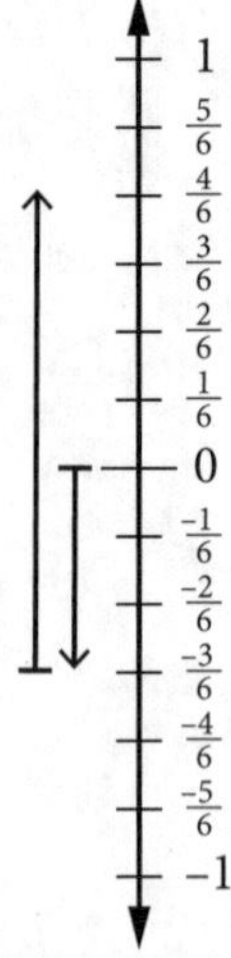

____________ + ____________ = ____________

7. $(\frac{3}{4})^3 =$ ____________

8. What is 18% as a fraction? ____________

Name: ____________________ Date: ____________________

Directions: Solve each problem.

1. What is 25% of $40? ____________

2. $7m - 6 = 22$

$m =$ ____________

3. What is the missing angle measure?

$x =$ ____________

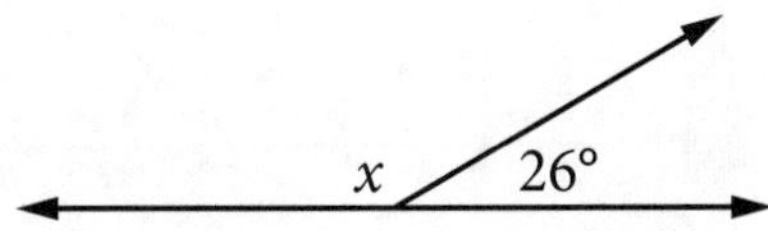

4. What is the area (A) of the trapezoid?

$A =$ ____________

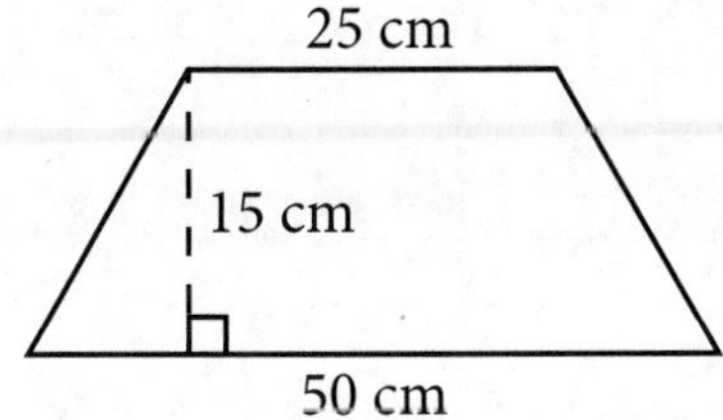

5. What is the volume (V) of the triangular prism?

$V =$ ____________

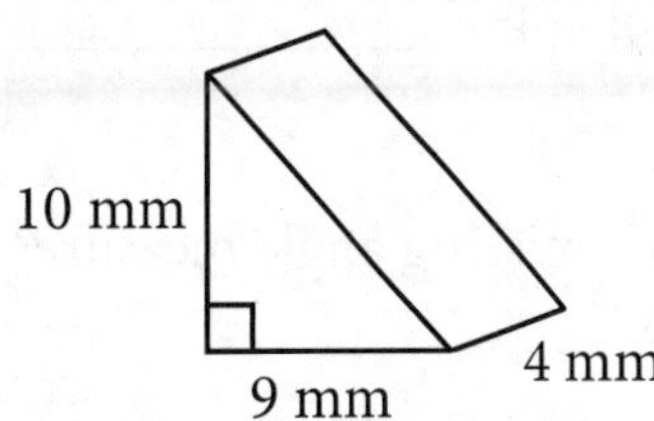

6. $-8.9 + 7.6 =$ ____________

7. Sebastian needed $\frac{1}{3}$ of a cup of pecans for $\frac{1}{2}$ of a cookie recipe. How many cups of pecans does he need for 1 full cookie recipe?

____

8. Write an equivalent expression.

$9(6.5x + 3.5) =$ ____________

Cumulative Review

REVIEW DAY 23

Name:____________________ Date:____________

Directions: Solve each problem.

1. Write the missing number to make a proportional relationship.

$\frac{48 \text{ crayons}}{3 \text{ boxes}} = \frac{\_\_\_\_}{9 \text{ boxes}}$

2. $[9 - (6 - 8)] + 4^2 =$ __________

3. What is the missing angle measure?

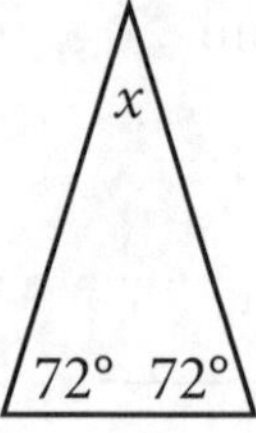

$x =$ __________

4. Write 28% as a fraction. __________

5. Akari is buying a game that costs \$55. Last week, the game was \$65. What percent did the price decrease? __________

6. Solve the inequality. Graph the solution to the inequality on the number line.

$-5x - 6 > -26$

$x =$ __________

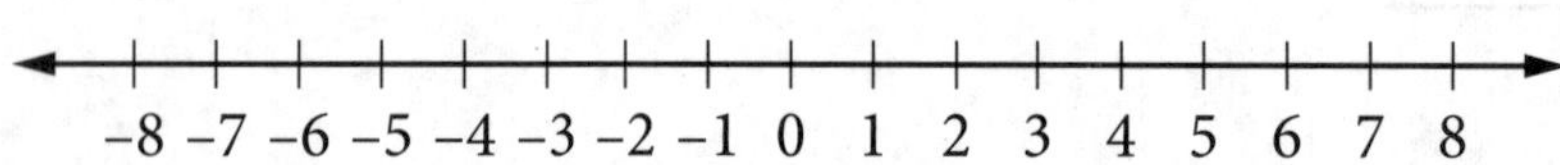

7. Find the volume (V) of the rectangular prism.

$V =$ __________

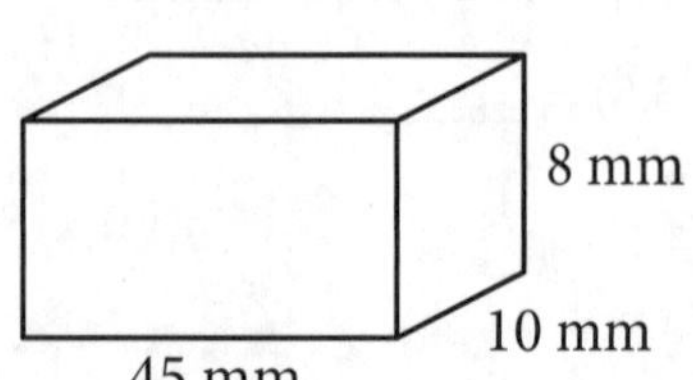

8. $-3 \times 15 =$ __________

Cumulative Review

Name: ______________________ Date: ______________

Directions: Solve each problem.

1. $\frac{12}{60} = \frac{x}{20}$

   $x =$ ______________

2. Write the equation for the problem represented on the horizontal number line.

   ______________ + ______________ = ______________

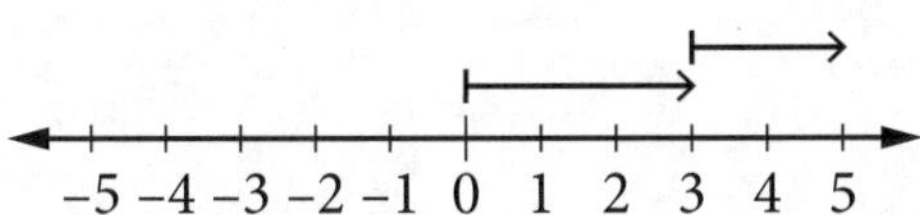

3. Write an equivalent expression.

   $6(4x + 5) =$ ______________

4. What is the radius of the circle? ______________

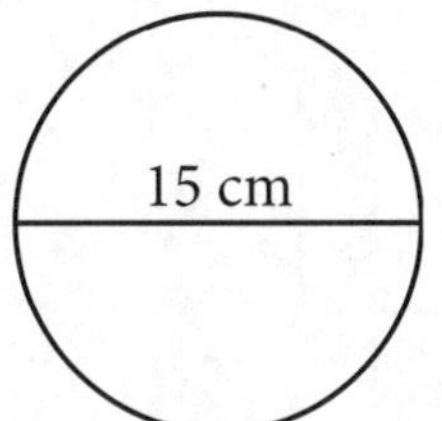

5. Write $\frac{6}{8}$ as a decimal. ______________

6. Benito is buying a new pair of jeans that are regularly $60. He has a 20% off coupon. How much will Benito pay for the jeans at the discounted price? ______________

7. What is the probability of spinning a 6 on the spinner and then flipping tails on a coin?

   ____

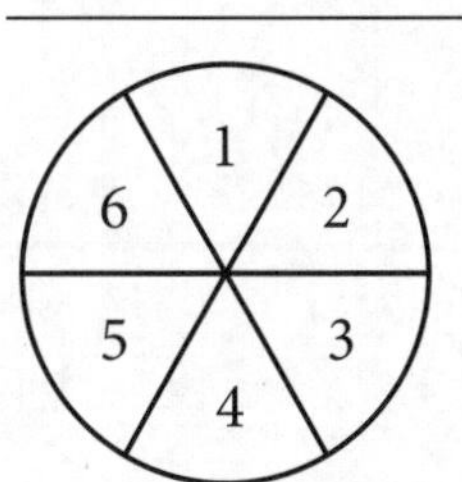

8. What is the volume (V) of the rectangular prism?

   $V =$ ______________

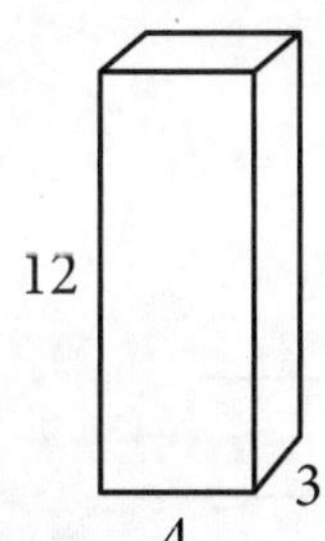

REVIEW DAY 25

Name: ______________________ Date: ______________

Directions: Solve each problem.

1. Write an equivalent expression.

$12(8x + 3) =$ ______________

2. Draw an example of a proportional relationship on the coordinate plane.

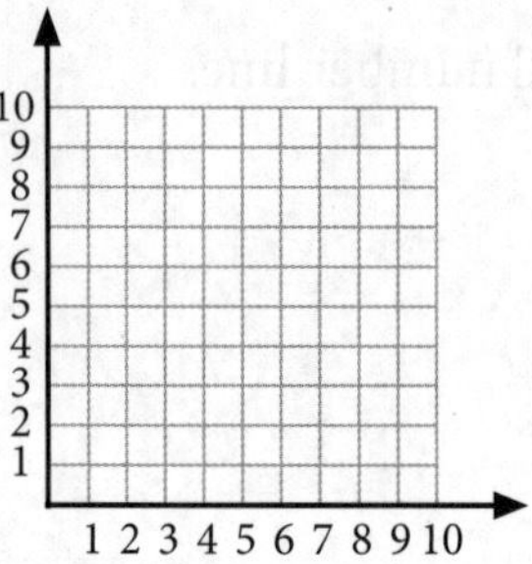

3. What is the constant of proportionality from the table?

$k =$ ________

x	y
0	0
2	5
4	10
6	15

4. $-5.4 - (-11.5) =$ ______________

5. Joon is buying a new speaker for $75. There is a tax of 7% on the speaker. What is the price of the speaker, including tax? ______________

6. Write an expression for *three times a number decreased by 12.* ______________

7. $6\frac{3}{5} \times 2\frac{3}{4} =$ ______________

8. Use the spinner to answer the questions.

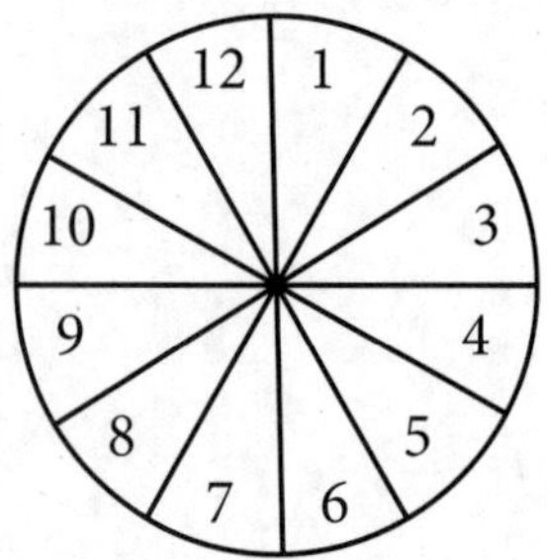

a. What is the probability of spinning a 4? ______________

b. What is the probability of spinning an even number? ______________

c. What is the probability of spinning a number less than 7? ______________

Cumulative Review

Standards Correlations

Shell Education is committed to producing educational materials that are research and standards based. To support this effort, this resource is correlated to the academic standards of all 50 states, the District of Columbia, the Department of Defense Dependent Schools, and the Canadian provinces. A correlation is also provided for key professional educational organizations.

To print a customized correlation report for your state, visit our website at **www.tcmpub.com/administrators/correlations** and follow the online directions. If you require assistance in printing correlation reports, please contact the Customer Service Department at 1-800-858-7339.

Standards Overview

The Every Student Succeeds Act (ESSA) mandates that all states adopt challenging academic standards that help students meet the goal of college and career readiness. While many states already adopted academic standards prior to ESSA, the act continues to hold states accountable for detailed and comprehensive standards. Standards are designed to focus instruction and guide adoption of curricula. They define the knowledge, skills, and content students should acquire at each level. Standards are also used to develop standardized tests to evaluate students' academic progress. State standards are used in the development of our resources, so educators can be assured they meet state academic requirements.

College and Career Readiness

Today's college and career readiness (CCR) standards offer guidelines for preparing K–12 students with the knowledge and skills that are necessary to succeed in postsecondary job training and education. CCR standards include the Common Core State Standards (CCSS) as well as other state-adopted standards such as the Texas Essential Knowledge and Skills. The standards found on pages 226–227 describe the content presented throughout this book.

English Language Development Standards

English language development standards are integrated within the practice pages to enable English learners to work toward proficiency in English while learning content—developing the skills and confidence in listening, speaking, reading, and writing.

Standards Correlations *(cont.)*

180 Days of Math for Seventh Grade offers a full page of mathematics practice activities for each day of the school year. Every unit provides questions tied to multiple math standards, giving students the opportunity for practice in a variety of mathematical concepts.

College and Career Readiness Standards

Ratios and Proportional Relationships
Calculate unit rates from rates in mathematical and real-world problems.
Recognize and represent proportional relationships between quantities. • Decide whether two quantities are in a proportional relationship. • Identify the constant of proportionality in tables, graphs, equations, diagrams, and verbal descriptions of proportional relationships. • Represent proportional relationships by equations. • Explain what a point (x, y) on the graph of a proportional relationship means in terms of the situation, with special attention to the points (0, 0) and $(1, r)$, where r is the unit rate.
Use proportional relationships to solve multistep ratio and percent problems.
The Number System
Add, subtract, multiply, and divide rational numbers fluently.
Describe situations in which opposite quantities combine to make 0.
Represent addition and subtraction of rational numbers on a horizontal or vertical number line diagram.
Understand subtraction of rational numbers as adding the additive inverse.
Apply properties of operations as strategies to add and subtract rational numbers.
Convert a rational number to a decimal using long division; know that the decimal form of a rational number terminates in 0s or eventually repeats.
Solve real-world and mathematical problems involving the four operations with rational numbers.
Expressions and Equations
Apply properties of operations as strategies to add, subtract, factor, and expand linear expressions with rational coefficients.
Solve multistep real-life and mathematical problems posed with positive and negative rational numbers in any form (whole numbers, fractions, and decimals), using tools strategically.
Solve word problems leading to equations of the form $px + q = r$ and $p(x + q) = r$, where p, q, and r are specific rational numbers.
Model and solve one-variable, two-step equations and inequalities.
Solve real-world and mathematical problems by writing and solving equations of the form $x + p = q$ and $px = q$ for cases in which p, q, and x are all nonnegative rational numbers.

Standards Correlations *(cont.)*

Solve word problems leading to inequalities of the form $px + q > r$ or $px + q < r$, where p, q, and r are specific rational numbers. Graph the solution set of the inequality, and interpret it in the context of the problem.
Use decimal notation for fractions with denominators 10 or 100.
Compare two decimals to hundredths by reasoning about their size.
Geometry
Solve problems involving scale drawings of geometric figures, including computing actual lengths and areas from a scale drawing and reproducing a scale drawing at a different scale.
Draw geometric shapes with given conditions.
Describe the two-dimensional figures that result from slicing three-dimensional figures, as in plane sections of right rectangular prisms and right rectangular pyramids.
Know the formulas for the area and circumference of a circle, and use them to solve problems.
Use facts about supplementary, complementary, vertical, and adjacent angles in a multistep problem to write and solve simple equations for an unknown angle in a figure.
Solve real-world and mathematical problems involving area, volume, and surface area of two- and three-dimensional objects composed of triangles, quadrilaterals, polygons, cubes, and right prisms.
Statistics and Probability
Use random sampling to draw inferences about a population.
Informally assess the degree of visual overlap of two numerical data distributions with similar variabilities, measuring the difference between the centers by expressing it as a multiple of a measure of variability.
Use measures of center and measures of variability for numerical data from random samples to draw informal comparative inferences about two populations.
Understand that the probability of a chance event is a number between 0 and 1 that expresses the likelihood of the event occurring.
Approximate the probability of a chance event by collecting data on the chance process that produces it and observing its long-run relative frequency, and predict the approximate relative frequency given the probability.
Develop a probability model and use it to find probabilities of events. Compare probabilities from a model to observe frequencies.
Find probabilities of compound events using organized lists, tables, tree diagrams, and simulation.
Design and use a simulation to generate frequencies for compound events.

References Cited

Cathcart, W. George, Yvonne M. Pothier, James H. Vance, and Nadine S. Bezuk. 2014. *Learning Mathematics in Elementary and Middle Schools: A Learning-Centered Approach*, 6th ed. Upper Saddle River: Prentice-Hall.

Durkin, Kelley, Bethany Rittle-Johnson, and Jon R. Star. 2017. "Using Comparison of Multiple Strategies in the Mathematics Classroom: Lessons Learned and Next Steps." *ZDM: The International Journal on Mathematics Education* 49, no. 4.

Ireland, Jo and Melissa Mouthaan. 2020. "Perspectives on Curriculum Design: Comparing the Spiral and the Network Models." *Research Matters: A Cambridge Assessment Publication,* 30: 7–12.

Marchitello, Max and Megan Wilhelm. 2014. "The Cognitive Science Behind the Common Core." Center for American Progress.

McNeil, Nicole, and Linda Jarvin. 2007. "When Theories Don't Add Up: Disentangling the Manipulatives Debate." *Theory into Practice* 46, no. 4: 309–316.

Answer Key

Grade 6 Review

Day 1 (page 10)

1. $\frac{3}{7}$, 3:7, 0.429
2. 10%
3. $7x + 5y$
4. 37.5 in.^{3}
5. 27
6. a. –2
   b. 2
7. 60
8. 10
9. $d = 3$
10. Quadrant II
11. $2.25
12. Option A is better.

Day 2 (page 11)

1. 90 cm^3
2. 246
3. 1,662.5
4. 28 m^2
5. 46
6. –5 –4 –3 –2 –1 0 1 2 3 4 5
7. They cannot because $3 + 5 < 9$.
8. 30
9. $x - 3$
10. –3
11. a. Additive
    b. $y = x + 4$
12. $2 \times 2 \times 2 \times 3$

Day 3 (page 12)

1.

Stem	Leaf
2	2, 2, 3, 4, 8
3	0, 5
4	2, 7
5	1
6	2

2. 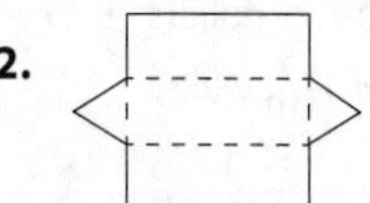

3. 55 miles
4. Unit Rate: $0.85, $21.25
5. 30 miles
6. 1,585.39
7. a. 0.28
   b. 28%
8. 20 cm^2
9. 4,000
10. 6

Day 4 (page 13)

1. 13
2. 13
3. 5
4. 36: 1, 2, 3, 4, (6), 9, 12, 18, 36
   42: 1, 2, 3, (6), 7, 14, 21, 42
5. Yes
6. (–4, –2)
7. –10
8. $7
9. 2(7 + 10)
10. $\frac{75}{20}$ or $3\frac{3}{4}$
11. 240 minutes
12. 0.25

Day 5 (page 14)

1. 0.75 raspberries to strawberries
2. square pyramid
3. 21 cm^2
4. 8
5. 55
6. 16
7. $m = 5$
8. –2,000
9. $\frac{144}{45}$ or $3\frac{1}{5}$
10. (2, –1)
11. a. 0.21
    b. 21%
12. 2.5 cm

Day 6 (page 15)

1. 3
2. $\frac{120}{5}$ or 24
3. 23
4. $2 \times 5 \times 5$
5. 215
6. a. 37.5%
   b. $\frac{5}{8}$
7. 21 feet
8. $3 : 1, \frac{3}{1}, 3$
9. $\frac{2}{5}$
10. 40 in.^{2}
11. a. 2 figures
    b. Yes
    c. $2\frac{1}{2} = \frac{5}{8} \div \frac{1}{4}$
12. a. $y = 144 \div 12$
    b. $y = 144 \times \frac{1}{12}$
    c. 12 home runs each

Day 7 (page 16)

1. $y = 3x$

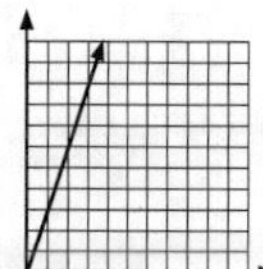

2. a. 25%
   b. $\frac{3}{4}$
   c. 0.25
3. Maril, $\frac{2}{3}$ is less than 1
4.

Fraction	Decimal	Percent
$\frac{11}{100}$	0.11	11%
$\frac{1}{10}$	0.1	10%
$\frac{1}{5}$	0.2	20%

5. $\frac{8}{65}$
6. 8.637
7. –5 –4 –3 –2 –1 0 1 2 3 4 5
8. 125
9. Quadrant IV
10. 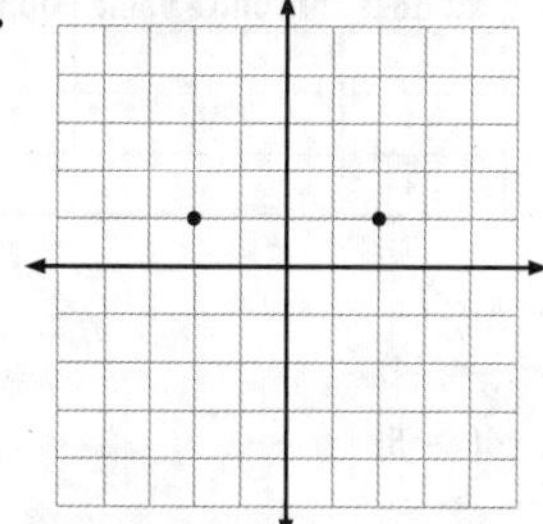

distance: 4

Day 8 (page 17)

1. a. 0.25
   b. 75%
2. Quadrant III
3. 55°
4. (–3, 1)
5. a. 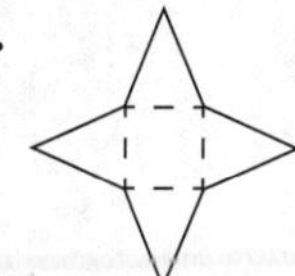
   b. 52 cm^2
6. a. 12 people
   b. 6–10
7. 24
8. 65

Answer Key (cont.)

Day 9 (page 18)

1. **a.** 40%
   b. 2 : 3
2. (3, –2)
3. **a.** 1
   b. 1
4. [diagram]
5. $8x + 80$
6. 20°
7. **a.** 5
   b. 7
   c. skewed
8. $8(2 + 3x)$ or $4(4 + 6x)$ or $2(8 + 12x)$

Day 10 (page 19)

1. **a.** 0.9
   b. 90%
2. Hallie, $\frac{9}{8}$ is greater than 1.
3. $5(2 + 7)$
4. 0.6 cups
5.

Number	Absolute Value	Opposite
6	6	–6
10	10	–10
–3	3	3

6. $x + 9$
7. (–4, –1)
8. $4(x + 5)$

Unit 1

Learn About Unit Rates
(page 20)

Example 1: 8
Example 2: 2
Example 3: $\frac{12}{2}$; 6 miles

Day 1 (page 21)

1. Rate: $\frac{\text{150 students}}{\text{15 tables}}$
   Unit Rate: $\frac{\text{10 students}}{\text{table}}$
2. Rate: $\frac{\text{56 hats}}{\text{8 packages}}$
   Unit Rate: $\frac{\text{7 hats}}{\text{package}}$
3. Rate: $\frac{\text{36 peaches}}{\text{3 boxes}}$
   Unit Rate: $\frac{\text{12 peaches}}{\text{box}}$
4. Rate: $\frac{\text{120 campers}}{\text{10 tents}}$
   Unit Rate: $\frac{\text{12 campers}}{\text{tent}}$
5. Rate: $\frac{\text{81 golf balls}}{\text{9 boxes}}$
   Unit Rate: $\frac{\text{9 golf balls}}{\text{box}}$
6. Rate: $\frac{\text{400 dollars}}{\text{20 hours of work}}$
   Unit Rate: $\frac{\text{20 dollars}}{\text{hour of work}}$
7. Rate: $\frac{\text{90 students}}{\text{3 classrooms}}$
   Unit Rate: $\frac{\text{30 students}}{\text{classroom}}$
8. Rate: $\frac{\text{12 birds}}{\text{4 nests}}$
   Unit Rate: $\frac{\text{3 birds}}{\text{nest}}$
9. Rate: $\frac{\text{48 lbs. of potatoes}}{\text{6 bags}}$
   Unit Rate: $\frac{\text{8 lbs. of potatoes}}{\text{bag}}$
10. Rate: $\frac{\text{60 books}}{\text{5 shelves}}$
    Unit Rate: $\frac{\text{12 books}}{\text{shelf}}$
11. Rate: $\frac{\text{35 juice boxes}}{\text{7 packages}}$
    Unit Rate: $\frac{\text{5 juice boxes}}{\text{package}}$
12. Rate: $\frac{\text{125 candles}}{\text{5 boxes}}$
    Unit Rate: $\frac{\text{25 candles}}{\text{box}}$

Day 2 (page 22)

1. $21
2. 3 dogs
3. $55.50
4. $8
5. 10 driveways snow plowed
6. 8 gallons
7. 12 miles
8. 44.8 pages
9. $12
10. 0.5 pizzas
11. 25 miles
12. $32
13. 50 words
14. 9 wins

Day 3 (page 23)

1. $32
2. 6 hot dogs
3. 50 cents or $0.50
4. 21 pages
5. 2 cups
6. $12
7. 24 problems
8. $1.50
9. 65 miles
10. 0.091 miles or $\frac{1}{11}$ miles
11. 2.143 lawns or $2\frac{1}{7}$ lawns
12. $10.99

Day 4 (page 24)

1. 12 miles
2. 12 miles
3. 20 bowls
4. 1.5 miles or $1\frac{1}{2}$ miles
5. 40 animals
6. 50 characters
7. 0.75 cups or $\frac{3}{4}$ cups
8. 0.25 inches or $\frac{2}{8}$ inches or $\frac{1}{4}$ inches
9. 3 games
10. 2 bags
11. 11.25 miles or $11\frac{1}{4}$ miles
12. 3.111 lawns or $3\frac{1}{9}$ lawns

Day 5 (page 25)

1. 2 miles
2. 6 miles
3. 8 miles
4. 0.333 dozen or $\frac{1}{3}$ dozen
5. 5 pillows
6. 16 cakes
7. 4 inches
8. $4
9. $18.25 or $18\frac{1}{4}$ dollars
10. 1.7 walls or $1\frac{7}{10}$ walls
11. 1.5 cups
12. 30 students

Learn About Proportional Relationships (page 26)

Example 1:
2. 8

Example 2:
1. 4, 4, 4
2. yes, yes

Answer Key *(cont.)*

Day 6 (page 27)

1. 12 cats
2. $390
3. 8 pencils
4. 240 problems
5. 112 points
6. 6 hours
7. 96 candy bars
8. 2 boxes
9. 30 cups sugar
10. 128 muffins
11. 84 players
12. 14 decks

Day 7 (page 28)

1. no
2. yes
3. yes
4. no
5. yes
6. no
7. no
8. yes

Day 8 (page 28)

1. no
2. no
3. yes
4. yes
5. no
6. yes
7. no
8. yes

Day 9 (page 30)

1.
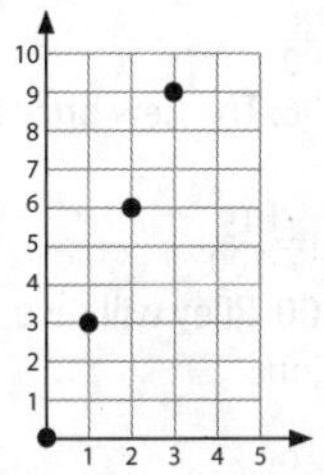

Proportional: yes

2.
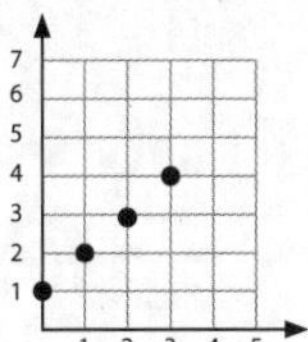

Proportional: no

3.
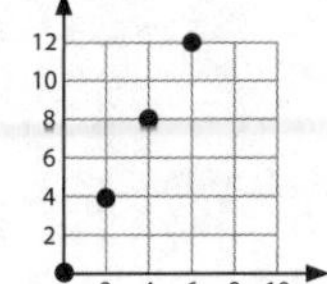

Proportional: yes

4.
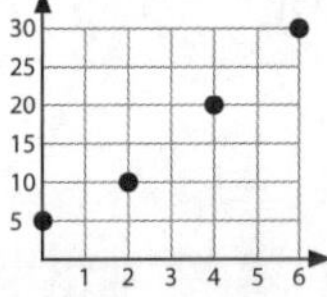

Proportional: no

5.

Proportional: yes

6.
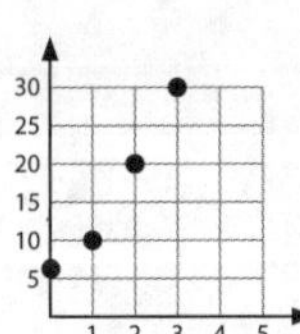

Proportional: no

Day 10 (page 31)

1. 12 cups
2. 120 sandwiches
3. 4 gallons
4. 600 gallons
5. $144
6. 16 mugs
7. 24 drawings
8. 24 lawns
9. 3 pies
10. $12
11. 5 shirts
12. 6 hours

Learn about Constant of Proportionality (page 32)

From a Table:

1. 1.25, 1.25, 1.25, 1.25
2. 1.25

From a Graph:

1. 1.30
2. Answers will vary.
3. 1.30
4. $1.30

From an Equation:

1. 5

Day 11 (page 33)

1. 1.5
2. 2.5
3. 9.3
4. 20
5. 4.5
6. 6

Day 12 (page 34)

1. 1
2. 15
3. 3
4. 1
5. 4
6. 2

Day 13 (page 35)

1. a. $k = 2$
   b. Every ounce of cheese costs $2.
2. a. $k = 0.5$
   b. Every pound of carrots costs $0.5.
3. a. $k = 7$
   b. Every pound of salami costs $7.
4. a. $k = 1.5$
   b. Every dozen of eggs costs $1.50.

Day 14 (page 36)

1. 3
2. 6
3. 1.5
4. –4
5. 4
6. –2
7. 9
8. 5
9. 1
10. 4
11. 21
12. 15
13. 3.5
14. 2

Day 15 (page 37)

1. 12
2. 4
3. –5
4. 9
5. 6
6. 11
7. 24
8. 3

Learn about Equations of Proportional Relationships (page 38)

Example 1:

2. 6
3. 6

Example 2:

2. 4
3. 4

Example 3:

1. Hours, Miles
2. 65
3. 65

Answer Key (cont.)

Day 16 (page 39)

1. 2
2. 7
3. 10
4. 3.8
5. 2.5
6. 4

Day 17 (page 40)

1. 6
2. 2
3. 15
4. 3
5. 5
6. 14

Day 18 (page 41)

1. 3
2. 7
3. 250
4. 18.5
5. 11
6. 2.5
7. 3.25
8. 10
9. 16
10. 9
11. 40
12. 30
13. 3
14. 7

Day 19 (page 42)

1.

0	0
1	25
2	50
3	75

Equation: $y = 25x$

2.

0	0
1	7.5
2	15
3	22.5

Equation: $y = 7.5x$

3.

0	0
1	12
10	120
20	240
50	600

Equation: $y = 12x$

4.

0	0
2	40
4	140
6	210

Equation: $y = 35x$

5.

0	0
3	90
6	180
9	270

Equation: $y = 30x$

6.

0	0
2	30
4	60
6	90

Equation: $y = 15x$

Day 20 (page 43)

1. $y = 9x$
2. $y = 65x$
3. $y = 15x$
4. $y = 5x$
5. $y = 6.5x$
6. $y = 16x$
7. $y = 1x$
8. $y = 11x$

Learn about Ratio and Percent Problems (page 44)

Total with Tip:

3. 1,300, 13
4. $13
5. $78

Discounted Price:

3. 250, 2.50
4. 25 – 2.50 = 22.50

Percent Increase:

3. 62.5

Converting Units:

2. 48
3. 48

Converting Units with Multiple Steps:

1. 86,400

Day 21 (page 46)

1. 15
2. 36
3. 5
4. 7
5. 21
6. 77
7. 8
8. 7
9. 5
10. 2
11. 8
12. 56

Day 22 (page 47)

1. a. $\frac{\text{30 students}}{\text{75 sandwiches}} = \frac{\text{120 students}}{x \text{ sandwiches}}$
   b. $x = 300$ sandwiches
2. a. $\frac{\text{9 dogs}}{\text{31.5 lbs. of food}} = \frac{\text{40 dogs}}{x \text{ lbs. of food}}$
   b. $x = 140$ lbs. of food
3. a. $\frac{\text{207 dollars}}{\text{18 hours}} = \frac{x \text{ dollars}}{\text{54 hours}}$
   b. $x = 621$ dollars
4. a. $\frac{\text{8 lbs. of strawberries}}{\text{3 hours}} = \frac{x \text{ lbs. of strawberries}}{\text{12 hours}}$
   b. $x = 32$ lbs. of strawberries
5. a. $\frac{\text{1,625 miles}}{\text{25 hours}} = \frac{\text{2,925 miles}}{x \text{ hours}}$
   b. $x = 45$ hours
6. a. $\frac{\text{15 cups}}{\text{6 cakes}} = \frac{x \text{ cups}}{\text{1 cake}}$
   b. $x = 2.5$ cups
7. a. $\frac{\text{16 hamburgers}}{\text{45 minutes}} = \frac{x \text{ hamburgers}}{\text{180 minutes}}$
   b. $x = 64$ hamburgers
8. a. $\frac{\text{4 packages}}{\text{5.56 dollars}} = \frac{x \text{ packages}}{\text{16.68 dollars}}$
   b. $x = 12$ packages

Day 23 (page 48)

1. a. $\frac{x}{90} = \frac{15}{100}$
   b. $x = 13.5$; Theresa should pay $103.50.
2. a. $\frac{x}{40} = \frac{25}{100}$
   b. $x = 10$; The discounted price is $30.
3. a. $\frac{x}{250} = \frac{22}{100}$
   b. $x = 55$; There will be 55 stamps with animals on them.
4. a. $\frac{x}{130} = \frac{10}{100}$
   b. $x = 13$; Mary's new weight is 117 pounds.
5. a. $\frac{x}{400} = \frac{5}{100}$
   b. $x = 20$; The total amount is $420.
6. a. $\frac{x}{350} = \frac{30}{100}$
   b. $x = 105$; The new price is $245.
7. a. $\frac{x}{72} = \frac{18}{100}$
   b. $x = 12.96$; The new price is $84.96.
8. a. $\frac{x}{20,000} = \frac{15}{100}$
   b. $x = 3,000$; Riley will save $3,000 on his tuition.

Day 24 (page 49)

1. 12%
2. –33.3%
3. 38.9%
4. 25%
5. –44.4%
6. –25%
7. –42%
8. –37.5%
9. –22.2%
10. 12.5%

Answer Key *(cont.)*

Day 25 (page 50)

1. 10,080 minutes
2. 10,800 seconds
3. 336 hours
4. 216 hours
5. 8,640 minutes
6. 63,360 inches
7. 42,240 feet
8. 36 feet
9. 1,814,400 seconds
10. 253,440 inches
11. 720 hours
12. 8,760 hours

Day 26 (page 51)

1. 5.6%
2. $20
3. a. $\frac{48 \text{ people}}{4 \text{ groups}}$
   b. $\frac{12 \text{ people}}{\text{group}}$
4. 36 problems
5. $k = 1$
6. $20
7. $9.54
8. 5,760 minutes
9. $x = 3$ cats
10. 45 gallons
11. $k = 3.5$
12. $k = 4.1$

Day 27 (page 52)

1. no
2. 2 books
3. yes
4. 12 hot dogs
5. $k = 9$
6. $k = 5$
7. $81
8. $600

Day 28 (page 53)

1. $k = 1.5$
2. 8 miles
3. $k = 7$
4. $7.99
5. no
6. a. $11.20
   b. $67.20
7. 240 apples
8. $k = 9$

x	y
1	$9
3	$27
6	$54
12	$108

Day 29 (page 54)

1. $y = 6x$
2. $12.50
3. no
4. no
5. 8%
6. $k = 12$
7. $y = 65x$
8. 432,000 seconds

Day 30 (page 55)

1. 7.5 miles
2. $y = 3x$
3. $22,500
4. 8,800 yards
5.

x	y
1	$15
2	$30
3	$45
4	$60

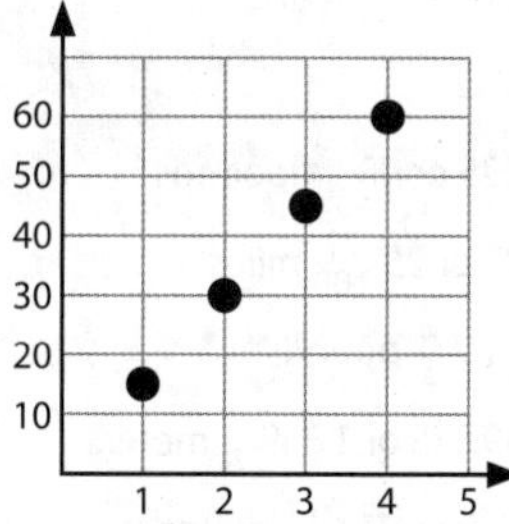

6. 128 beads
7. a. $3.60
   b. $48.60
8. $k = 15$

Unit 2

Learn about Adding and Subtracting Rational Numbers (page 56)

Example 1: 2

Example 2: $10 + (-10) = 0$

Example 3: -11

Example 4:

1. -3 and 1
2. 4, 4

Day 1 (page 58)

1. $\frac{1}{4} + (-\frac{3}{4}) = -\frac{2}{4}$ or $-\frac{1}{2}$
2. $\frac{3}{4} + (-\frac{6}{4}) = -\frac{3}{4}$
3. $-2 + 6 = 4$
4. $1\frac{1}{2} + (-2\frac{1}{2}) = -1$
5. $-1 + 2 = 1$
6. $\frac{3}{8} + (-\frac{5}{8}) = -\frac{2}{8}$

Day 2 (page 59)

1. $\frac{3}{4} + (-\frac{7}{4}) = -1$
2. $-\frac{5}{6} + \frac{9}{6} = \frac{4}{6}$
3. $-4 + 8 = 4$
4. $-1 + \frac{7}{4} = \frac{3}{4}$
5. $-5 + 8 = 3$
6. $-3 + 4\frac{1}{2} = 1\frac{1}{2}$

Day 3 (page 60)

1. $-35 + 35 = 0$
2. $-1{,}000 + 1{,}000 = 0$
3. $8 + (-8) = 0$
4. $30{,}000 + (-30{,}000) = 0$
5. $6 + (-6) = 0$
6. $50 + (-50) = 0$
7. -9
8. 3
9. -25
10. 100

Day 4 (page 61)

1. $9 + (-7) = 2$
2. $-12 + (-6) = -18$
3. $-7 + (3) = -4$
4. $14 + (-15) = -1$
5. $-11 + (-12) = -23$
6. $24 + (-30) = -6$
7. $18 + (6) = 24$
8. $14 + (6) = 20$
9. $-5 + (-6) = -11$
10. $-2 + (2) = 0$
11. $2\frac{1}{2} + (-5\frac{1}{2}) = -3$
12. $-8\frac{1}{3} + (-2\frac{2}{3}) = -11$
13. $9 + (-10\frac{1}{4}) = -1\frac{1}{4}$
14. $7\frac{1}{4} + (-6) = 1\frac{1}{4}$

Answer Key *(cont.)*

Day 5 (page 62)

1. $-1 - 2 = -3$ or $2 - (-1) = 3$
   Absolute value: 3
2. $-\frac{4}{5} - \frac{3}{5} = -\frac{7}{5}$ or $\frac{3}{5} - (-\frac{4}{5}) = \frac{7}{5}$
   Absolute value: $\frac{7}{5}$
3. $-\frac{3}{4} - \frac{1}{4} = -1$ or $\frac{1}{4} - (-\frac{3}{4}) = -1$
   Absolute value: 1
4. $-\frac{2}{6} - \frac{4}{6} = -1$ or $\frac{4}{6} - (-\frac{2}{6}) = 1$
   Absolute value: 1
5. $-3 - 2 = -5$ or $2 - (-3) = 5$
   Absolute value: 5
6. $-2.5 - 1.5 = -4$ or $1.5 - (-2.5) = 4$
   Absolute value: 4

Day 6 (page 63)

1. $25\frac{13}{40}$
2. -3.1
3. 3
4. -11
5. -6.3
6. $59\frac{7}{9}$
7. $10\frac{1}{2}$
8. -4.1
9. $1\frac{3}{10}$
10. $-6\frac{2}{9}$
11. -43.6
12. $1\frac{3}{8}$
13. 655
14. 117

Day 7 (page 64)

1. $3\frac{3}{4}$ pounds
2. 1.5 miles
3. 69.2 miles
4. $46\frac{1}{10}$ laps
5. $11\frac{5}{9}$ hours
6. 19.45 miles or $19\frac{9}{20}$ miles
7. 0.05 of the weeds or $\frac{1}{20}$
8. 0.15 or $\frac{3}{20}$
9. 19 minutes
10. 0.1 or $\frac{1}{10}$

Day 8 (page 65)

1. positive
2. negative
3. negative
4. negative
5. positive
6. positive
7. positive
8. negative
9. negative
10. positive
11. negative
12. negative
13. positive
14. negative

Day 9 (page 66)

1. -9.7 or $-9\frac{7}{10}$
2. -1
3. 14
4. $-1\frac{3}{5}$
5. 6.45 or $6\frac{9}{20}$
6. $13\frac{1}{3}$
7. 14.05 or $14\frac{1}{20}$
8. 3
9. 0.1 or $\frac{1}{10}$
10. -58.25 or $-58\frac{1}{4}$
11. $-4\frac{3}{4}$
12. 18.1 or $18\frac{1}{10}$
13. 18.06 or $18\frac{3}{50}$
14. 24.9 or $24\frac{9}{10}$

Day 10 (page 67)

1. 18.5 or $18\frac{1}{2}$ quarts
2. $107.12
3. 40.225 or $40\frac{9}{40}$ pounds
4. 25.77 or $25\frac{77}{100}$ miles
5. 7.8 or $7\frac{4}{5}$ pounds
6. 1,349.375 or $1{,}349\frac{3}{8}$ meters
7. 572.85 or $572\frac{17}{20}$ pounds
8. 2.225 or $2\frac{9}{40}$ miles
9. 0.083 or $\frac{1}{12}$ of the cake
10. $19.50

Learn about Multiplying and Dividing Rational Numbers
(page 68)

Example 1:

1. 4.5
2. negative
3. -4.5

Example 2:

2. -63

Example 3:

2. $-\frac{21}{15} \times \frac{15}{7} = -9$

Example 4:

1. 9
2. negative
3. -9

Example 5:

$-\frac{1}{5}, \frac{(-1)}{5}, \frac{1}{(-5)},$

Day 11 (page 70)

1. $6\frac{1}{3}$
2. $1\frac{1}{4}$
3. 20.02
4. $\frac{2}{5}$
5. $\frac{42}{55}$
6. 3
7. $14\frac{2}{3}$
8. 42
9. 32.2368
10. 2
11. $1\frac{1}{4}$
12. 3.075 or $3\frac{3}{40}$
13. $2\frac{13}{40}$
14. 17

Day 12 (page 71)

1. -32
2. 9
3. 30
4. -6
5. -2
6. 24
7. 9
8. 16
9. 0
10. -6
11. 7
12. 22
13. -12
14. 5

Day 13 (page 72)

1. -25
2. $-7 \times 3 + -7 \times -6 = 21$
3. $-\frac{1}{5} \times 10 + -\frac{1}{5} \times -5 = -1$
4. $1\frac{2}{3} \times -6 + 1\frac{2}{3} \times 3 = -5$
5. $-1.5 \times 2.8 + -1.5 \times -4 = 1.8$
6. $\frac{8}{9} \times -27 + \frac{8}{9} \times 18 = -8$
7. $-6 \times \frac{1}{3} + -6 \times 8 = -50$
8. $-\frac{4}{5} \times -10 + -\frac{4}{5} \times 20 = -8$
9. $6.5 \times -2.1 + 6.5 \times 4 = 12.35$
10. $2 \times -2 + 2 \times 5 = 6$
11. $-\frac{3}{4} \times 24 + -\frac{3}{4} \times -12 = -9$
12. $-7 \times 5.4 + -7 \times 2 = -51.8$
13. $-2\frac{2}{3} \times -9 + -2\frac{2}{3} \times 12 = -8$
14. $5 \times -8 + 5 \times -4 = -60$

Answer Key *(cont.)*

Day 14 (page 73)

1. 8
2. 4^4, 256
3. 3^6; 729
4. 1
5. 15
6. 6^1, 6
7. 5^5; 3,125
8. 2^6, 64
9. 9^2, 81
10. 1
11. 5^6; 15,625
12. 7^3; 343
13. 4^3; 64
14. 5^3; 125

Day 15 (page 74)

1. 10 miles
2. 9 laps
3. 4 lawns
4. 3 bags
5. 65 cookies
6. 49.8 minutes
7. 9 cups
8. 48 papers
9. 18 batches
10. 19.5 miles

Learn about Converting Rational Numbers to Decimals (page 75)

1. 40/100
2. 0.4

Day 16 (page 76)

1. repeating
2. terminating
3. repeating
4. repeating
5. terminating
6. repeating
7. repeating
8. terminating
9. repeating
10. terminating
11. terminating
12. terminating
13. repeating
14. terminating

Day 17 (page 77)

1. $0.\overline{33}$; repeating
2. 0.375; terminating
3. 0.2; terminating
4. $0.\overline{44}$; repeating
5. 0.6; terminating
6. $0.\overline{11}$; repeating
7. $0.\overline{66}$; repeating
8. 0.875; terminating
9. 0.25; terminating
10. 0.4; terminating

Day 18 (page 78)

1. $\frac{3}{10}$
2. 0.25
3. $3.\overline{33}$
4. 80%
5. 82%
6. 50%
7. $\frac{45}{100}$
8. $\frac{95}{100}$
9. 150%
10. $\frac{35}{100}$
11. 0.12
12. $\frac{50}{100}$
13. 62.5%
14. 75%

Day 19 (page 79)

Fraction	Decimal	Percent
$\frac{3}{5}$	0.6	60%
$\frac{8}{10}$	0.8	80%
$\frac{12}{100}$	0.12	12%
$\frac{7}{8}$	0.875	87.5%
$1\frac{2}{5}$	1.4	140%
$2\frac{1}{5}$	2.2	220%
$\frac{3}{4}$	0.75	75%
$\frac{3}{10}$	0.3	30%
$\frac{72}{100}$	0.72	72%
$2\frac{1}{4}$	2.25	225%
$3\frac{1}{2}$	3.5	350%
$\frac{38}{100}$	0.38	38%
$\frac{9}{10}$	0.90	90%
$\frac{1}{100}$	0.01	1%

Day 20 (page 80)

1. a. 90%
   b. 0.9
   c. terminating
2. a. 0.85
   b. terminating
   c. $\frac{85}{100}$
3. a. $0.\overline{66}$
   b. repeating
   c. $66.\overline{66}\%$
4. a. terminating
   b. $\frac{2}{5}$
   c. 40%
5. a. 1.1
   b. terminating
   c. 110%
6. a. 0.55
   b. terminating
   c. $\frac{55}{100}$

Learn about Solving Problems with Rational Numbers (page 81)

Example 1:

1. \$440
2. \$550 – \$440
3. \$110

Example 2:

1. \$37.50
2. \$37.50

Day 21 (page 82)

1. \$10.54
2. $\frac{11}{20}$ more
3. 12.35 or $12\frac{7}{20}$
4. $\frac{3}{20}$ of the garage
5. 97.5 or $97\frac{1}{2}$ miles
6. \$75.30
7. 0.075 or $\frac{3}{40}$ more
8. 5.25 or $5\frac{1}{4}$ more
9. $4\frac{11}{20}$ pounds
10. $15\frac{3}{10}$ quarts

Answer Key *(cont.)*

Day 22 (page 83)

1. $50
2. $1,200
3. 30 problems
4. 7 seeds
5. 15 flowers
6. 10 hours
7. $7\frac{1}{5}$ hours
8. 6 miles
9. 40 students
10. 2.6 miles

Day 23 (page 84)

1. $90
2. $24
3. $127.50
4. $132.50
5. $54\frac{1}{6}$ miles
6. 6 packs
7. $17.50
8. $15.70
9. $2,550
10. $29.96

Day 24 (page 85)

1. 24
2. –1
3. 13
4. 76
5. 40
6. 1.5
7. 1
8. 38
9. 3.65 or $3\frac{13}{20}$
10. $6\frac{1}{8}$
11. $\frac{1}{3}$
12. 5.41 or $5\frac{41}{100}$

Day 25 (page 86)

1. $87.50
2. $2.03
3. 6.5 miles
4. 48 servings
5. 180 minutes
6. $150
7. 6
8. 17
9. 14.64 or $14\frac{16}{25}$
10. 91
11. 15
12. 0

Day 26 (page 87)

1. **a.** $\frac{75 \text{ dogs}}{15 \text{ kennels}}$
   b. $\frac{5 \text{ dogs}}{\text{kennel}}$
2. 4 miles
3. $k = 1.5$
4. 13
5. **a.** $\frac{3}{5}$
   b. 0.6
6. 16
7. 432,000 seconds
8. $9.75
9. 14.6
10. $9\frac{19}{45}$
11. $k = 7$
12. no

Day 27 (page 88)

1. $-\frac{3}{4} + \frac{7}{4} = 1$
2. $k = 12$
3. 2.4 or $2\frac{2}{5}$
4. no
5. $k = 0.45$

14	$6.30
16	$7.20
18	$8.10

6. 72 muffins
7. no
8. $3 \times -5 + 3 \times 4 = -15 + 12 = -3$

Day 28 (page 89)

1. 15 cupcakes
2. $-\frac{3}{5} + 1\frac{3}{5} = 1$
3. $-2 \times 3 + -2 \times 6 = -6 + -12 = -18$
4. $k = 1.5$
5. 162 chairs
6. $y = 10x$
7. **a.** positive
   b. positive
8. $y = 20x$

Day 29 (page 90)

1. 4 driveways
2. $80
3. 17
4. $3 + (-7) = -4$
5. 25%
6. 6
7. $2 + (-6) = -4$
8. 0.064 or $\frac{8}{125}$
9. $5\frac{7}{12}$
10. $10,200
11. –5
12. 681

Day 30 (page 91)

1. $1\frac{1}{2}$ cups
2. $k = 1$
3. $200
4. $y = 5x$
5. $7.73
6. 8
7. 2,401
8. $1\frac{1}{2} + (-3) = -1\frac{1}{2}$

Unit 3

Learn about Equivalent Expressions (page 92)

Example 1:

2. $4m - 7$

Example 2:

2. $6a$, 18
3. $6a + 18$

Example 3:

4. $3(6 + a)$

Example 4:

1. $18x$, 24, $18x + 24$
2. no

Answer Key (cont.)

Day 1 (page 94)

1. $-4b + 1$
2. $16v - 11w$
3. $-2k + 3$
4. $7a - 2b + 8$
5. $-6x - 9y$
6. $13p - 3d$
7. $5c - 6a$
8. $28a + 15$
9. $3q - 6p + 7$
10. $2f - 20$
11. $11m + 6n - 6$
12. $-12j - 4$

Day 2 (page 95)

1. $12x + 18$
2. $40m + 72$
3. $12a + 18b + 24$
4. $6a + 18b + 18$
5. $21m + 33$
6. $120a + 140$
7. $15x + 250$
8. $24p + 56$

Day 3 (page 96)

1. $50x + 35$
2. $-12a - 8b - 8$
3. $2a - 12b$
4. $80b - 70c$
5. $-8a + 16b$
6. $18a + 12b - 9c$
7. $-20m + 200$
8. $31k + 7$
9. $22b - 121$
10. $12a - 24b$
11. $12 - 16x$
12. $-12x - 24$
13. $9a - 6b + 18$
14. $-42a - 98$

Day 4 (page 97)

1. $2(x + 5y + 15)$
2. $5(p + 5 + 9q)$
3. $6(q + 5)$
4. $4(n + 4 + 6m)$
5. $6(m + 9)$
6. $3(a + 4b + 13)$
7. $8(2 + 4a + 5b)$
8. $3(b + 4a + 2)$

Day 5 (page 98)

1. no
2. yes
3. yes
4. yes
5. yes
6. yes
7. no
8. no
9. no
10. yes
11. no
12. no

Learn about Multistep Problems with Rational Numbers (page 99)

Multistep Word Problem:

2. \$52.50
4. $\$52.50 \cdot 1.08 = \$56.70$

Solutions to Inequalities:

1. 10
2. yes, yes

Using Estimation:

1. 1,500
2. no
3. 1,500 is more than 1,200

Day 6 (page 100)

1. -3.74
2. 6
3. $-9\frac{2}{15}$
4. 34
5. 3
6. $106.5\overline{33}$ or $106\frac{8}{15}$
7. $-3\frac{3}{8}$
8. -85
9. $10\frac{9}{20}$
10. 78
11. -68.55
12. $22\frac{9}{10}$

Day 7 (page 101)

1. \$215
2. \$12.09 (if tip is paid on whole price) or \$11.87 (if tip is paid on discount price)
3. 11.009 pints or $11\frac{9}{1,000}$ pints
4. \$158.70
5. \$217.50
6. \$2,220
7. \$900
8. \$96.53

Day 8 (page 102)

1. yes
2. no
3. no
4. yes
5. yes
6. no
7. no
8. yes
9. no
10. yes

Day 9 (page 103)

1. a. \$2.40
   b. \$158.40
2. a. \$33.75
   b. \$191.25
   c. \$18
   d. \$209.25
3. a. $\frac{1}{2}$ foot
   b. $2\frac{4}{5}$ feet
   c. 6.6 or $6\frac{3}{5}$ feet
4. a. \$328.80
   b. \$167.44

Day 10 (page 104)

1. a. no
   b. 7×10 is more than 60
2. a. yes
   b. 8×6 is 48
3. a. no
   b. 3×5 is 15
4. a. no
   b. $\frac{6}{4} = 1.5$ and 1.5×30 is 45
5. a. no
   b. 4×5 is 20
6. a. yes
   b. 1.5×4 is 6

Learn about Using Variables (page 105)

Example 1:

1. Sample answer: x
2. Answers should match the variable in #1.

Example 3:

3. $y = 2x + 4$

Example 4:

2. the number of stamps Marcia's friend has

Answer Key *(cont.)*

Day 11 (page 106)

1. $6x = 12$
2. $k - 4$
3. $4(y + 2)$
4. $9x = 49$
5. $3x + 8 = 30$
6. $2x - 9 = 50$
7. $30x = 270$
8. $8x - 14 = 30$
9. $11x > 132$
10. $7x + 18$
11. $10x + 6 \leq 40$
12. $4x - 90 = 100$
13. $70x > 350$
14. $x + 15 \geq 60$

Day 12 (page 107)

1. $200 = x + 3x$
2. $18 = x + 0.5x$
3. $200 \leq 50x$
4. $45 = 2x + x$
5. $48 \leq x$
6. $75 \geq 7x + 35$
7. $60 > 5x$
8. $80 = 7x$
9. $95 = 1x + 65$
10. $112 = 14x$

Day 13 (page 108)

1. $y = x + 4$
2. $y = 3x + 3$
3. $y = 4x + 8$
4. $y = x + 2$

Day 14 (page 109)

1. $y = 12x + 12$
2. $y = x + 0.5$
3. $y = 3x + 4$
4. $y = 2x + 8$
5. $y = 3x + 3$
6. $y = 1x + 10$
7. $y = 2x + 7$
8. $y = 5x + 5$

Day 15 (page 110)

1. Answers should reflect real-word situations.
2. Answers should reflect real-word situations.
3. Answers should reflect real-word situations.
4. Answers should reflect real-word situations.
5. Answers should reflect real-word situations.
6. Answers should reflect real-word situations.
7. Answers should reflect real-word situations.
8. Answers should reflect real-word situations.
9. Answers should reflect real-word situations.
10. Answers should reflect real-word situations.
11. Answers should reflect real-word situations.
12. Answers should reflect real-word situations.

Learn about Solving Equations (page 111)

Example 1:

2. 39, 13

Example 2:

1. $8y - 24$
3. 8
4. Point at 8

Example 3:

3. 275, 11

Day 16 (page 113)

1. $m = 3$
2. $b = 2.\overline{88}$
3. $y = 27$
4. $p = 15$
5. $x = 1.25$
6. $m = 5$
7. $w = 6$
8. $q = 2$
9. $x = 19$
10. $p = 17$
11. $x = 1$
12. $r = 2$

Day 17 (page 114)

1. $c = 0$
2. $x = 2$
3. $m = 5$
4. $w = 3$
5. $x = 13$
6. $t = 7$
7. $v = 14$
8. $x = 5$
9. $k = 10$
10. $b = 15$
11. $q = 7$
12. $x = 5$

Day 18 (page 115)

1. a. $5x - 30 = 275$
   b. $x = \$61$
2. a. $330 = 7x + 120$
   b. $x = 30$ hours
3. a. $87.25 = x(25) - 0.5(25)$
   b. $x = \$3.99$
4. a. $335 = 40x + 15$
   b. $x = 8$ months
5. a. $425 = 75x + 200$
   b. $x = 3$ months
6. a. $300 = 18x - 60$
   b. $x = 20$ pillows

Day 19 (page 116)

1.

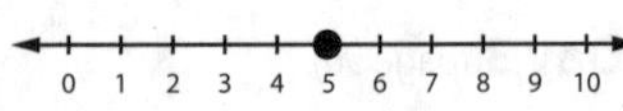

2.

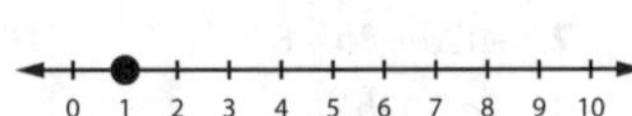

3.

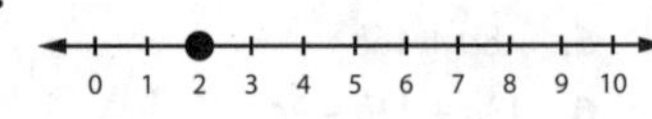

4.

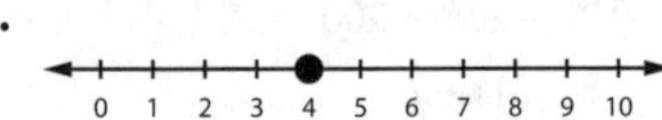

5.

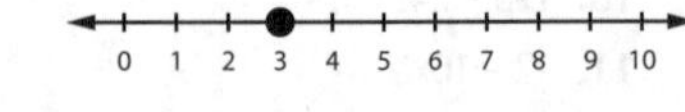

6.

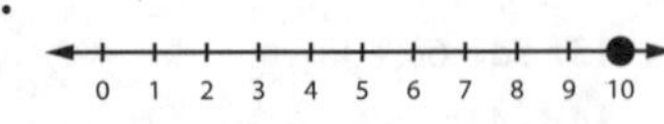

7.

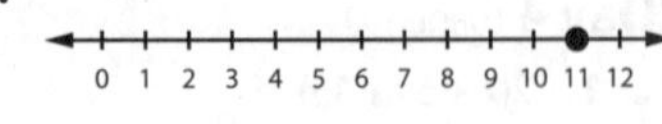

8.

–5 –4 –3 –2 –1 0 1 2 3 4 5

Answer Key (cont.)

Day 20 (page 117)

1. 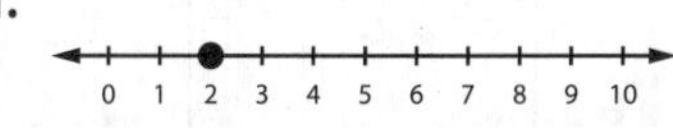
2. 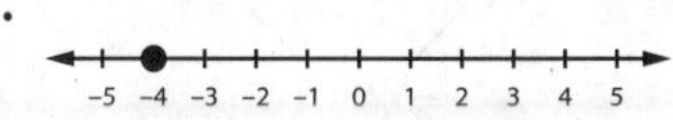
3. 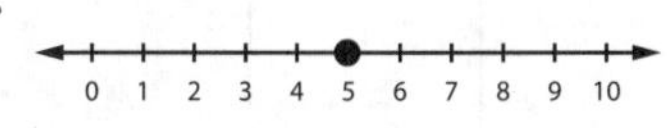
4. 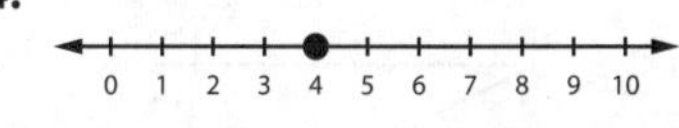
5. 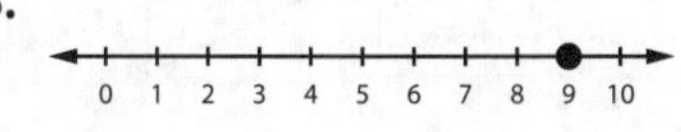
6. 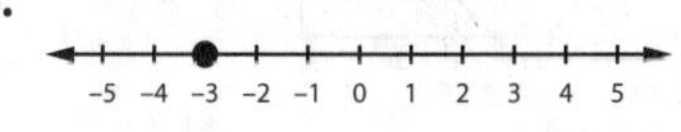
7. 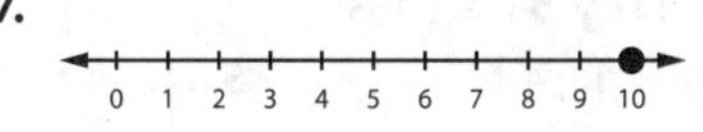
8. 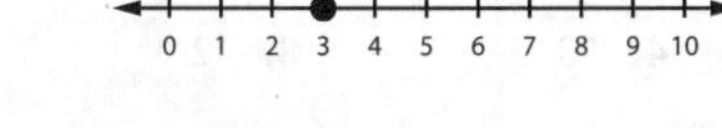

Learn about Solving Inequalities (page 118)

Example 1:

2. 7
3. right

Example 2:

2. right

Day 21 (page 119)

1. $x > 6$
2. $v \le 2$
3. $x < 13$
4. $x < -6$
5. $d \le 5$
6. $j < 15$
7. $f \ge -5$
8. $k \ge 9$
9. $y < 11$
10. $g < 4$
11. $n \le 2$
12. $h > 14$

Day 22 (page 120)

1. a. $350 \le 6x + 80$
   b. $x \ge 45$ tickets
   c. They need to sell 45+ tickets.
2. a. $280 < 4x + 40$
   b. $x > 60$ bracelets
   c. They need to sell 61 or more bracelets.
3. a. $300 < 13x - 25$
   b. $x > 25$
   c. He needs to work more than 25 hours.
4. a. $48 \le 4x + 32$
   b. $x \ge 4$
   c. He needs to have grown at least 4 inches a year.

Day 23 (page 121)

1. 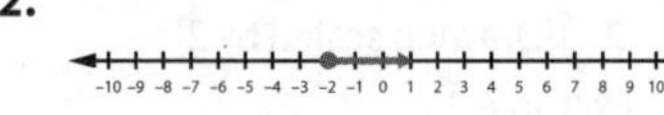
2. 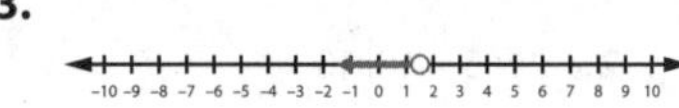
3. 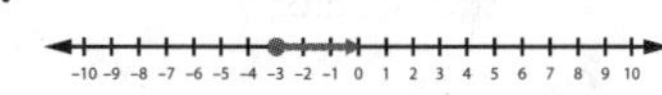
4. 
5. 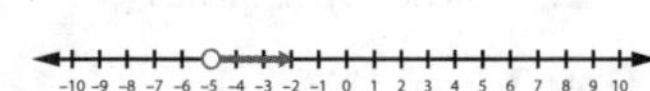
6. 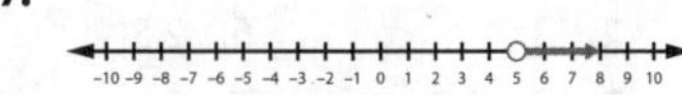
7. 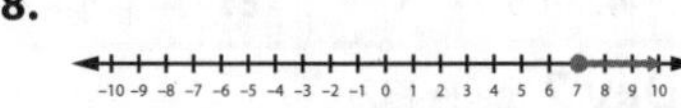
8.

Day 24 (page 122)

1. 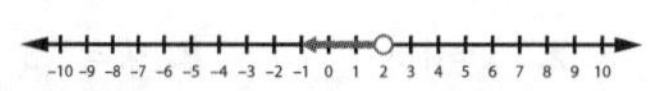
2. 
3. 
4. 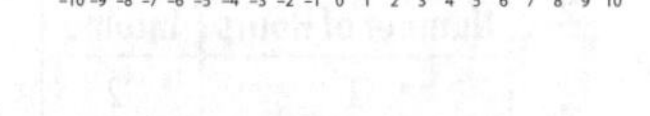
5. 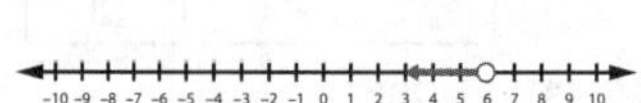
6.
7. 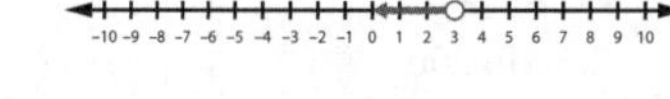
8. 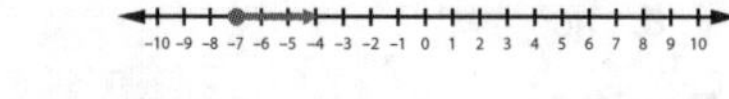

Day 25 (page 123)

1. a. $48 \le 5x + 18$
   b. $x \ge 6$
   c. 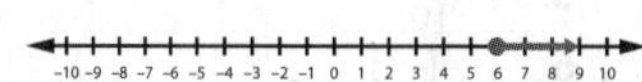
2. a. $400 \le 25x + 90$
   b. $x \ge 12.4$, rounds to 13 chairs
   c. 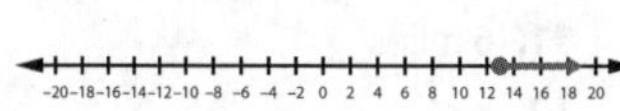
3. a. $105 \le 5x - 10$
   b. $x \ge 23$
   c. 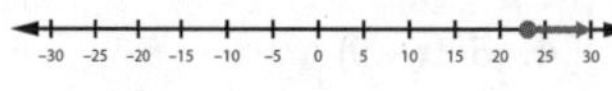
4. a. $75 \le 5x + 15$
   b. $x \ge 12$
   c.

Answer Key *(cont.)*

Day 26 (page 124)

1. $m = 6$
2. $x = 18$
3. 12 mugs
4. 55 miles
5. no
6. 96 hours
7. −8
8. $k = 2.5$
9. $x > 6$
10. $3(x + 8)$
11. $y = 2x + 2$
12. $12x + 12$

Day 27 (page 125)

1. a. $\frac{2}{10}$
   b. 0.2
2.

Number of Hours	Income
2	22
4	44
6	66
8	88

3. $y = 20x$
4. 36
5. $k = 5$
6. $16,200
7. 120
8. no

Day 28 (page 126)

1. $2x + 8$
2. $3(x + 10)$
3. $600
4. $5\frac{5}{7}$ recipes
5. $14\frac{7}{10}$
6. $1 + (-4) = -3$
7. 0.625
8. $k = 30$
9. 15,625
10. $16
11. 6 miles
12. $x < 2$

Day 29 (page 127)

1. $y = 0.5x + 3$
2. −48
3. $70.20
4. $5(2x + 9)$
5. $4 - 9 = -5$
6. a. 0.35
   b. $\frac{35}{100}$
7. 6 books
8. $11
9. −18
10. 23

Day 30 (page 128)

1. $88.50
2. 0.8
3. $4 - (-1) = 5$
4. $13.50
5. no
6. $11.\overline{33}$ or $11\frac{1}{3}$
7. $36m + 90$
8. $150
9. Points at (1, 2), (2, 4), (3, 6), (4, 8), (5, 10)
10. −8

Unit 4

Learn about Scale Drawings
(page 129)

Example 1:

2. 2, 2
3. 2

Example 2:

2. [Drawing scaled by 2]

Example 3:

1. 5
2. $2 \times 5 = 10$, 10

Example 4:

1. 8 square units
2. 9
3. 72 square units

Example 5:

1. 8, 12
2. 8 inches by 12 inches

Day 1 (page 131)

1. 2
2. 3
3. 2
4. 1.5
5. 5
6. 2.5
7. 1.8
8. 3

Day 2 (page 132)

1.
2. 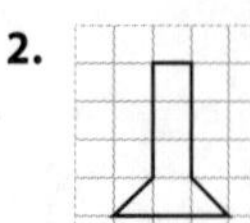
3. 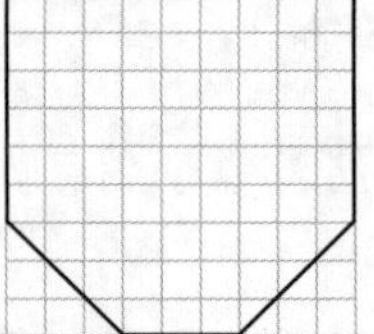
4. 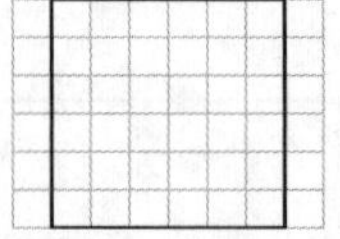
5.
6.

Day 3 (page 133)

1. 4
2. 21
3. 2
4. 10
5. 10
6. 10.5
7. 20
8. 12

Day 4 (page 134)

1. 256 units^2
2. 36 units^2
3. 108 units^2
4. 3 units^2
5. 50 units^2
6. 12 units^2

Day 5 (page 135)

1. 60 in. × 75 in.
2. 900 miles
3. 24 in. × 40 in.
4. 24 in. × 24 in.
5. 7
6. 12 in. × 18 in.
7. 5 ft.
8. 3 ft. × 4 ft.

Learn about 2D and 3D Shapes (page 136)

Triangles:

1. one

Cross-Sections:

2. rectangle

Answer Key *(cont.)*

Day 6 (page 137)

1. 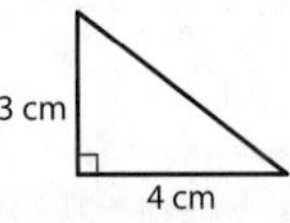

2. 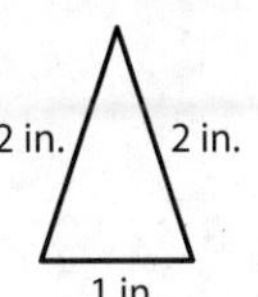

3. 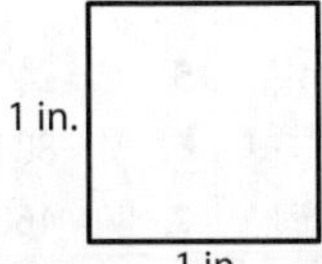

4. 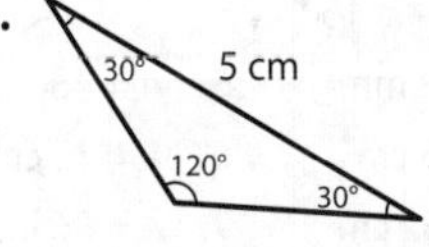

5. 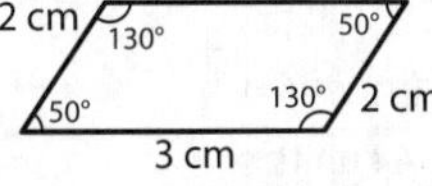

6. 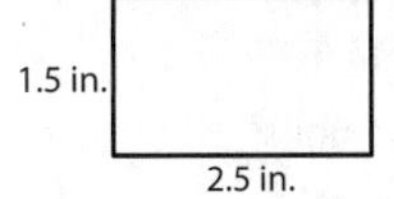

Day 7 (page 138)

1. yes
2. yes
3. yes
4. no
5. yes
6. no
7. no
8. no
9. yes
10. no
11. yes
12. yes
13. yes
14. yes

Day 8 (page 139)

1. more than 1
2. 1 triangle
3. more than 1
4. no triangle
5. 1 triangle
6. 1 triangle
7. more than 1
8. no triangle

Day 9 (page 140)

1. triangle
2. rectangle
3. rectangle
4. triangle
5. circle
6. triangle

Day 10 (page 141)

1. no
2. more than one
3. 180 degrees
4. no
5. zero
6. 30°, 3 cm, 130°
7. 1 in., 3 in.
8. rectangle

Learn about Circles (page 142)

Example 1:

1. 6 cm
3. 18.84 cm

Example 2:

1. 9
3. 28.26 cm^2

Example 3:

2. 12.56 $ft.^2$

Example 4:

1. 28
2. 14

Day 11 (page 143)

1. **a.** 20π yd.
   b. 62.8 yd.
2. **a.** 2.4π cm
   b. 7.5 cm
3. **a.** 11π mm
   b. 34.5 mm
4. **a.** 4.2π cm
   b. 13.2 cm
5. **a.** 14π yd.
   b. 44.0 yd.
6. **a.** 12π mm
   b. 37.7 mm
7. **a.** 4π in.
   b. 12.6 in.
8. **a.** 14π mm
   b. 44.0 mm

Day 12 (page 144)

1. **a.** 36(3.14) mm^2
   b. 113.04 mm^2
2. **a.** 4.41(3.14) cm^2
   b. 13.85 cm^2
3. **a.** 25(3.14) $in.^2$
   b. 78.5 $in.^2$
4. **a.** 49(3.14) mm^2
   b. 153.86 mm^2
5. **a.** 16(3.14) $yd.^2$
   b. 50.24 $yd.^2$
6. **a.** 16(3.14) $in.^2$
   b. 50.24 $in.^2$
7. **a.** 51.84(3.14) $in.^2$
   b. 162.78 $in.^2$
8. **a.** 81(3.14) m^2
   b. 254.34 m^2

Day 13 (page 145)

1. circumference: 25.12 in.
2. area: 12.56 $ft.^2$
3. area: 200.96 $ft.^2$
4. area: 113.04 $in.^2$
5. circumference: 87.92 in.
6. circumference: 21.98 in.
7. area: 50.24 $ft.^2$
8. circumference: 12.56 in.

Day 14 (page 146)

1. 7
2. 78
3. 9
4. 18
5. 27
6. 12
7. 5
8. 100
9. 16
10. 46

Day 15 (page 147)

1. **a.** 16π mm
   b. 50.24 mm
2. 45
3. 94.2 ft.
4. 22
5. **a.** 37.21π cm^2
   b. 116.8 cm^2
6. 31.4 ft.
7. 29
8. 12

Answer Key *(cont.)*

Learn about Angles (page 148)

Example 2:

2. 115°

Example 3:

2. 75°

Example 4:

3. 48°

Example 5:

3. 75°

Day 16 (page 150)

1. adjacent
2. supplementary, adjacent
3. supplementary, adjacent
4. supplementary, vertical
5. complementary, adjacent
6. adjacent

Day 17 (page 151)

1. **a.** $x + 75 = 180$
   b. $x = 105°$
2. **a.** $x + 45 = 180$
   b. $x = 135°$
3. **a.** $x + 90 = 180$
   b. $x = 90°$
4. **a.** $x + 105 = 180$
   b. $x = 75°$
5. **a.** $x + 165 = 180$
   b. $x = 15°$
6. **a.** $x + 35 = 180$
   b. $x = 145°$

Day 18 (page 152)

1. **a.** $x + 65 = 90$
   b. $x = 25°$
2. **a.** $x + 80 = 90$
   b. $x = 10°$
3. **a.** $x + 72 = 90$
   b. $x = 18°$
4. **a.** $x + 30 = 90$
   b. $x = 60°$
5. **a.** $x + 53 = 90$
   b. $x = 37°$
6. **a.** $x + 67 = 90$
   b. $x = 23°$

Day 19 (page 153)

1. **a.** $40 + 22 + x = 90$
   b. $x = 28°$
2. **a.** $x + 45 = 90$
   b. $x = 45°$
3. **a.** $95 + x + 60 = 180$
   b. $x = 25°$
4. **a.** $50 + 110 + x = 180$
   b. $x = 20°$
5. **a.** $x + 50 + 12 = 90$
   b. $x = 28°$
6. **a.** $60 + 90 + x = 180$
   b. $x = 30°$

Day 20 (page 154)

1. **a.** $70 + 70 + x = 180$
   b. $x = 40°$
2. **a.** $90 + 60 + x = 180$
   b. $x = 30°$
3. **a.** $30 + 120 + x = 180$
   b. $x = 30°$
4. **a.** $60 + 60 + x = 180$
   b. $x = 60°$
5. **a.** $43 + 89 + x = 180$
   b. $x = 48°$
6. **a.** $15 + 150 + x = 180$
   b. $x = 15°$

Learn about Area, Volume, and Surface Area (page 155)

Example 1:

2. 14

3. 14, 70, 70

Example 2:

1. $73\frac{1}{3}$

Example 3:

2. 28

Example 4:

2. 16, 3

3. 19

Day 21 (page 157)

1. $A = 54 \text{ in.}^2$
2. $A = 12 \text{ ft.}^2$
3. $A = 69 \text{ yd.}^2$
4. $A = 400 \text{ mm}^2$
5. $A = 10 \text{ m}^2$
6. $A = 49 \text{ mm}^2$
7. $A = 96 \text{ ft.}^2$
8. $A = 35 \text{ in.}^2$

Day 22 (page 158)

1. $V = 800 \text{ cm}^3$
2. $V = 266.67 \text{ cm}^3$
3. $V = 210 \text{ m}^3$
4. $V = 70 \text{ m}^3$
5. $V = 432 \text{ cm}^3$
6. $V = 144 \text{ cm}^3$
7. $V = 200 \text{ mm}^3$
8. $V = 66.67 \text{ mm}^3$

Day 23 (page 159)

1. $V = 270 \text{ cm}^3$
2. $V = 90 \text{ cm}^3$
3. $V = 112 \text{ in.}^3$
4. $V = 56 \text{ in.}^3$
5. $V = 240 \text{ in.}^3$
6. $V = 80 \text{ in.}^3$
7. $V = 468 \text{ mm}^3$
8. $V = 156 \text{ mm}^3$

Day 24 (page 160)

1. $A = 88 \text{ mm}^2$
2. $A = 45 \text{ cm}^2$
3. $A = 152 \text{ cm}^2$
4. $A = 280 \text{ in.}^2$
5. $A = 486 \text{ cm}^2$
6. $A = 72 \text{ cm}^2$
7. $A = 96 \text{ in.}^2$
8. $A = 40 \text{ m}^2$

Day 25 (page 161)

1. $A = 44 \text{ units}^2$
2. $A = 27 \text{ units}^2$
3. $A = 23 \text{ units}^2$
4. $A = 12.5 \text{ units}^2$
5. $A = 8 \text{ units}^2$
6. $A = 16 \text{ units}^2$
7. $A = 29 \text{ units}^2$
8. $A = 16 \text{ units}^2$

Day 26 (page 162)

1. $x \leq 4$

   –10 –9 –8 –7 –6 –5 –4 –3 –2 –1 0 1 2 3 4 5 6 7 8 9 10
2. 15°
3. $35
4. **a.** $\frac{144 \text{ players}}{6 \text{ teams}}$
   b. $\frac{24 \text{ players}}{\text{team}}$
5. 4 paragraphs
6. no
7. 17
8. $64.90
9. $0.\overline{55}$
10. $380

Answer Key (cont.)

Day 27 (page 163)

1. 1,050 mm^3
2. 7,776
3. –32.5
4. 150°
5. 30 cats
6. $2,000
7. 70°
8. 4.5
9. $4\frac{5}{56}$
10. 144 units^2

Day 28 (page 164)

1. complimentary
2. $22
3. 18 units^3
4. 7
5. $11\frac{1}{5}$
6. a. 0.85
   b. $\frac{85}{100}$
7. $7x-7$
8. $x=4$
9. $1\frac{23}{40}$
10. 5

Day 29 (page 165)

1. no
2. $30x+42$
3. 12
4. $k=0.25$
5. $2-(-1)=3$
6. –13
7. 35°
8. rectangle

Day 30 (page 166)

1. $5(a+5)$
2. 46
3. a. $k=3$
   b. $y=3x$
4. 273 in.^{2}
5. no
6. $200
7.

Fraction	Decimal	Percent
$\frac{1}{5}$	0.2	20%
$\frac{9}{10}$	0.9	90%
$\frac{18}{100}$	0.18	18%

8. $26\frac{3}{5}$
9. 2
10. $38.25

Unit 5

Learn about Sampling and Making Inferences (page 167)

Example 1: d

Example 2: b

Example 3:

1. yes
2. yes

Example 4: blue, blue, red

Day 1 (page 169)

1. B
2. C
3. D
4. B
5. C
6. B

Day 2 (page 170)

1. A
2. A
3. C
4. B
5. C
6. B

Day 3 (page 171)

1. No, it is skewed to her homeroom.
2. yes
3. No, it is skewed to houses on the streets.
4. yes
5. No, it is skewed to students with better grades.
6. yes
7. No, it is skewed to Saturday morning shoppers.
8. yes

Day 4 (page 172)

Exmples:

1. Dogs are most popular.
2. Art is the most popular.
3. Saturday is the most popular.
4. D is the most common grade.
5. Country music is the most popular.
6. Beach-themed is the most popular.

Day 5 (page 173)

1. 110 students
2. 1,950 residents
3. 50 parents
4. 1,275 customers
5. 1,600 people
6. 90 students

Learn about Data and Graphs (page 174)

Example 1:

1. softball: median is 15, range is 9
   baseball: median is 13.5, range is 9
2. softball
3. the teams have the same range
4. softball

Day 6 (page 175)

1. 60 people
2. 11–15 years
3. 16–20 years
4. $165
5. $250
6. $85
7. 10 people
8. 4
9. 1 ticket

Day 7 (page 176)

1. 12
2. 8
3. ages 16–29
4. 8 miles
5. 8 miles
6. 8 miles is the median number of miles run for both groups.
7. ages 30–50

Day 8 (page 177)

1. 17 workers
2. 24
3. 18
4. 18
5. 30
6. 15
7. 25
8. 10
9. 25 times

Day 9 (page 178)

1. 40
2. 70
3. Yes, the numbers have a large range from low to high.
4. 40, it is the median value.
5. 7
6. No, it is really grouped up at the lower end.
7. 2
8. 1.875 pets
9. 2 pets, it is the most common number.

Answer Key *(cont.)*

Day 10 (page 179)

1. Class 1
2. Class 2
3. same for both classes
4. Class 2
5. Class 1
6. 2022
7. 2020
8. 2020
9. 2020
10. 2022

Learn about Probability
(page 180)

Example 1: 100%

Example 2: $0.25 \times 200 = 50$ times

Day 11 (page 181)

1. $\frac{1}{2}$
2. Answers should reflect a low probability.
3. Answers should reflect a low probability.
4. Answers should reflect a low probability.
5. $\frac{1}{4}$
6. $\frac{1}{4}$
7. $\frac{1}{6}$
8. 100%
9. 0%
10. Answers should reflect a reasonable probability.
11. Answers should reflect a reasonable probability.
12. $\frac{4}{5}$
13. $\frac{1}{2}$
14. Answers should reflect a reasonable probability.

Day 12 (page 182)

1. $\frac{3}{5}$
2. $\frac{2}{5}$
3. $\frac{2}{5}$
4. $\frac{3}{5}$
5. $\frac{1}{4}$
6. $\frac{3}{4}$
7. $\frac{1}{8}$
8. $\frac{7}{8}$

Day 13 (page 183)

1. 50 times
2. 100 times
3. 200 times
4. 100 times
5. 50 times
6. 100 times
7. 150 times
8. 100 times

Day 14 (page 184)

1. $\frac{1}{2}$
2. $\frac{1}{8}$
3. $\frac{1}{4}$
4. $\frac{1}{8}$
5. **a.** <
   b. >
   c. <
   d. =
6. $\frac{1}{8}$
7. $\frac{3}{8}$
8. $\frac{1}{2}$
9. **a.** >
   b. =
   c. >

Day 15 (page 185)

1. $\frac{5}{8}$
2. $\frac{10}{12}$ or $\frac{5}{6}$
3. $\frac{25}{30}$ or $\frac{5}{6}$
4. $\frac{19}{24}$
5. 10 times
6. 35 times
7. **a.** =
   b. >
   c. =
8. **a.** 0%
   b. $\frac{1}{3}$
   c. 100%

Learn about Probability Models (page 186)

Example 1:

1. {1, 2, 3, 4}
2. 1, $\frac{1}{4}$

Example 2:

2. $\frac{4}{20}$

Example 3:

1. chips, cookie, chips, cookie
2. 6

Example 4:

2. 6

Day 16 (page 188)

1. **a.** 1, 2, 3, 4, 5
   b. $\frac{1}{5}$
2. **a.** green, green, green, blue, blue
   b. $\frac{2}{5}$
3. **a.** P, A, R, T, Y
   b. $\frac{1}{5}$
4. **a.** 1, 2, 3, 4, 5, 6
   b. $\frac{1}{2}$
5. **a.** yellow, yellow, yellow, yellow, yellow, red, red, red, green
   b. $\frac{1}{9}$
6. **a.** 1, 2, 3, 4, 5, 6, 7, 8
   b. $\frac{1}{8}$
7. **a.** 1, 2, 3, 4, 5, 6, 7, 8, 9, 10, 11, 12
   b. $\frac{1}{2}$
8. **a.** heads, tails
   b. $\frac{1}{2}$

Day 17 (page 189)

1. 28%
2. 65%
3. 50%
4. $\frac{1}{3}$
5. $\frac{64}{75}$
6. $\frac{2}{75}$ or $2.\overline{66}$
7. $\frac{3}{10}$
8. $\frac{2}{5}$
9. $\frac{2}{5}$

Day 18 (page 190)

1.
   - elephant < smiley, heart
   - lion < smiley, heart
   - tiger < smiley, heart
   - penguin < smiley, heart

   8 possible outcomes

2.
   - kickball < ice cream, snow cone
   - tennis < ice cream, snow cone
   - laser tag < ice cream, snow cone
   - basketball < ice cream, snow cone

   8 possible outcomes

3.
   - pizza < broccoli, asparagus, peas
   - steak < broccoli, asparagus, peas
   - pork chops < broccoli, asparagus, peas
   - pasta < broccoli, asparagus, peas

   12 possible outcomes

4.
   - 1 < heads, tails
   - 2 < heads, tails
   - 3 < heads, tails
   - 4 < heads, tails
   - 5 < heads, tails
   - 6 < heads, tails

   12 possible outcomes

Answer Key (cont.)

Day 19 (page 191)

1. 12 possible outcomes
2. 12 possible outcomes
3. 9 possible outcomes
4. 12 possible outcomes

Day 20 (page 192)

1.

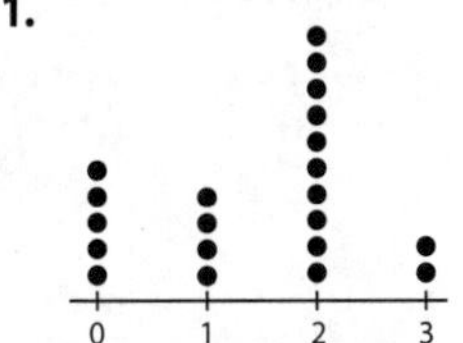

2.

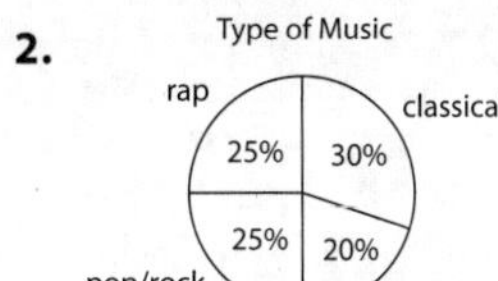

3.

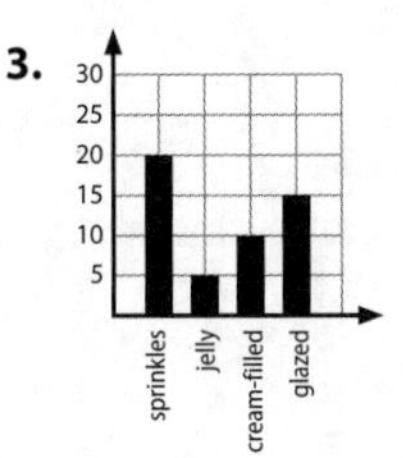

4.

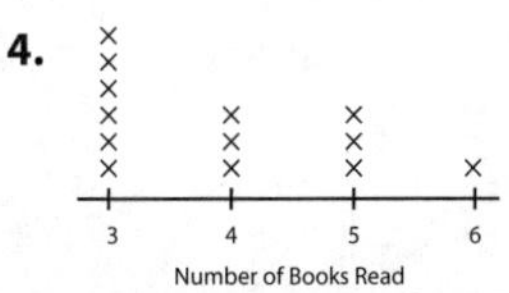

Learn about Finding Probability (page 193)

Example 1:

1. heads, tails, heads, tails, heads, tails
2. $\frac{1}{8}$

Example 2:

2. 4
3. 1, 3

Example 3:

1. $\frac{1}{10}$
2. 20
3. $\frac{20}{200}$

Example 4:

1. 50, $\frac{8}{50}$
2. $\frac{8}{50}$, 16

Day 21 (page 195)

1. $\frac{1}{18}$
2. Shun wins: $\frac{7}{12}$; Sister wins: $\frac{5}{12}$
3. $\frac{1}{8}$
4. $\frac{1}{6}$

Day 22 (page 196)

1. Spinner with 10 parts, six shaded for successful shots
2. Answers should reflect a reasonable simulation design.
3. Spinner with 4 parts, 3 shaded for rain
4. 4 blocks, 1 blue, 3 red
5. Flip a coin 40 times, heads for tennis, tails for golf
6. Answers should reflect a reasonable simulation design.

Day 23 (page 197)

	1	2	3	4	5	6
1	2	3	4	5	6	7
2	3	4	5	6	7	8
3	4	5	6	7	8	9
4	5	6	7	8	9	10
5	6	7	8	9	10	11
6	7	8	9	10	11	12

1. $\frac{21}{36}$
2. $\frac{15}{36}$
3. $\frac{1}{2}$

	1	2	3	4	5	6
1	1	2	3	4	5	6
2	2	4	6	8	10	12
3	3	6	9	12	15	18
4	4	8	12	16	20	24
5	5	10	15	20	25	30
6	6	12	18	24	30	36

4. $\frac{17}{36}$
5. $\frac{19}{36}$
6. $\frac{27}{36}$ or $\frac{3}{4}$

Day 24 (page 198)

1. $\frac{8}{50}$
2. $\frac{19}{50}$
3. $\frac{23}{50}$
4. $\frac{42}{50}$
5. $\frac{1}{4}$
6. $\frac{3}{4}$
7. $\frac{34}{40}$
8. $\frac{36}{40}$
9. $\frac{28}{60}$
10. $\frac{32}{60}$
11. $\frac{5}{60}$
12. $\frac{8}{60}$

Day 25 (page 199)

1. 8
2. $\frac{1}{4}$
3. $\frac{3}{8}$
4. $\frac{3}{8}$
5. $\frac{1}{5}$
6. $\frac{32}{40}$
7. $\frac{11}{40}$
8. $\frac{27}{40}$

Cumulative Review

Day 1 (page 200)

1. 24π ft.
2. 308 mm^2
3. hexagon
4. 16.2
5. $21,250
6. yes
7. $x < 8$

   -10 -9 -8 -7 -6 -5 -4 -3 -2 -1 0 1 2 3 4 5 6 7 8 9 10
8. 7 people

Day 2 (page 201)

1. $k = 8$
2. $\frac{1}{5}$
3. 48 units^2
4. **a.** 6
   b. 9
   c. 9 times
5. 28 – 12
6. 13.65
7. 0.8
8. yes

Day 3 (page 202)

1. 45
2. 60°
3. **a.** 20
   b. 50
   c. 80
4. yes
5. 25 miles
6. 105°
7. 4
8. 0.14

Answer Key (cont.)

Day 4 (page 203)

1. a. $\frac{81 \text{ pencils}}{27 \text{ students}}$
   b. $\frac{3 \text{ pencils}}{\text{student}}$
2. yes
3. –38
4. 60°
5. 32°
6. 27 days
7. 49π in.^{2}
8. $7x + 4 = 14$

Day 5 (page 204)

1. 2.7 recipes
2.

Fraction	Decimal	Percent
$\frac{1}{5}$	0.2	20%
$\frac{55}{100}$	0.55	55%
$\frac{84}{100}$	0.84	84%

3. 20°
4. Scale factor = 4, $x = 9$
5. a. middle school
   b. middle school
6. 50%
7. 120 mm^2
8. 360 cm^3

Day 6 (page 205)

1. 72
2. 16 units^2
3. 20°
4. $x \geq 4$

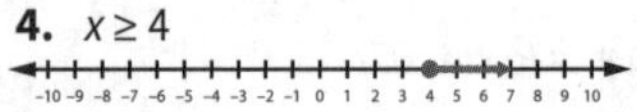

5. 27
6. no
7. a. 18
   b. 324

Day 7 (page 206)

1. a. ages 4–18
   b. ages 14–18
   c. ages 14–18
2. $11(x + 5)$
3. a. $\frac{1}{8}$
   b. $\frac{1}{2}$
   c. $\frac{3}{8}$
4. 12
5. $x = 3$
6. $3x + 6 = 32$
7. 18.75 or $18\frac{3}{4}$
8. 20

Day 8 (page 207)

1. 9.3π
2. more than one
3. 4
4. 95 cm^2
5. 36 mm^2
6. 200 tables
7. 24 mm^3
8. 24

Day 9 (page 208)

1. 288 cm^3
2. 17°
3. $24a + 48$
4. $x < 1$

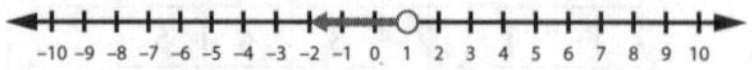

5. $k = 7$

x	y
1	7
20	140
50	350
80	560

6. no
7. $30\frac{2}{5}$
8. 5

Day 10 (page 209)

1. 30°
2. $15x + 21y + 27$
3. –14
4. square
5. a. 121π
   b. 379.94 cm^2
6. 6.3
7. no
8. 6

Day 11 (page 210)

1. 9
2. 16.5 units^2
3. a. 12
   b. 8
   c. 2
4. 420 football players
5. $k = 8$
6. $6\frac{9}{10}$
7. –6
8. no

Day 12 (page 211)

1. 5
2. $17\frac{1}{4}$
3. –2
4. 22
5. 10°
6. no
7. 990 mm^3
8. $382.50
9. $9v + 72$
10. $k = 3$

Day 13 (page 212)

1. adjacent
2. yes
3. a. 4
   b. 2
4. 70 m^2
5. 1,250 points
6. 3
7. 42 ft.^{3}
8. 27

Day 14 (page 213)

1. 175 yd.^{2}
2. 60 ft.^{3}
3. 124 ft.^{2}
4. $y = 5x$
5. $-\frac{1}{3}$
6. 59°
7. 36π ft.^{2}
8. –2

Answer Key *(cont.)*

Day 15 (page 214)

1. 32 in.^{3}
2. –5.5
3. 10
4. 10.2π in.
5. $y = 6x$
6. $3\frac{1}{5}$
7. 48
8. –39

Day 16 (page 215)

1. 65°
2. $\frac{1}{3}$
3. $\frac{3}{4} + (-1\frac{3}{4}) = -1$
4. 17°
5. $4(9 + c)$
6. no
7. $26.60
8. 14

Day 17 (page 216)

1. supplementary, adjacent
2. $y = 1x$
3. 91 mm^2
4. $3x + 24$
5. $\frac{95}{100}$
6. no
7. 90 people
8. 4

Day 18 (page 217)

1. $-1\frac{1}{3} + 2\frac{1}{3} = 1$
2. 20°
3. $64.9
4. 294 cm^2
5. no
6. **a.** 10.4π m
   b. 32.656 m
7. 12
8. –6

Day 19 (page 218)

1. 9
2. 180 inches
3. 51
4. no
5. triangle
6. **a.** 448 ft.^{3}
   b. 400 ft.^{2}
7. 39
8. 5

Day 20 (page 219)

1. **a.** 1.96π mm^2
   b. 6.15 mm^2
2. 59°
3. 65 miles
4. $12a + 8b + 20$
5. **a.** 0.35
   b. $\frac{35}{100}$
6. 31
7. –14
8. 3

Day 21 (page 220)

1. 65 miles
2. $73a + 15$
3. $\frac{1}{4}$
4. 512
5. $9.45
6. $-\frac{4}{6} + \frac{7}{6} = \frac{4}{6}$
7. $\frac{27}{64}$
8. $\frac{18}{100}$

Day 22 (page 221)

1. $10
2. $m = 4$
3. 154°
4. 562.5 cm^2
5. 180 mm^3
6. –1.3
7. $\frac{2}{3}$ cups
8. $58.5x + 31.5$

Day 23 (page 222)

1. 144 crayons
2. 27
3. 36°
4. $\frac{28}{100}$
5. 15.4%
6. $x < 4$, line going left from 4 with open circle
7. 3,600 mm^3
8. –45

Day 24 (page 223)

1. 4
2. $3 + 2 = 5$
3. $24x + 30$
4. 7.5 cm
5. 0.75
6. $48
7. $\frac{1}{12}$
8. 144 units^3

Day 25 (page 224)

1. $96x + 36$
2. Answers should reflect a proportional relationship.
3. $k = 2.5$
4. 6.1
5. $80.25
6. $3x - 12$
7. $18\frac{3}{20}$
8. **a.** $\frac{1}{12}$
   b. $\frac{1}{2}$
   c. $\frac{1}{2}$

Digital Resources

Accessing the Digital Resources

The digital resources can be downloaded by following these steps:

1. Go to **www.tcmpub.com/digital**
2. Use the 13-digit ISBN number to redeem the digital resources.
3. Respond to the questions using the book.
4. Follow the prompts on the Content Cloud website to sign in or create a new account.
5. The content redeemed will now be on your My Content screen. Click on the product to look through the digital resources. All resources are available for download. Select files can be previewed, opened, and shared.

For questions and assistance with your ISBN redemption, please contact Teacher Created Materials.

email: customerservice@tcmpub.com

phone: 800-858-7339

Contents of the Digital Resources

- Standards Correlations
- Class and Individual Analysis Sheets
- Math Learning Resources

